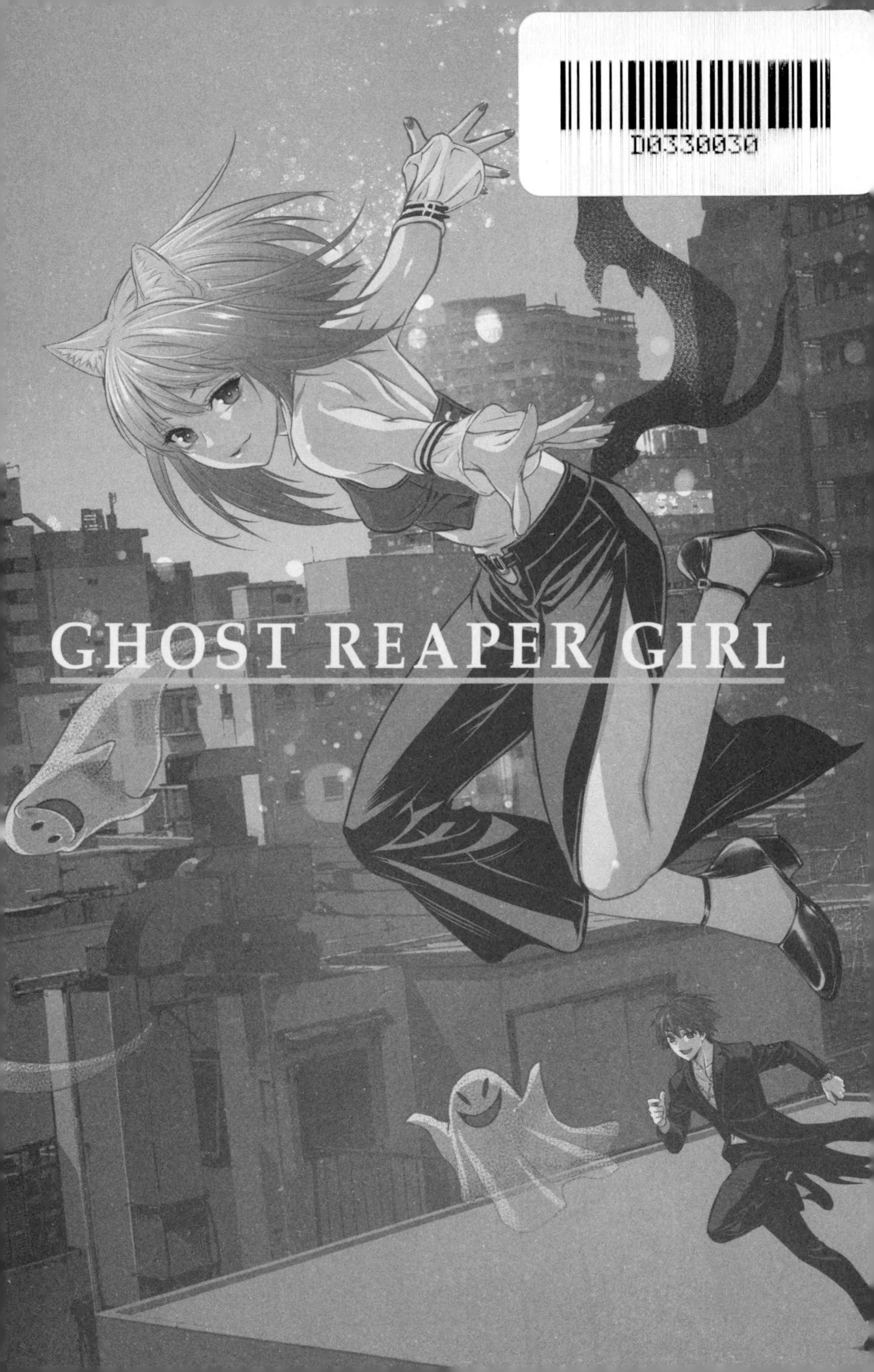
GHOST REAPER GIRL

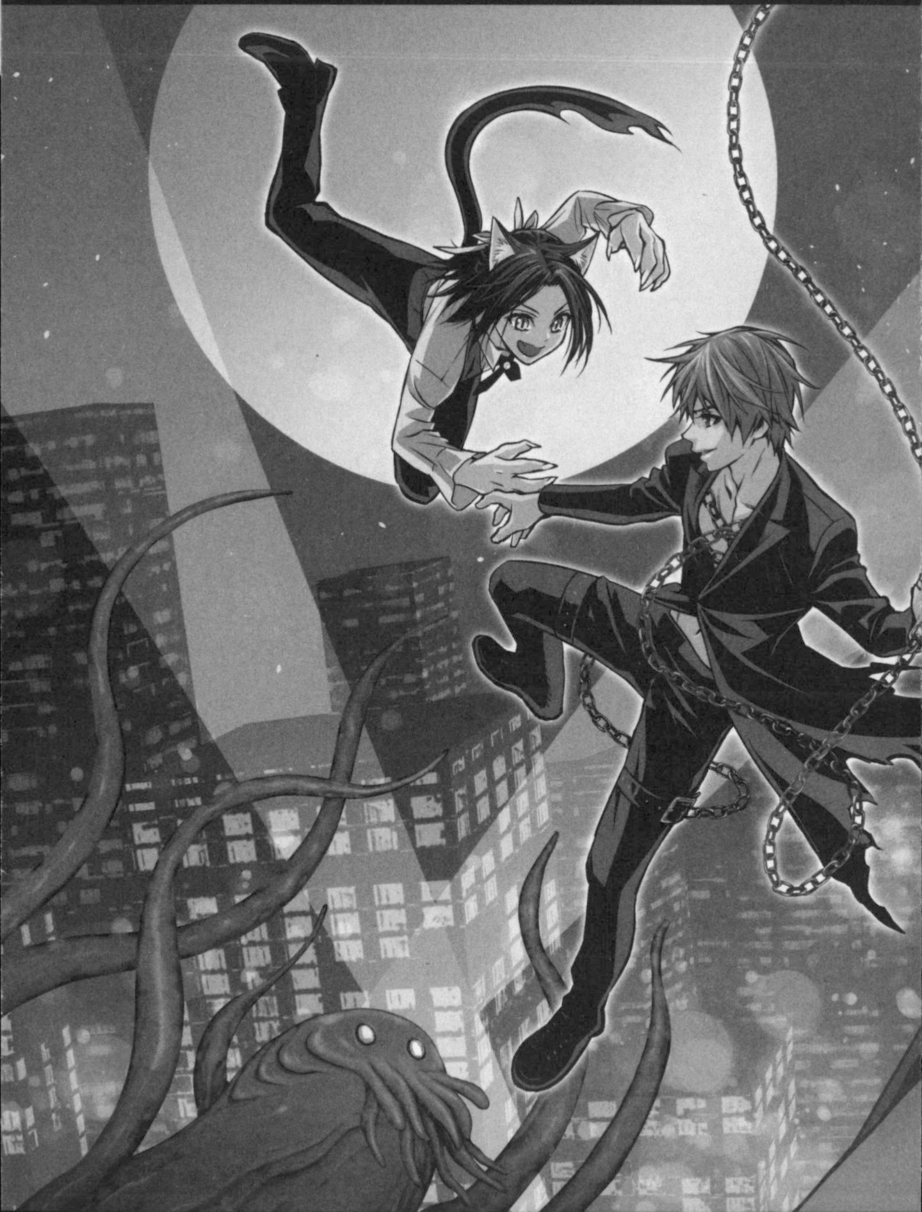

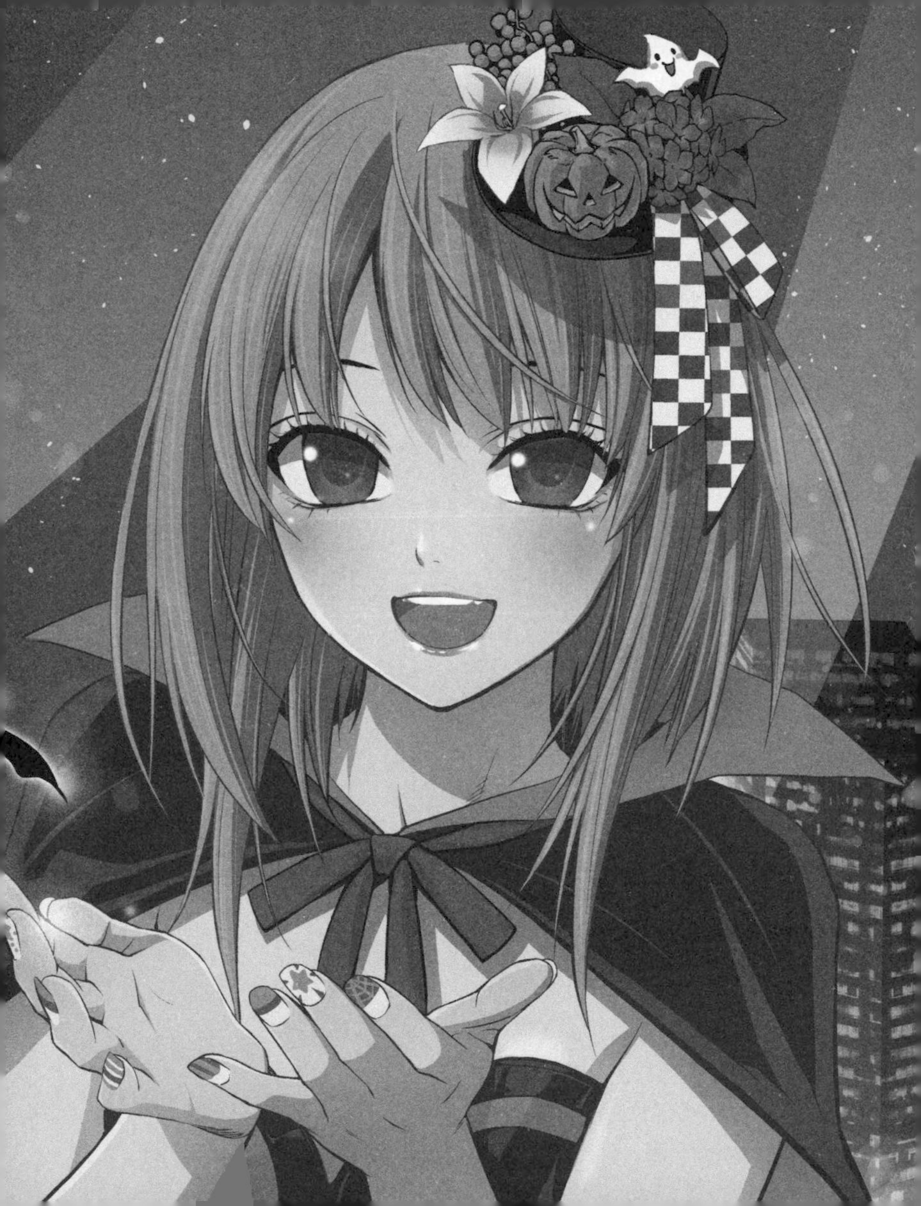

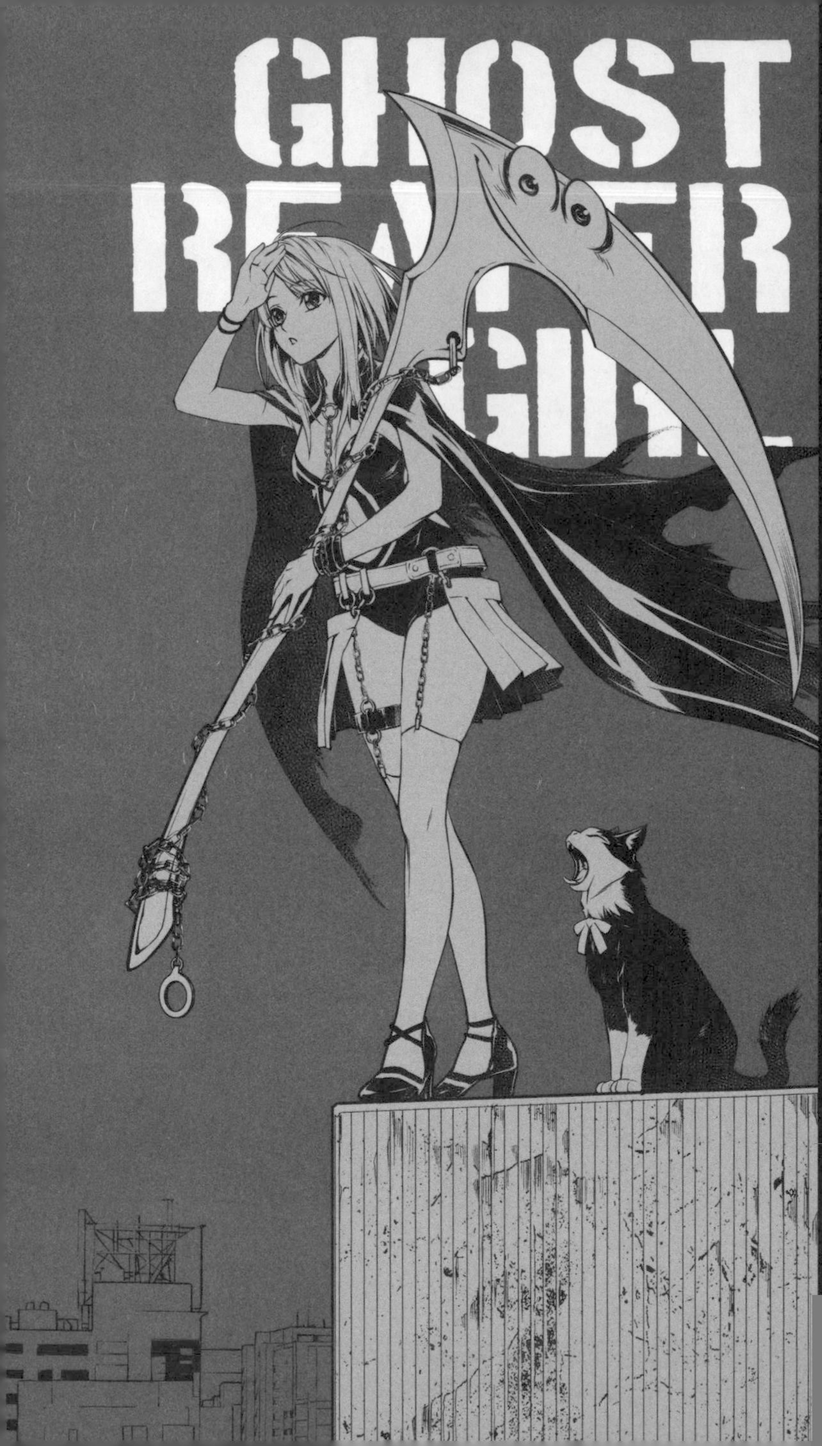
GHOST

CHARACTERS

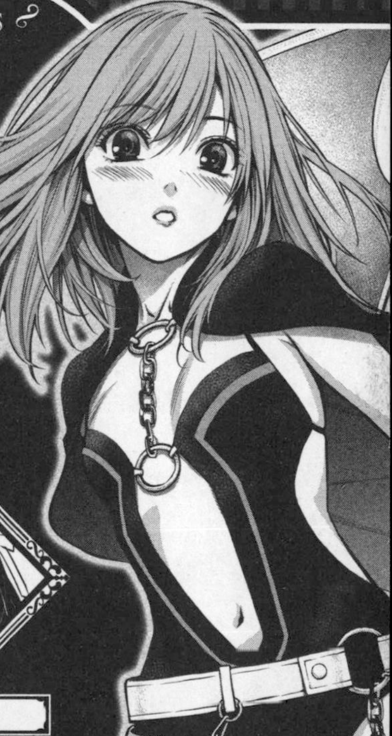

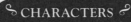

Chloé Love

After her rare genetic makeup as a spirit medium led to her meeting Kai, Chloé was thrust into the world of ghost reaping. She can let Kai or Noel possess her to transform and fight!

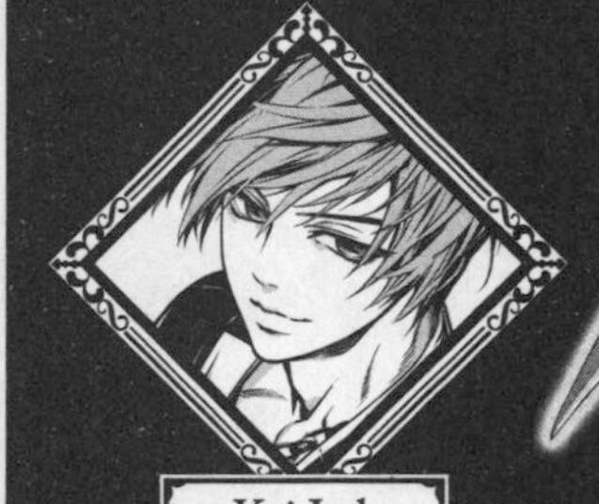

Kai Iod

A spirit and a ghost reaper. A huge fan of Chloé's acting, he volunteered to be her familiar.

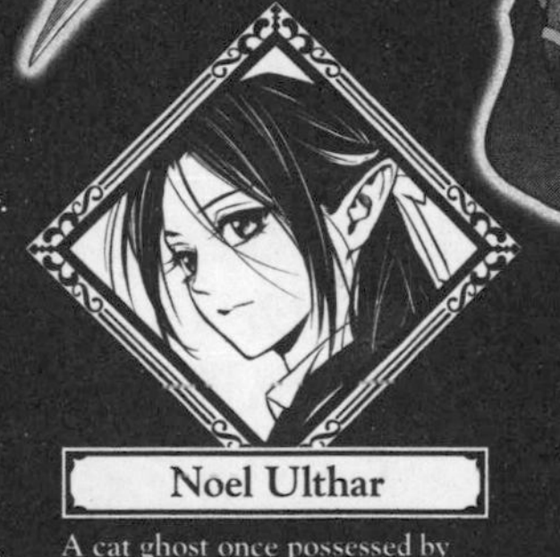

Noel Ulthar

A cat ghost once possessed by an evil spirit. Stuck around as Chloé's familiar after she saved him.

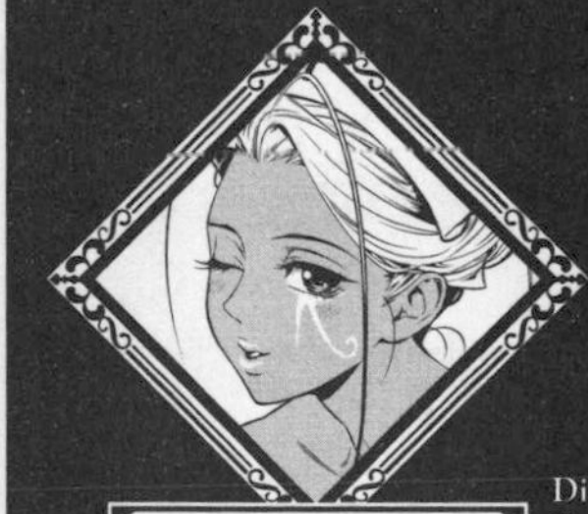

Nyarlathotep

Director of Arkham Bullet's Far East Branch. She seems to know Kai...?

STORY

When evil spirits escape from their jail in Hades, they return to the real world and plunge it into chaos. Meanwhile, unknown actress Chloé has hit a wall at age 28, until an encounter with ghost reaper Kai finds her falling into a role practically written for her—battling evil spirits! Chloé, Kai, and Noel visit Arkham Bullet to make the new job official, only to find out Chloé is wanted thanks to the video of her first fight going viral. After Noel takes a fatal attack from Nyarlathotep, Chloé orders him to possess her...

GHOST REAPER GIRL

2

CONTENTS

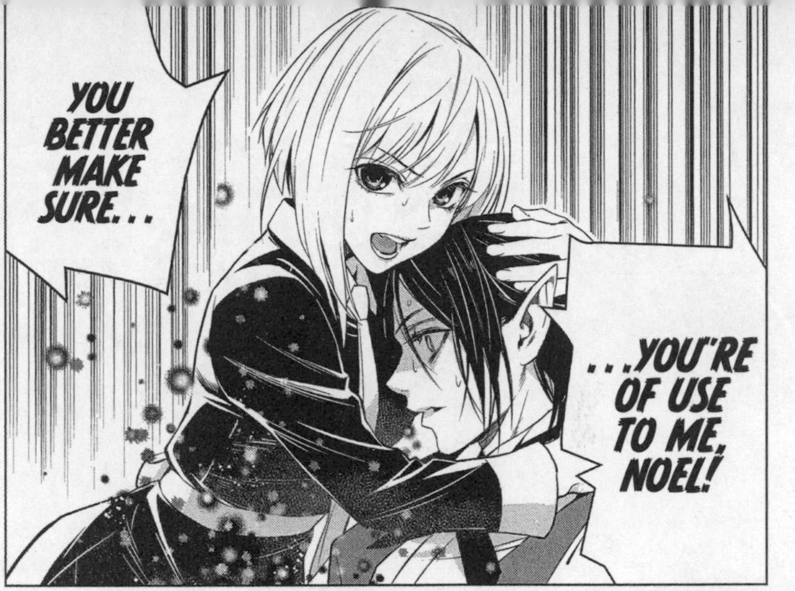
YOU BETTER MAKE SURE...
...YOU'RE OF USE TO ME, NOEL!

#5: Catfight

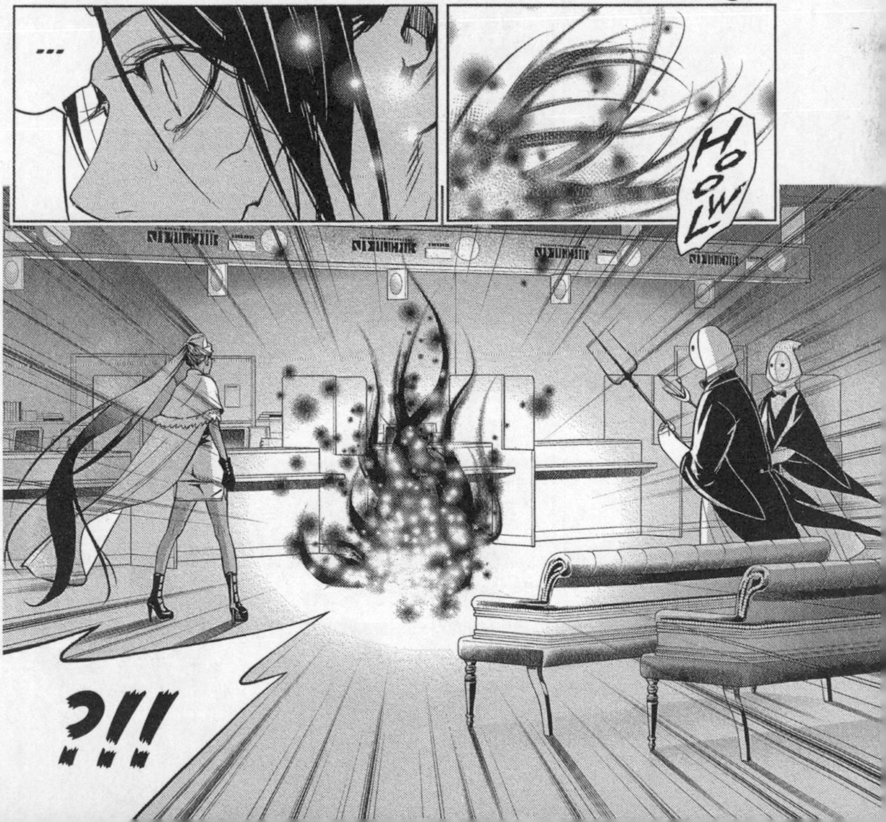
HOOWL
...
?!!

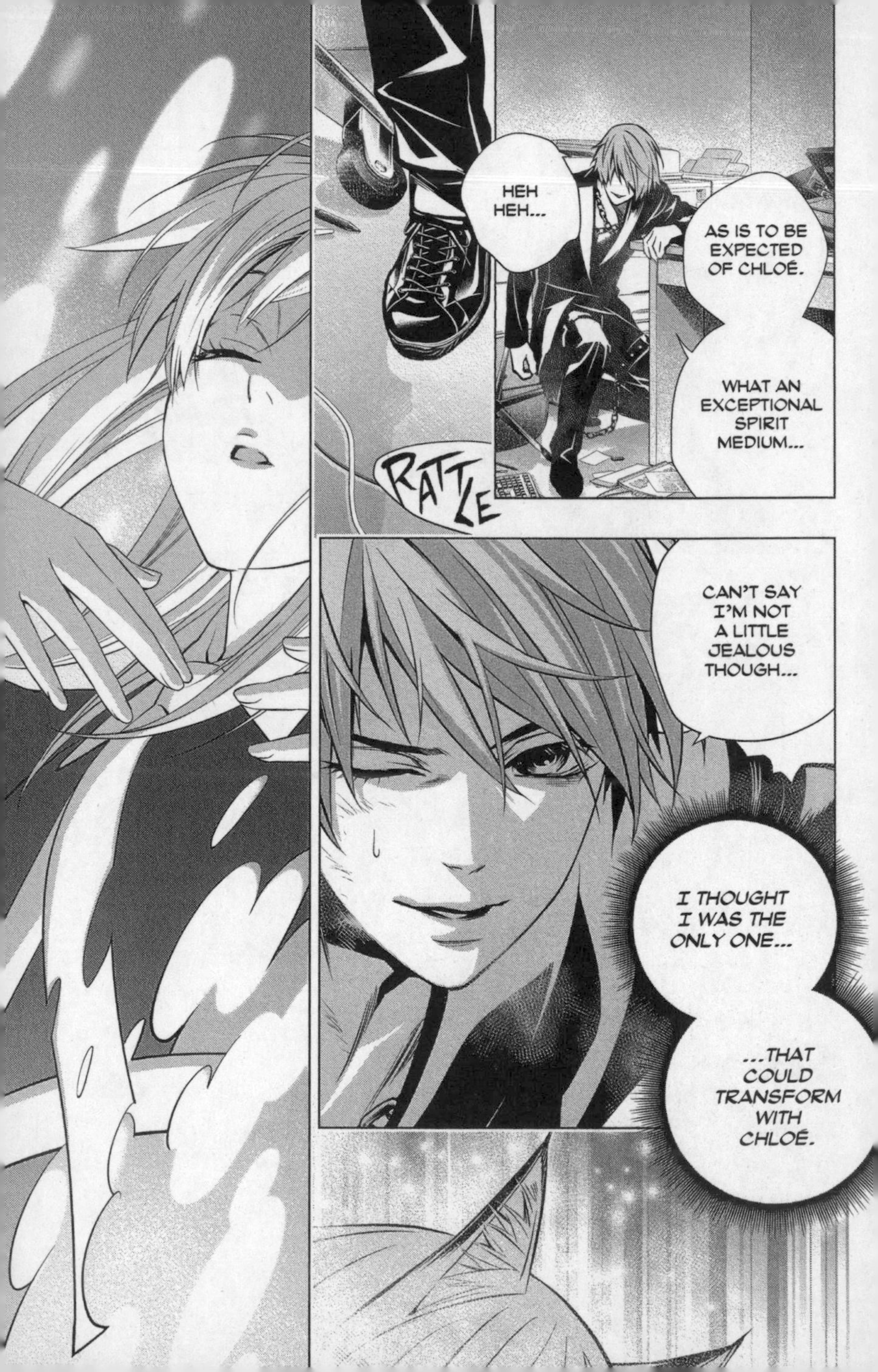
HEH HEH...
AS IS TO BE EXPECTED OF CHLOÉ.
WHAT AN EXCEPTIONAL SPIRIT MEDIUM...
RATTLE
CAN'T SAY I'M NOT A LITTLE JEALOUS THOUGH...
I THOUGHT I WAS THE ONLY ONE...
...THAT COULD TRANSFORM WITH CHLOÉ.

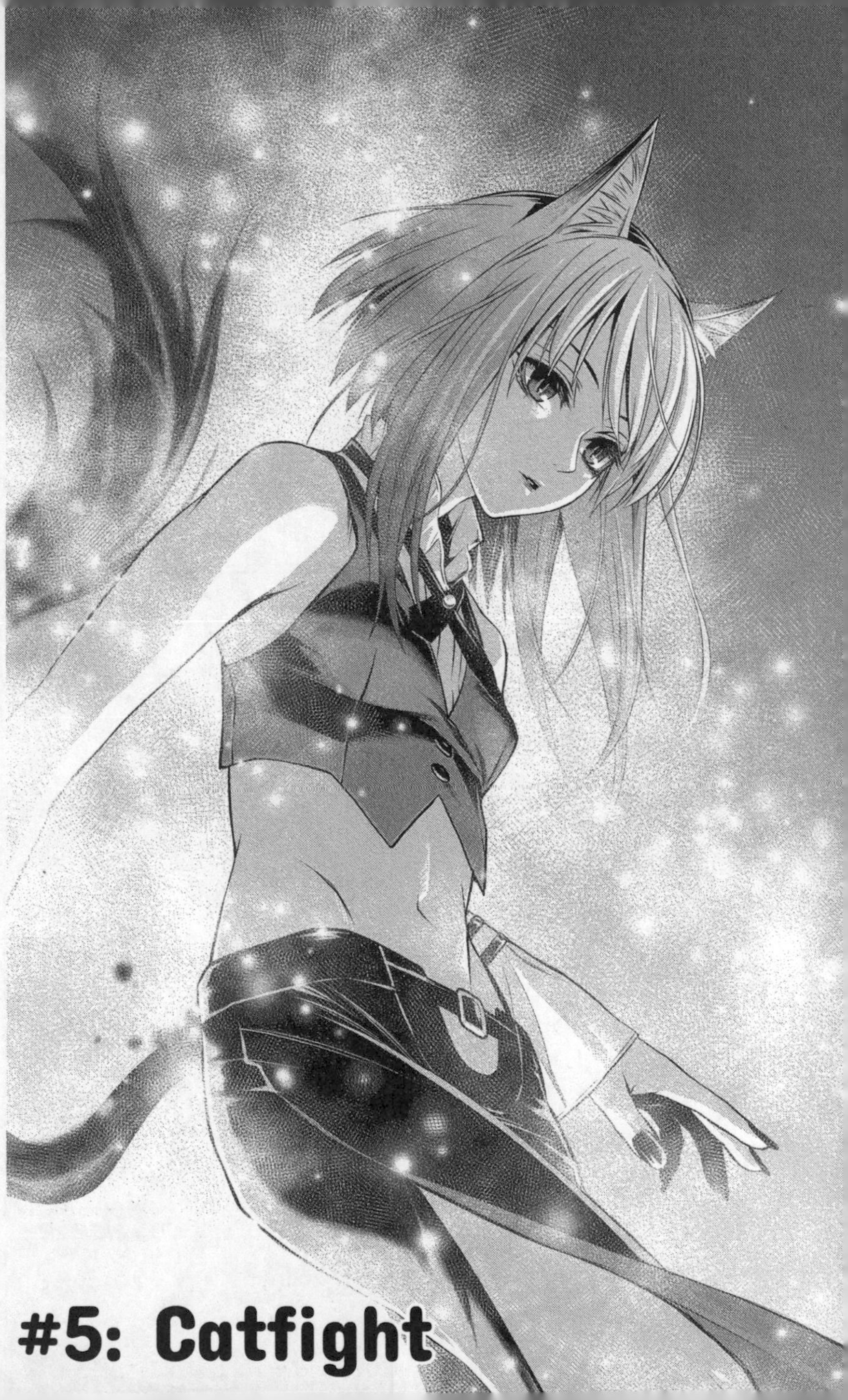

#5: Catfight

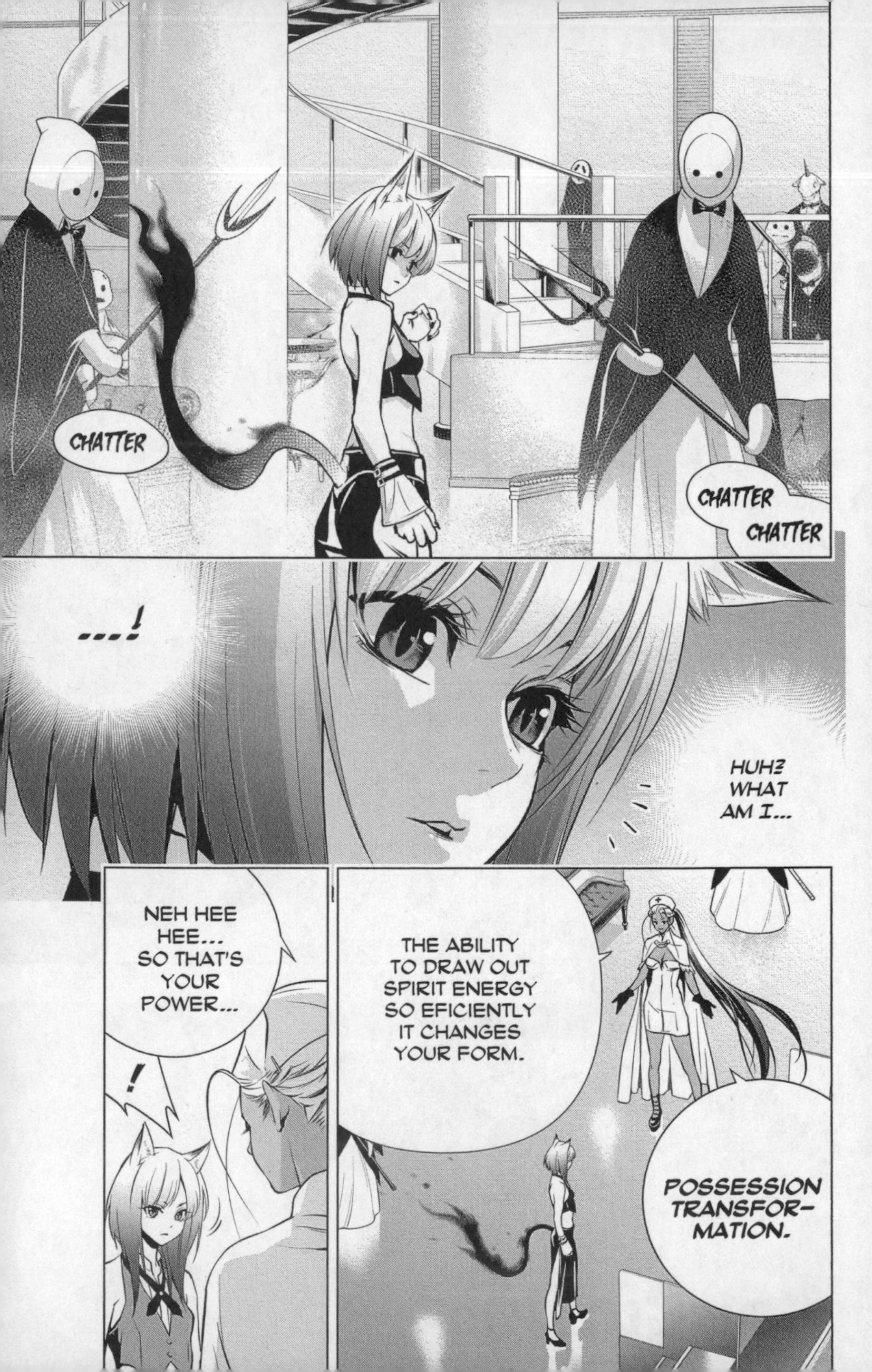
CHATTER
CHATTER CHATTER
...!
HUH? WHAT AM I...
NEH HEE HEE... SO THAT'S YOUR POWER...
!
THE ABILITY TO DRAW OUT SPIRIT ENERGY SO EFICIENTLY IT CHANGES YOUR FORM.
POSSESSION TRANSFOR-MATION.

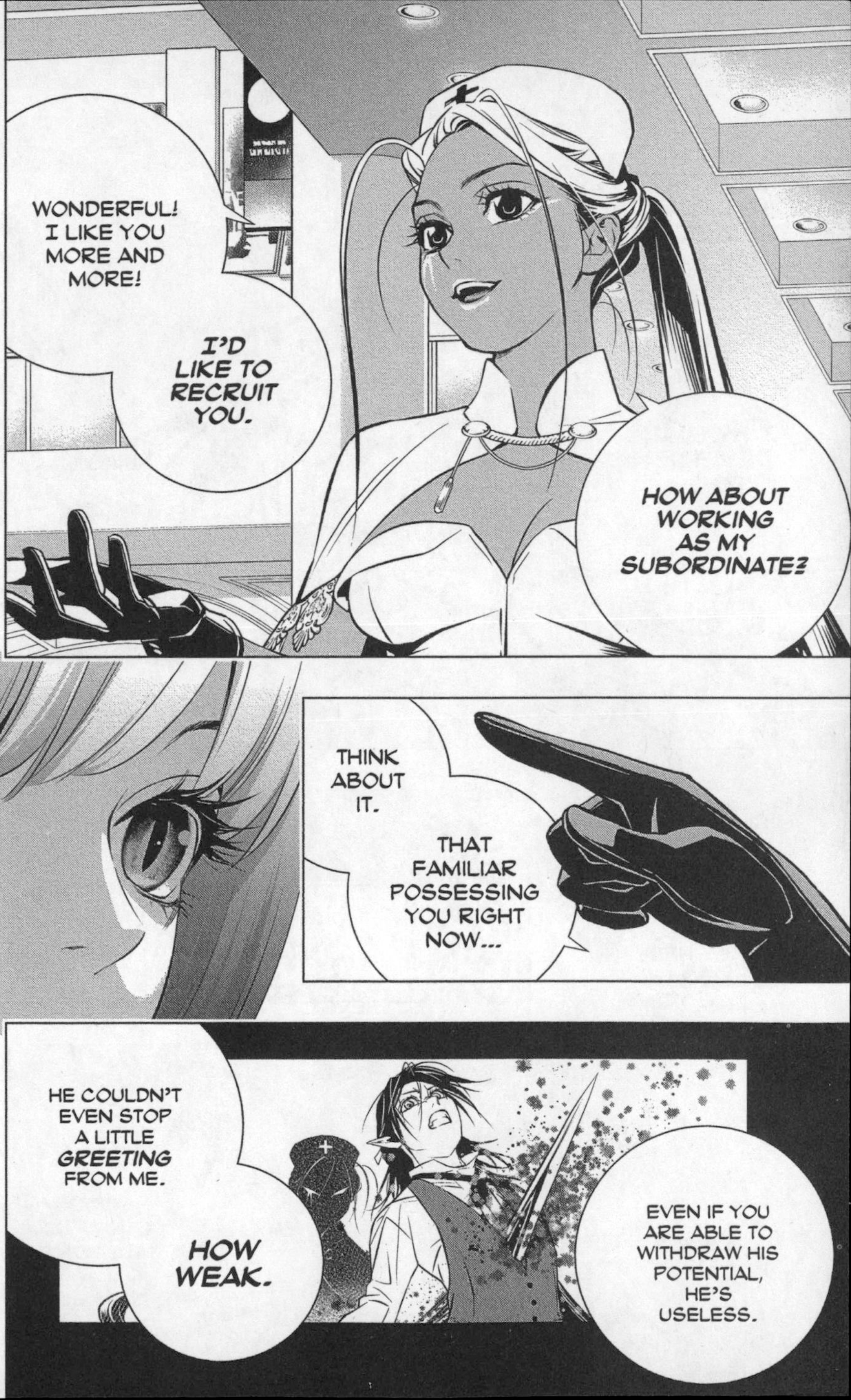
WONDERFUL! I LIKE YOU MORE AND MORE!
I'D LIKE TO RECRUIT YOU.
HOW ABOUT WORKING AS MY SUBORDINATE?
THINK ABOUT IT.
THAT FAMILIAR POSSESSING YOU RIGHT NOW...
HE COULDN'T EVEN STOP A LITTLE *GREETING* FROM ME.
HOW WEAK.
EVEN IF YOU ARE ABLE TO WITHDRAW HIS POTENTIAL, HE'S USELESS.

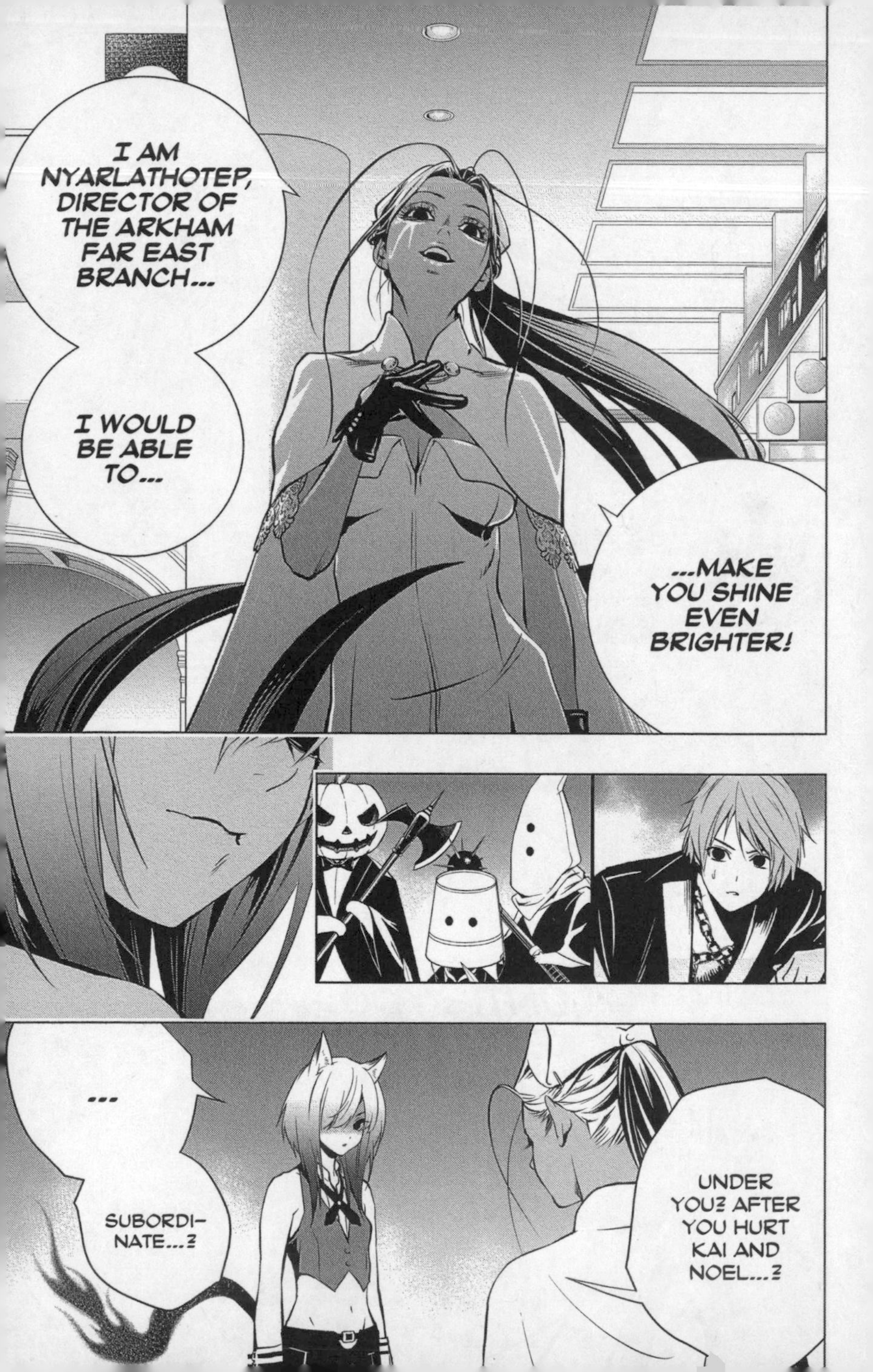
I AM NYARLATHOTEP, DIRECTOR OF THE ARKHAM FAR EAST BRANCH...
I WOULD BE ABLE TO...
...MAKE YOU SHINE EVEN BRIGHTER!
UNDER YOU? AFTER YOU HURT KAI AND NOEL...?
...
SUBORDI-NATE...?

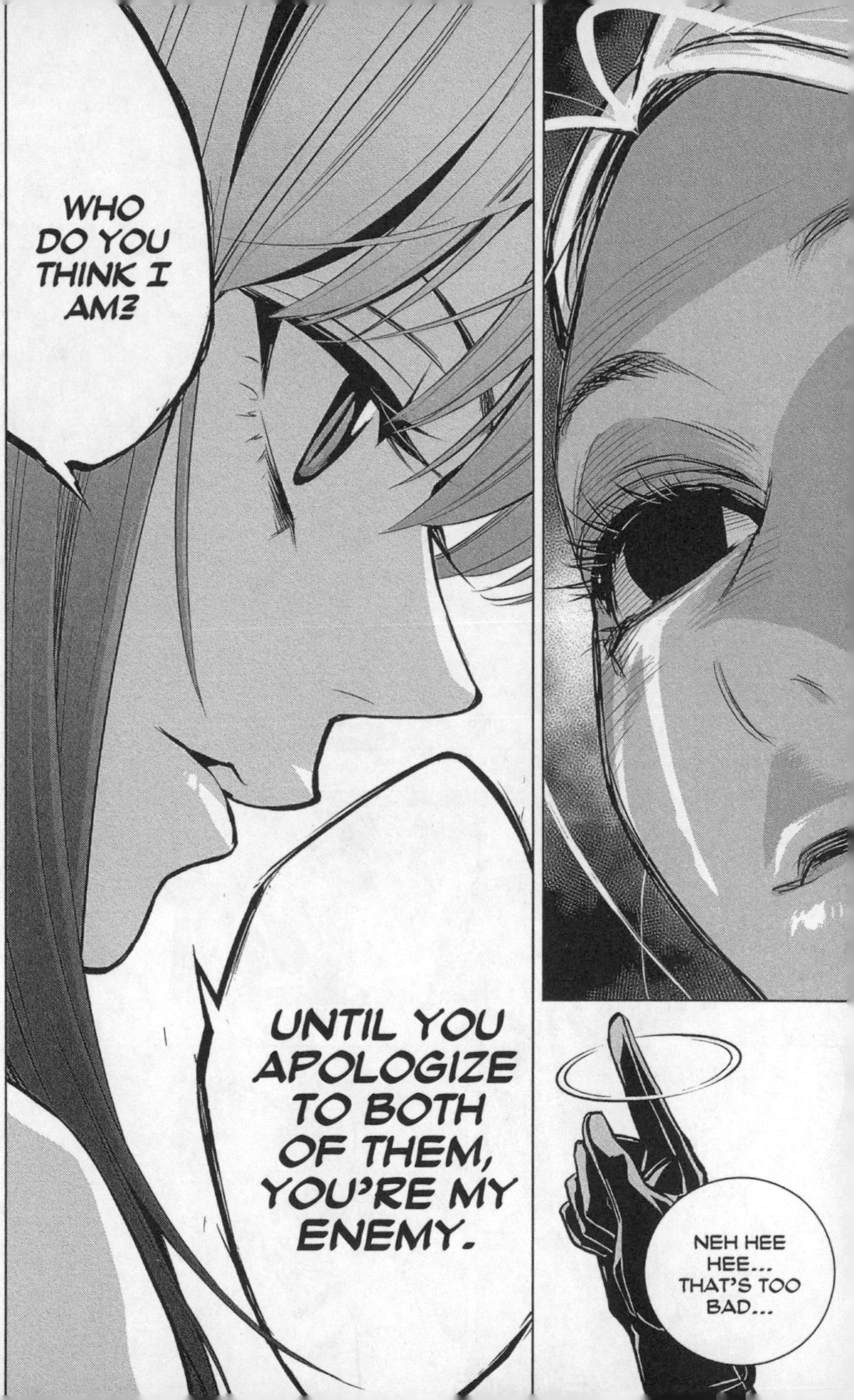
WHO DO YOU THINK I AM?
UNTIL YOU APOLOGIZE TO BOTH OF THEM, YOU'RE MY ENEMY.
NEH HEE HEE... THAT'S TOO BAD...

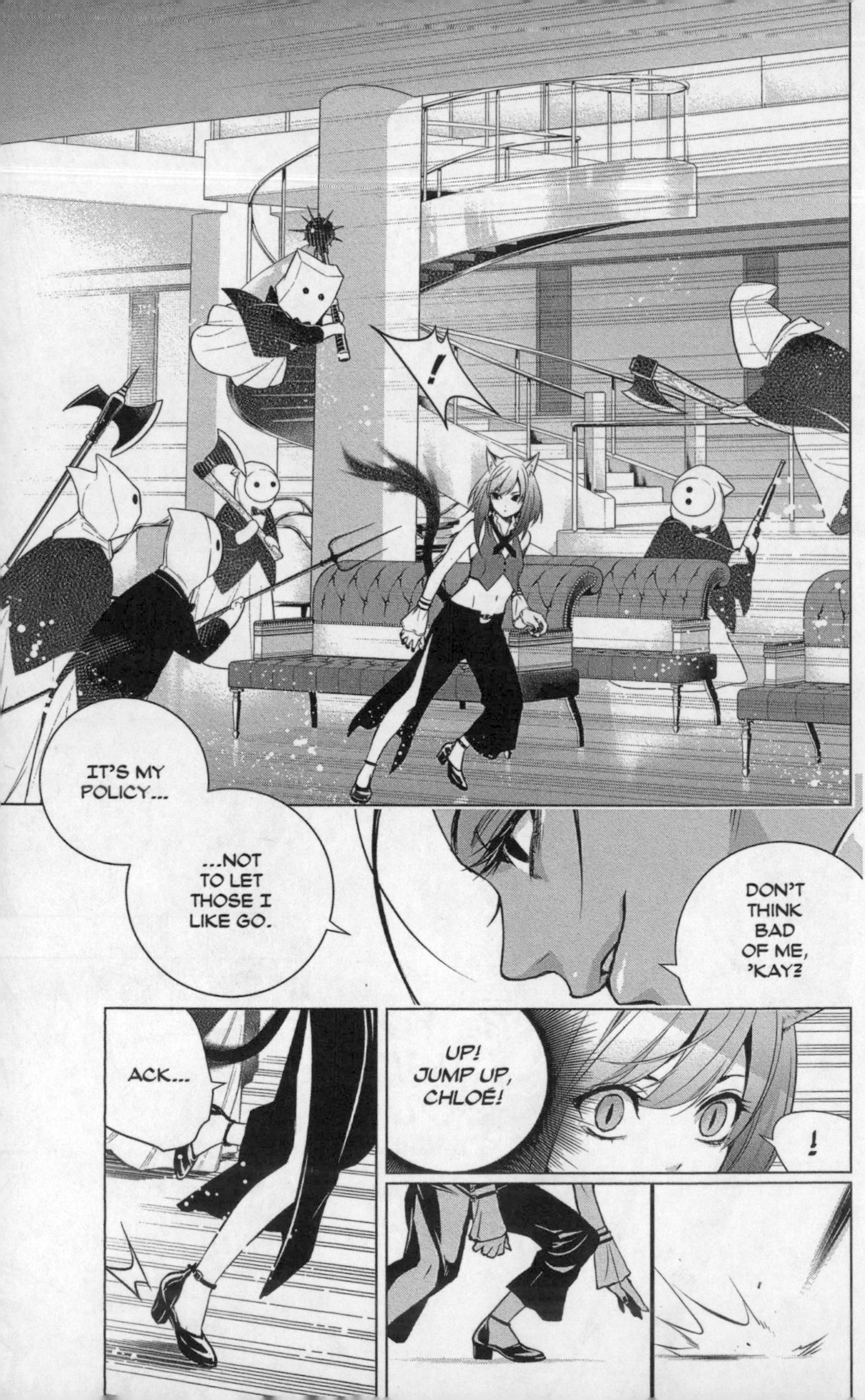
!
IT'S MY POLICY...
...NOT TO LET THOSE I LIKE GO.
DON'T THINK BAD OF ME, 'KAY?
UP! JUMP UP, CHLOÉ!
!
ACK...

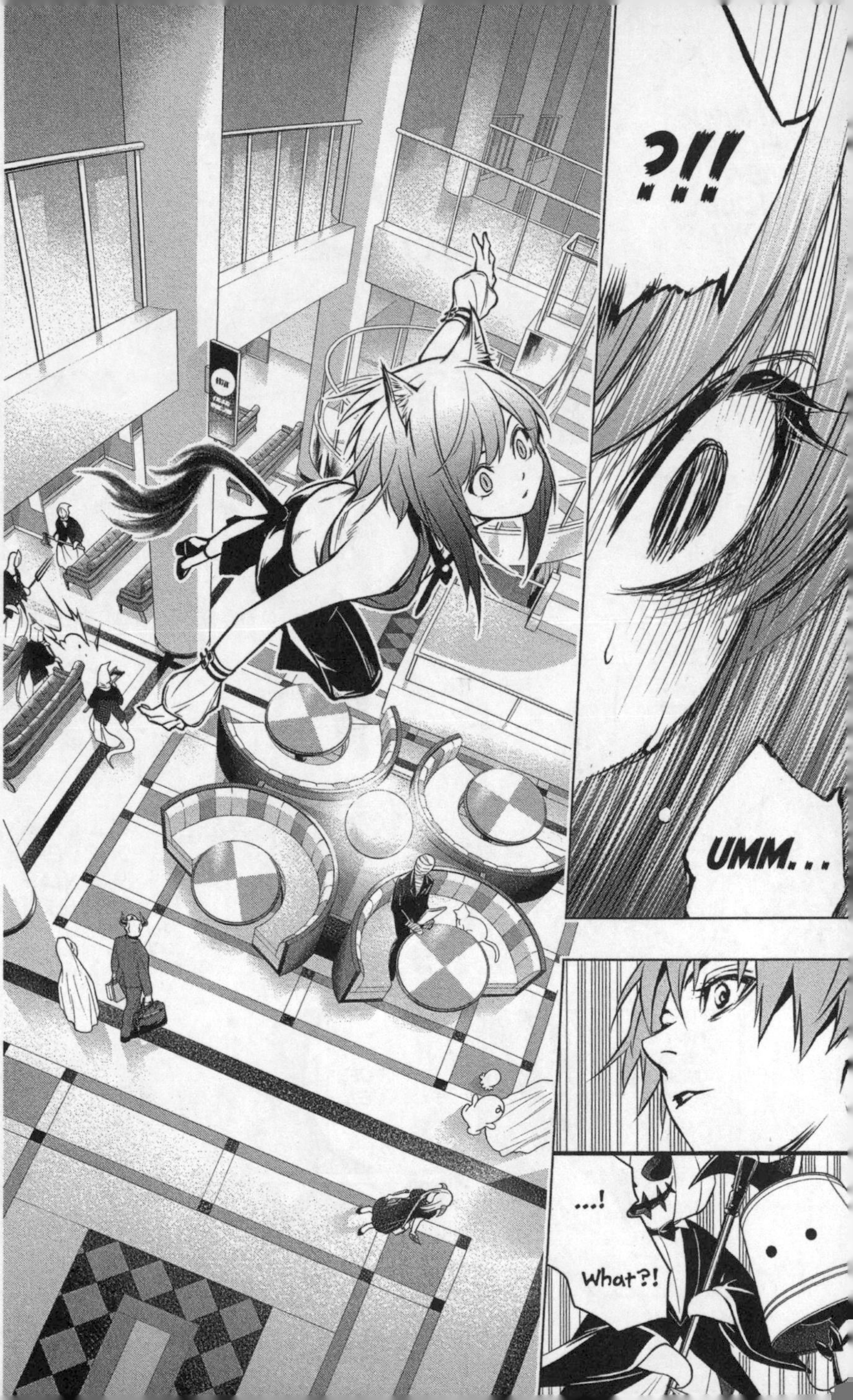
?!!
UMM...
...!
What?!

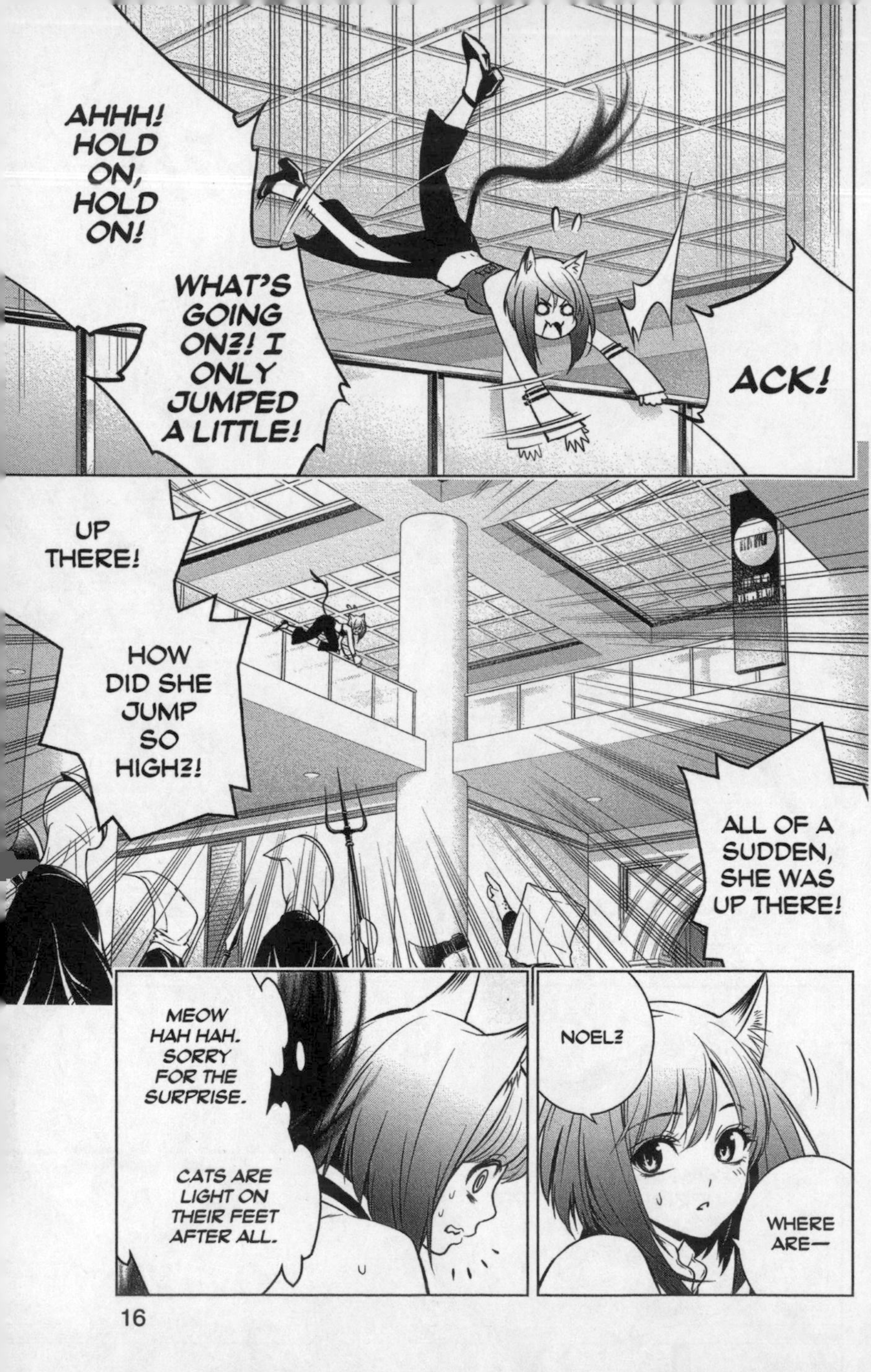
ACK!
AHHH! HOLD ON, HOLD ON!
WHAT'S GOING ON?! I ONLY JUMPED A LITTLE!
UP THERE!
HOW DID SHE JUMP SO HIGH?!
ALL OF A SUDDEN, SHE WAS UP THERE!
NOEL?
WHERE ARE—
MEOW HAH HAH. SORRY FOR THE SURPRISE.
CATS ARE LIGHT ON THEIR FEET AFTER ALL.

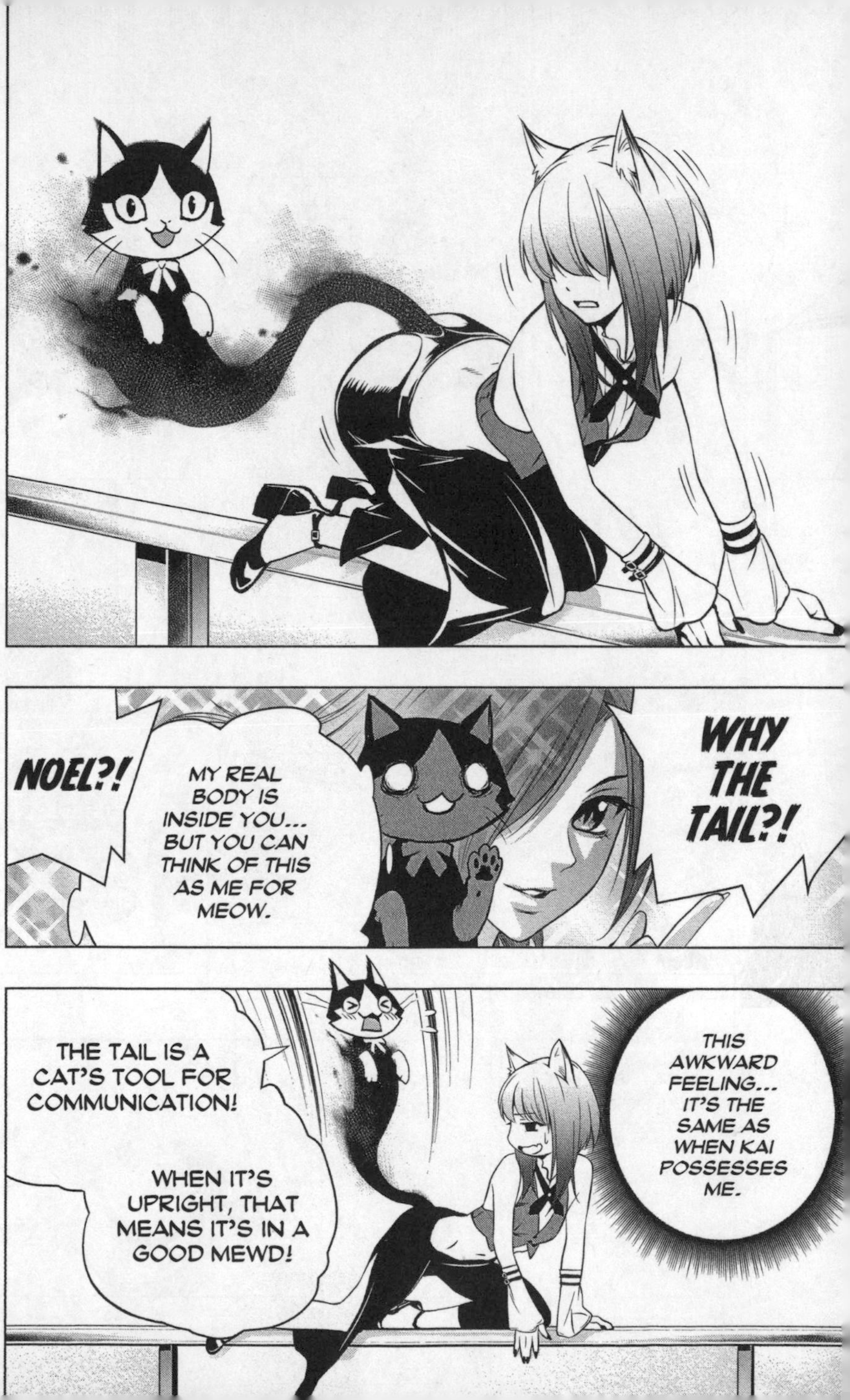
WHY THE TAIL?!
MY REAL BODY IS INSIDE YOU... BUT YOU CAN THINK OF THIS AS ME FOR MEOW.
NOEL?!
THIS AWKWARD FEELING... IT'S THE SAME AS WHEN KAI POSSESSES ME.
THE TAIL IS A CAT'S TOOL FOR COMMUNICATION!
WHEN IT'S UPRIGHT, THAT MEANS IT'S IN A GOOD MEWD!

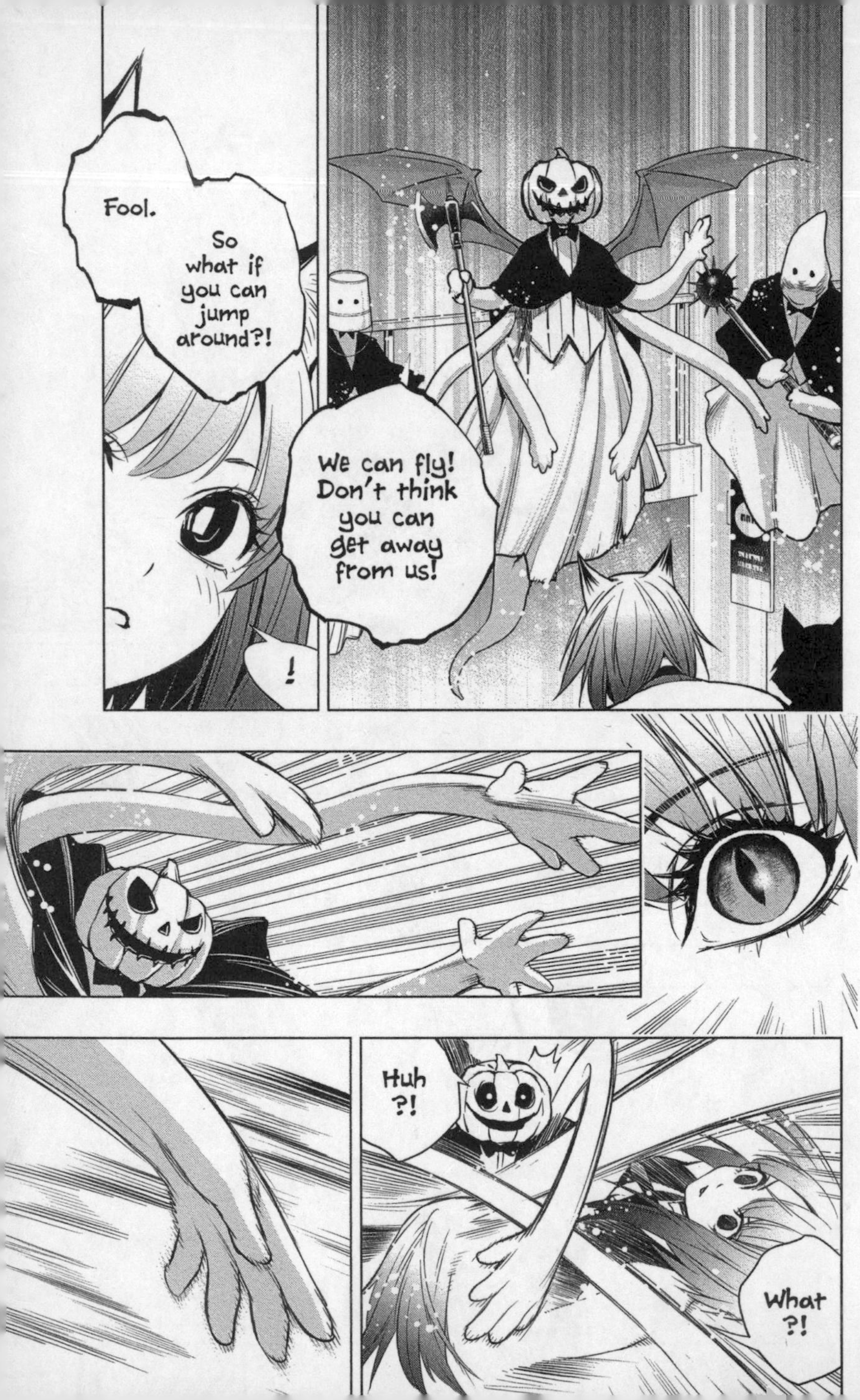
Fool.
So what if you can jump around?!
We can fly! Don't think you can get away from us!
!
Huh ?!
What ?!

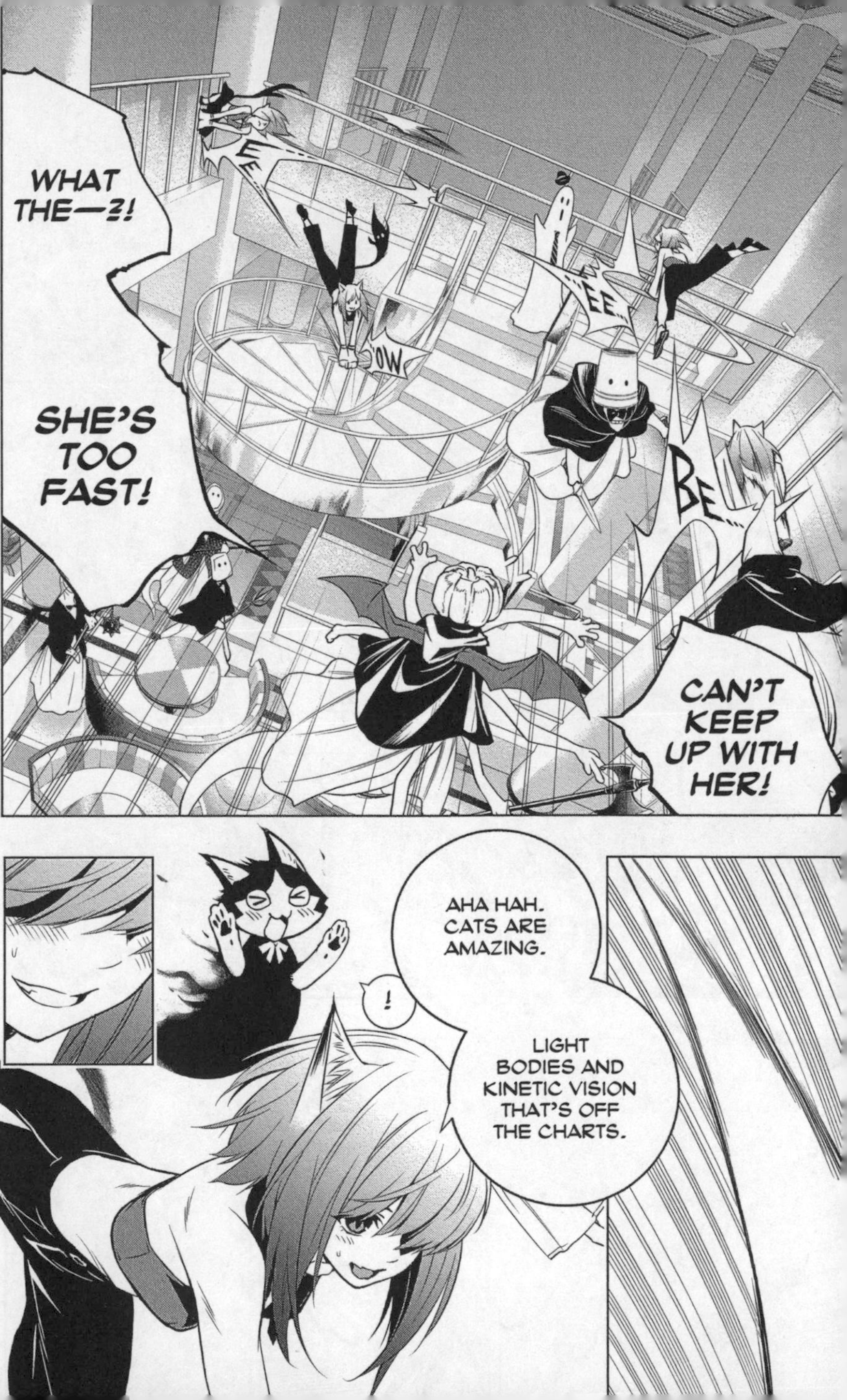
WHAT THE—?!
EE...
...EE...
OW
SHE'S TOO FAST!
BE...
CAN'T KEEP UP WITH HER!
AHA HAH. CATS ARE AMAZING.
!
LIGHT BODIES AND KINETIC VISION THAT'S OFF THE CHARTS.

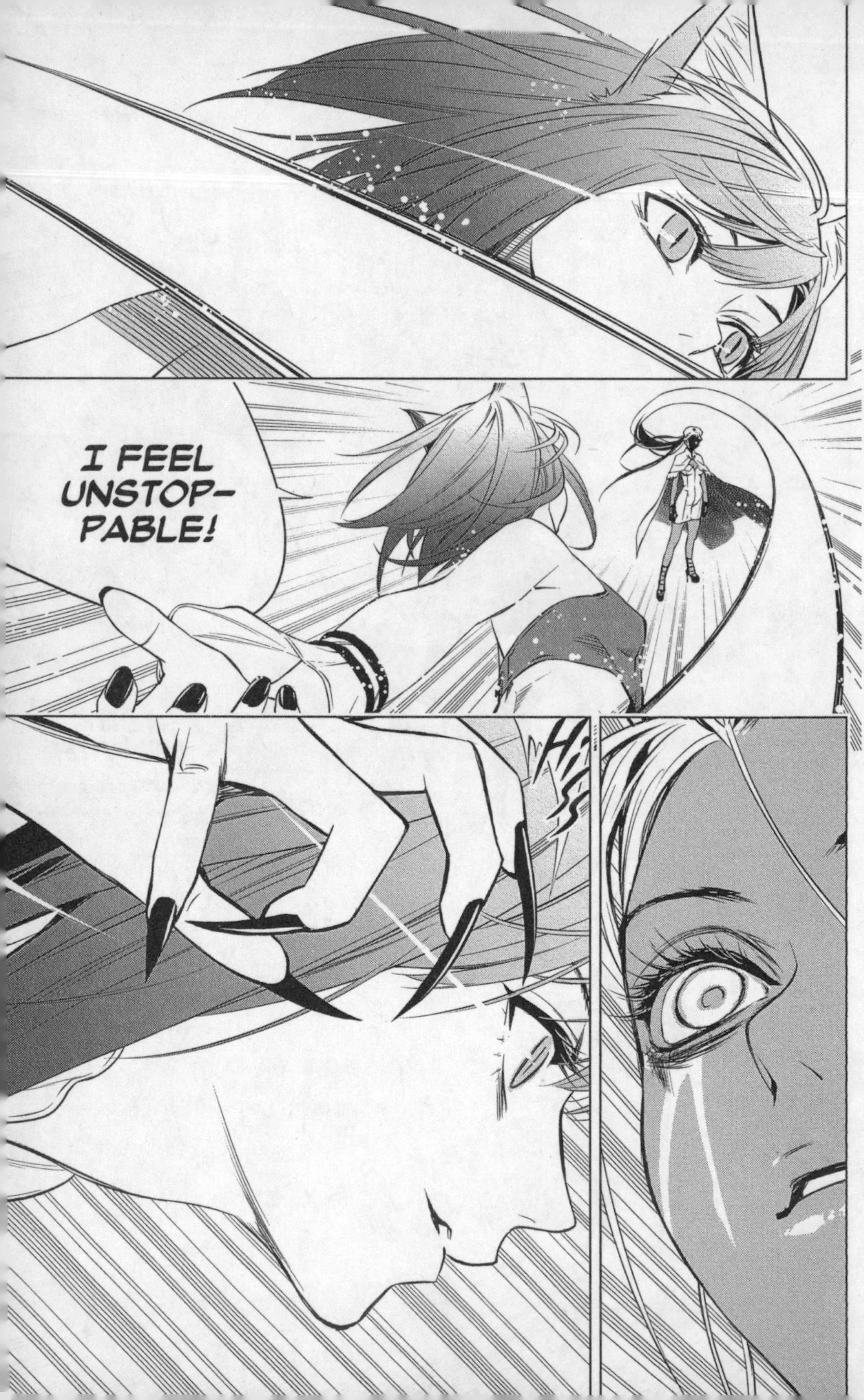
I FEEL UNSTOP-PABLE!

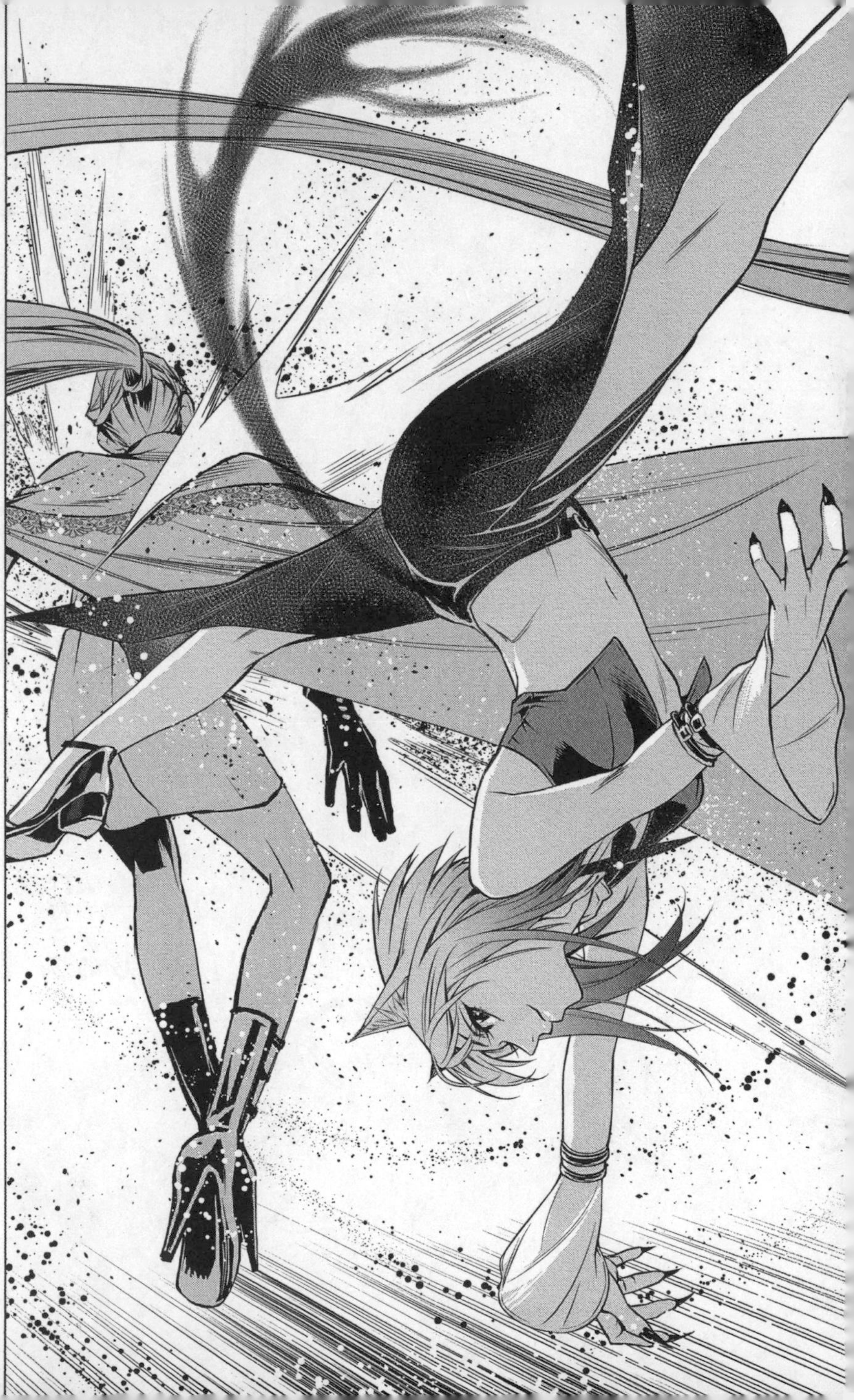

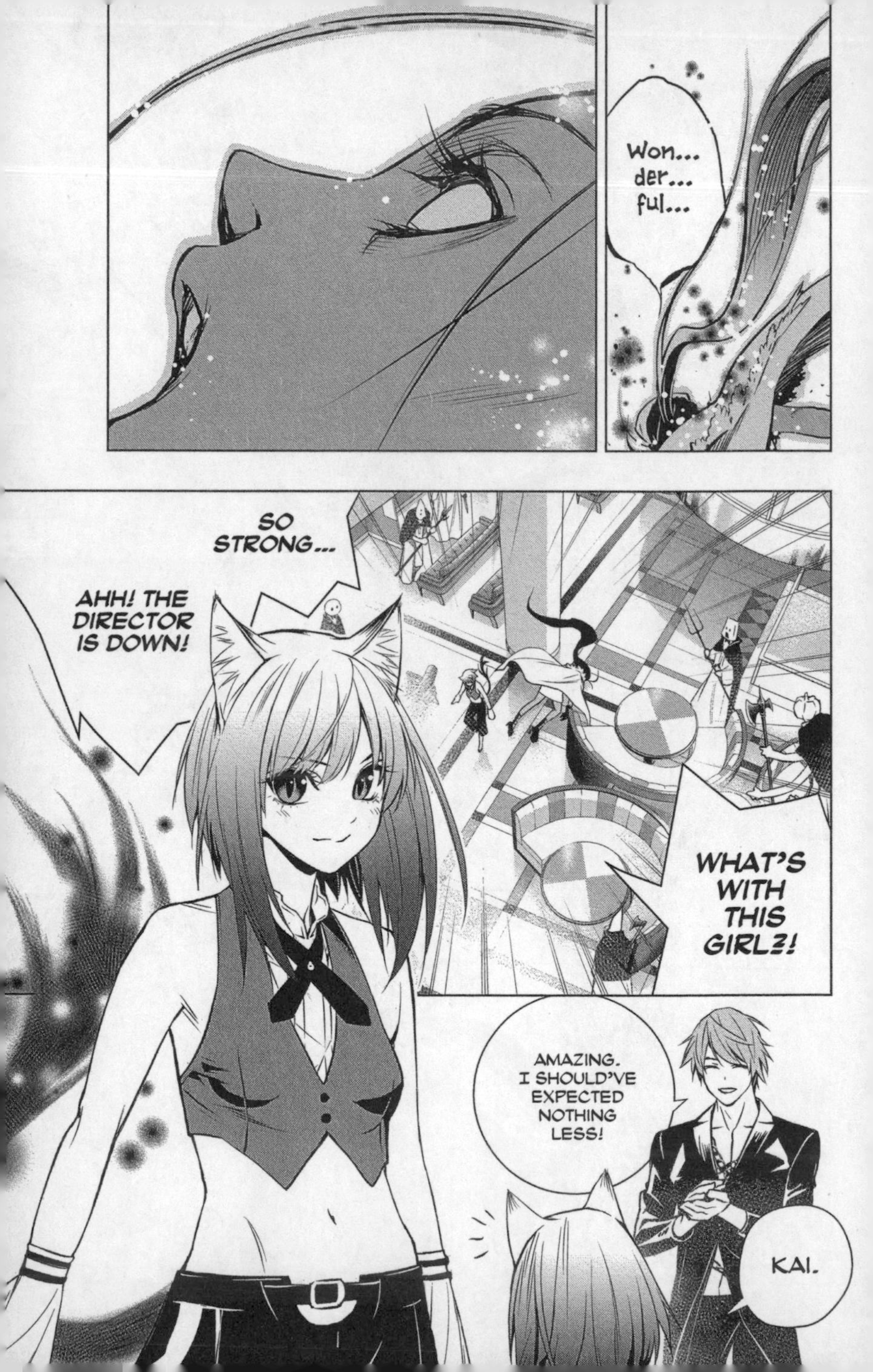
Won... der... ful...
SO STRONG...
AHH! THE DIRECTOR IS DOWN!
WHAT'S WITH THIS GIRL?!
AMAZING. I SHOULD'VE EXPECTED NOTHING LESS!
KAI.

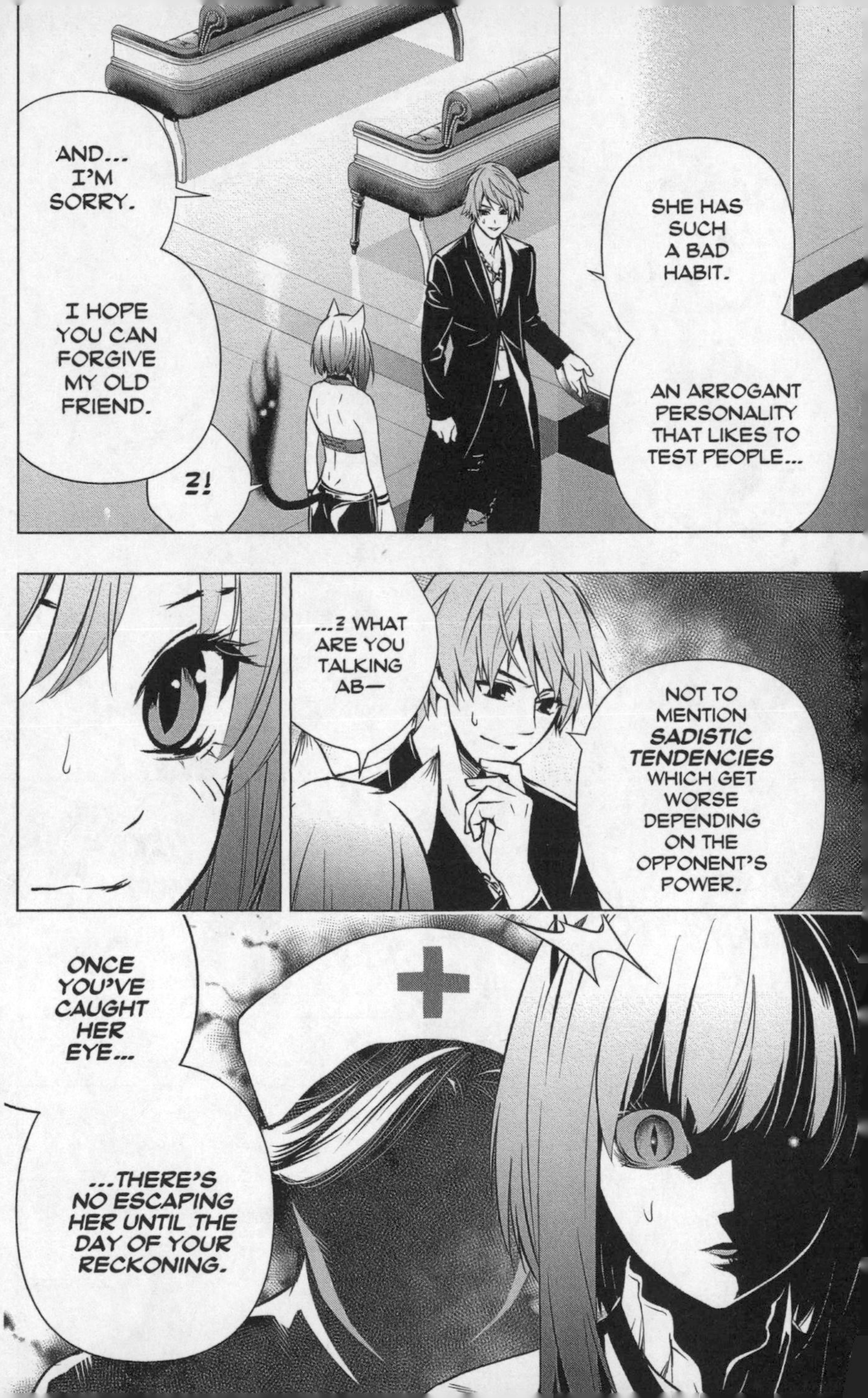
SHE HAS SUCH A BAD HABIT.
AN ARROGANT PERSONALITY THAT LIKES TO TEST PEOPLE...
AND... I'M SORRY.
I HOPE YOU CAN FORGIVE MY OLD FRIEND.
?!
...? WHAT ARE YOU TALKING AB—
NOT TO MENTION *SADISTIC TENDENCIES* WHICH GET WORSE DEPENDING ON THE OPPONENT'S POWER.
ONCE YOU'VE CAUGHT HER EYE...
...THERE'S NO ESCAPING HER UNTIL THE DAY OF YOUR RECKONING.

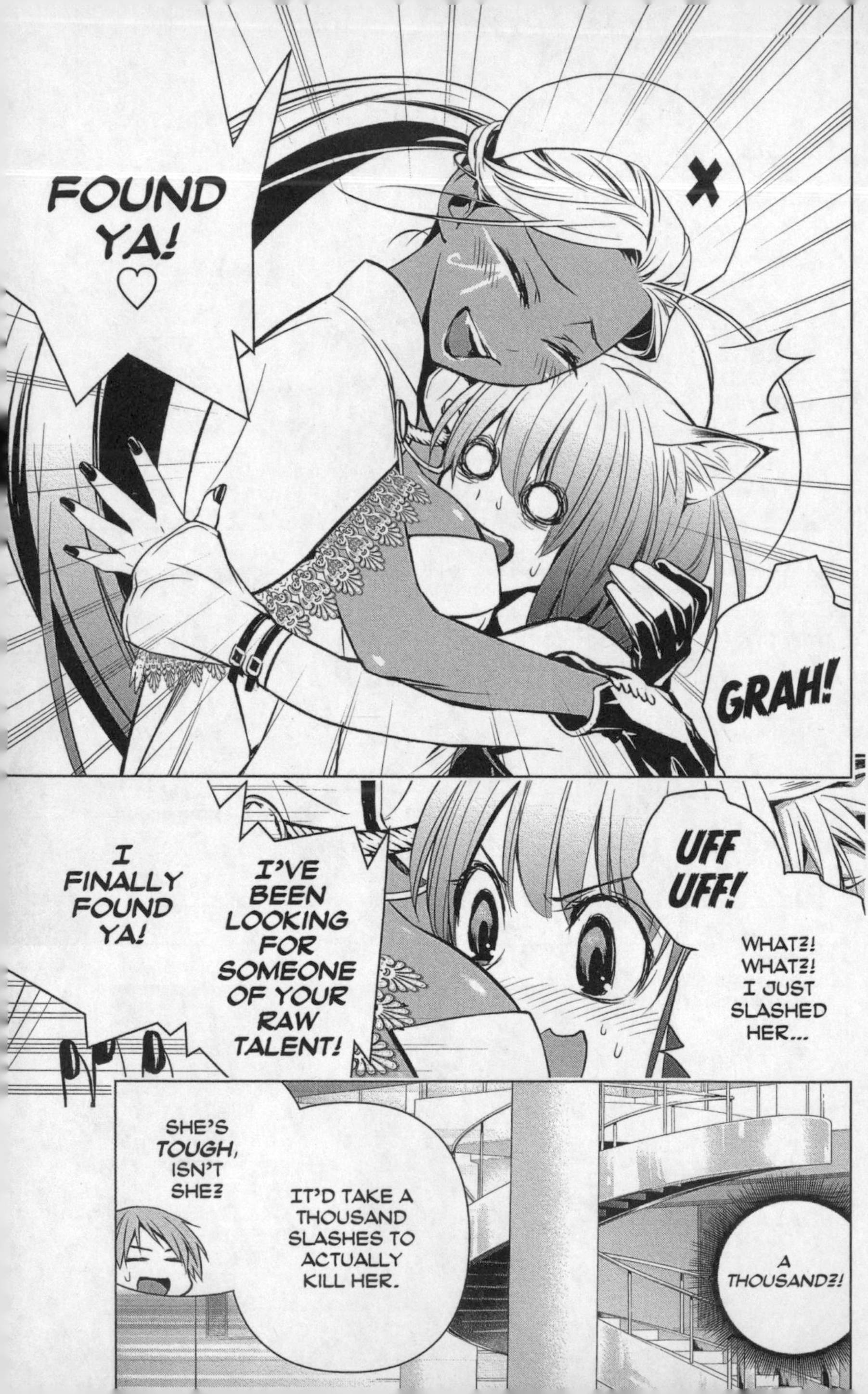
FOUND YA! ♡
GRAH!
I FINALLY FOUND YA!
I'VE BEEN LOOKING FOR SOMEONE OF YOUR RAW TALENT!
UFF UFF!
WHAT?! WHAT?! I JUST SLASHED HER...
SHE'S TOUGH, ISN'T SHE?
IT'D TAKE A THOUSAND SLASHES TO ACTUALLY KILL HER.
A THOUSAND?!

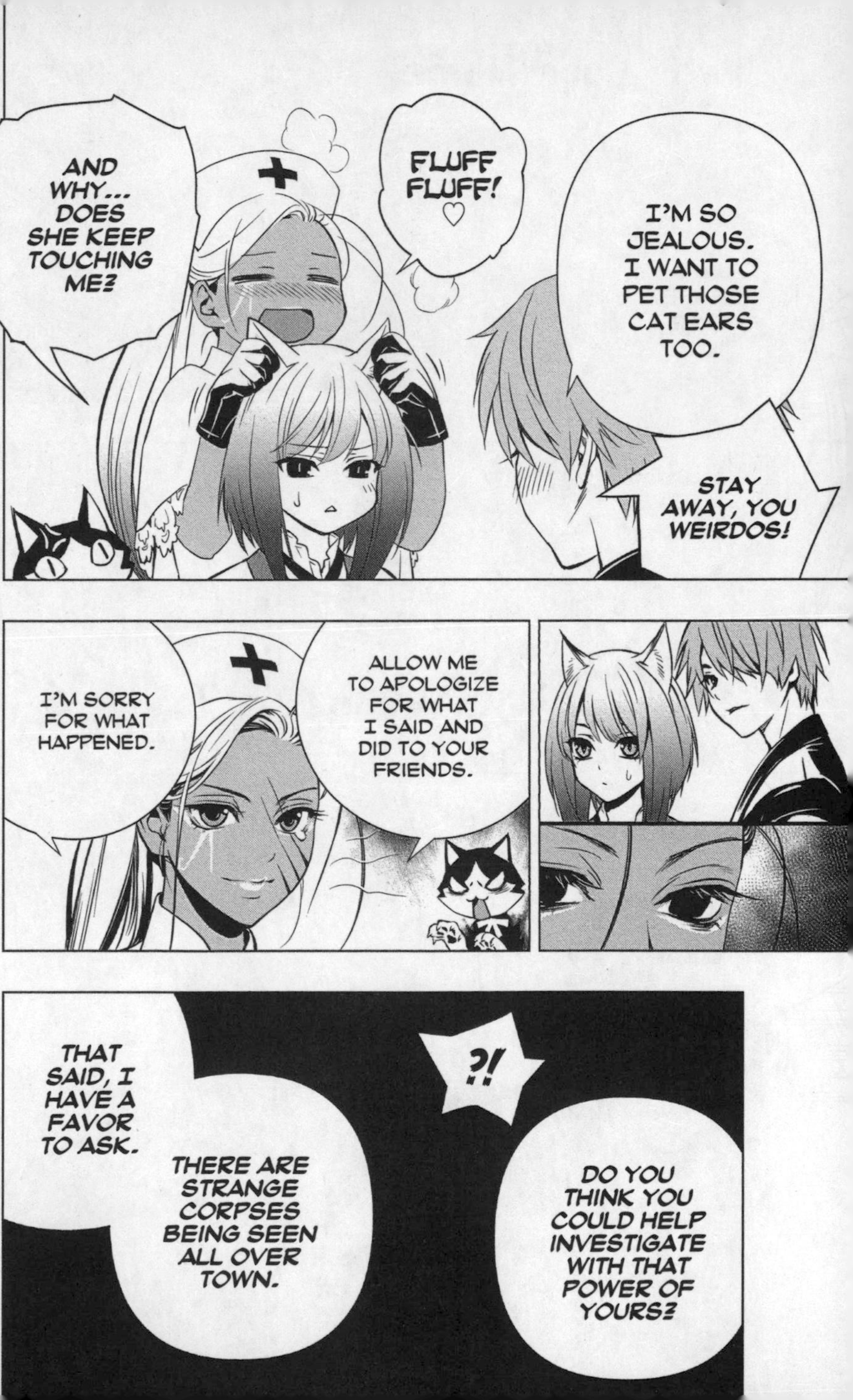
AND WHY... DOES SHE KEEP TOUCHING ME?
FLUFF FLUFF! ♡
I'M SO JEALOUS. I WANT TO PET THOSE CAT EARS TOO.
STAY AWAY, YOU WEIRDOS!
I'M SORRY FOR WHAT HAPPENED.
ALLOW ME TO APOLOGIZE FOR WHAT I SAID AND DID TO YOUR FRIENDS.
THAT SAID, I HAVE A FAVOR TO ASK.
THERE ARE STRANGE CORPSES BEING SEEN ALL OVER TOWN.
DO YOU THINK YOU COULD HELP INVESTIGATE WITH THAT POWER OF YOURS?
?!

#6: Code Name

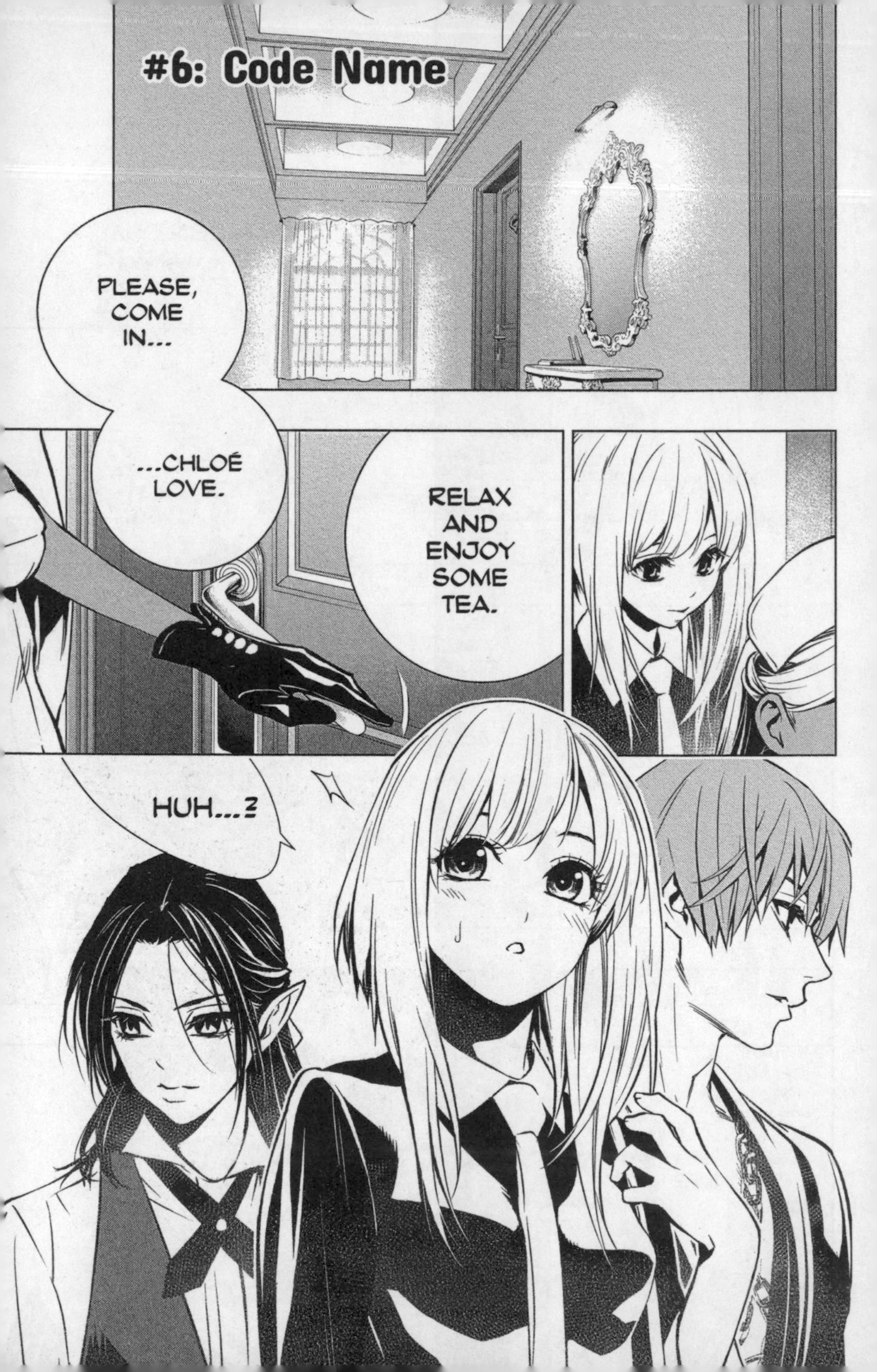
PLEASE, COME IN...
...CHLOÉ LOVE.
RELAX AND ENJOY SOME TEA.
HUH...?

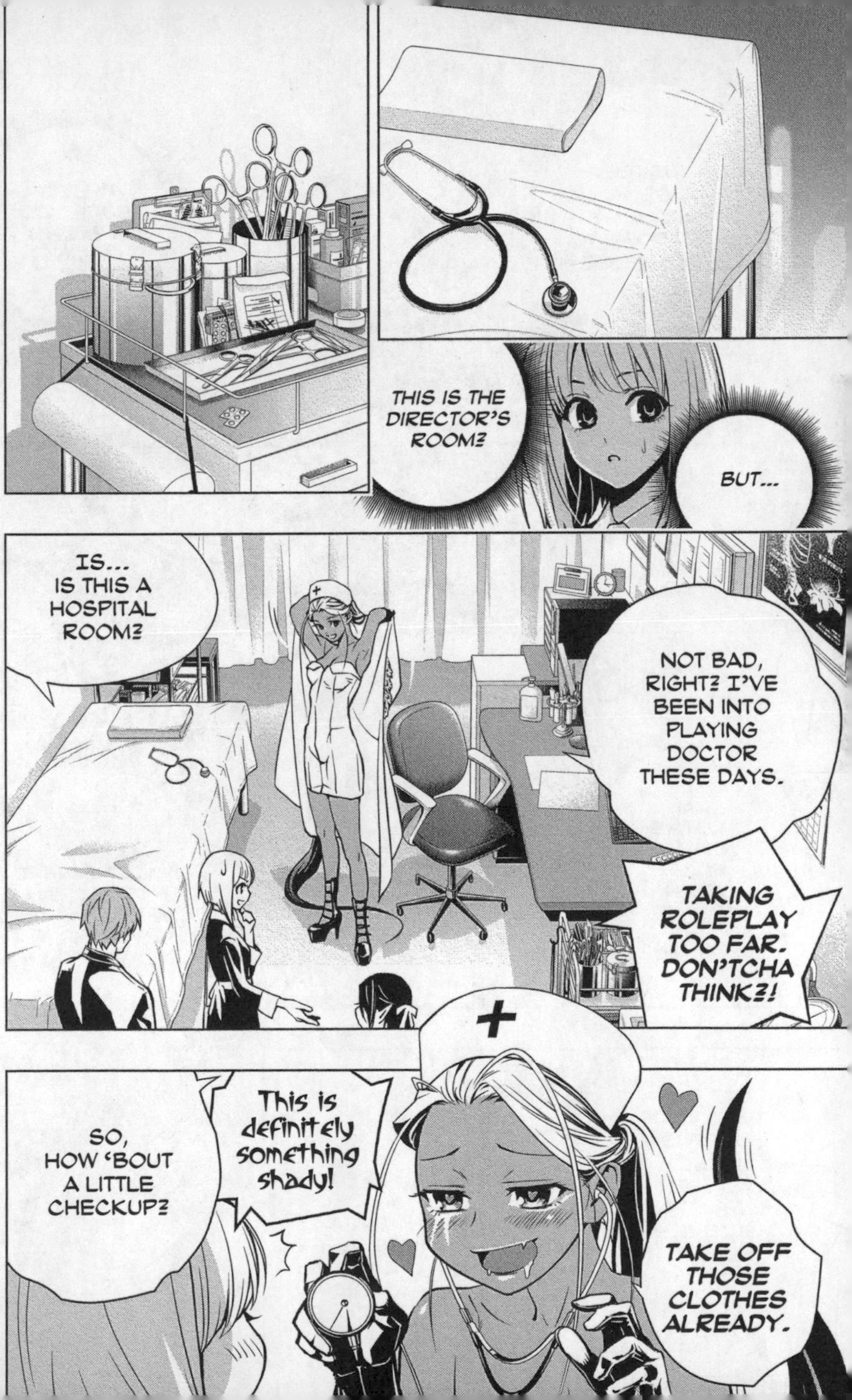
THIS IS THE DIRECTOR'S ROOM?
BUT...
IS... IS THIS A HOSPITAL ROOM?
NOT BAD, RIGHT? I'VE BEEN INTO PLAYING DOCTOR THESE DAYS.
TAKING ROLEPLAY TOO FAR. DON'TCHA THINK?!
SO, HOW 'BOUT A LITTLE CHECKUP?
TAKE OFF THOSE CLOTHES ALREADY.
This is definitely something shady!

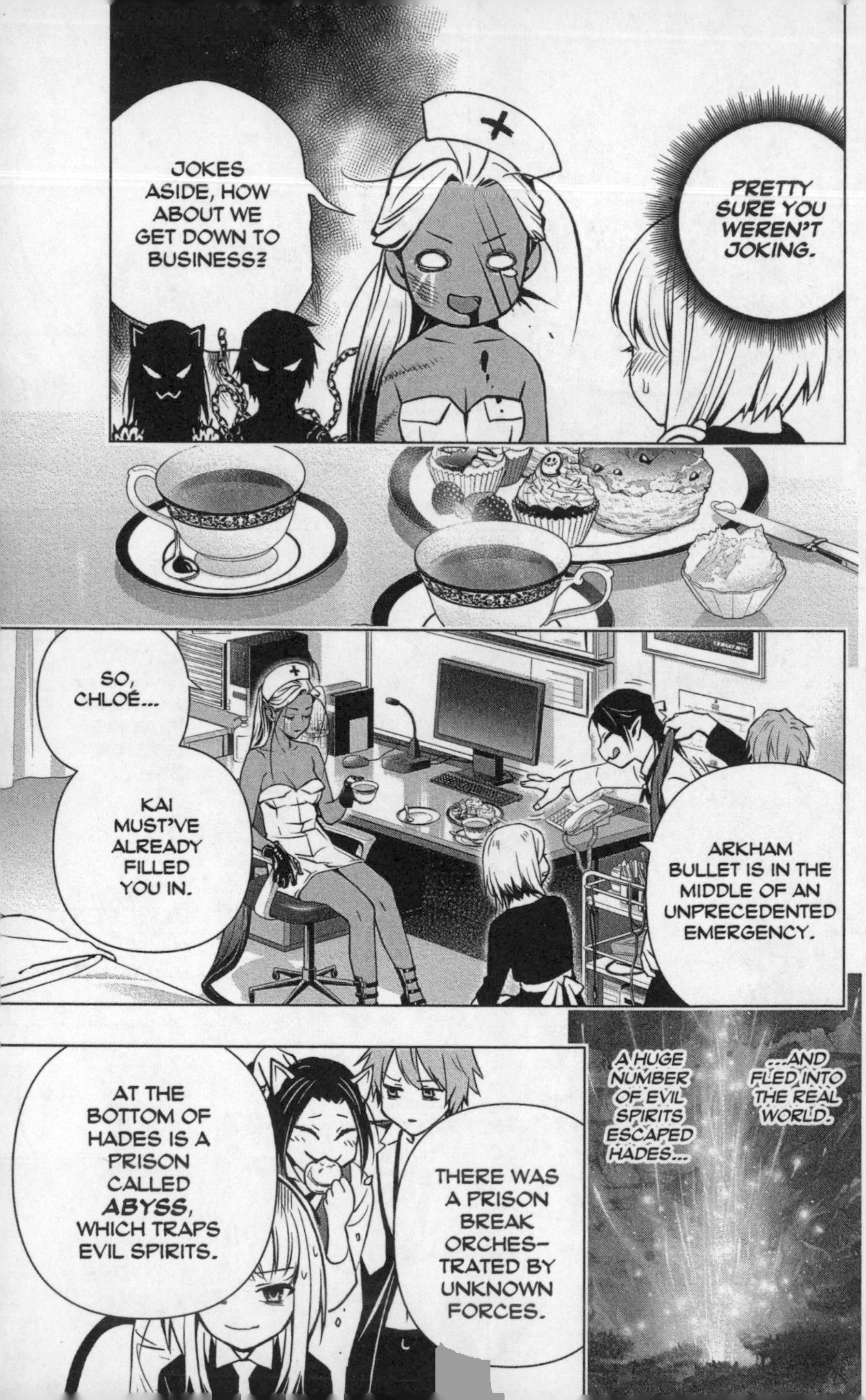
JOKES ASIDE, HOW ABOUT WE GET DOWN TO BUSINESS?
PRETTY SURE YOU WEREN'T JOKING.
SO, CHLOÉ...
KAI MUST'VE ALREADY FILLED YOU IN.
ARKHAM BULLET IS IN THE MIDDLE OF AN UNPRECEDENTED EMERGENCY.
AT THE BOTTOM OF HADES IS A PRISON CALLED ABYSS, WHICH TRAPS EVIL SPIRITS.
THERE WAS A PRISON BREAK ORCHES-TRATED BY UNKNOWN FORCES.
A HUGE NUMBER OF EVIL SPIRITS ESCAPED HADES...
...AND FLED INTO THE REAL WORLD.

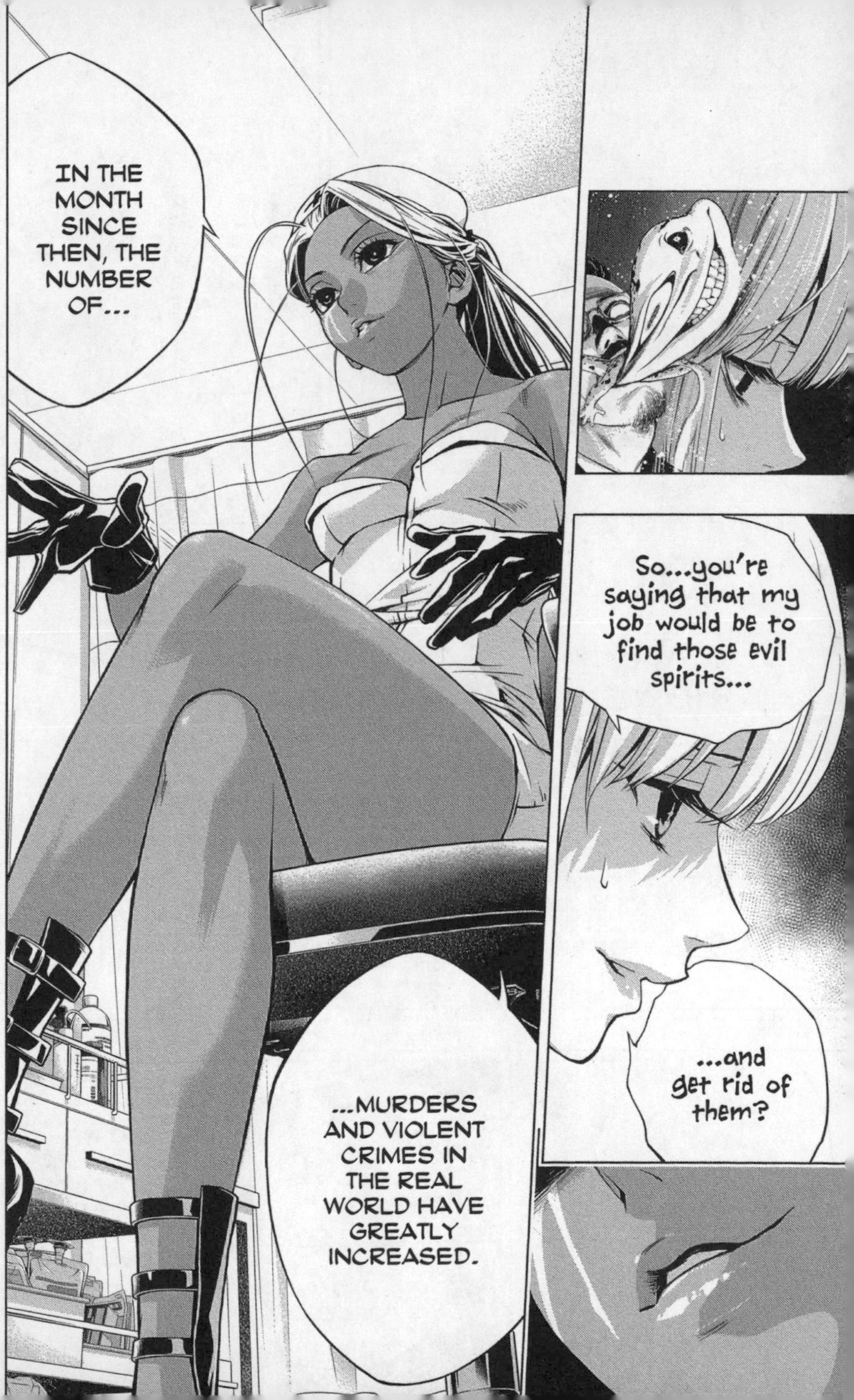
IN THE MONTH SINCE THEN, THE NUMBER OF...
...MURDERS AND VIOLENT CRIMES IN THE REAL WORLD HAVE GREATLY INCREASED.
So...you're saying that my job would be to find those evil spirits...
...and get rid of them?

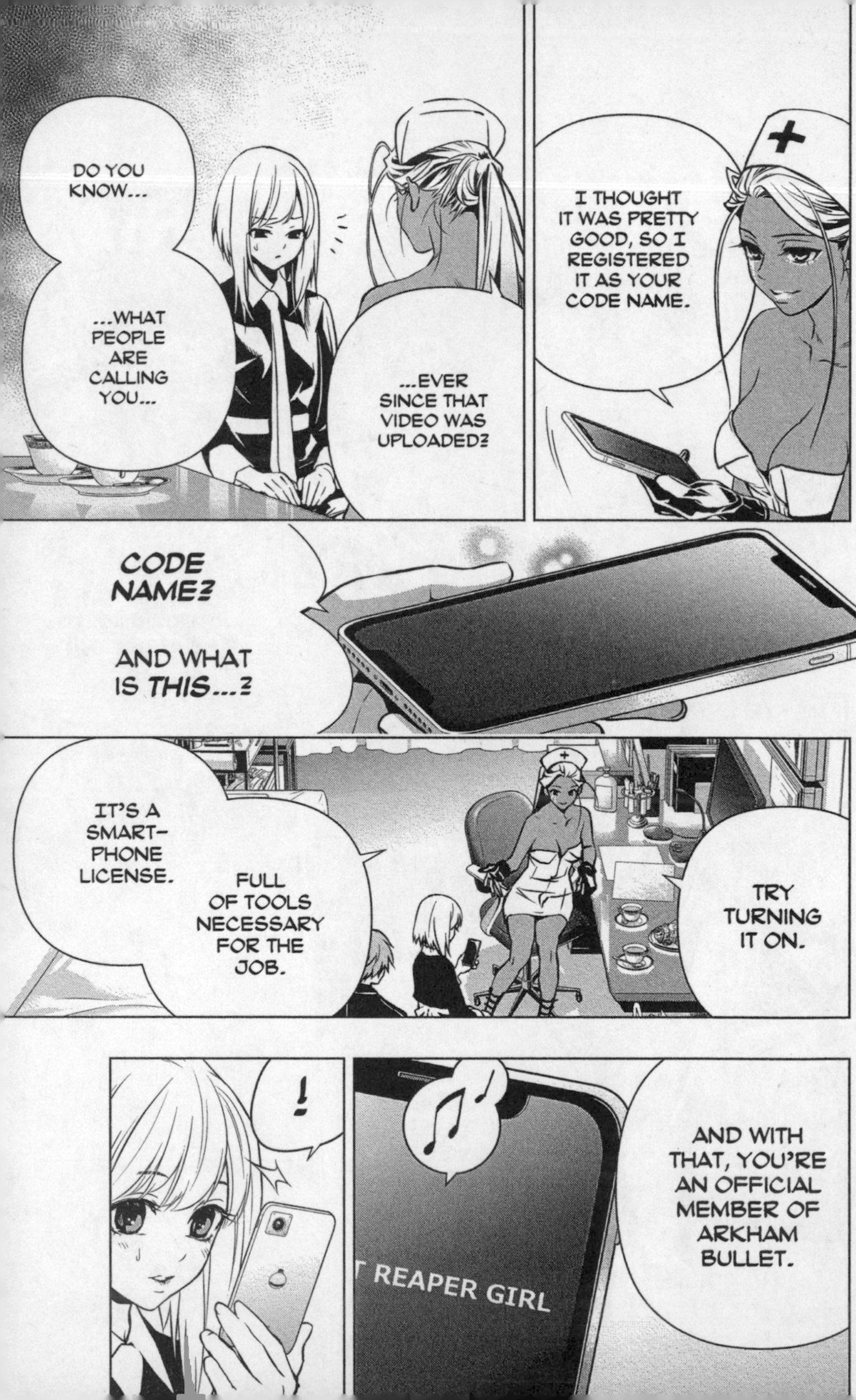
DO YOU KNOW...
...WHAT PEOPLE ARE CALLING YOU...
...EVER SINCE THAT VIDEO WAS UPLOADED?
I THOUGHT IT WAS PRETTY GOOD, SO I REGISTERED IT AS YOUR CODE NAME.
CODE NAME?
AND WHAT IS THIS...?
IT'S A SMART-PHONE LICENSE.
FULL OF TOOLS NECESSARY FOR THE JOB.
TRY TURNING IT ON.
!
T REAPER GIRL
AND WITH THAT, YOU'RE AN OFFICIAL MEMBER OF ARKHAM BULLET.

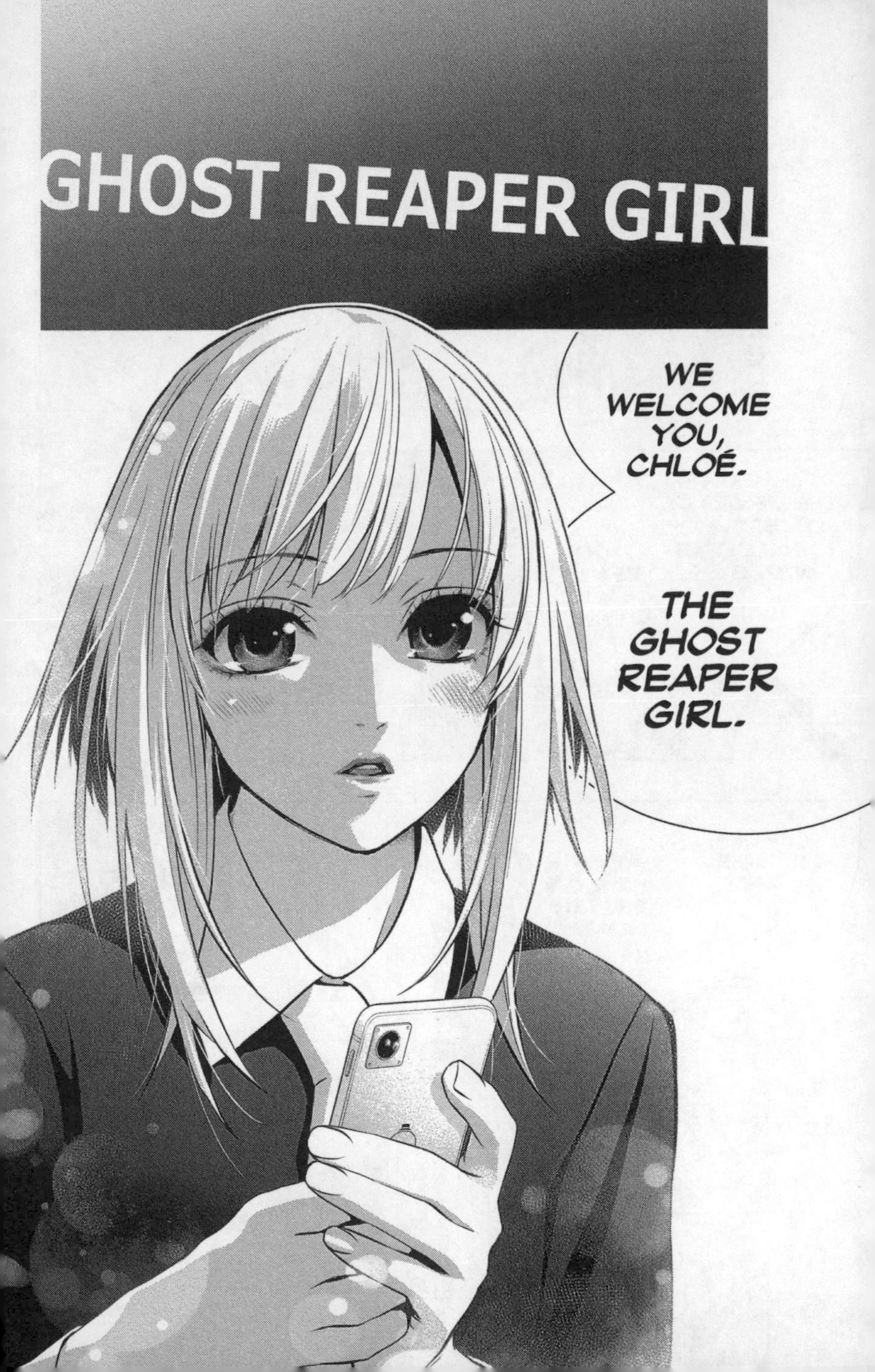
GHOST REAPER GIRL
WE WELCOME YOU, CHLOÉ.
THE GHOST REAPER GIRL.

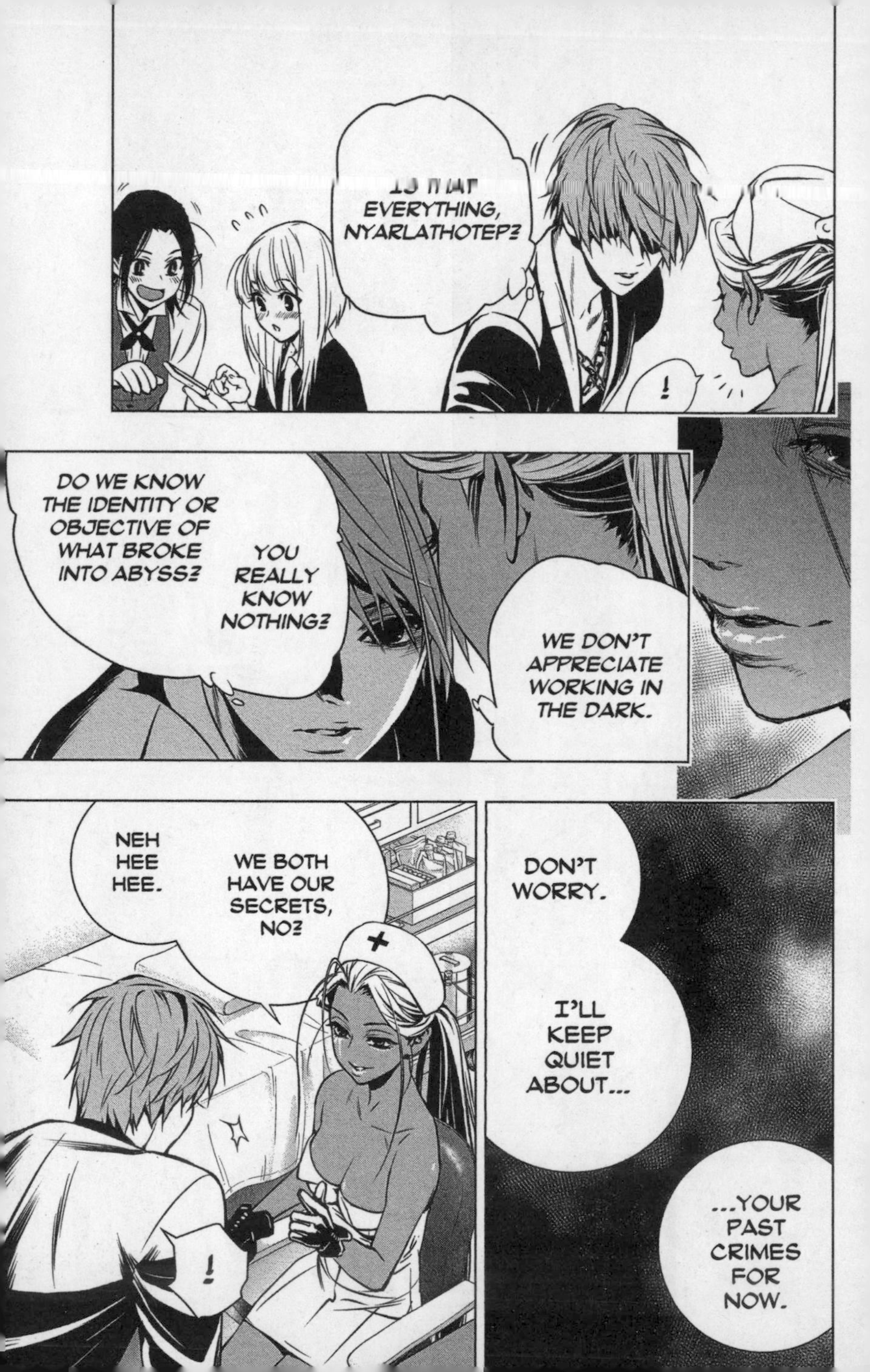
EVERYTHING, NYARLATHOTEP?
!
DO WE KNOW THE IDENTITY OR OBJECTIVE OF WHAT BROKE INTO ABYSS?
YOU REALLY KNOW NOTHING?
WE DON'T APPRECIATE WORKING IN THE DARK.
DON'T WORRY.
I'LL KEEP QUIET ABOUT...
...YOUR PAST CRIMES FOR NOW.
NEH HEE HEE.
WE BOTH HAVE OUR SECRETS, NO?
!

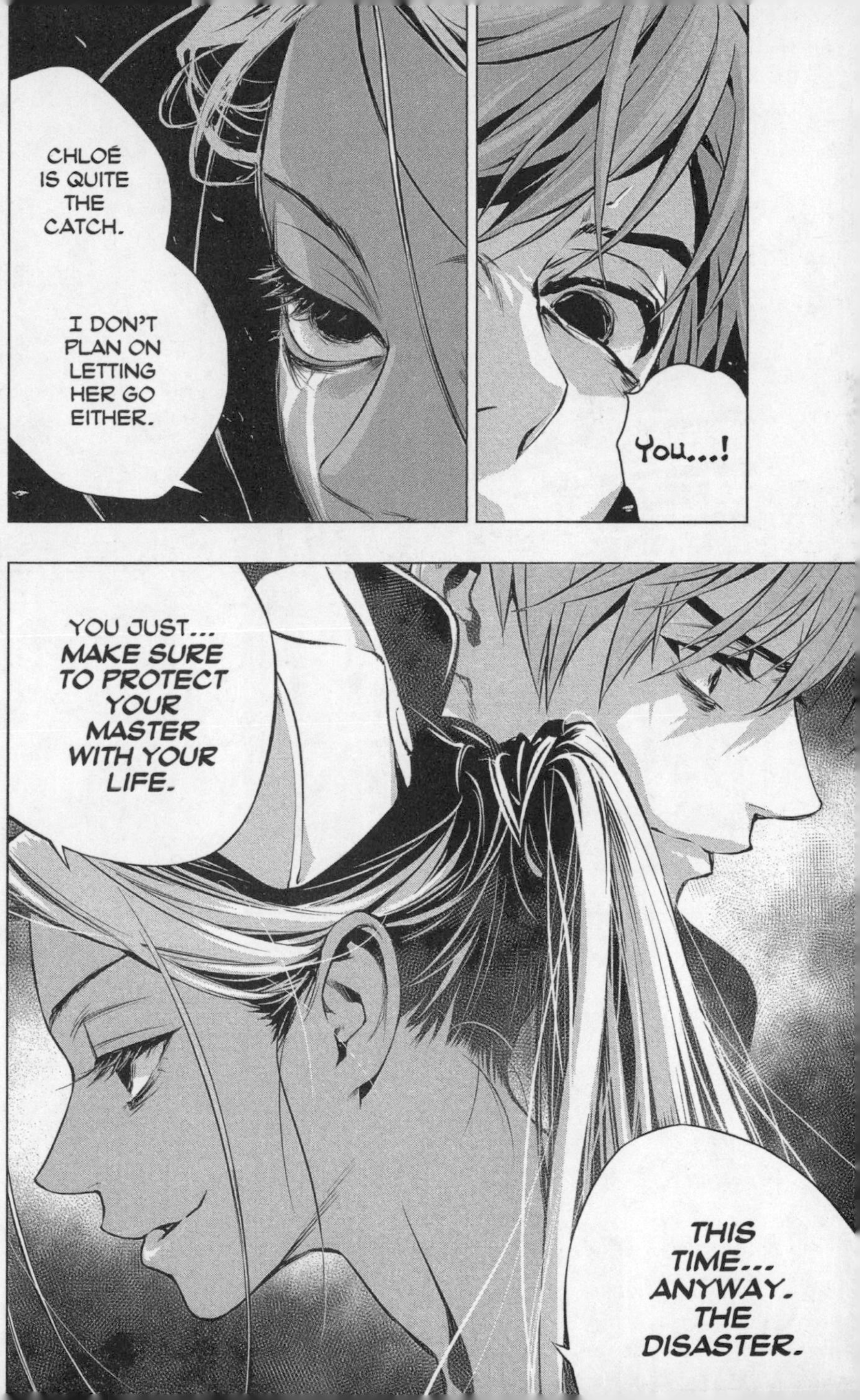
CHLOÉ IS QUITE THE CATCH.
I DON'T PLAN ON LETTING HER GO EITHER.
You...!
YOU JUST... MAKE SURE TO PROTECT YOUR MASTER WITH YOUR LIFE.
THIS TIME... ANYWAY. THE DISASTER.

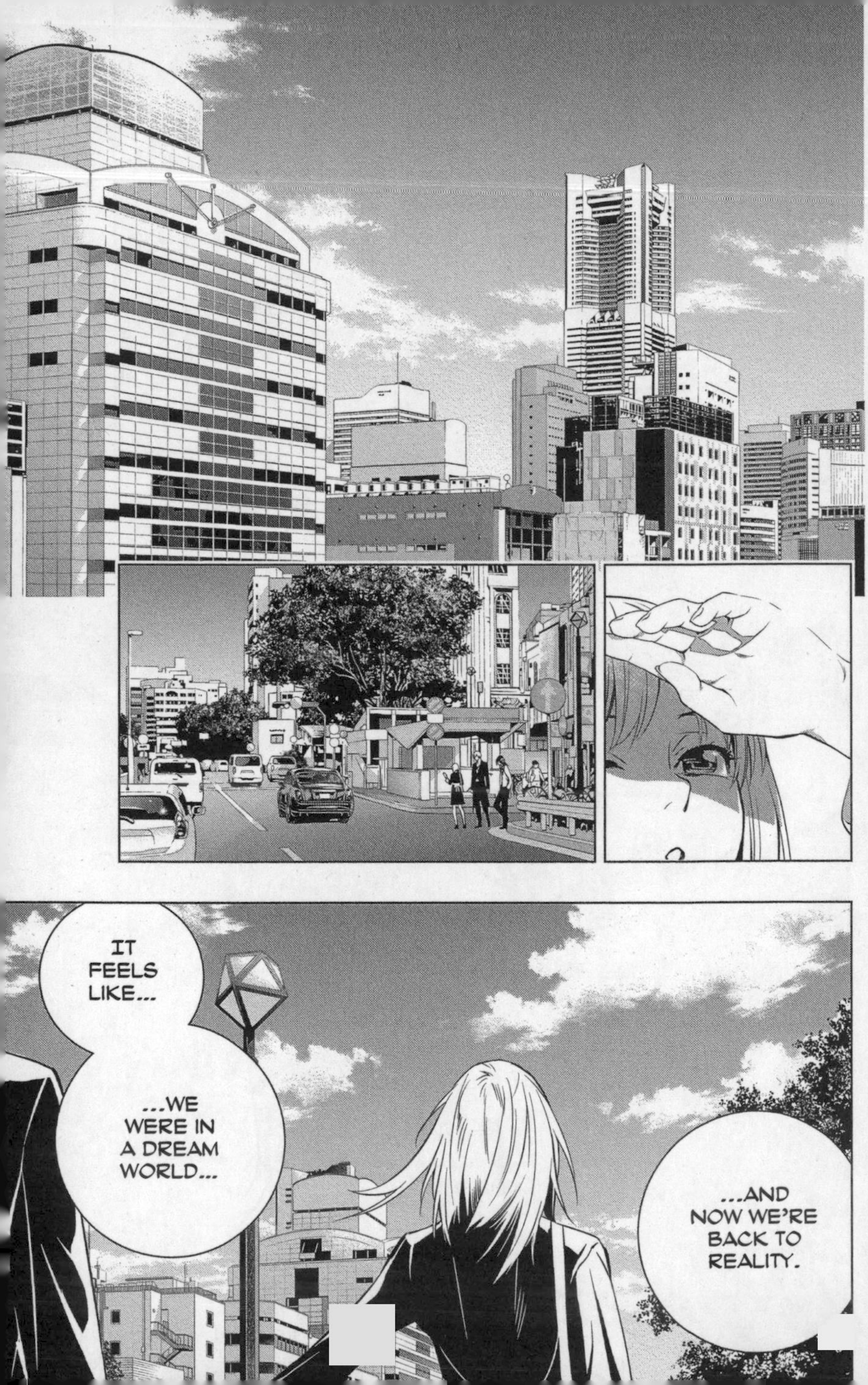
IT FEELS LIKE...
...WE WERE IN A DREAM WORLD...
...AND NOW WE'RE BACK TO REALITY.

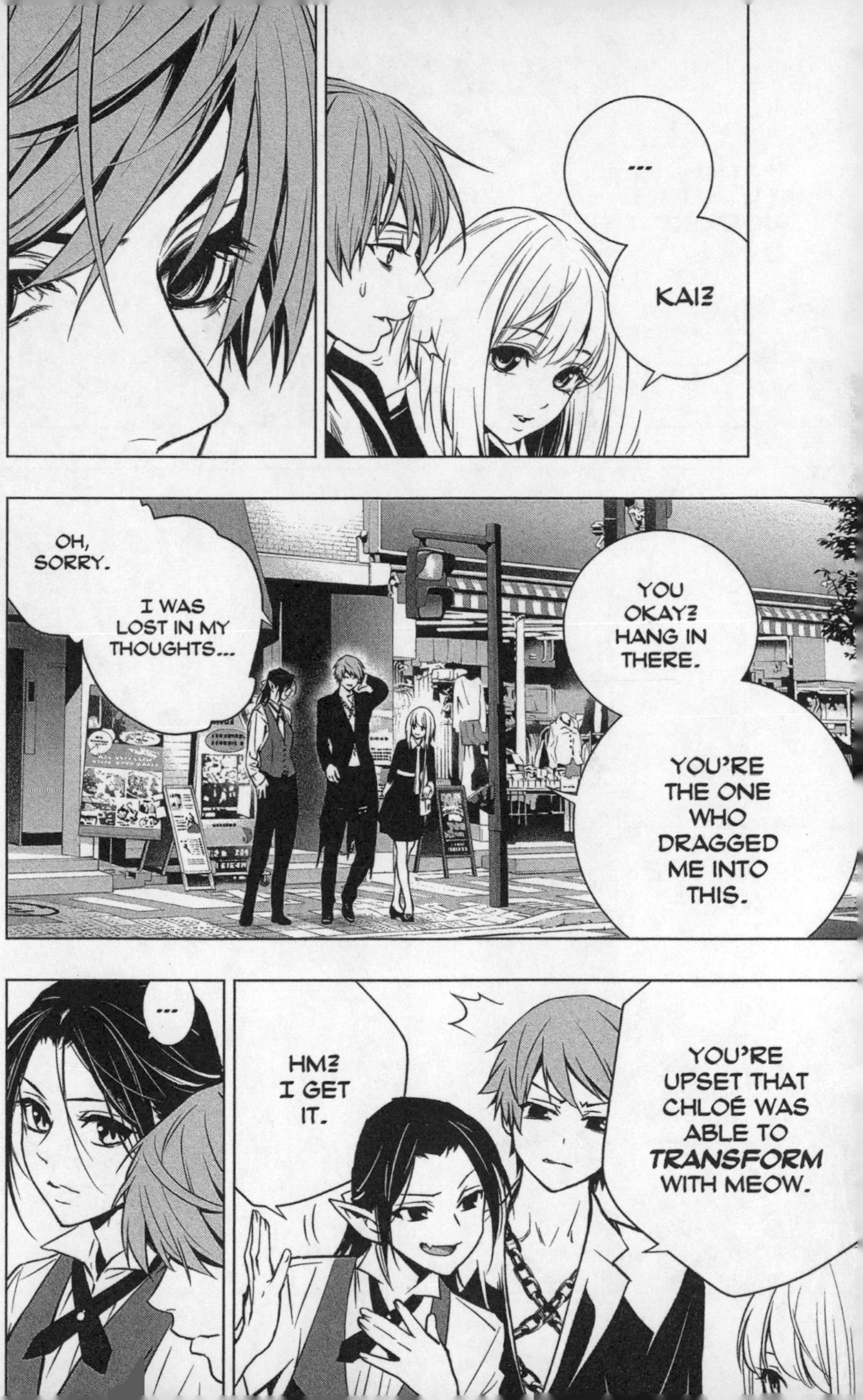
...
KAI?
OH, SORRY.
I WAS LOST IN MY THOUGHTS...
YOU OKAY? HANG IN THERE.
YOU'RE THE ONE WHO DRAGGED ME INTO THIS.
...
HM? I GET IT.
YOU'RE UPSET THAT CHLOÉ WAS ABLE TO *TRANSFORM* WITH MEOW.

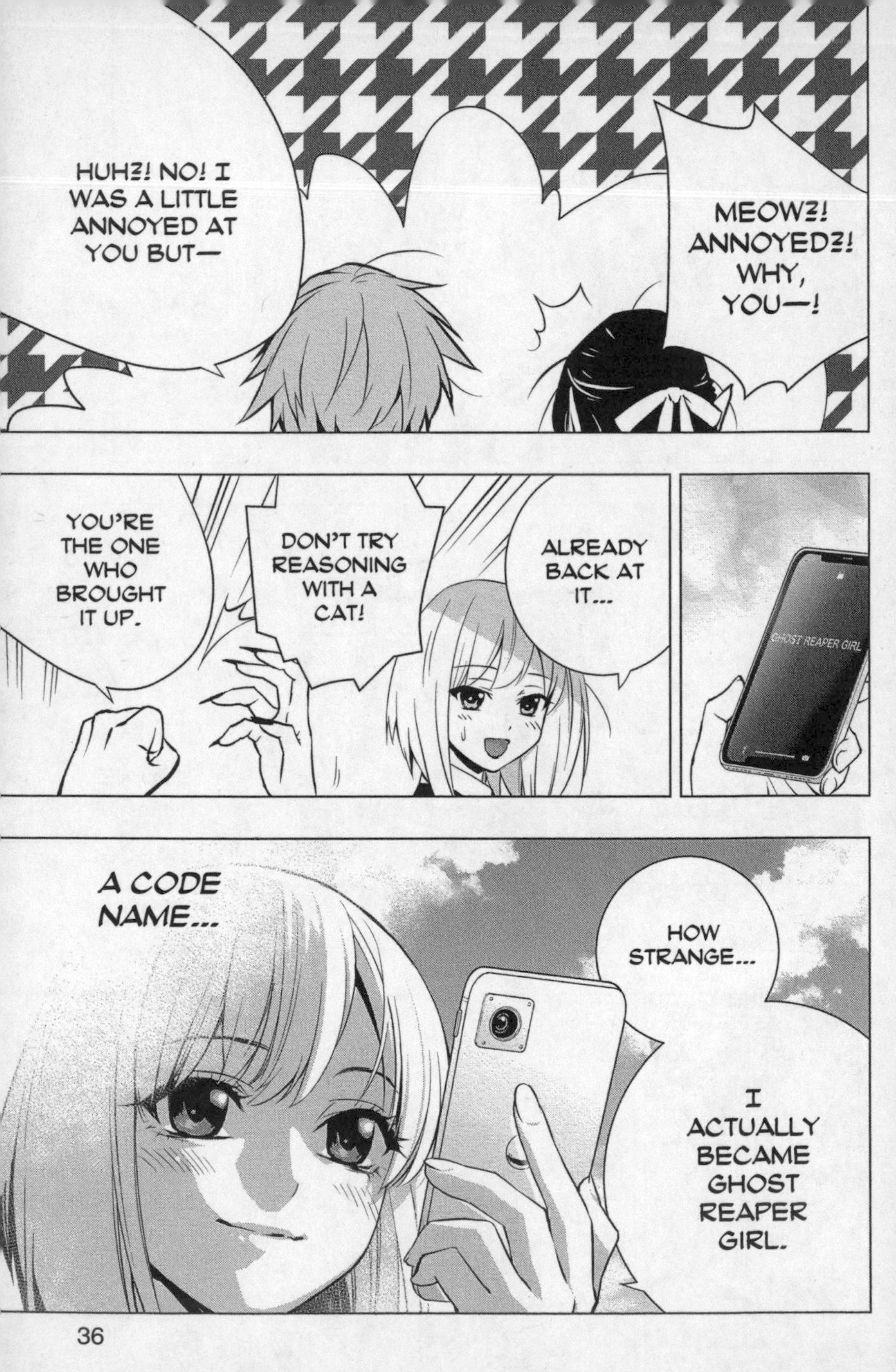
HUH?! NO! I WAS A LITTLE ANNOYED AT YOU BUT—
MEOW?! ANNOYED?! WHY, YOU—!
YOU'RE THE ONE WHO BROUGHT IT UP.
DON'T TRY REASONING WITH A CAT!
ALREADY BACK AT IT...
GHOST REAPER GIRL
A CODE NAME...
HOW STRANGE...
I ACTUALLY BECAME GHOST REAPER GIRL.

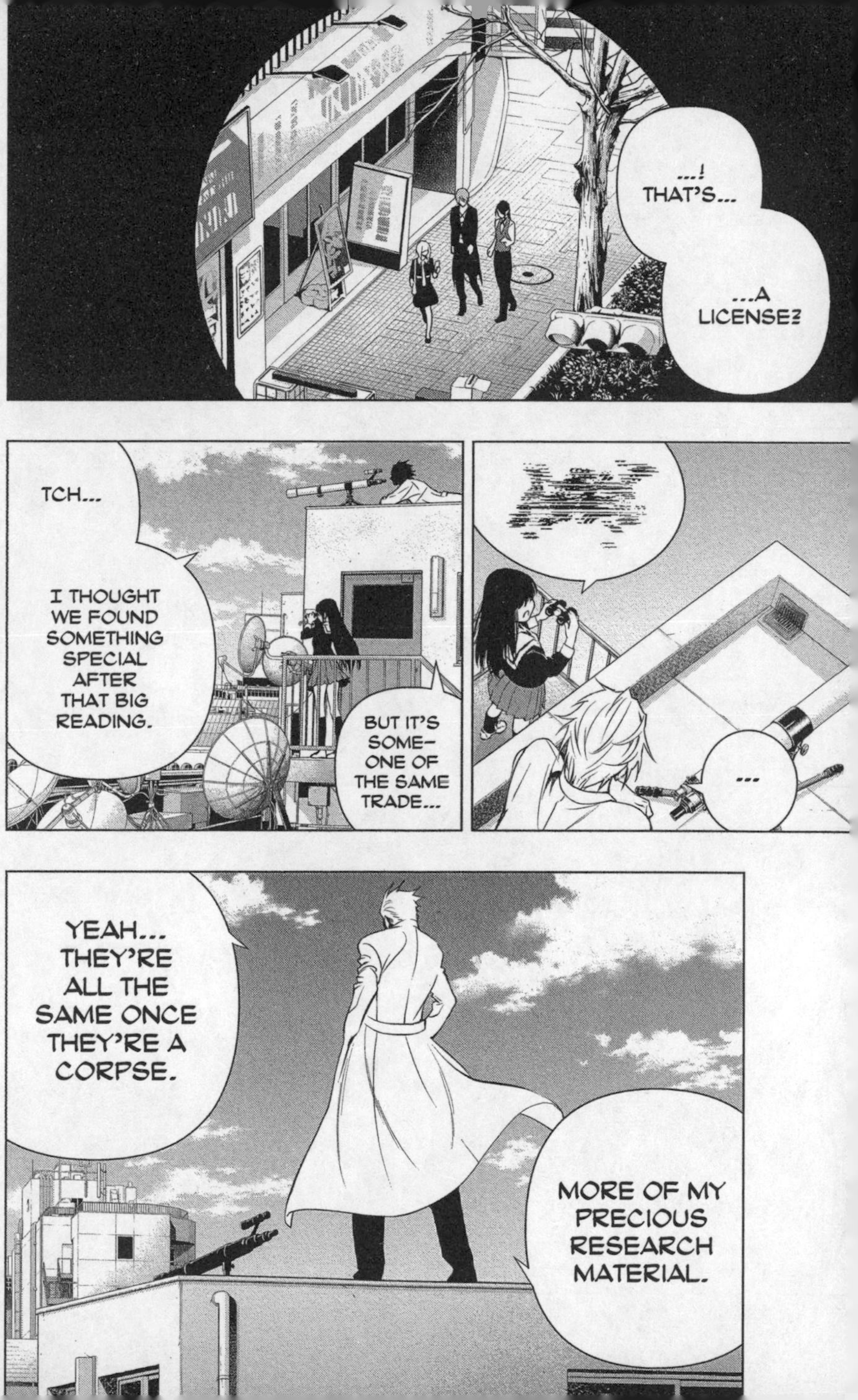
...! THAT'S...
...A LICENSE?
...
TCH...
I THOUGHT WE FOUND SOMETHING SPECIAL AFTER THAT BIG READING.
BUT IT'S SOME-ONE OF THE SAME TRADE...
YEAH... THEY'RE ALL THE SAME ONCE THEY'RE A CORPSE.
MORE OF MY PRECIOUS RESEARCH MATERIAL.

#7: Level Up

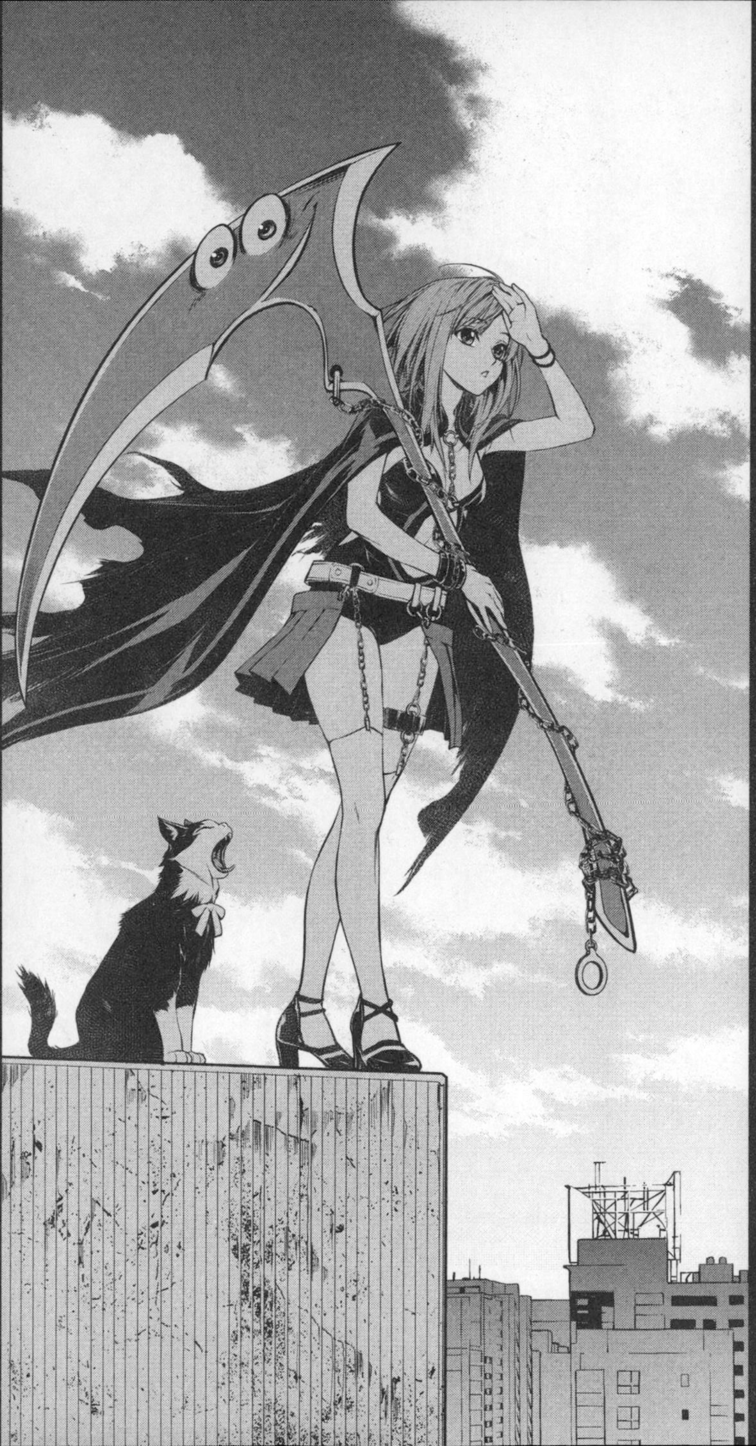

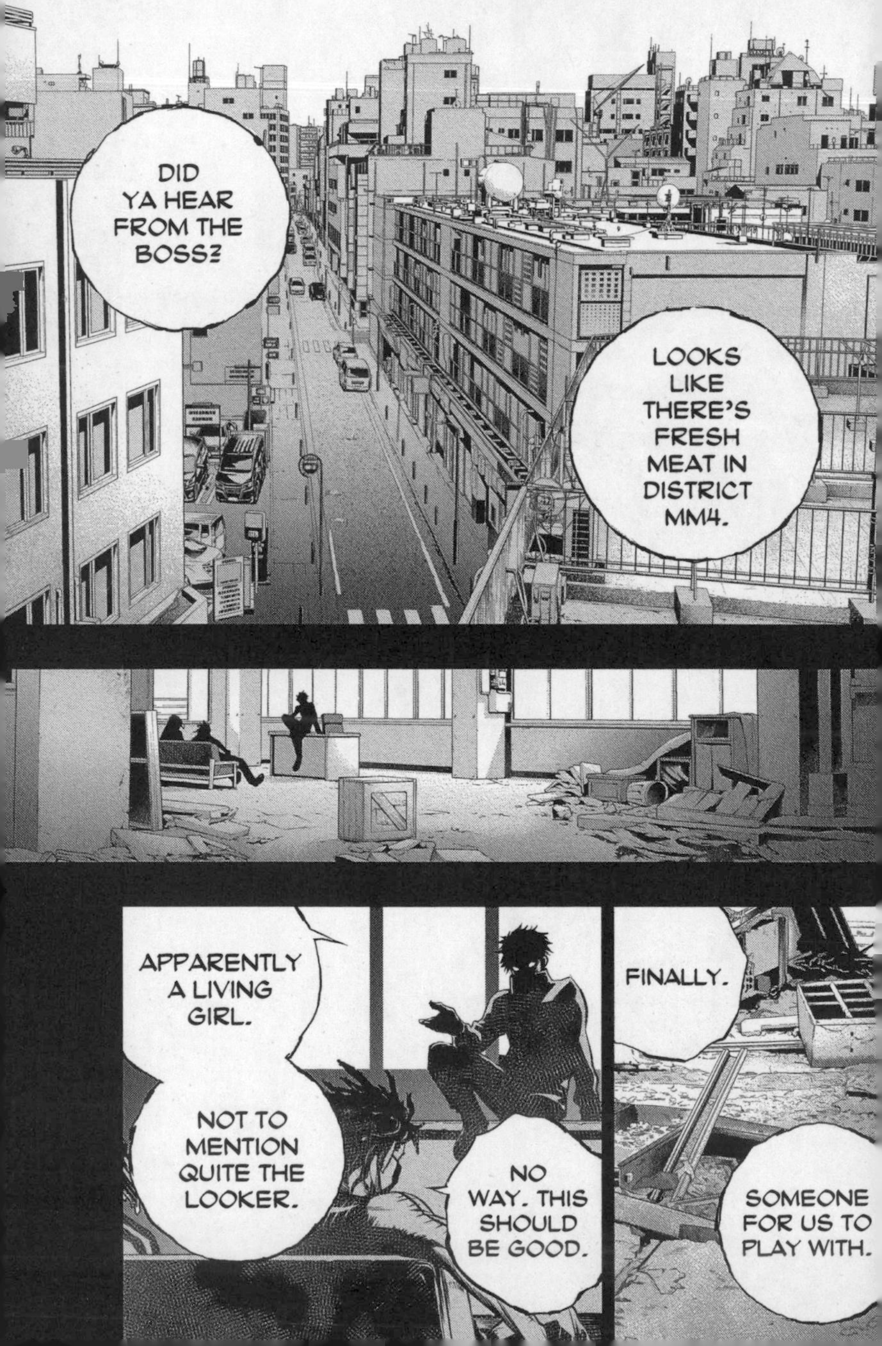
DID YA HEAR FROM THE BOSS?
LOOKS LIKE THERE'S FRESH MEAT IN DISTRICT MM4.
FINALLY.
SOMEONE FOR US TO PLAY WITH.
APPARENTLY A LIVING GIRL.
NOT TO MENTION QUITE THE LOOKER.
NO WAY. THIS SHOULD BE GOOD.

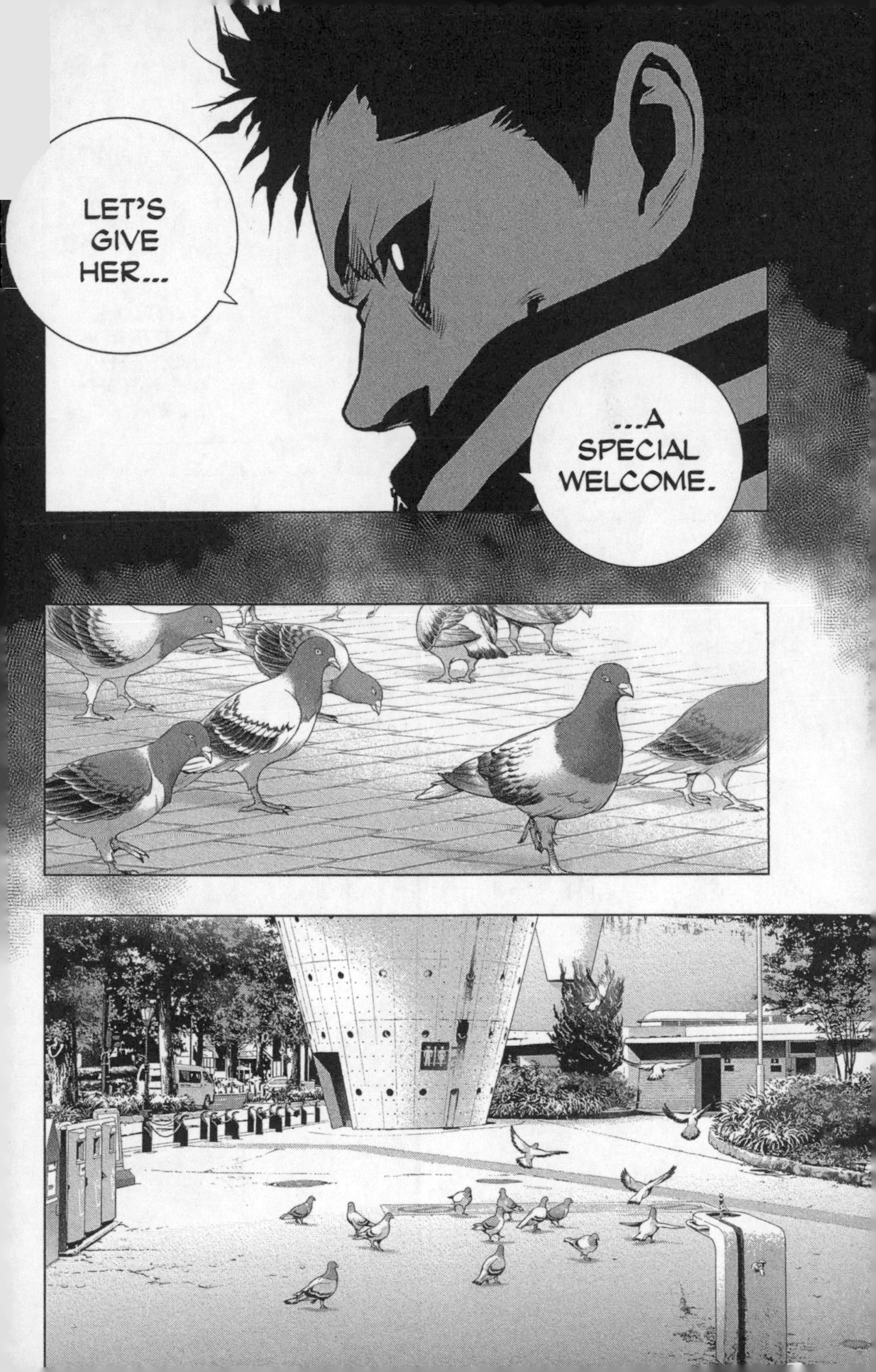
LET'S GIVE HER...
...A SPECIAL WELCOME.

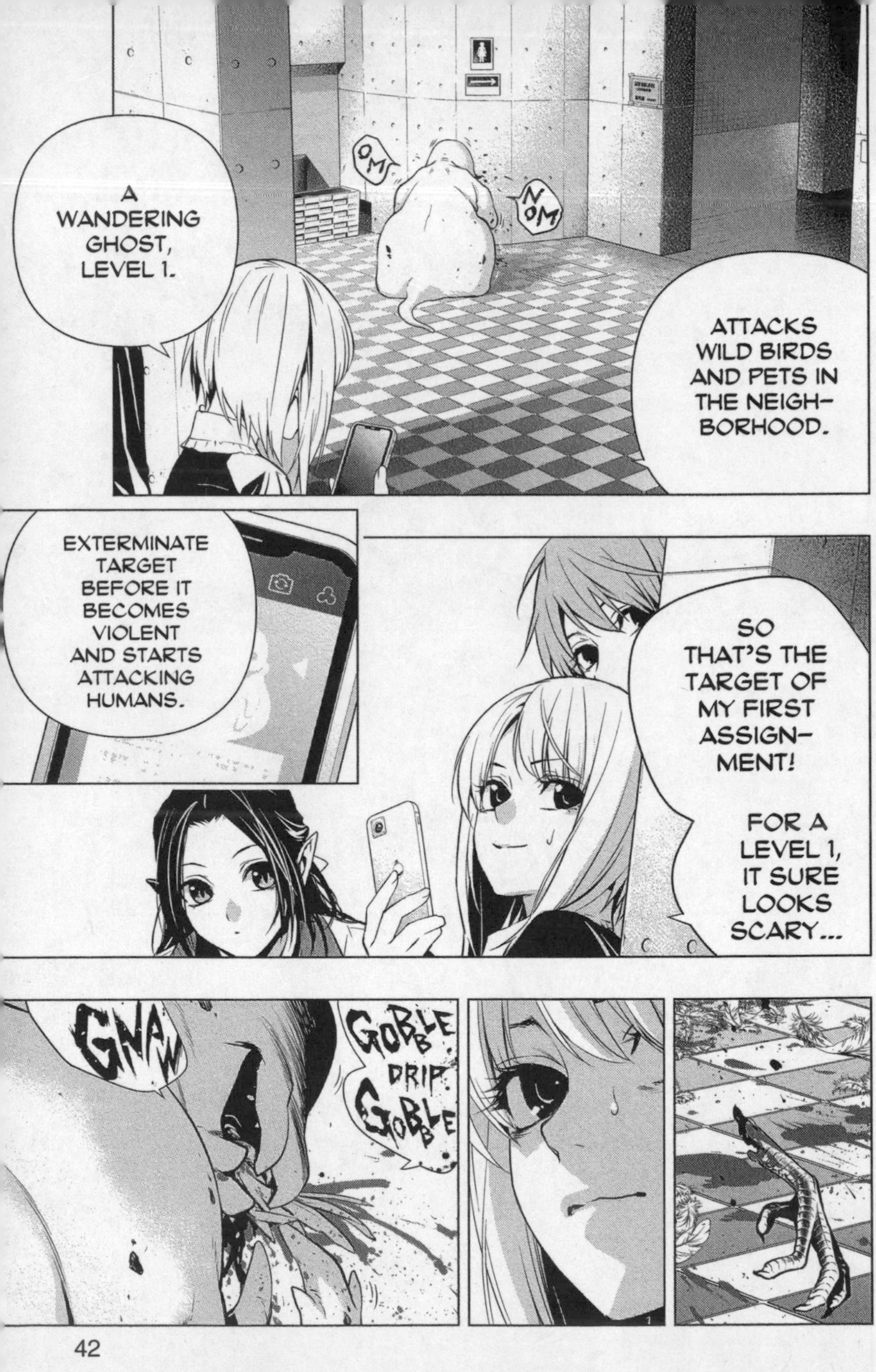
OM
NOM
A WANDERING GHOST, LEVEL 1.
ATTACKS WILD BIRDS AND PETS IN THE NEIGH-BORHOOD.
EXTERMINATE TARGET BEFORE IT BECOMES VIOLENT AND STARTS ATTACKING HUMANS.
SO THAT'S THE TARGET OF MY FIRST ASSIGN-MENT!
FOR A LEVEL 1, IT SURE LOOKS SCARY...
GOBBLE DRIP GOBBLE
GNAW

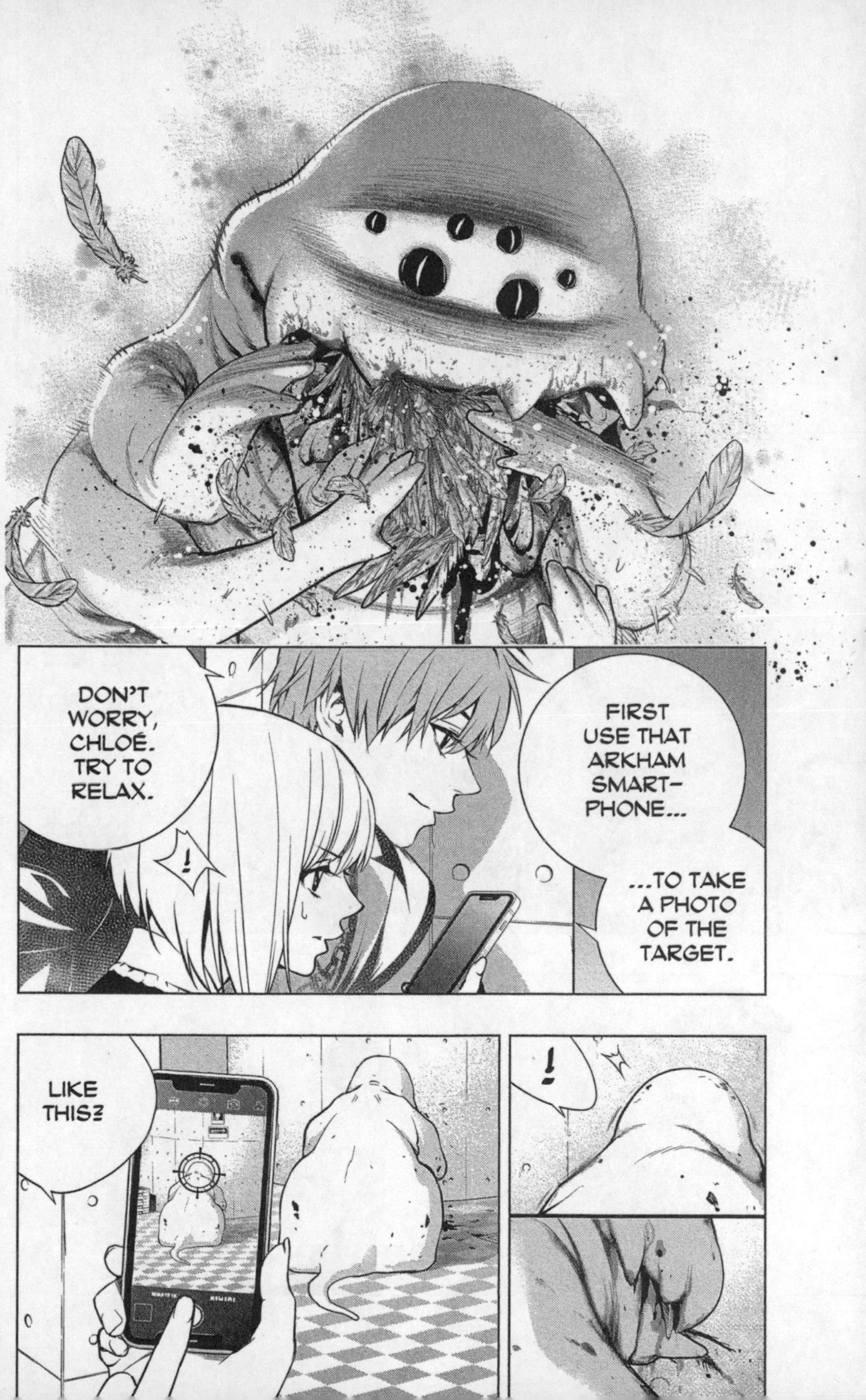
FIRST USE THAT ARKHAM SMART-PHONE...
...TO TAKE A PHOTO OF THE TARGET.
DON'T WORRY, CHLOÉ. TRY TO RELAX.
!
!
LIKE THIS?

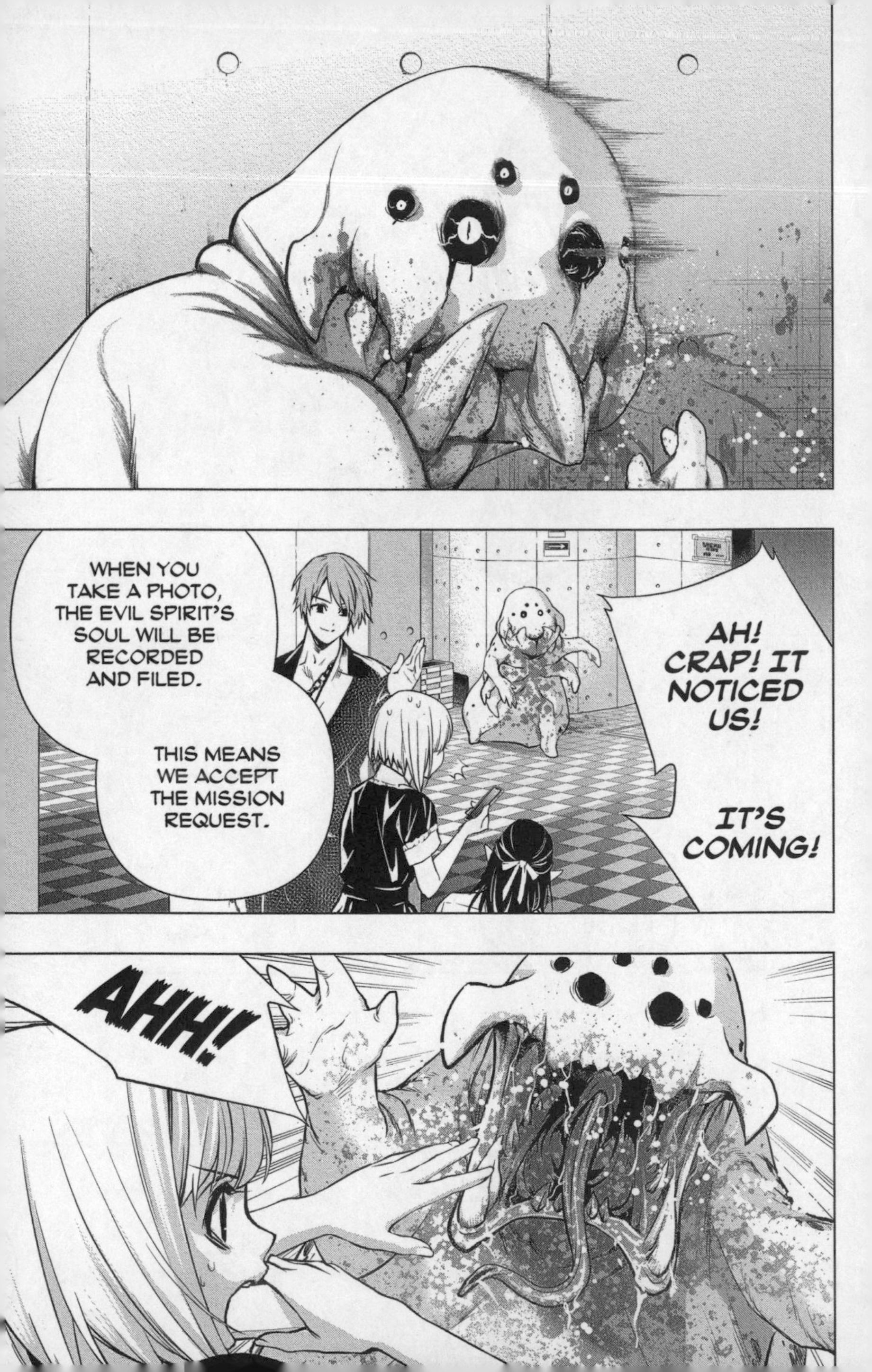
AH! CRAP! IT NOTICED US!
IT'S COMING!
WHEN YOU TAKE A PHOTO, THE EVIL SPIRIT'S SOUL WILL BE RECORDED AND FILED.
THIS MEANS WE ACCEPT THE MISSION REQUEST.
AHH!

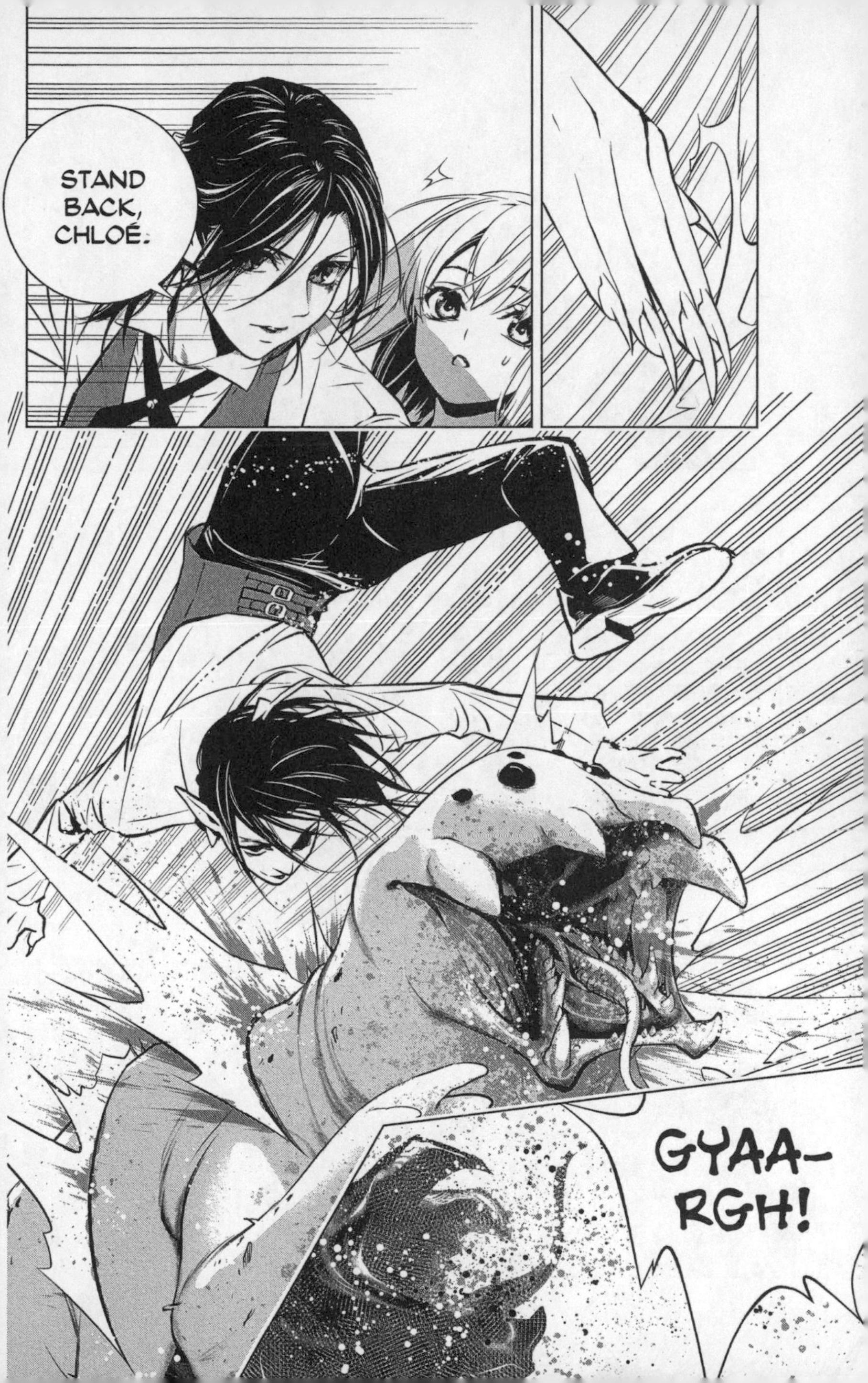
STAND BACK, CHLOÉ.
GYAA-RGH!

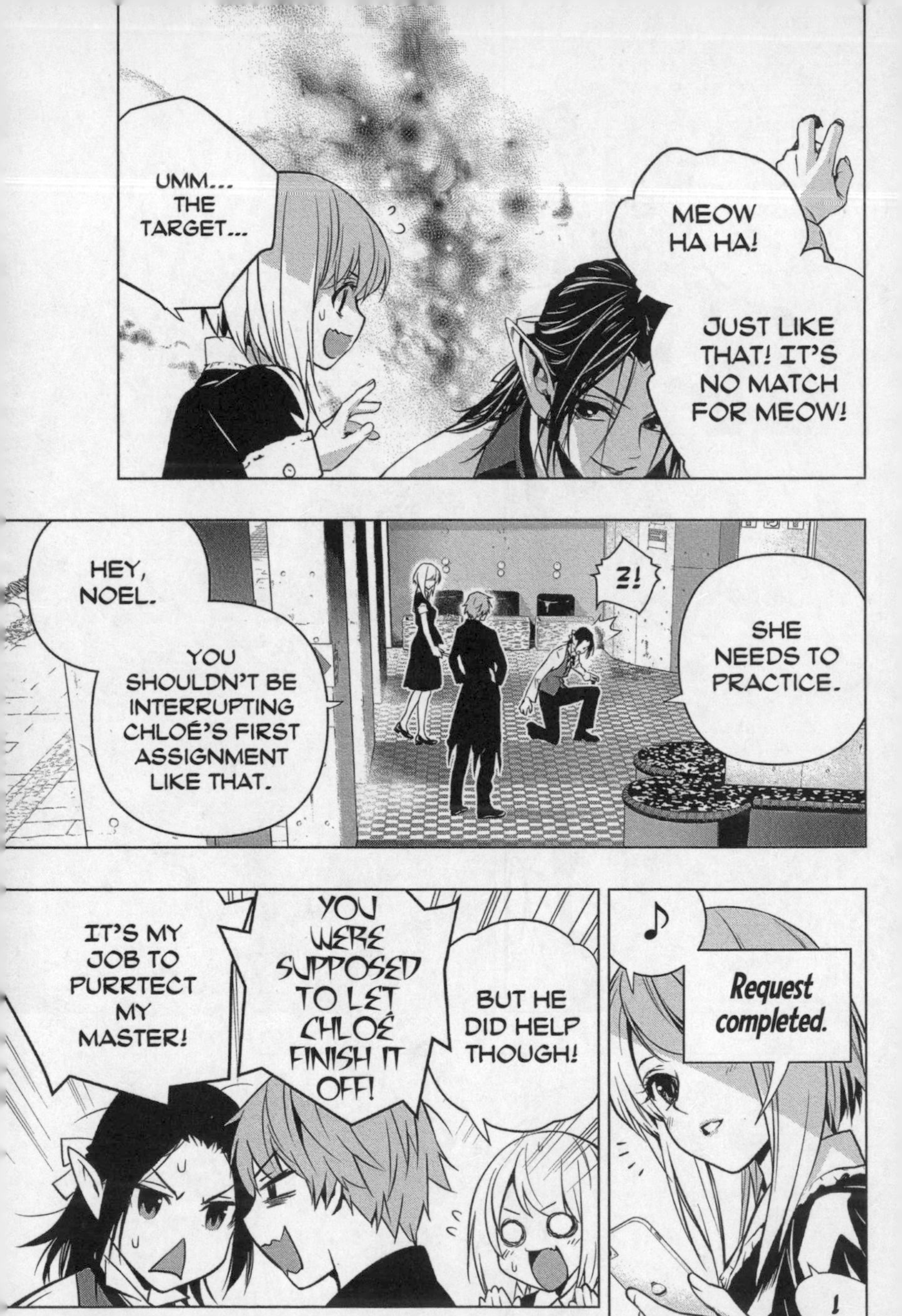
UMM... THE TARGET...
MEOW HA HA!
JUST LIKE THAT! IT'S NO MATCH FOR MEOW!
SHE NEEDS TO PRACTICE.
?!
HEY, NOEL.
YOU SHOULDN'T BE INTERRUPTING CHLOÉ'S FIRST ASSIGNMENT LIKE THAT.
♪
Request completed.
!
BUT HE DID HELP THOUGH!
YOU WERE SUPPOSED TO LET CHLOÉ FINISH IT OFF!
IT'S MY JOB TO PURRTECT MY MASTER!

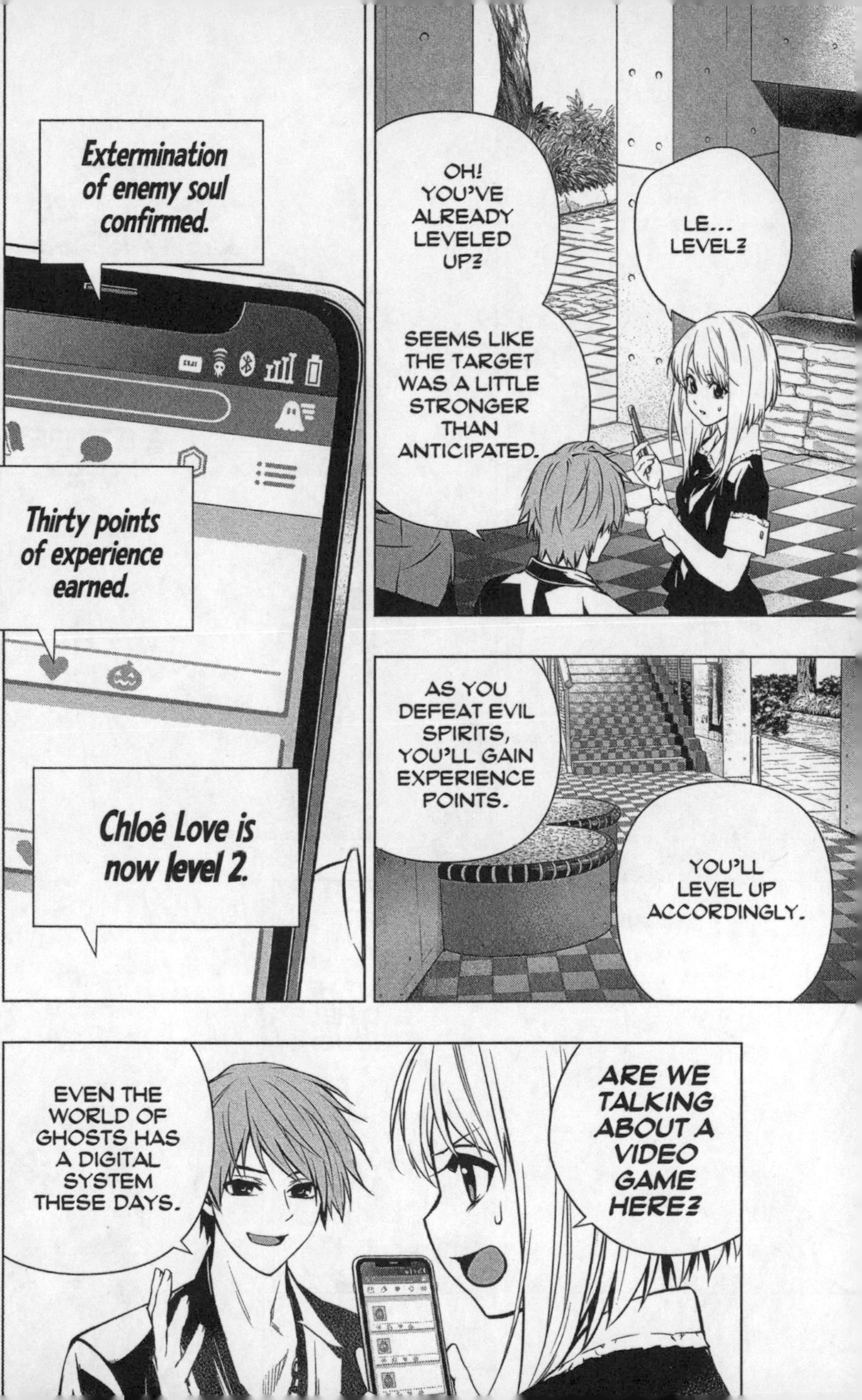
OH! YOU'VE ALREADY LEVELED UP?
LE... LEVEL?
SEEMS LIKE THE TARGET WAS A LITTLE STRONGER THAN ANTICIPATED.
AS YOU DEFEAT EVIL SPIRITS, YOU'LL GAIN EXPERIENCE POINTS.
YOU'LL LEVEL UP ACCORDINGLY.
Extermination of enemy soul confirmed.
Thirty points of experience earned.
Chloé Love is now level 2.
ARE WE TALKING ABOUT A VIDEO GAME HERE?
EVEN THE WORLD OF GHOSTS HAS A DIGITAL SYSTEM THESE DAYS.

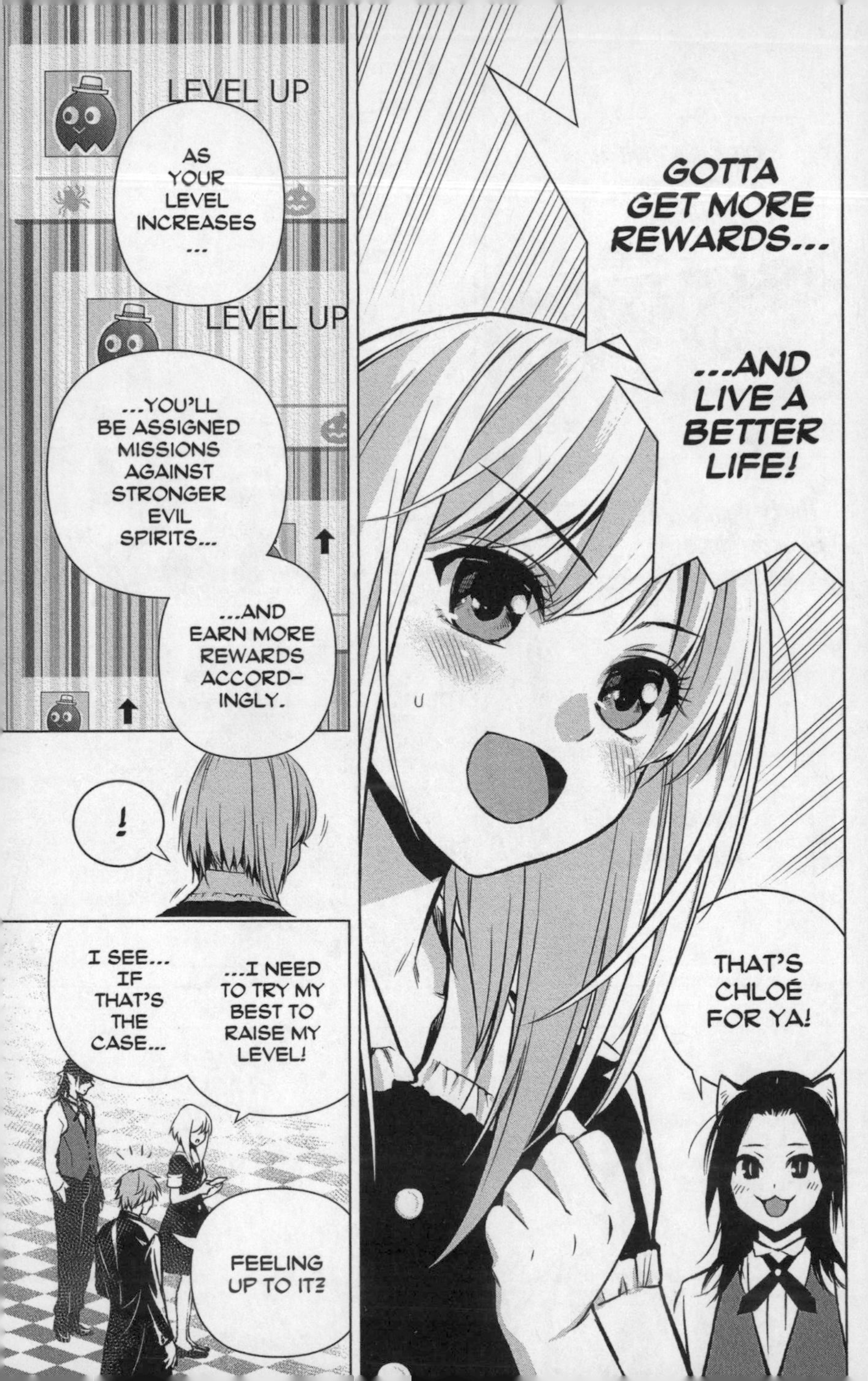
LEVEL UP
AS YOUR LEVEL INCREASES ...
LEVEL UP
...YOU'LL BE ASSIGNED MISSIONS AGAINST STRONGER EVIL SPIRITS...
...AND EARN MORE REWARDS ACCORD-INGLY.
!
I SEE... IF THAT'S THE CASE...
...I NEED TO TRY MY BEST TO RAISE MY LEVEL!
FEELING UP TO IT?
GOTTA GET MORE REWARDS...
...AND LIVE A BETTER LIFE!
THAT'S CHLOÉ FOR YA!

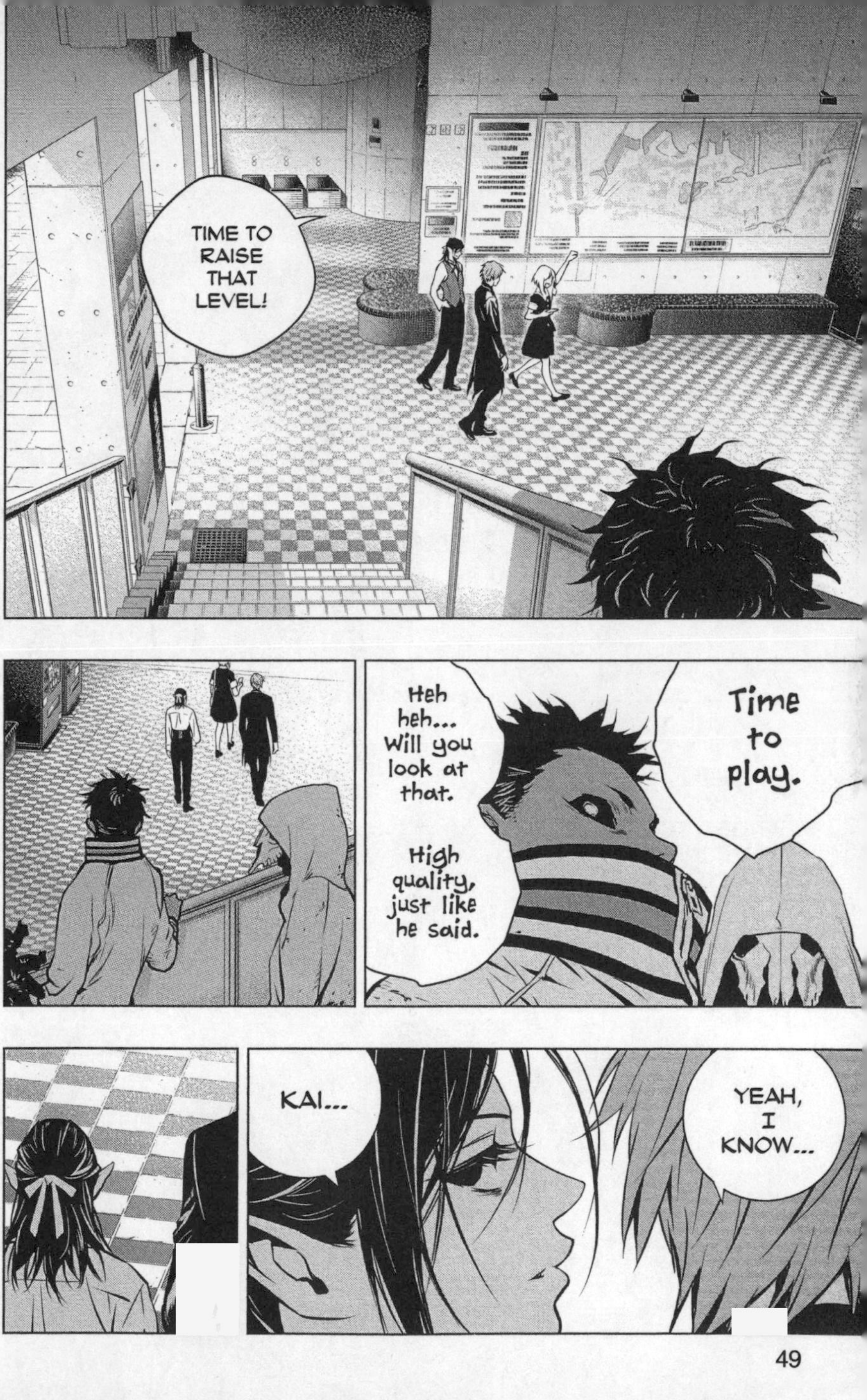
TIME TO RAISE THAT LEVEL!
Heh heh... Will you look at that.
High quality, just like he said.
Time to play.
KAI...
YEAH, I KNOW...

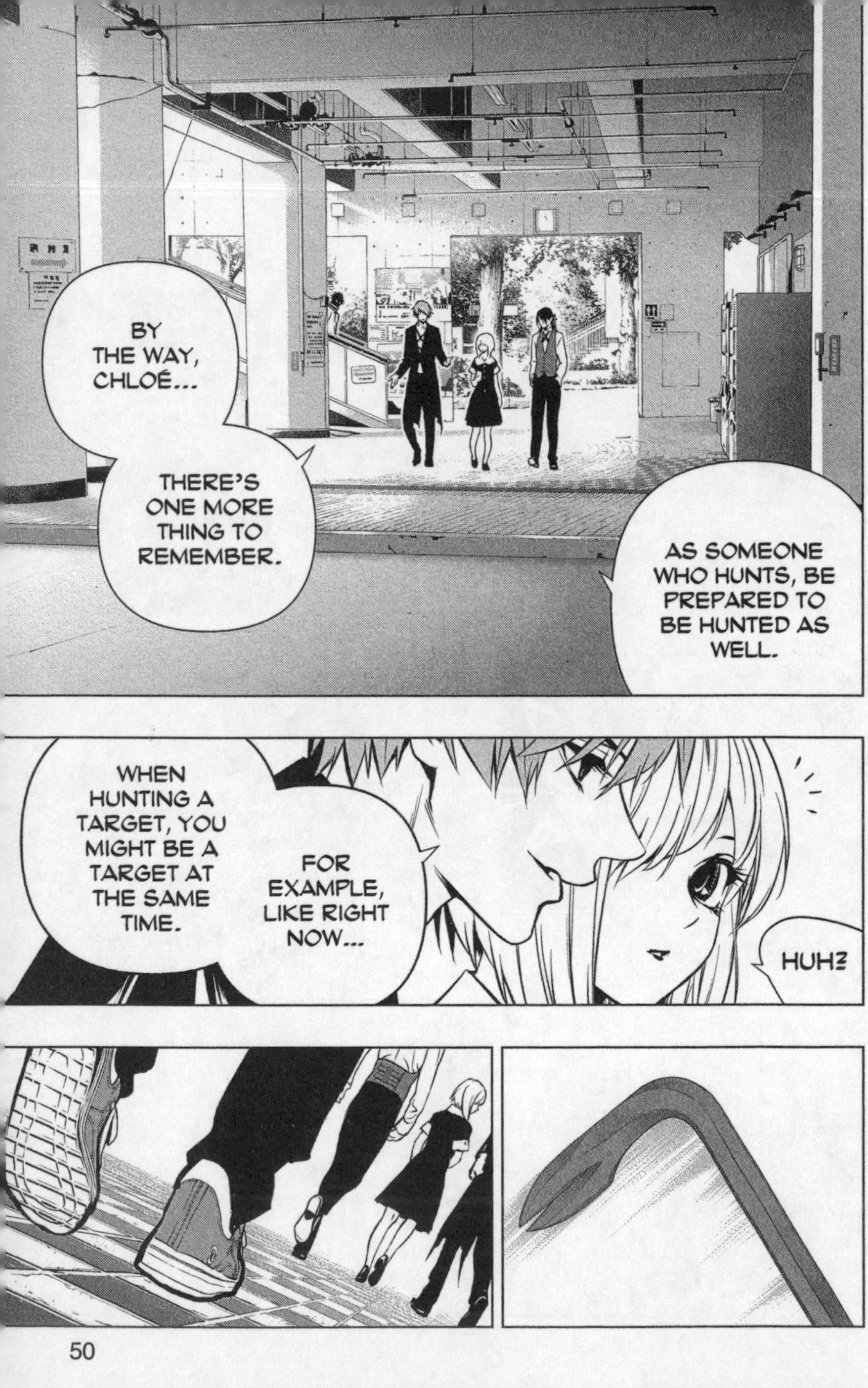
BY THE WAY, CHLOÉ...
THERE'S ONE MORE THING TO REMEMBER.
AS SOMEONE WHO HUNTS, BE PREPARED TO BE HUNTED AS WELL.
WHEN HUNTING A TARGET, YOU MIGHT BE A TARGET AT THE SAME TIME.
FOR EXAMPLE, LIKE RIGHT NOW...
HUH?

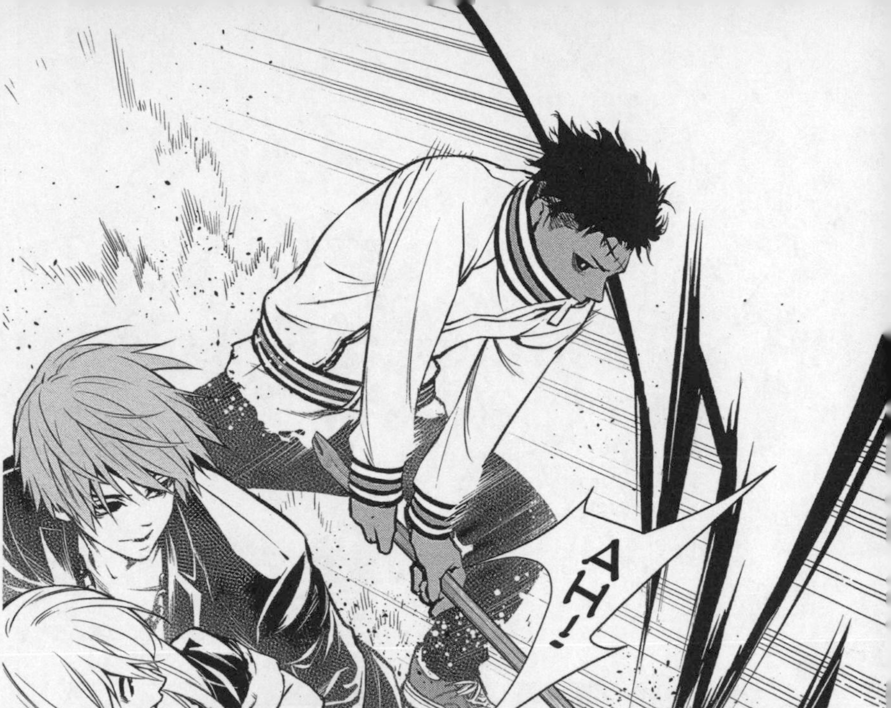
AH!!

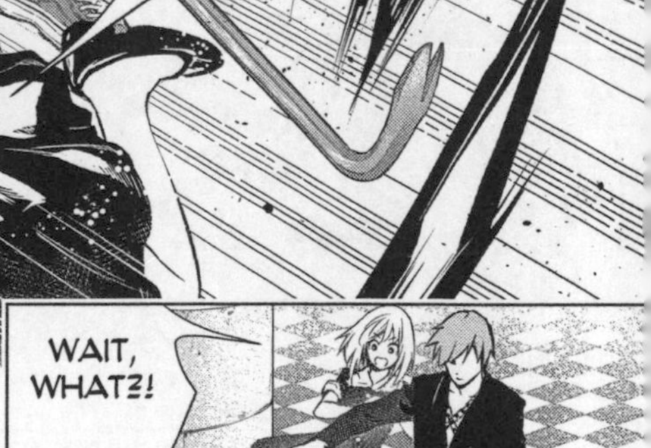
WAIT, WHAT?!
WHO ARE THESE GUYS?!
Tch...

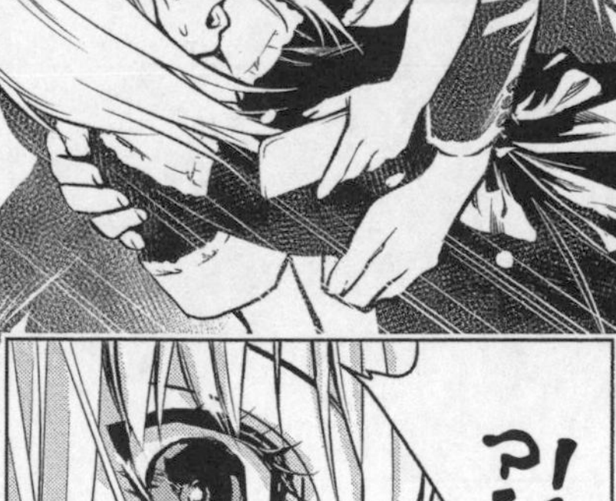
?!

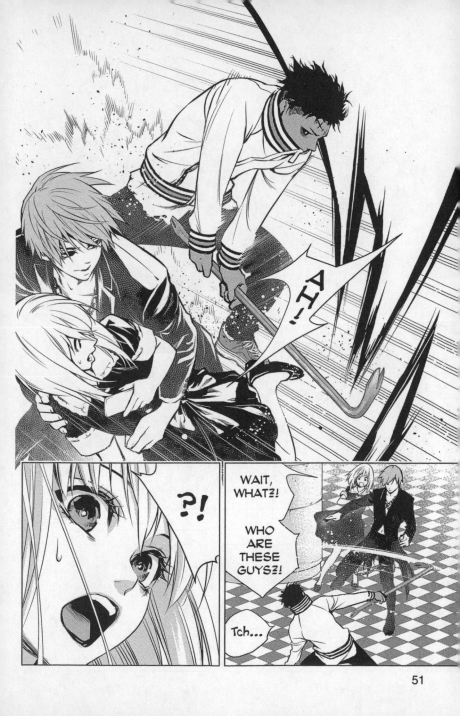

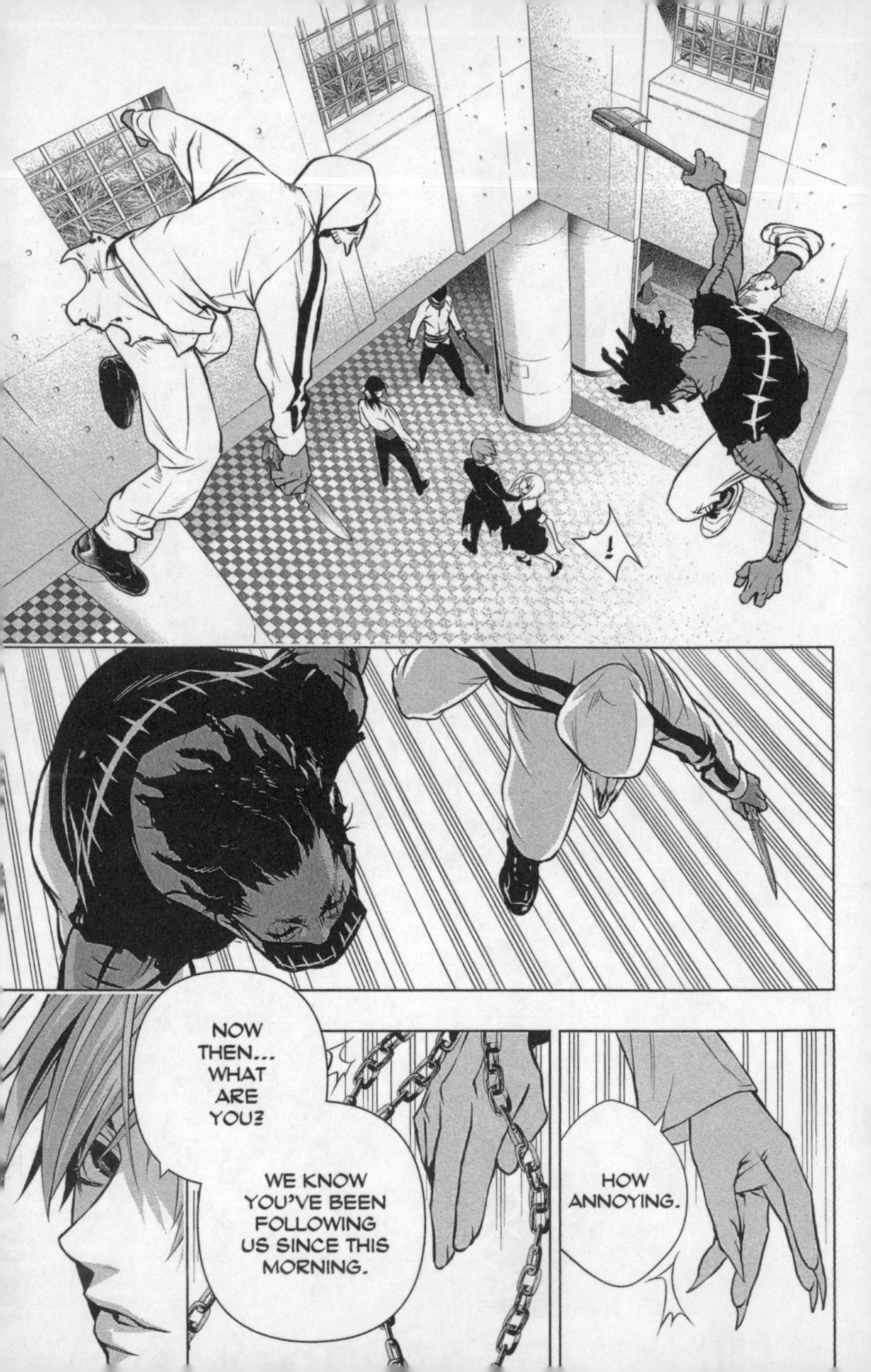
!
NOW THEN... WHAT ARE YOU?
WE KNOW YOU'VE BEEN FOLLOWING US SINCE THIS MORNING.
HOW ANNOYING.

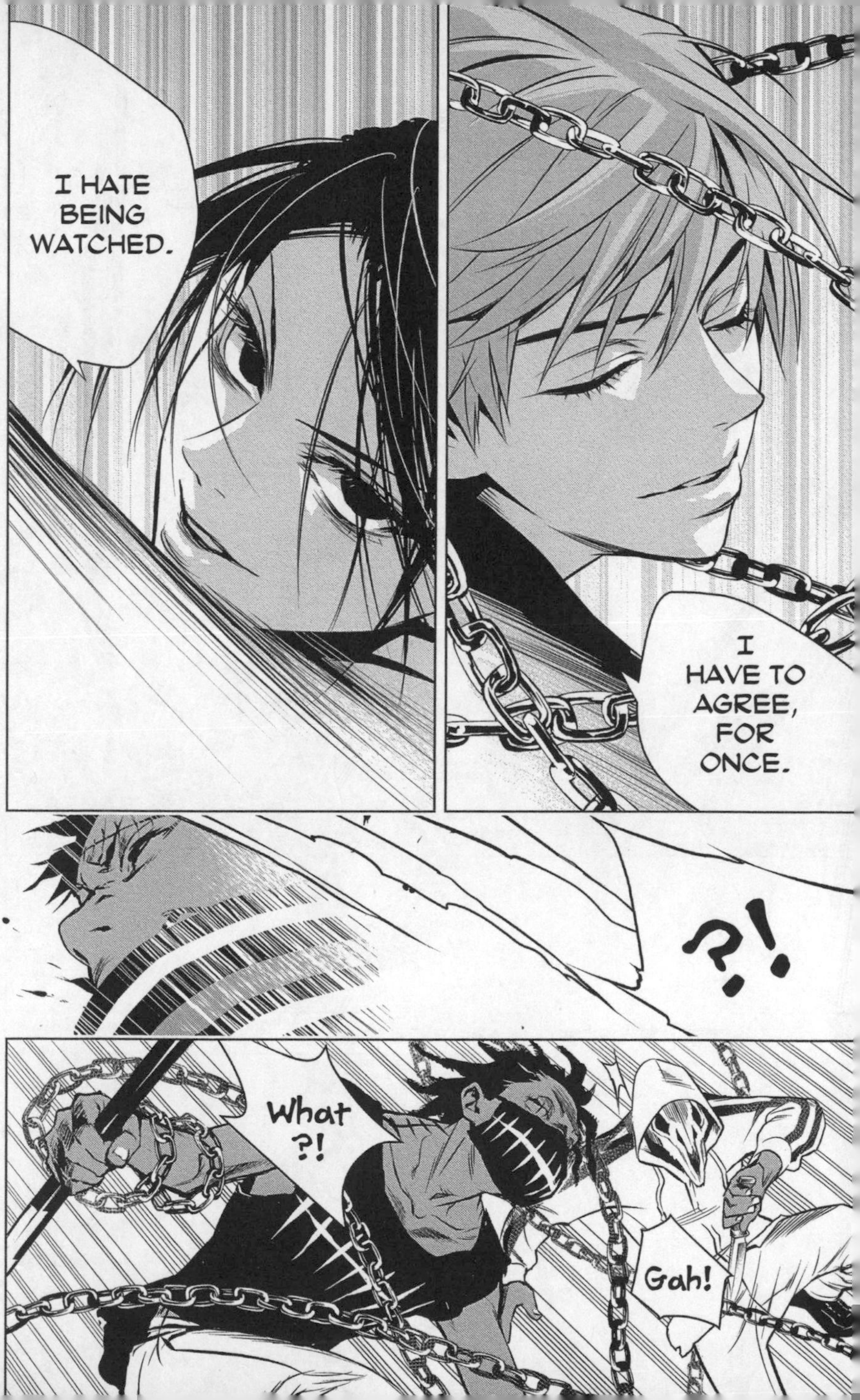
I HATE BEING WATCHED.
I HAVE TO AGREE, FOR ONCE.
?!
What ?!
Gah!

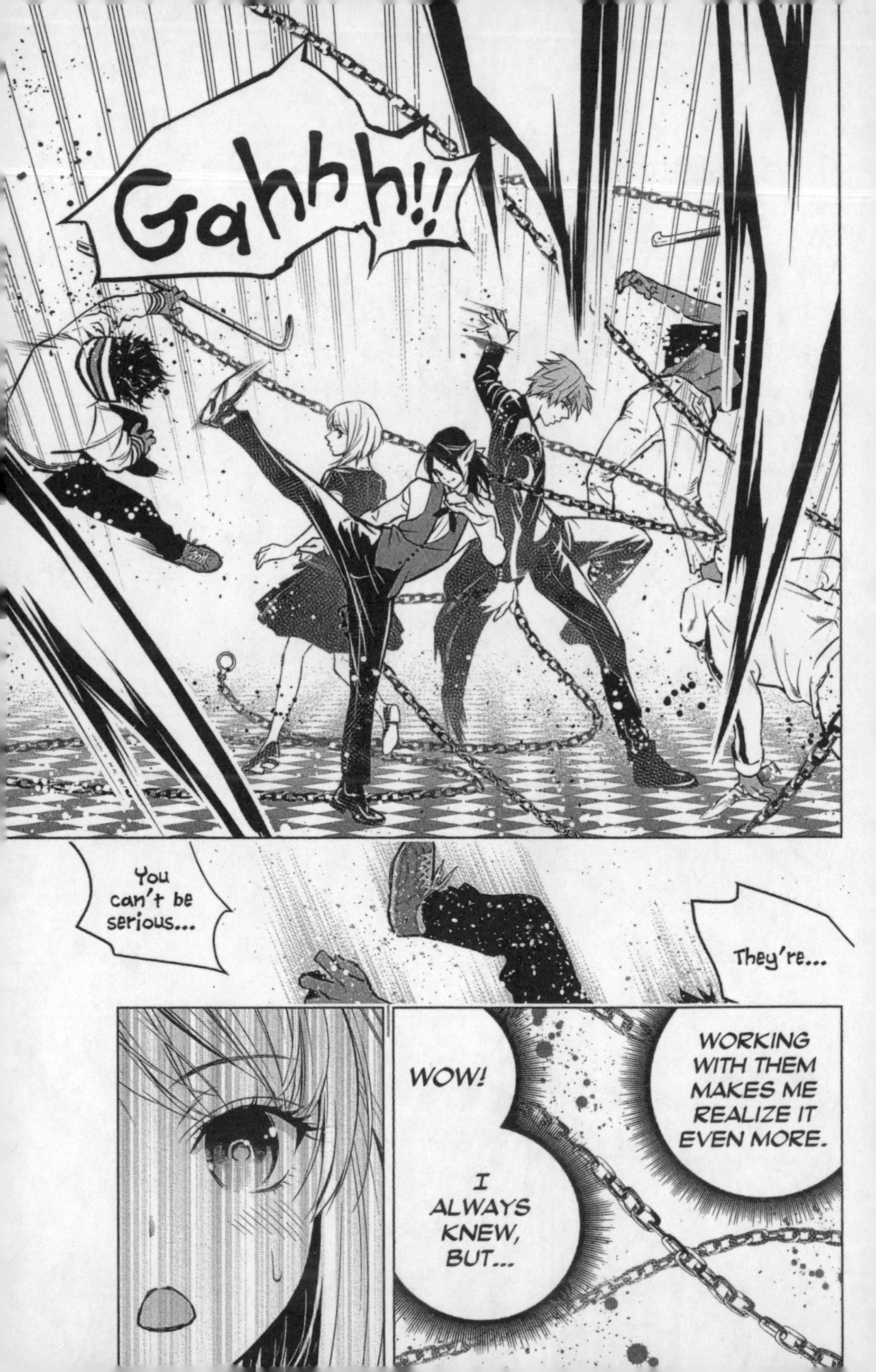
Gahhh!!
They're...
You can't be serious...
WOW!
I ALWAYS KNEW, BUT...
WORKING WITH THEM MAKES ME REALIZE IT EVEN MORE.

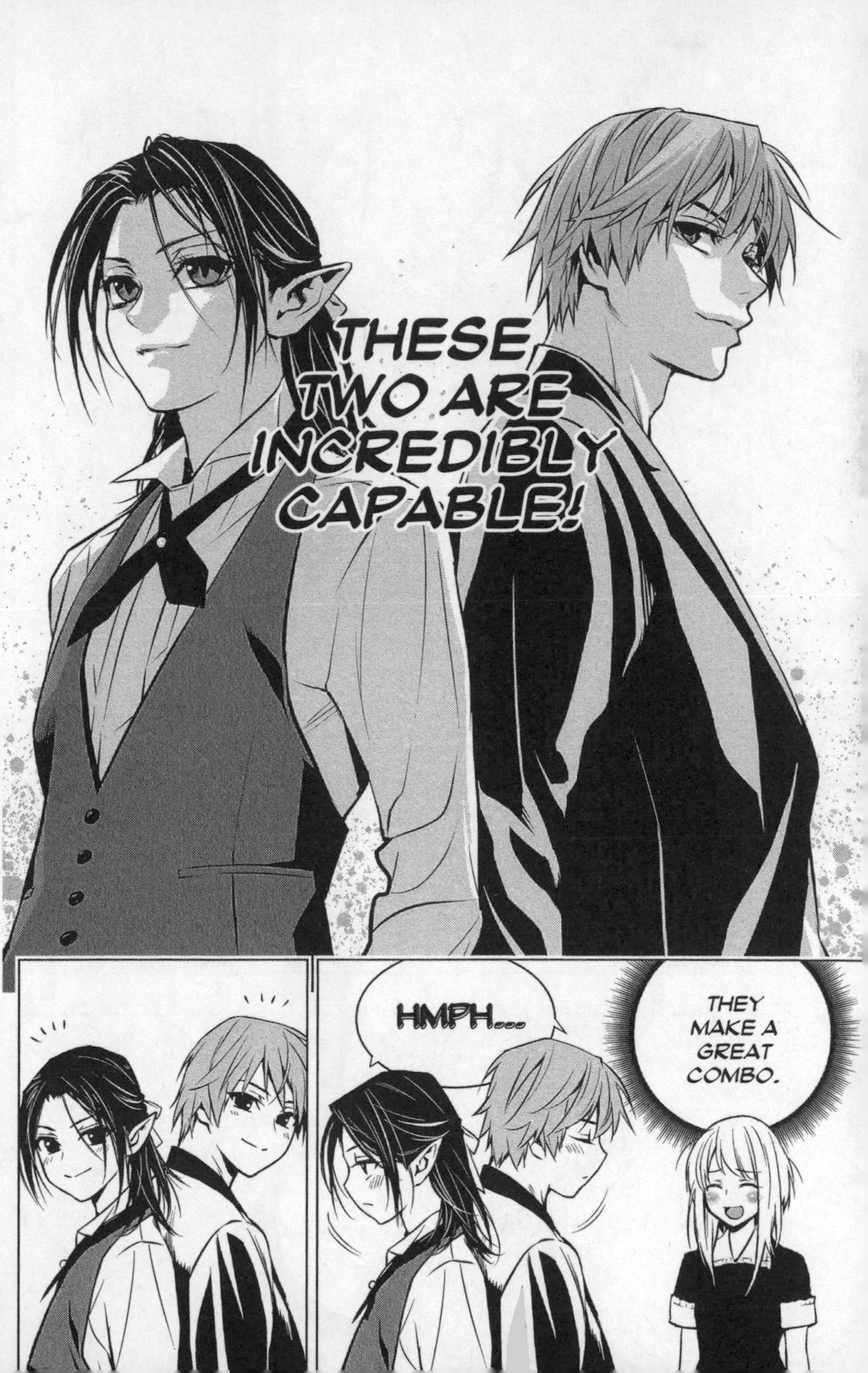
THESE TWO ARE INCREDIBLY CAPABLE!
THEY MAKE A GREAT COMBO.
HMPH...

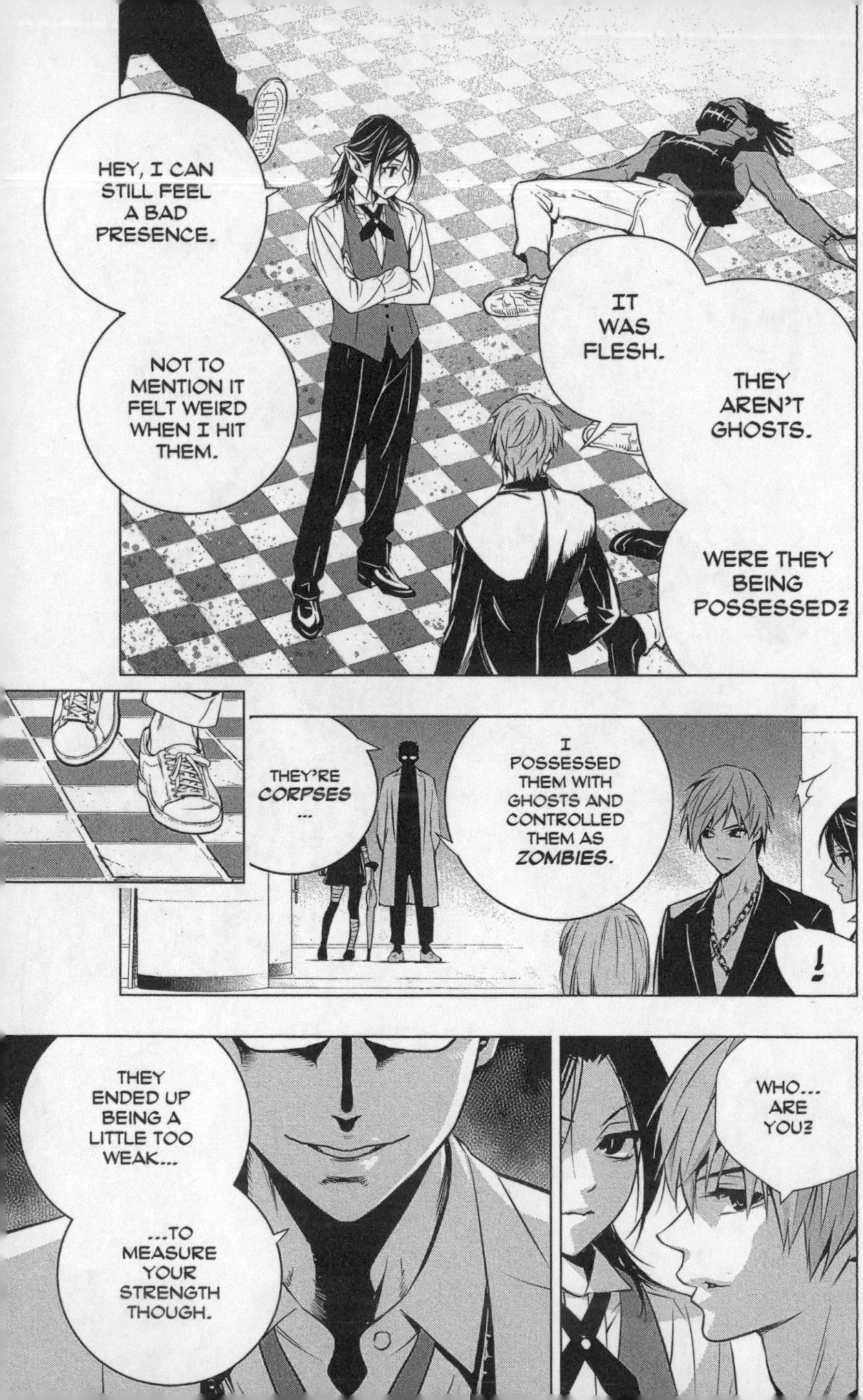
HEY, I CAN STILL FEEL A BAD PRESENCE.
NOT TO MENTION IT FELT WEIRD WHEN I HIT THEM.
IT WAS FLESH.
THEY AREN'T GHOSTS.
WERE THEY BEING POSSESSED?
THEY'RE *CORPSES* ...
I POSSESSED THEM WITH GHOSTS AND CONTROLLED THEM AS *ZOMBIES*.
!
THEY ENDED UP BEING A LITTLE TOO WEAK...
...TO MEASURE YOUR STRENGTH THOUGH.
WHO... ARE YOU?

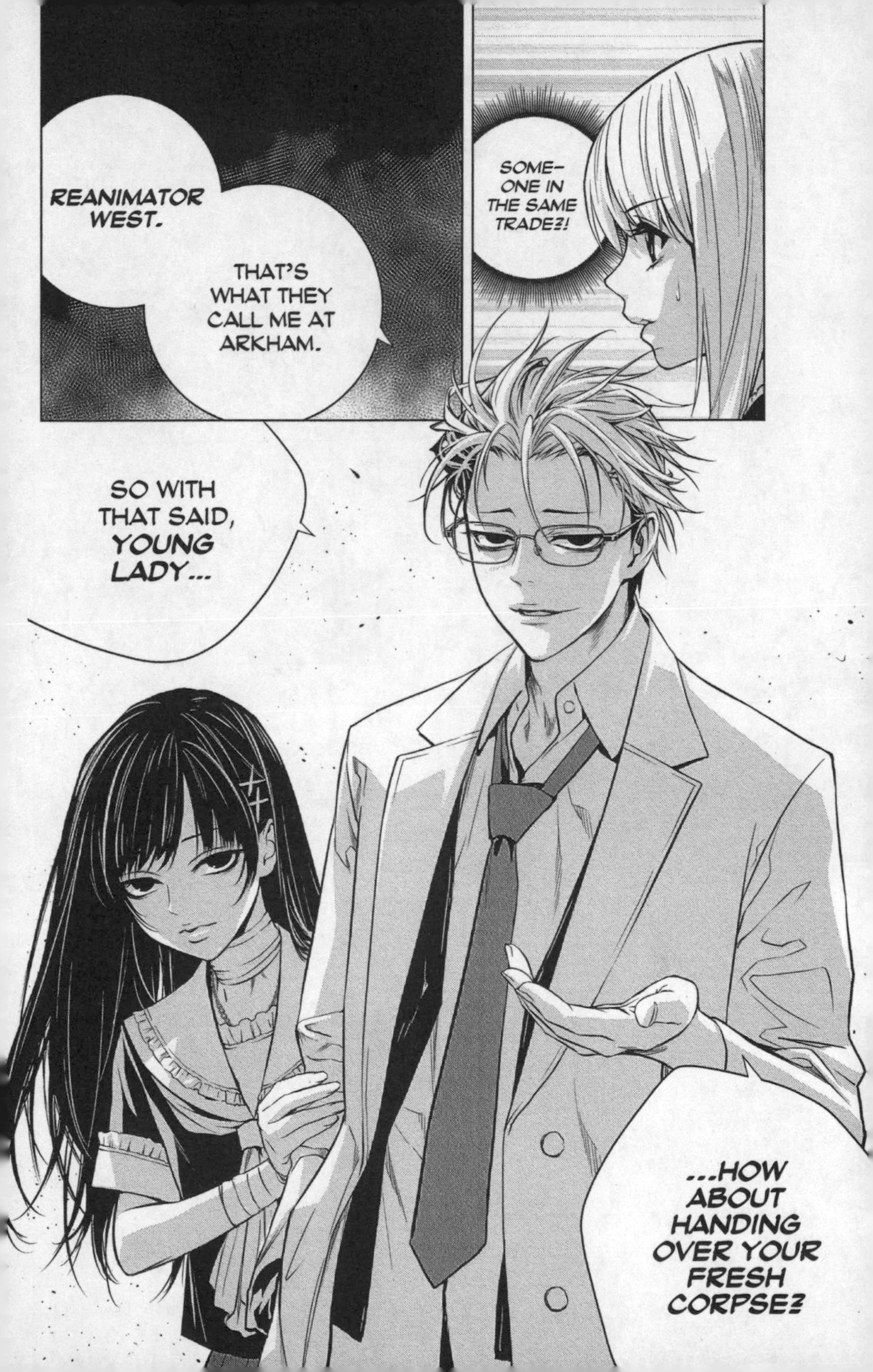
SOME-ONE IN THE SAME TRADE?!
REANIMATOR WEST.
THAT'S WHAT THEY CALL ME AT ARKHAM.
SO WITH THAT SAID, YOUNG LADY...
...HOW ABOUT HANDING OVER YOUR FRESH CORPSE?

#8: Game of the Dead

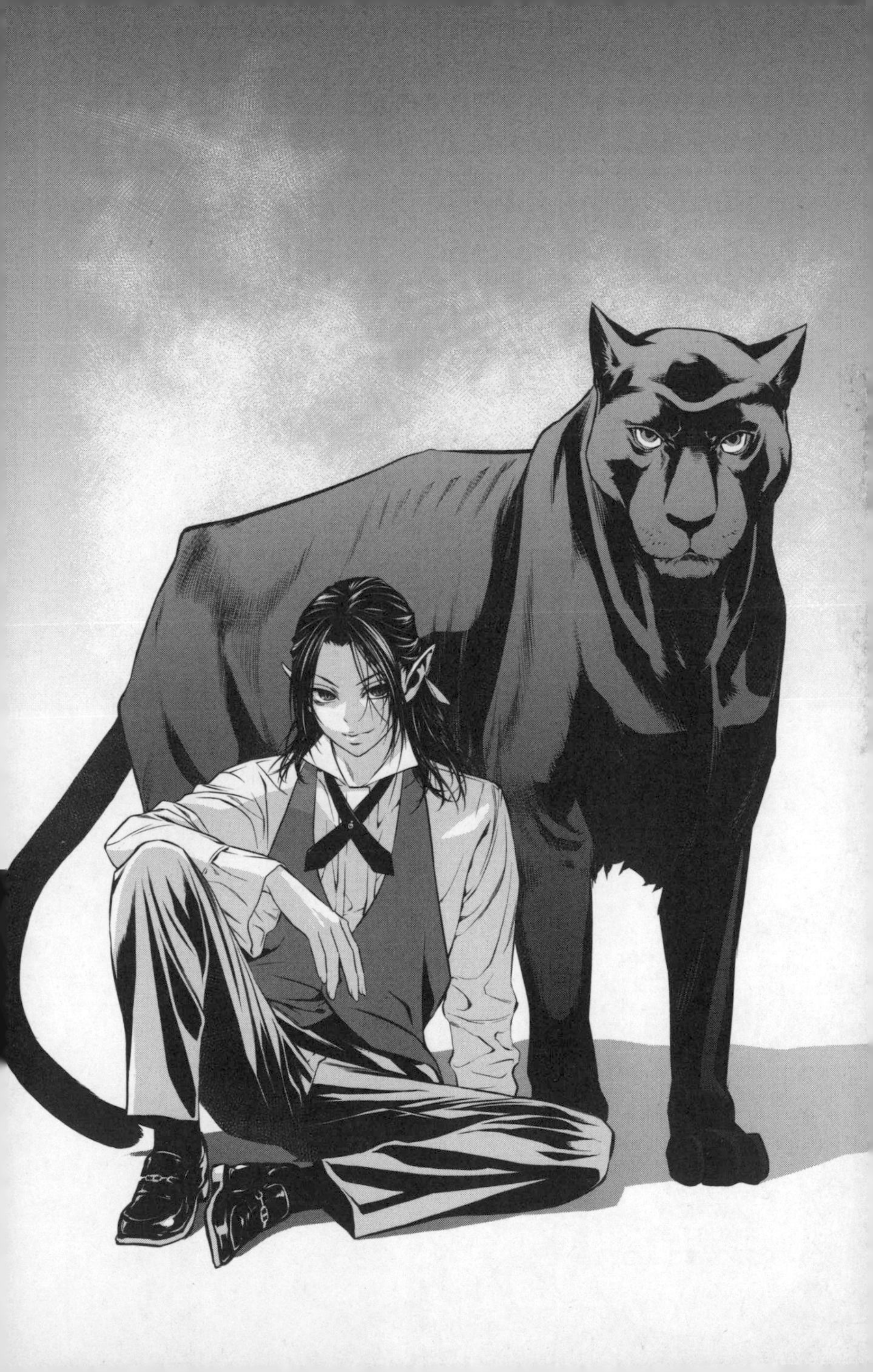

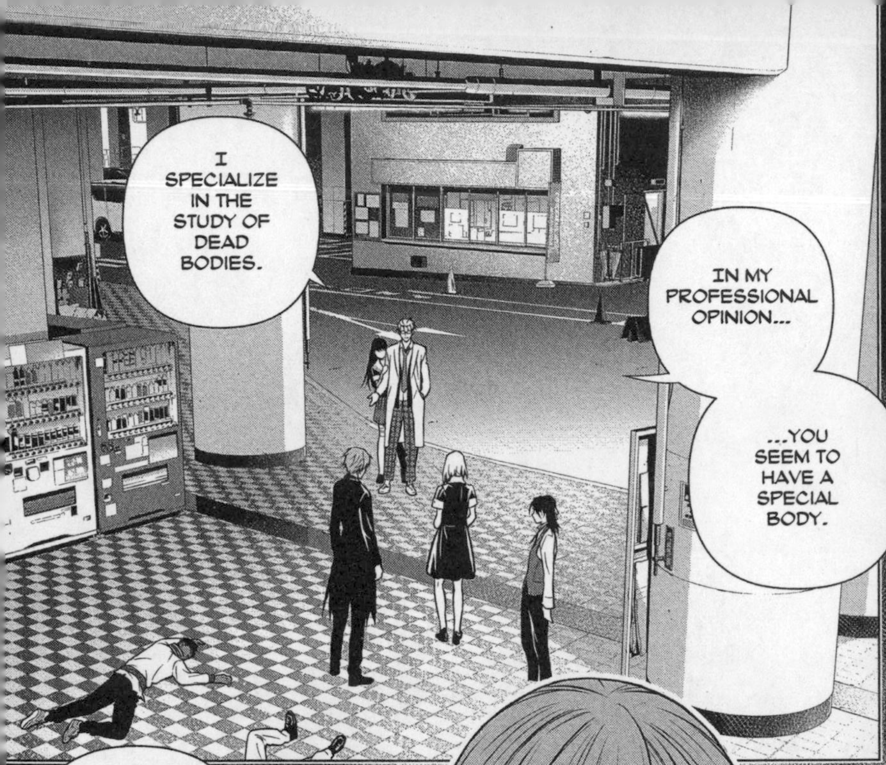
I SPECIALIZE IN THE STUDY OF DEAD BODIES.
IN MY PROFESSIONAL OPINION...
...YOU SEEM TO HAVE A SPECIAL BODY.
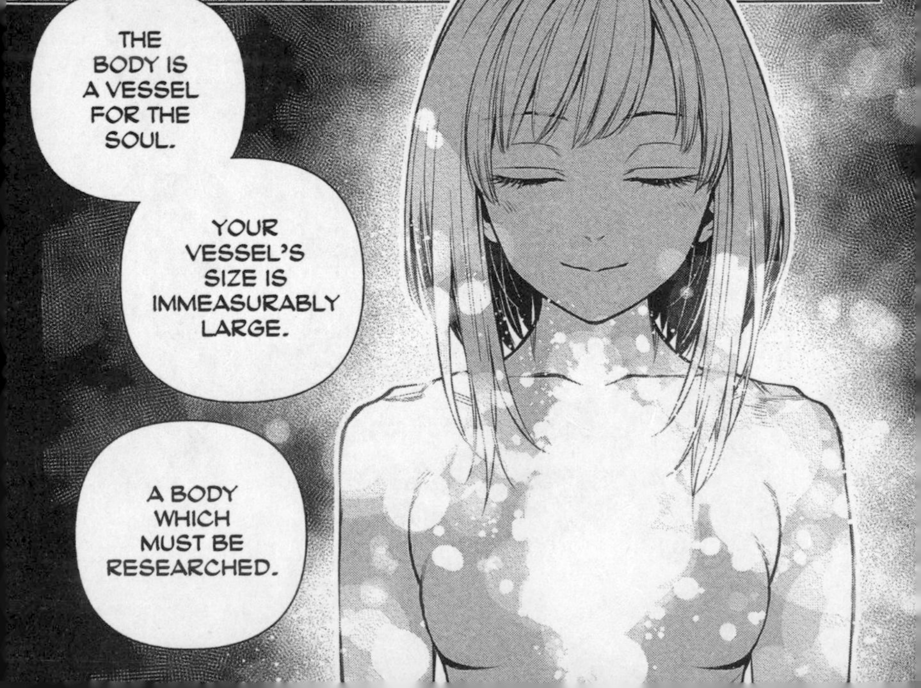
THE BODY IS A VESSEL FOR THE SOUL.
YOUR VESSEL'S SIZE IS IMMEASURABLY LARGE.
A BODY WHICH MUST BE RESEARCHED.

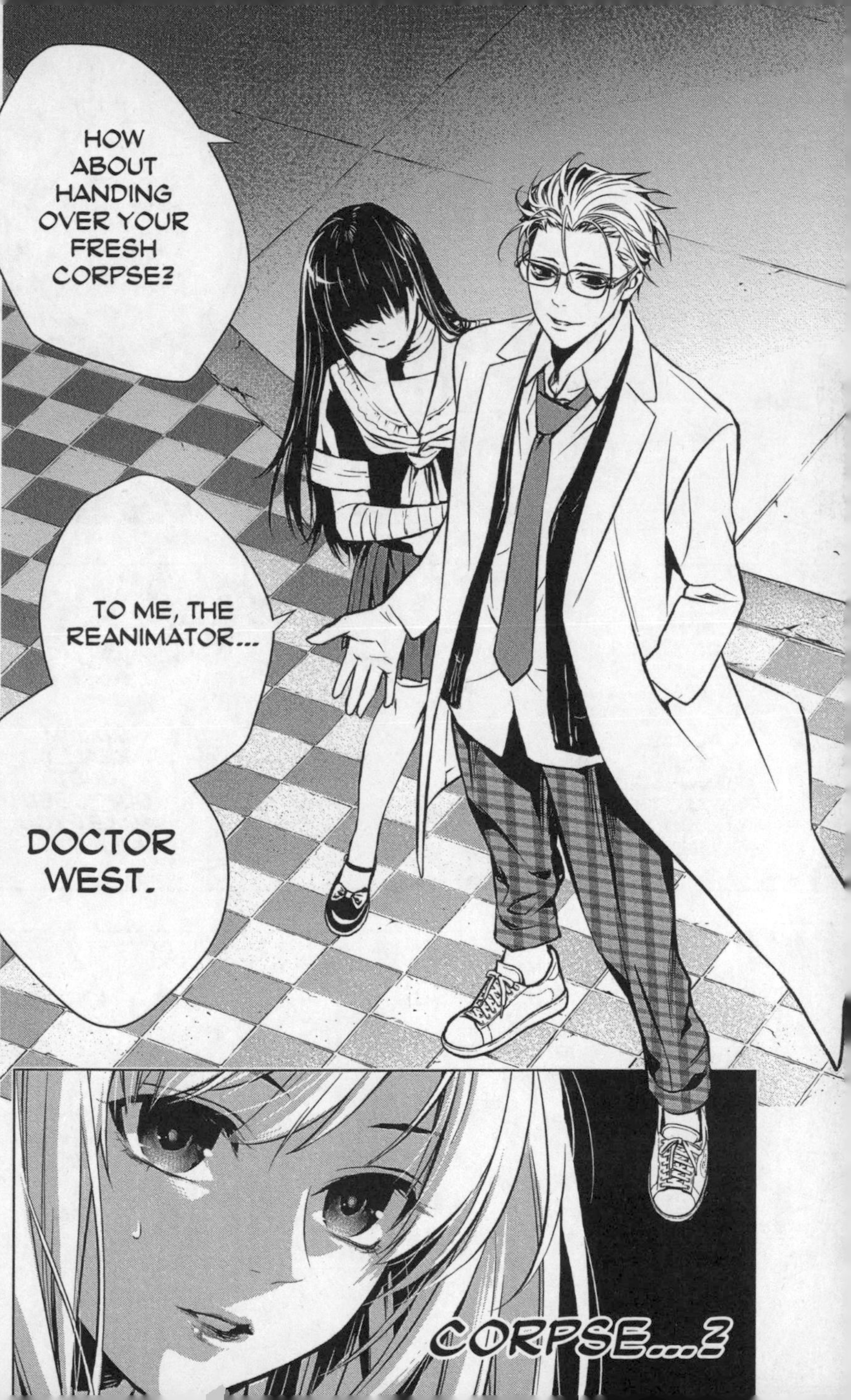
HOW ABOUT HANDING OVER YOUR FRESH CORPSE?
TO ME, THE REANIMATOR...
DOCTOR WEST.
CORPSE...?

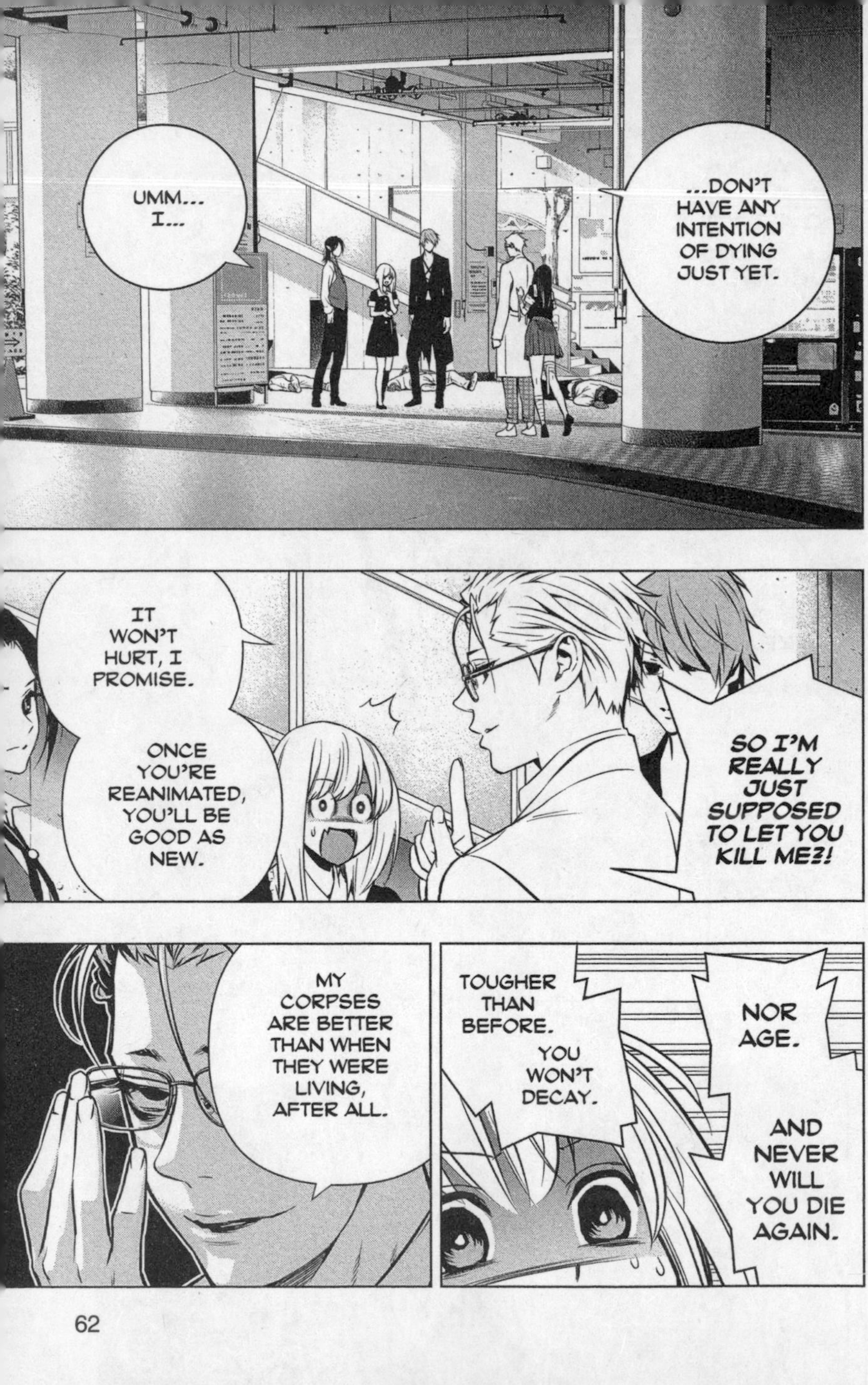
UMM... I...
...DON'T HAVE ANY INTENTION OF DYING JUST YET.
IT WON'T HURT, I PROMISE.
ONCE YOU'RE REANIMATED, YOU'LL BE GOOD AS NEW.
SO I'M REALLY JUST SUPPOSED TO LET YOU KILL ME?!
MY CORPSES ARE BETTER THAN WHEN THEY WERE LIVING, AFTER ALL.
TOUGHER THAN BEFORE.
YOU WON'T DECAY.
NOR AGE.
AND NEVER WILL YOU DIE AGAIN.

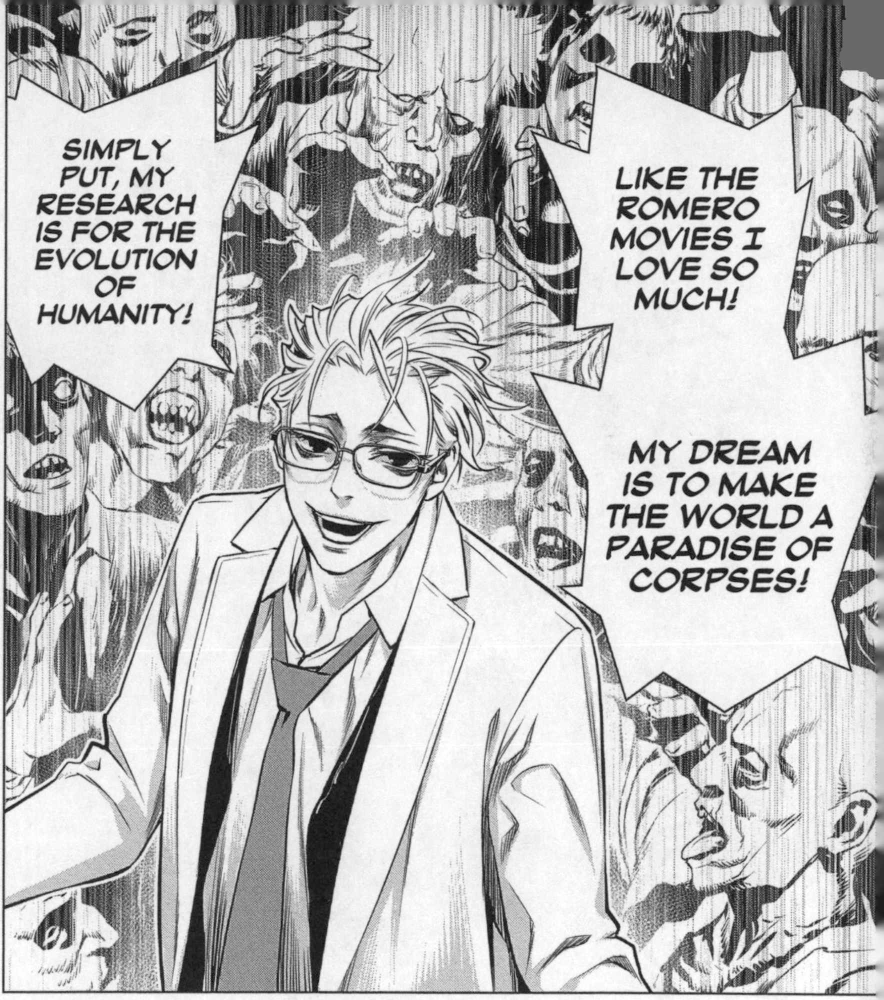
SIMPLY PUT, MY RESEARCH IS FOR THE EVOLUTION OF HUMANITY!
MY DREAM IS TO MAKE THE WORLD A PARADISE OF CORPSES!
LIKE THE ROMERO MOVIES I LOVE SO MUCH!

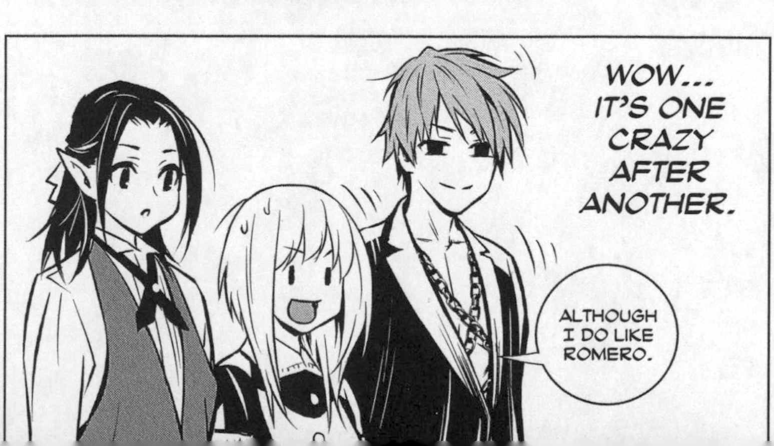
WOW... IT'S ONE CRAZY AFTER ANOTHER.
ALTHOUGH I DO LIKE ROMERO.

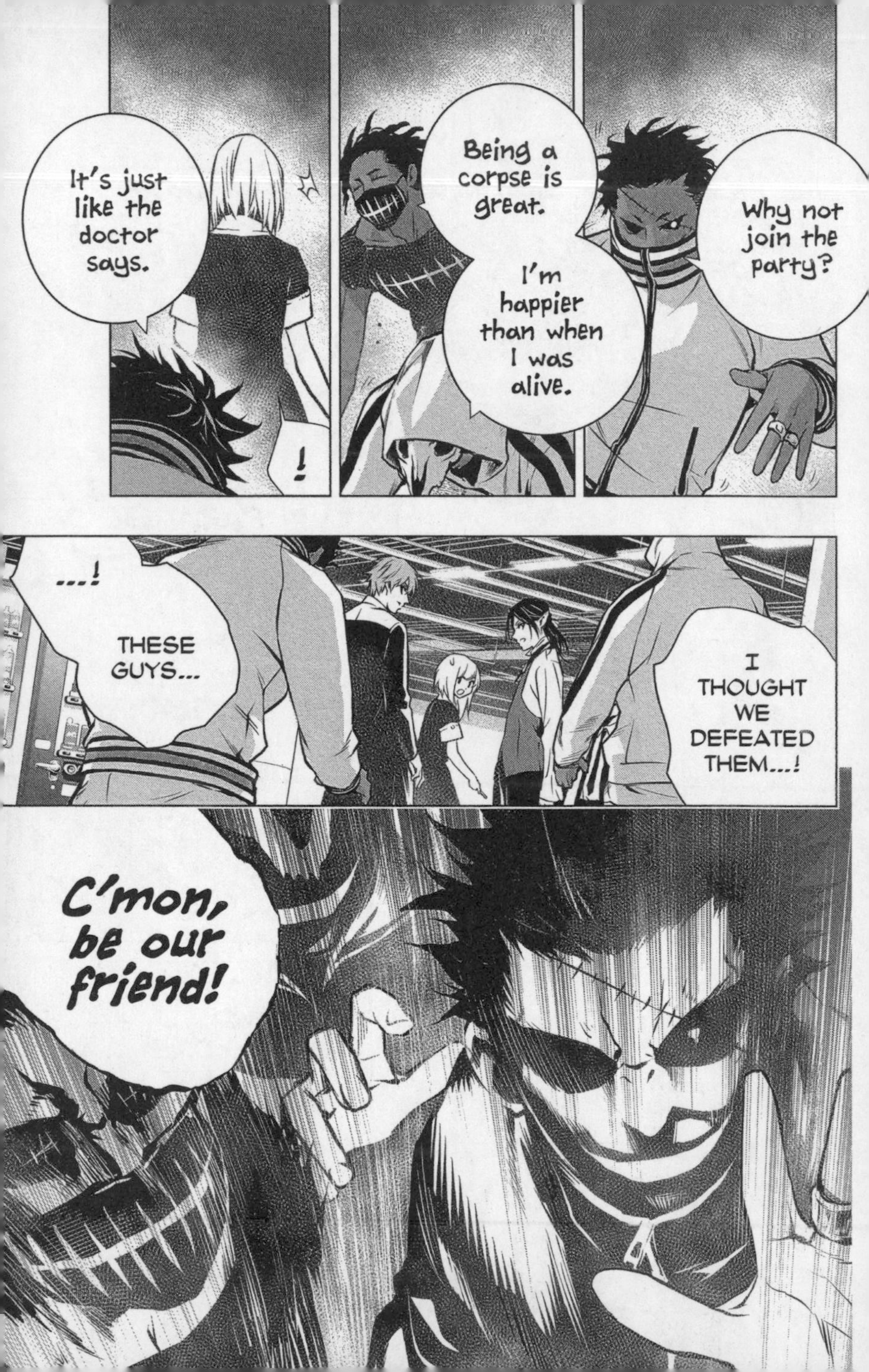

Why not join the party?
Being a corpse is great.
I'm happier than when I was alive.
It's just like the doctor says.
!
...!
THESE GUYS...
I THOUGHT WE DEFEATED THEM...!
C'mon, be our friend!

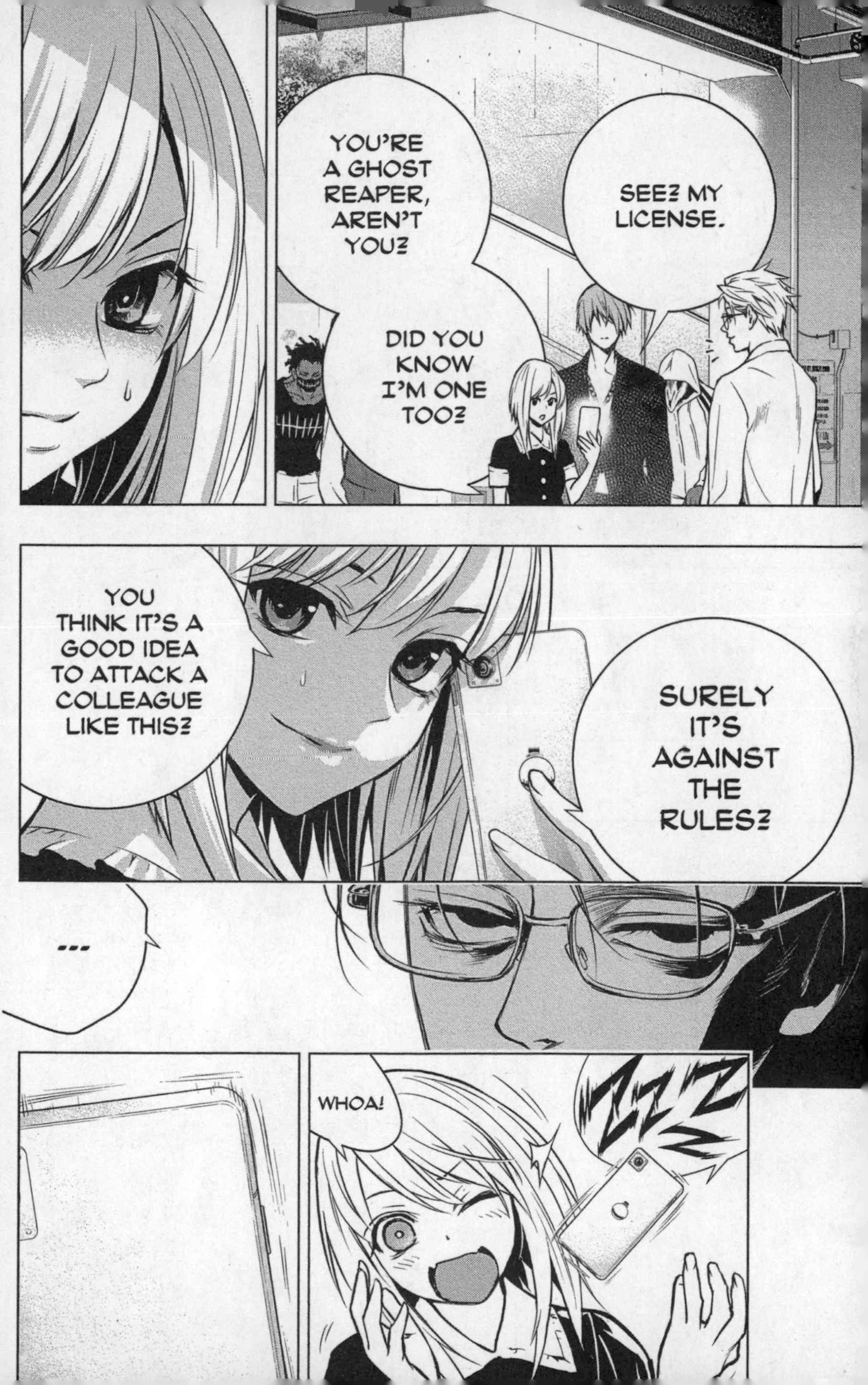
YOU'RE A GHOST REAPER, AREN'T YOU?
DID YOU KNOW I'M ONE TOO?
SEE? MY LICENSE.
YOU THINK IT'S A GOOD IDEA TO ATTACK A COLLEAGUE LIKE THIS?
SURELY IT'S AGAINST THE RULES?
...
WHOA!
ZZZ

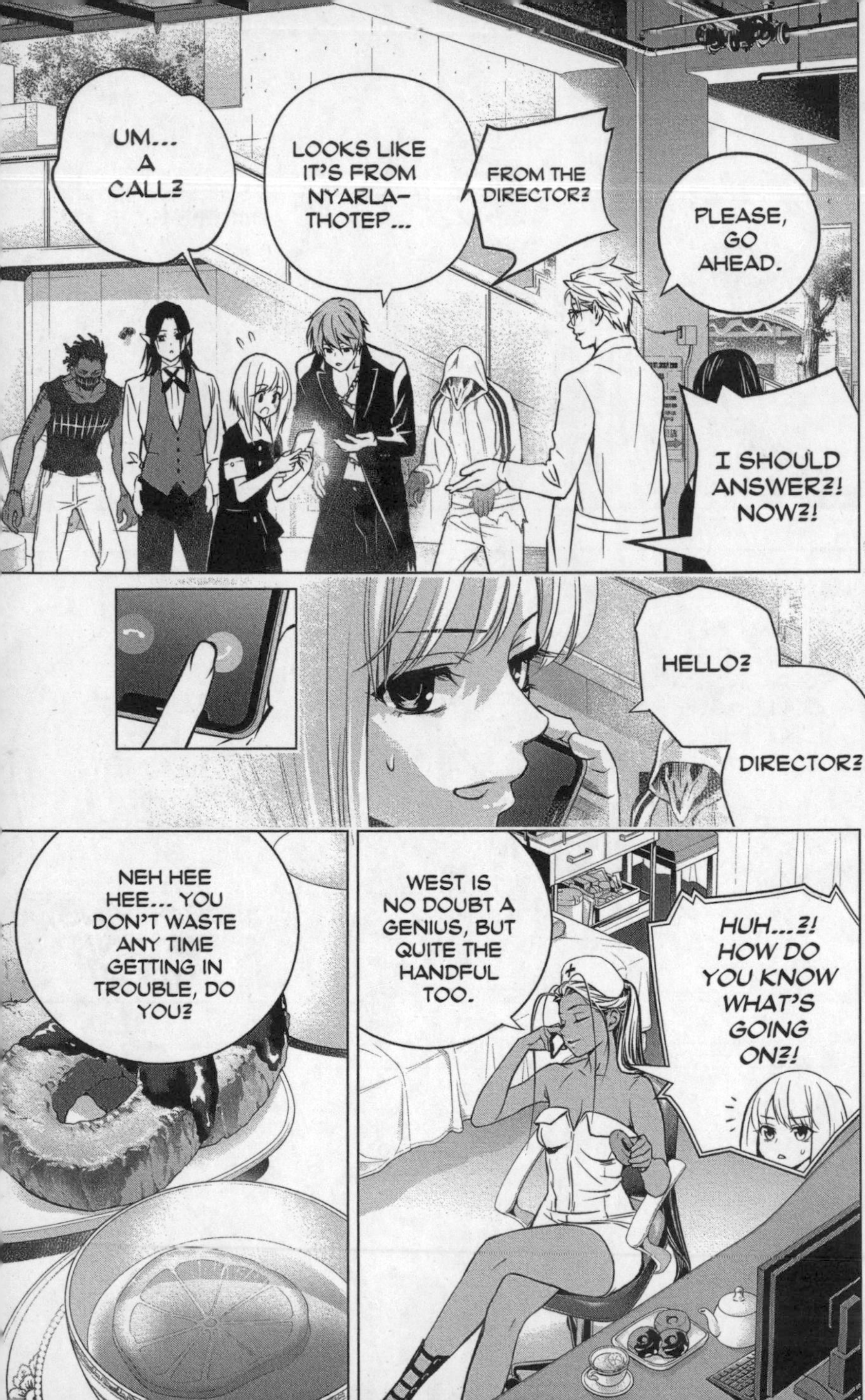
UM... A CALL?
LOOKS LIKE IT'S FROM NYARLA-THOTEP...
FROM THE DIRECTOR?
PLEASE, GO AHEAD.
I SHOULD ANSWER?! NOW?!
HELLO?
DIRECTOR?
NEH HEE HEE... YOU DON'T WASTE ANY TIME GETTING IN TROUBLE, DO YOU?
WEST IS NO DOUBT A GENIUS, BUT QUITE THE HANDFUL TOO.
HUH...?! HOW DO YOU KNOW WHAT'S GOING ON?!

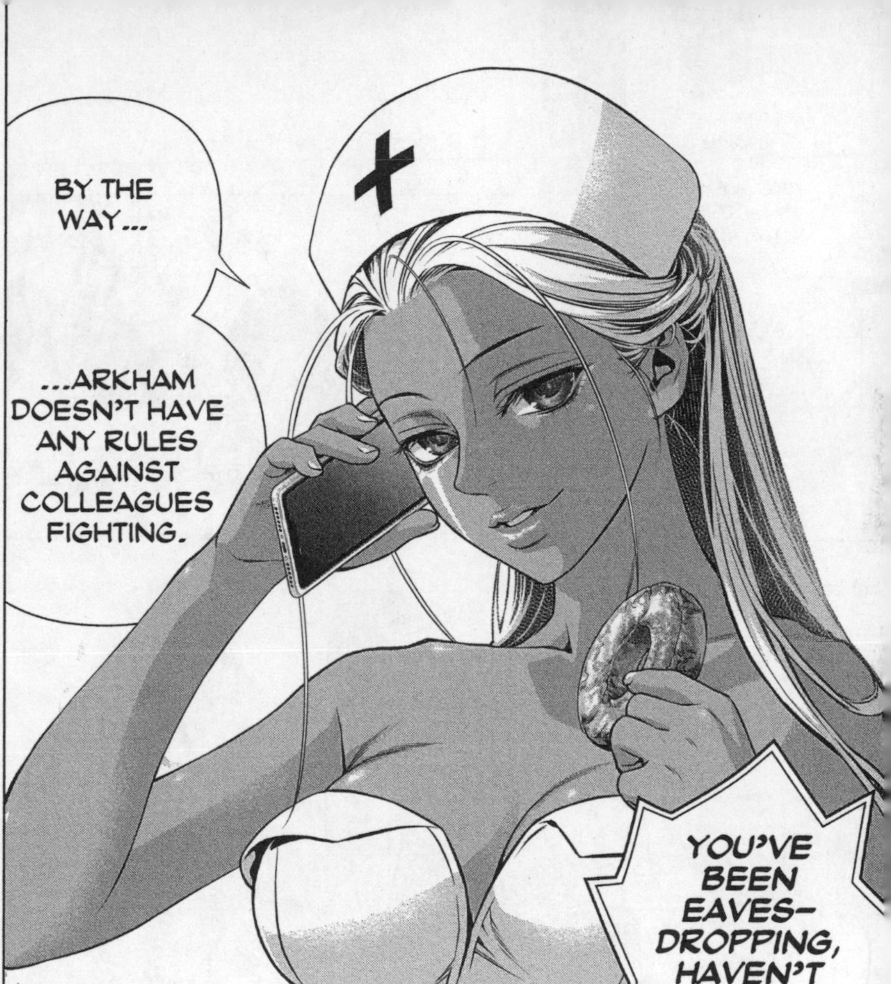
BY THE WAY...
...ARKHAM DOESN'T HAVE ANY RULES AGAINST COLLEAGUES FIGHTING.
YOU'VE BEEN EAVES-DROPPING, HAVEN'T YOU?!

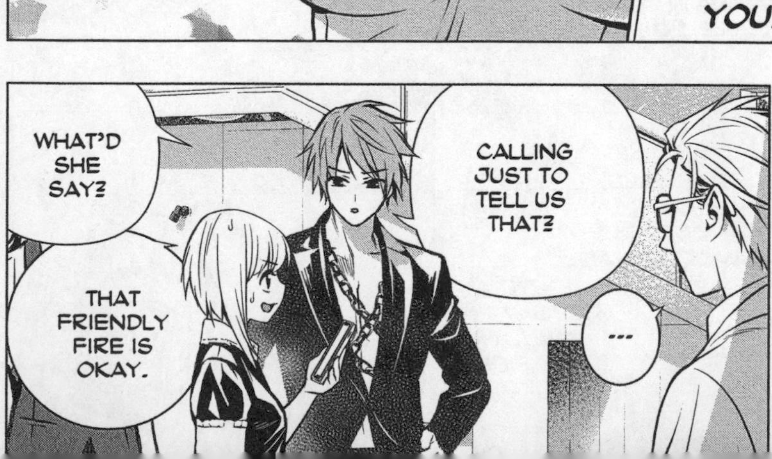
CALLING JUST TO TELL US THAT?
WHAT'D SHE SAY?
THAT FRIENDLY FIRE IS OKAY.
...

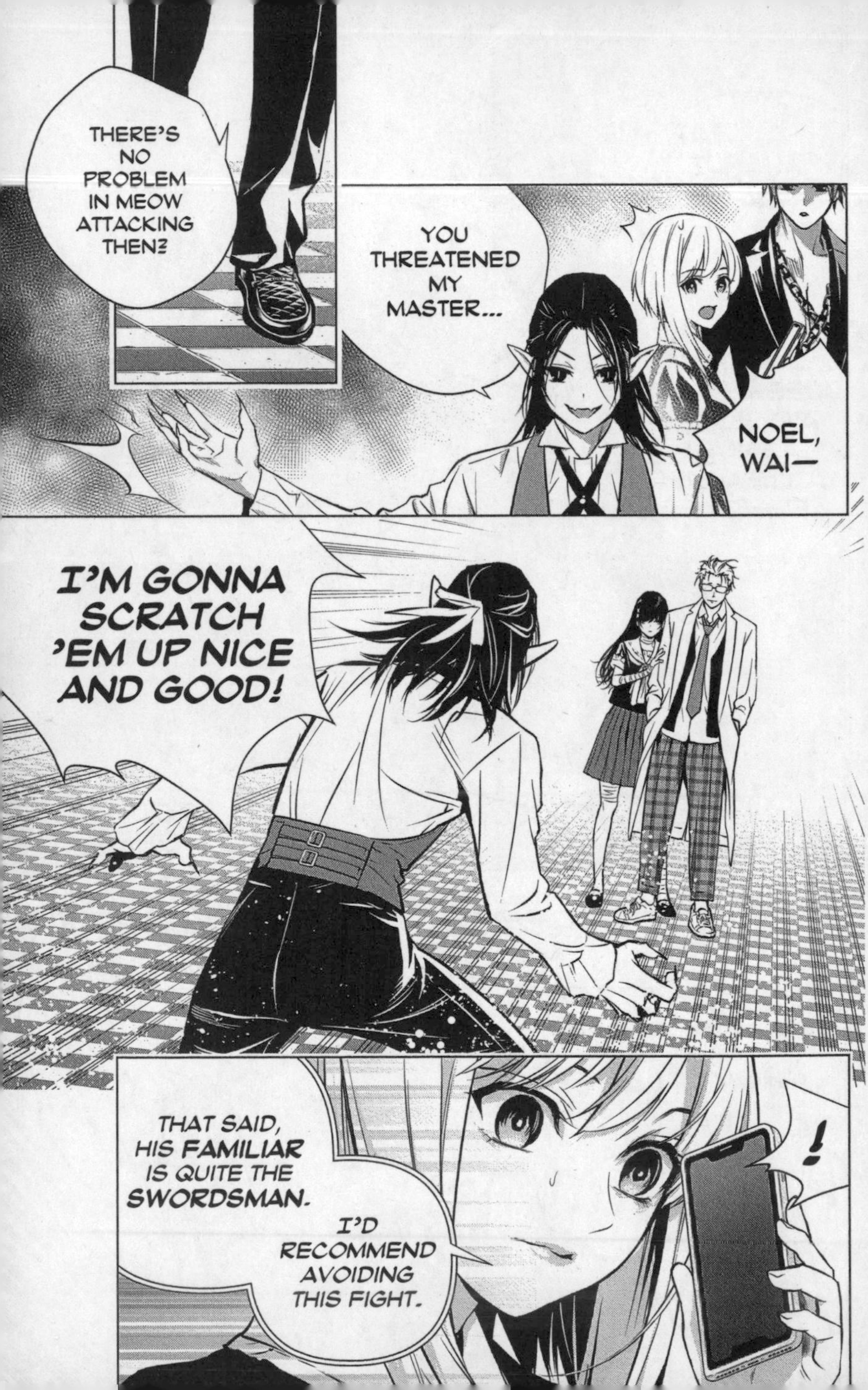
THERE'S NO PROBLEM IN MEOW ATTACKING THEN?
YOU THREATENED MY MASTER...
NOEL, WAI—
I'M GONNA SCRATCH 'EM UP NICE AND GOOD!
!
THAT SAID, HIS FAMILIAR IS QUITE THE SWORDSMAN.
I'D RECOMMEND AVOIDING THIS FIGHT.

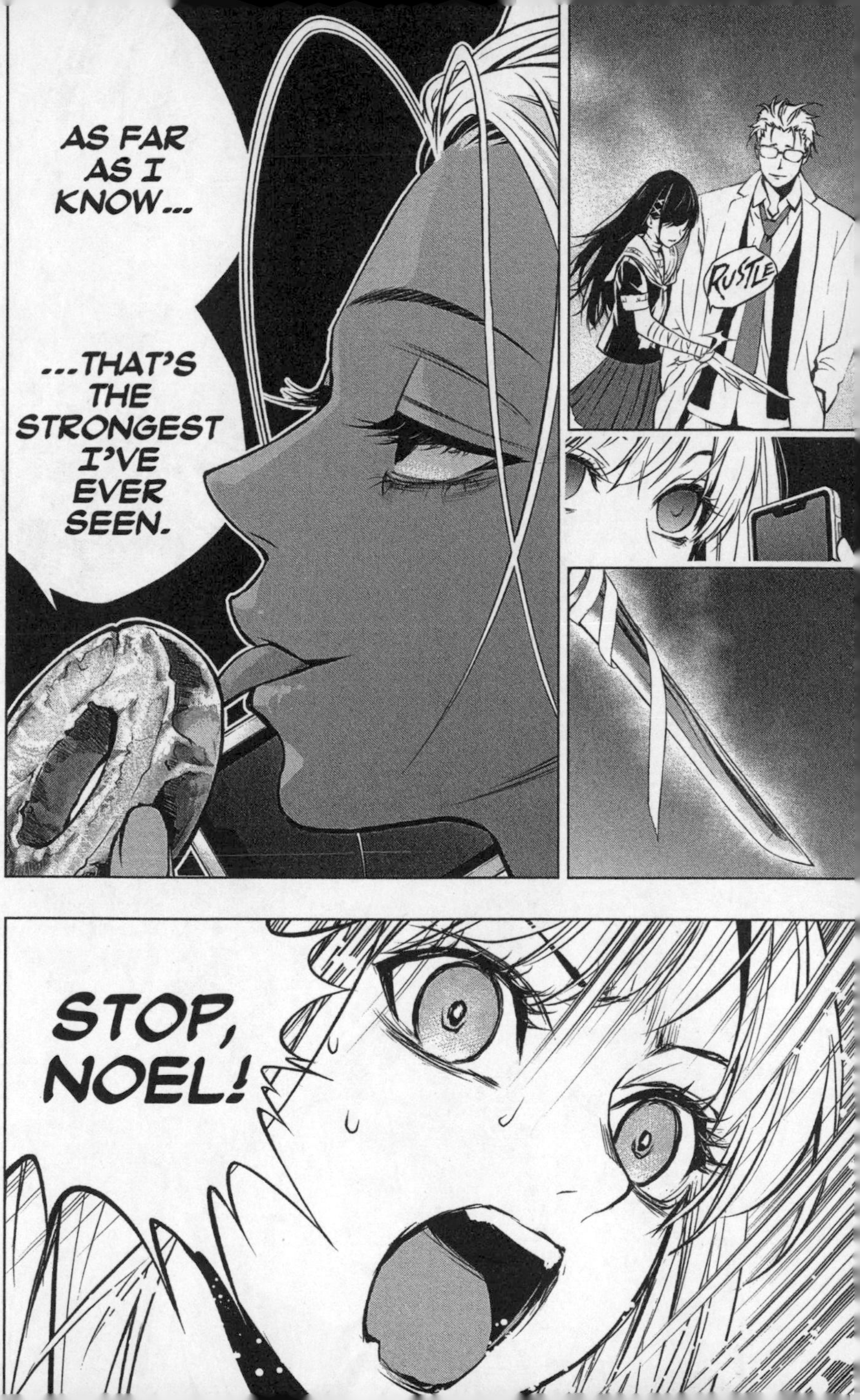
RUSTLE
AS FAR AS I KNOW...
...THAT'S THE STRONGEST I'VE EVER SEEN.
STOP, NOEL!

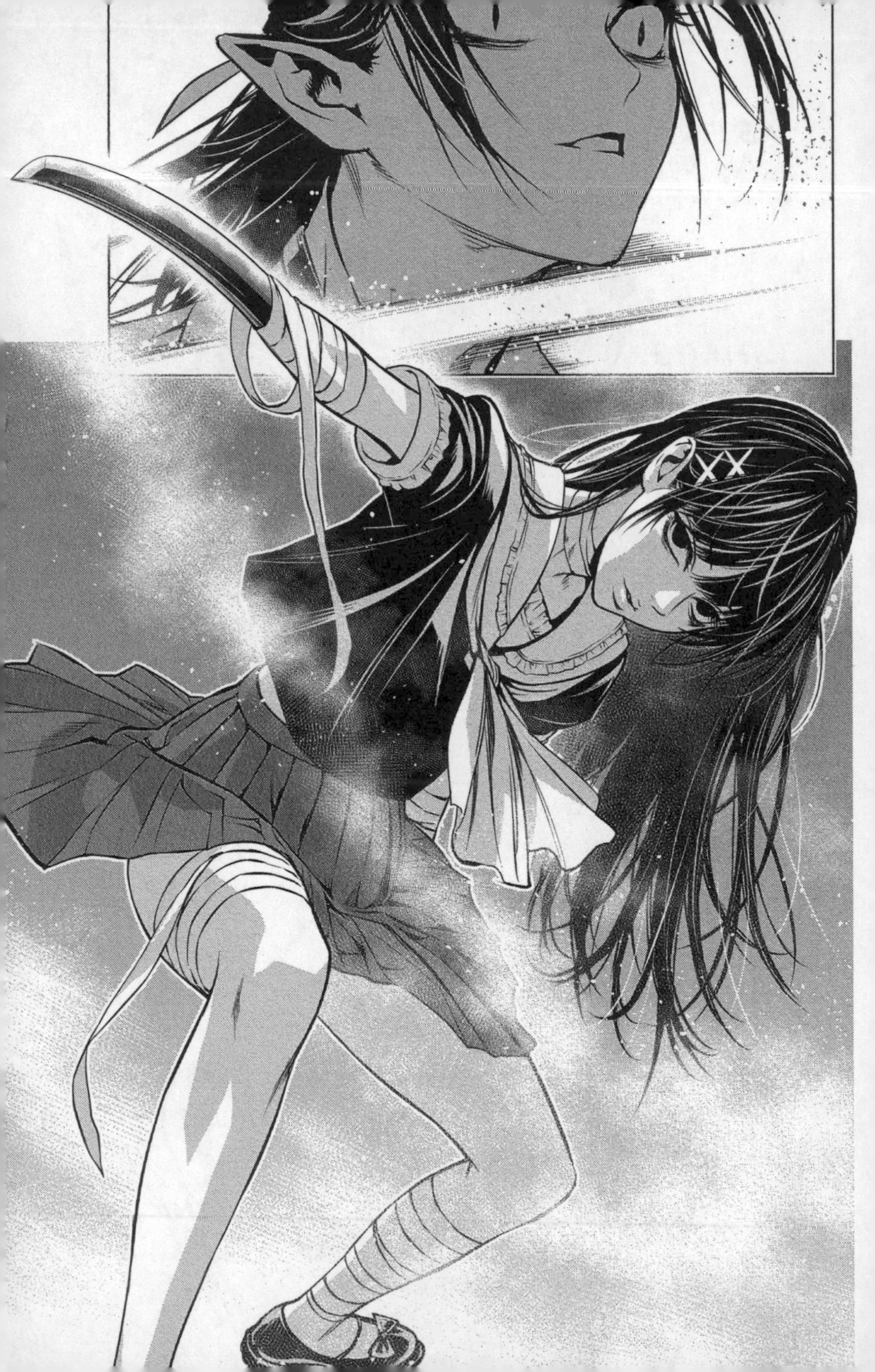

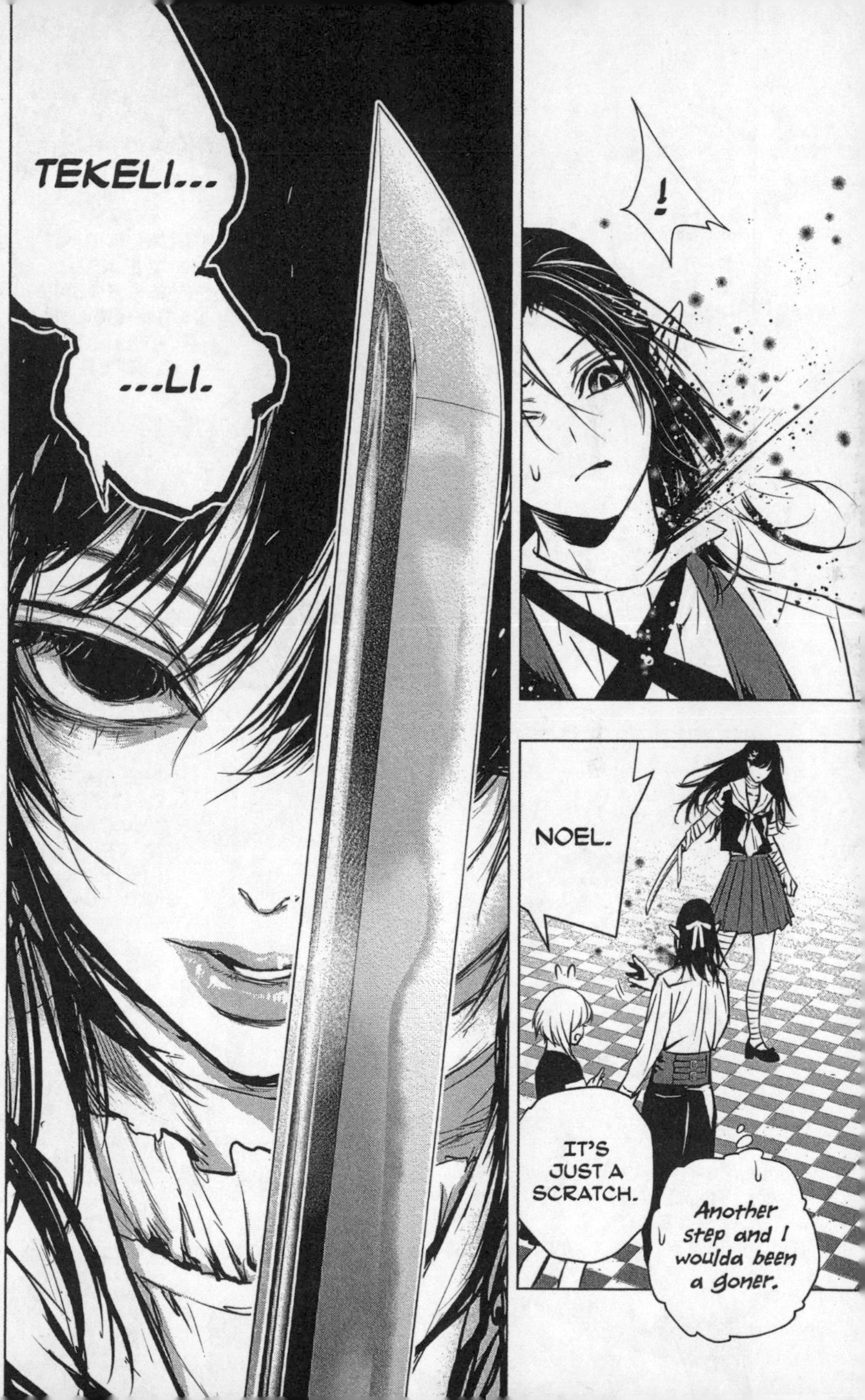
!
NOEL.
IT'S JUST A SCRATCH.
Another step and I woulda been a goner.
TEKELI...
...LI.

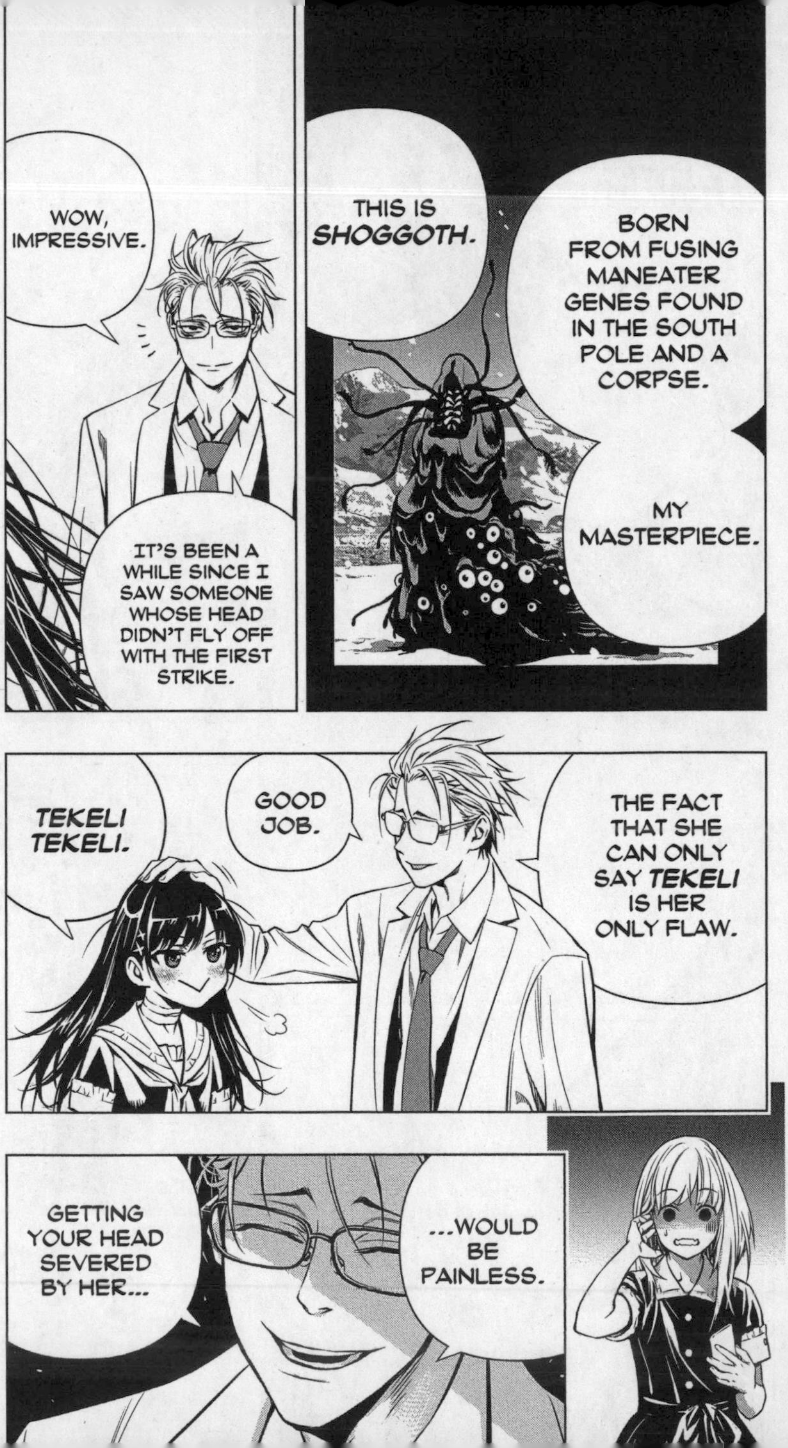
WOW, IMPRESSIVE.
IT'S BEEN A WHILE SINCE I SAW SOMEONE WHOSE HEAD DIDN'T FLY OFF WITH THE FIRST STRIKE.
THIS IS *SHOGGOTH*.
BORN FROM FUSING MANEATER GENES FOUND IN THE SOUTH POLE AND A CORPSE.
MY MASTERPIECE.
TEKELI TEKELI.
GOOD JOB.
THE FACT THAT SHE CAN ONLY SAY *TEKELI* IS HER ONLY FLAW.
GETTING YOUR HEAD SEVERED BY HER...
...WOULD BE PAINLESS.

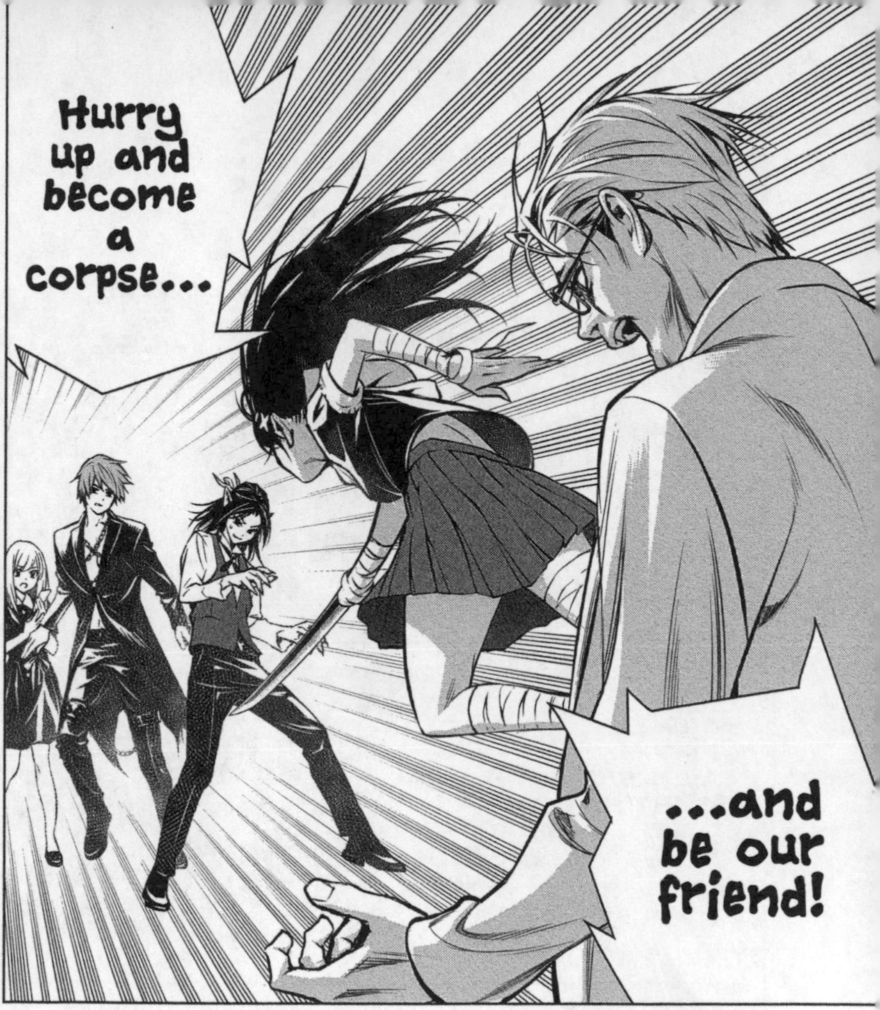
Hurry up and become a corpse...
...and be our friend!

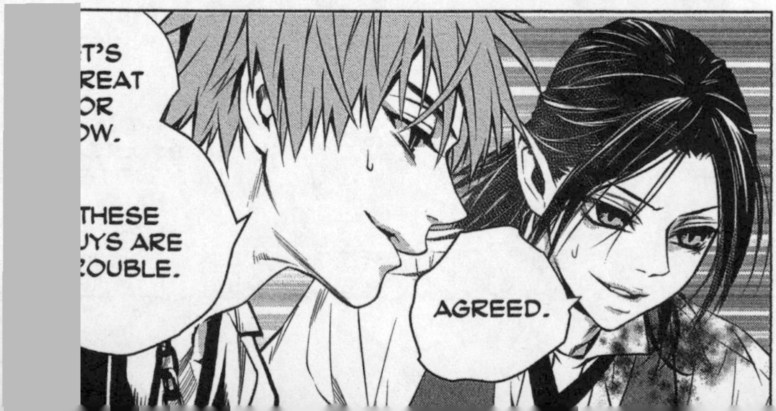
T'S REAT OR OW.
THESE UYS ARE ROUBLE.
AGREED.

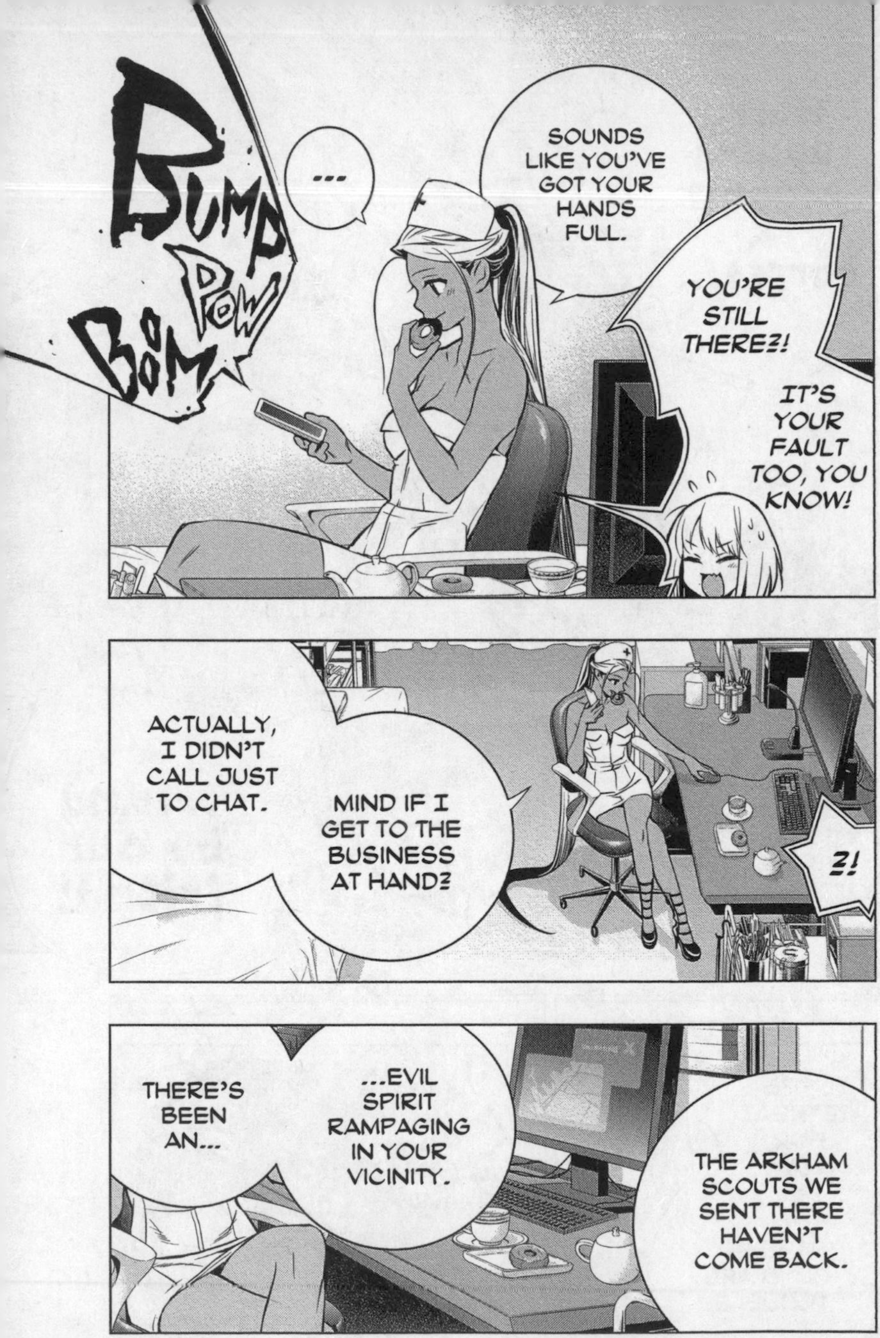
SOUNDS LIKE YOU'VE GOT YOUR HANDS FULL.
...
BUMP POW BOOM
YOU'RE STILL THERE?!
IT'S YOUR FAULT TOO, YOU KNOW!
?!
ACTUALLY, I DIDN'T CALL JUST TO CHAT.
MIND IF I GET TO THE BUSINESS AT HAND?
THERE'S BEEN AN...
...EVIL SPIRIT RAMPAGING IN YOUR VICINITY.
THE ARKHAM SCOUTS WE SENT THERE HAVEN'T COME BACK.

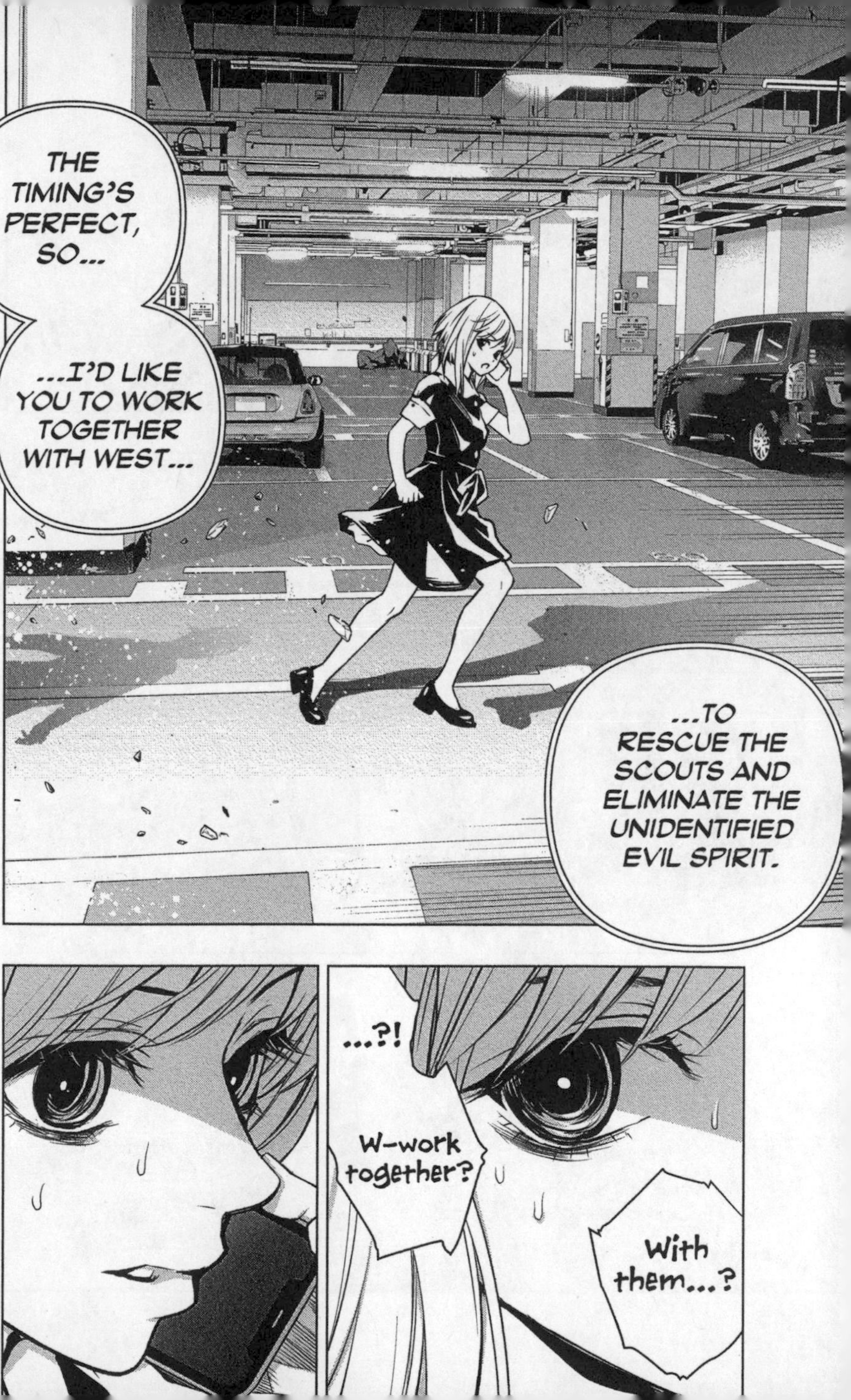
THE TIMING'S PERFECT, SO...
...I'D LIKE YOU TO WORK TOGETHER WITH WEST...
...TO RESCUE THE SCOUTS AND ELIMINATE THE UNIDENTIFIED EVIL SPIRIT.
...?!
W-work together?
With them...?

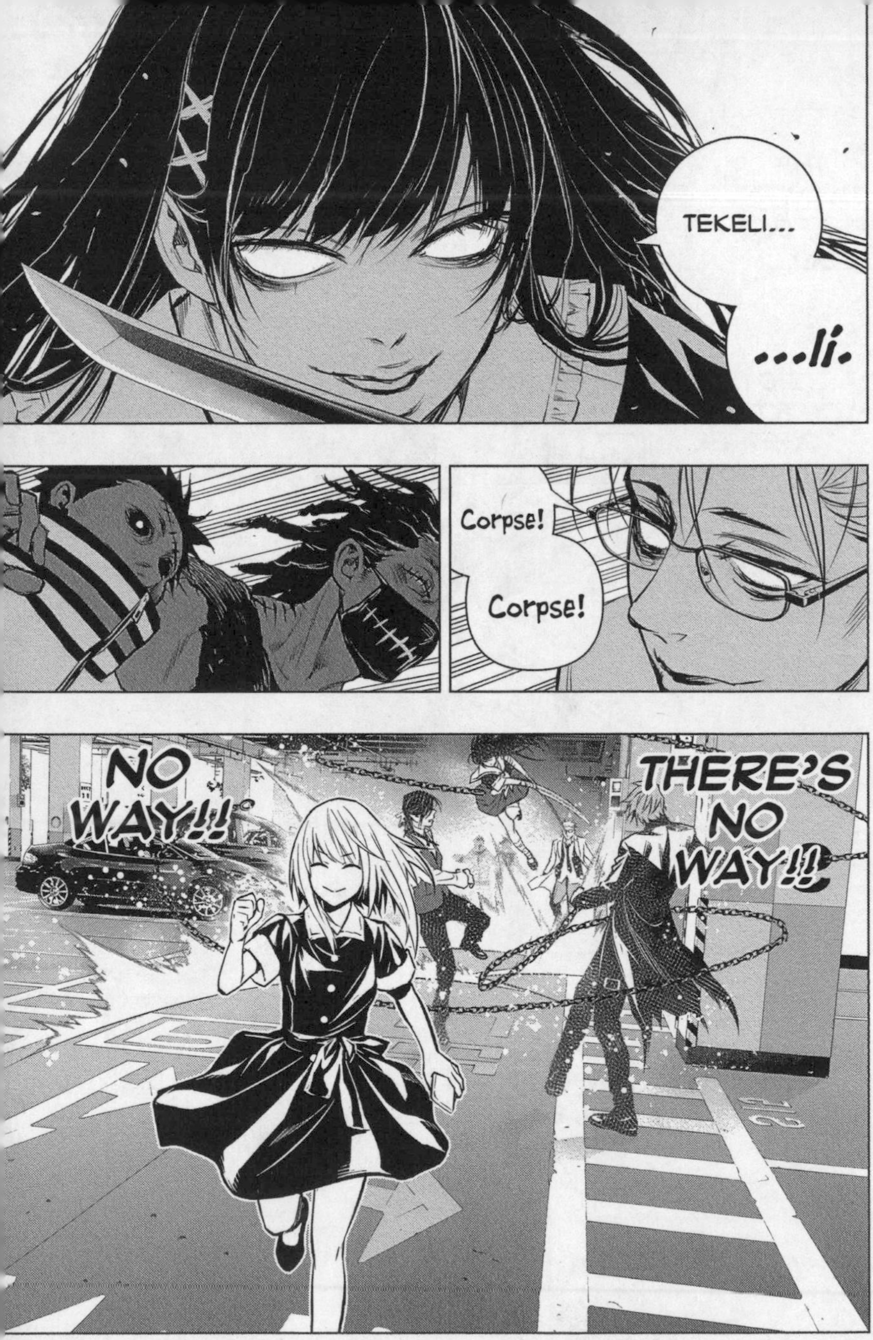
TEKELI...
...li.
Corpse!
Corpse!
THERE'S NO WAY!!
NO WAY!!

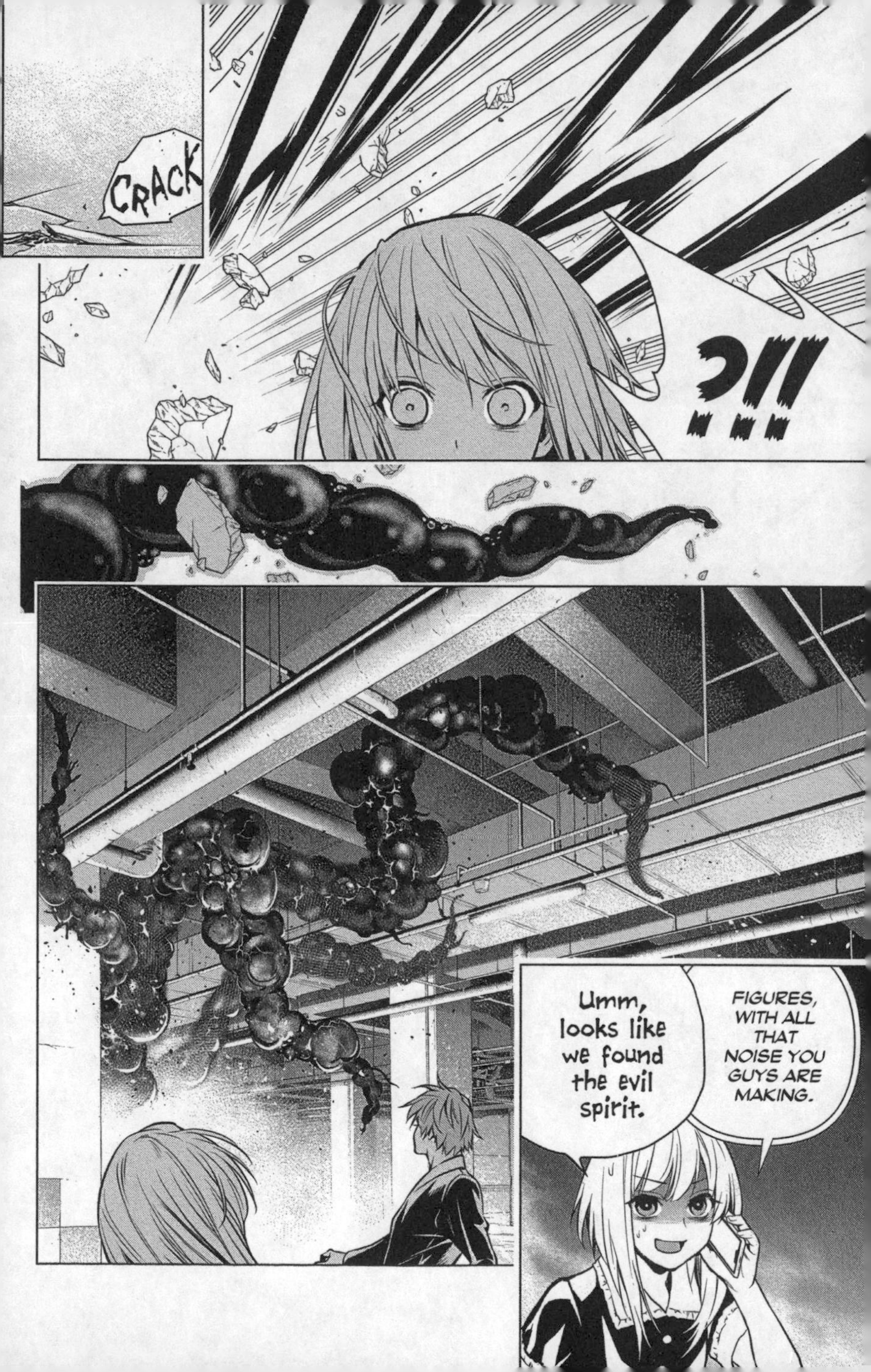
?!!
CRACK
FIGURES, WITH ALL THAT NOISE YOU GUYS ARE MAKING.
Umm, looks like we found the evil spirit.

GHOST REAPER GIRL

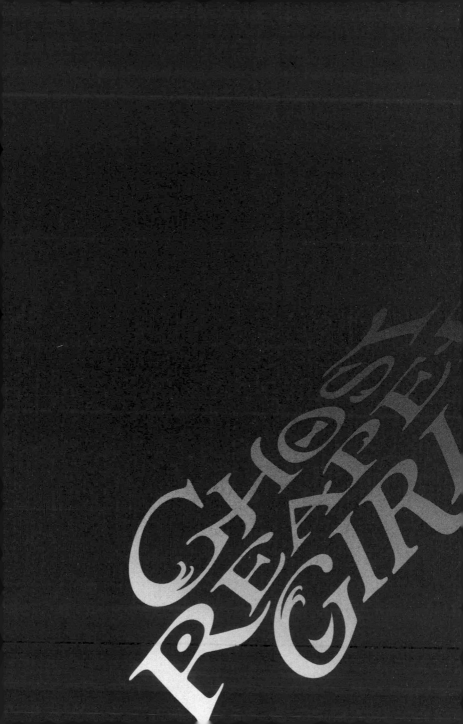

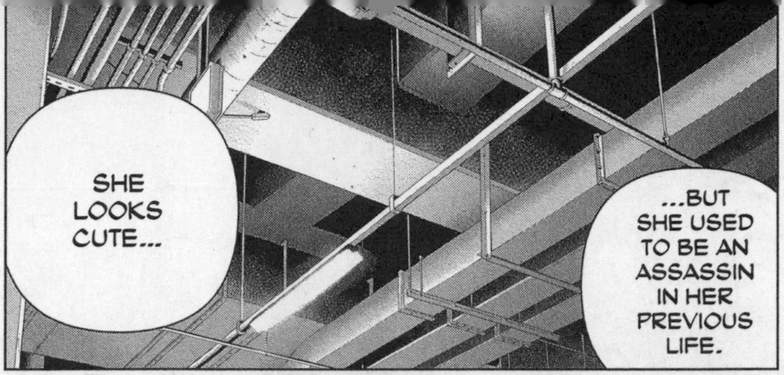
SHE LOOKS CUTE...
...BUT SHE USED TO BE AN ASSASSIN IN HER PREVIOUS LIFE.

#9: The Killing Doll

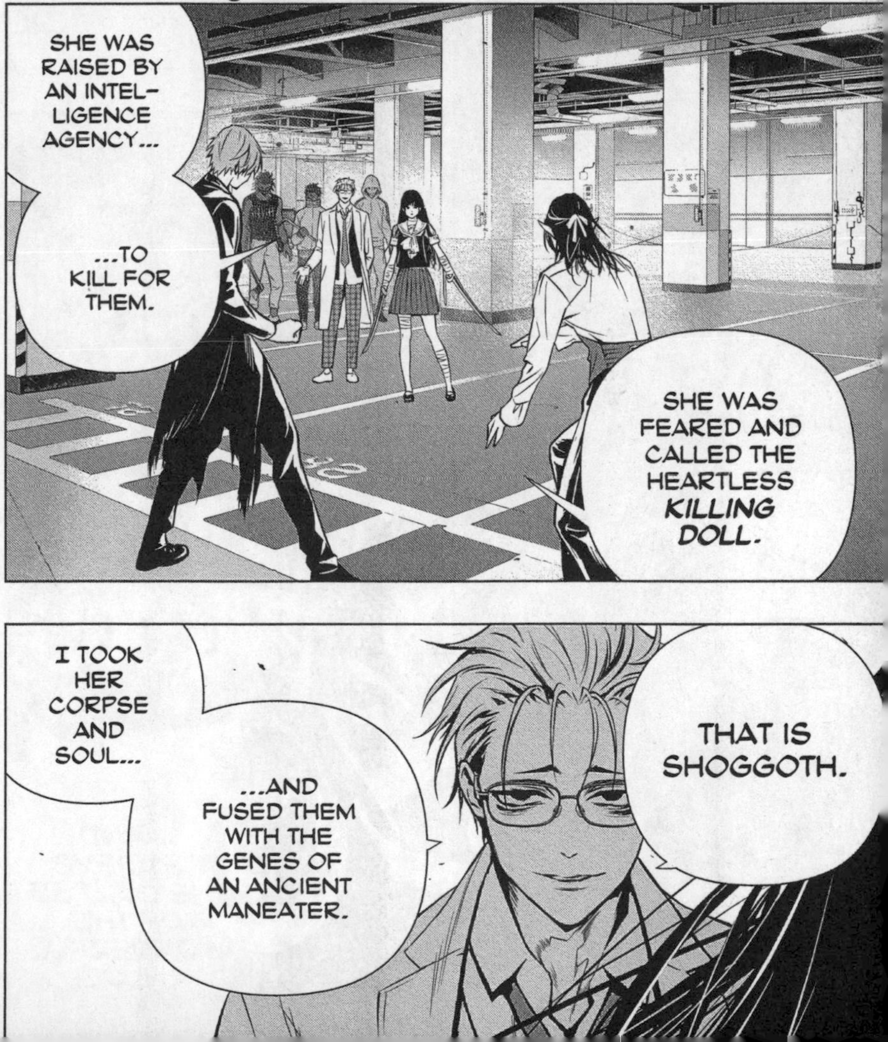
SHE WAS RAISED BY AN INTEL-LIGENCE AGENCY...
...TO KILL FOR THEM.
SHE WAS FEARED AND CALLED THE HEARTLESS KILLING DOLL.
I TOOK HER CORPSE AND SOUL...
...AND FUSED THEM WITH THE GENES OF AN ANCIENT MANEATER.
THAT IS SHOGGOTH.

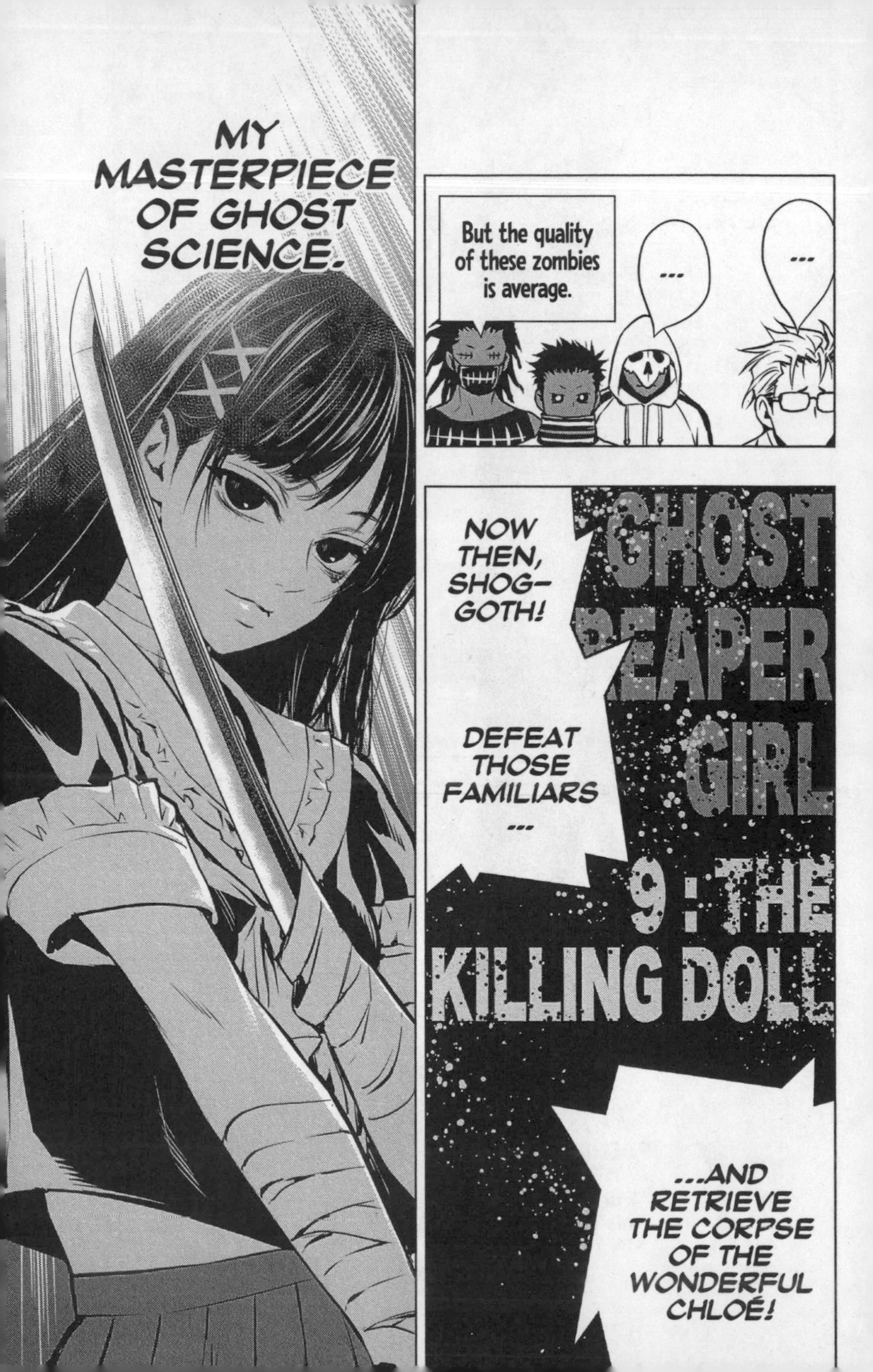
MY MASTERPIECE OF GHOST SCIENCE.
But the quality of these zombies is average.
...
...
NOW THEN, SHOG-GOTH!
GHOST REAPER GIRL 9 : THE KILLING DOLL
DEFEAT THOSE FAMILIARS ...
...AND RETRIEVE THE CORPSE OF THE WONDERFUL CHLOÉ!

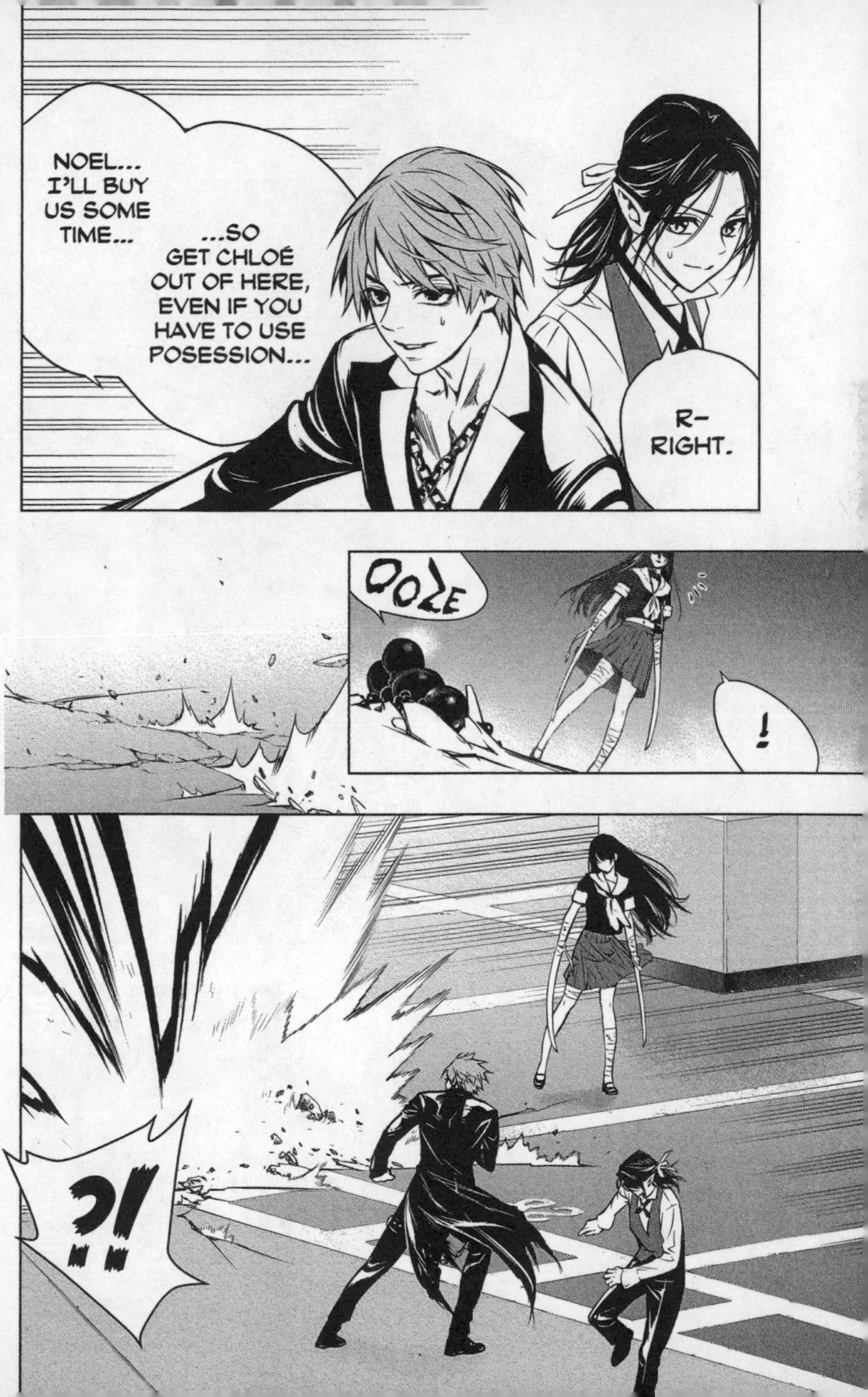
NOEL... I'LL BUY US SOME TIME...
...SO GET CHLOÉ OUT OF HERE, EVEN IF YOU HAVE TO USE POSESSION...
R-RIGHT.
OOZE
!
?!!

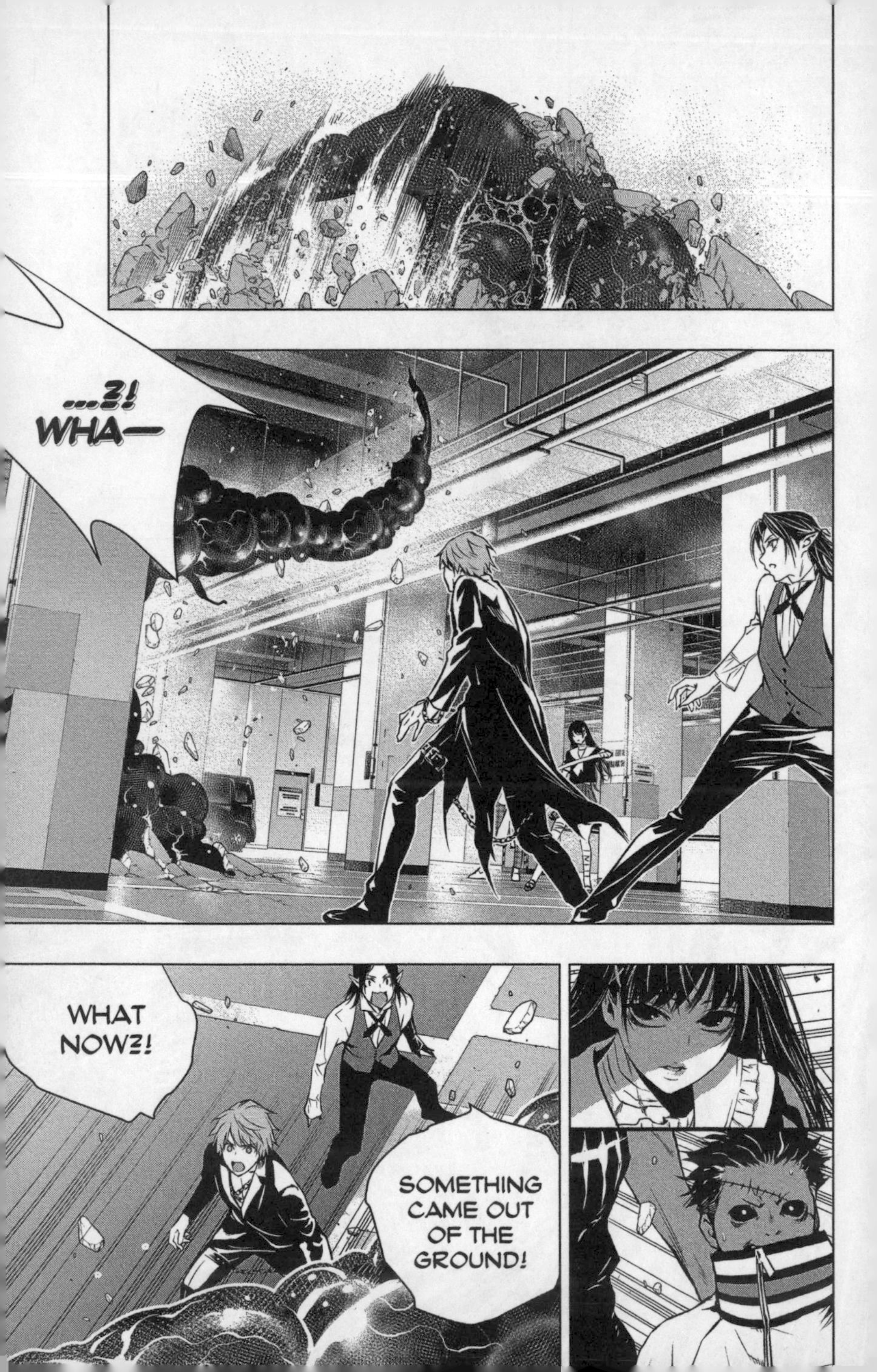
...?!
WHA—
WHAT NOW?!
SOMETHING CAME OUT OF THE GROUND!

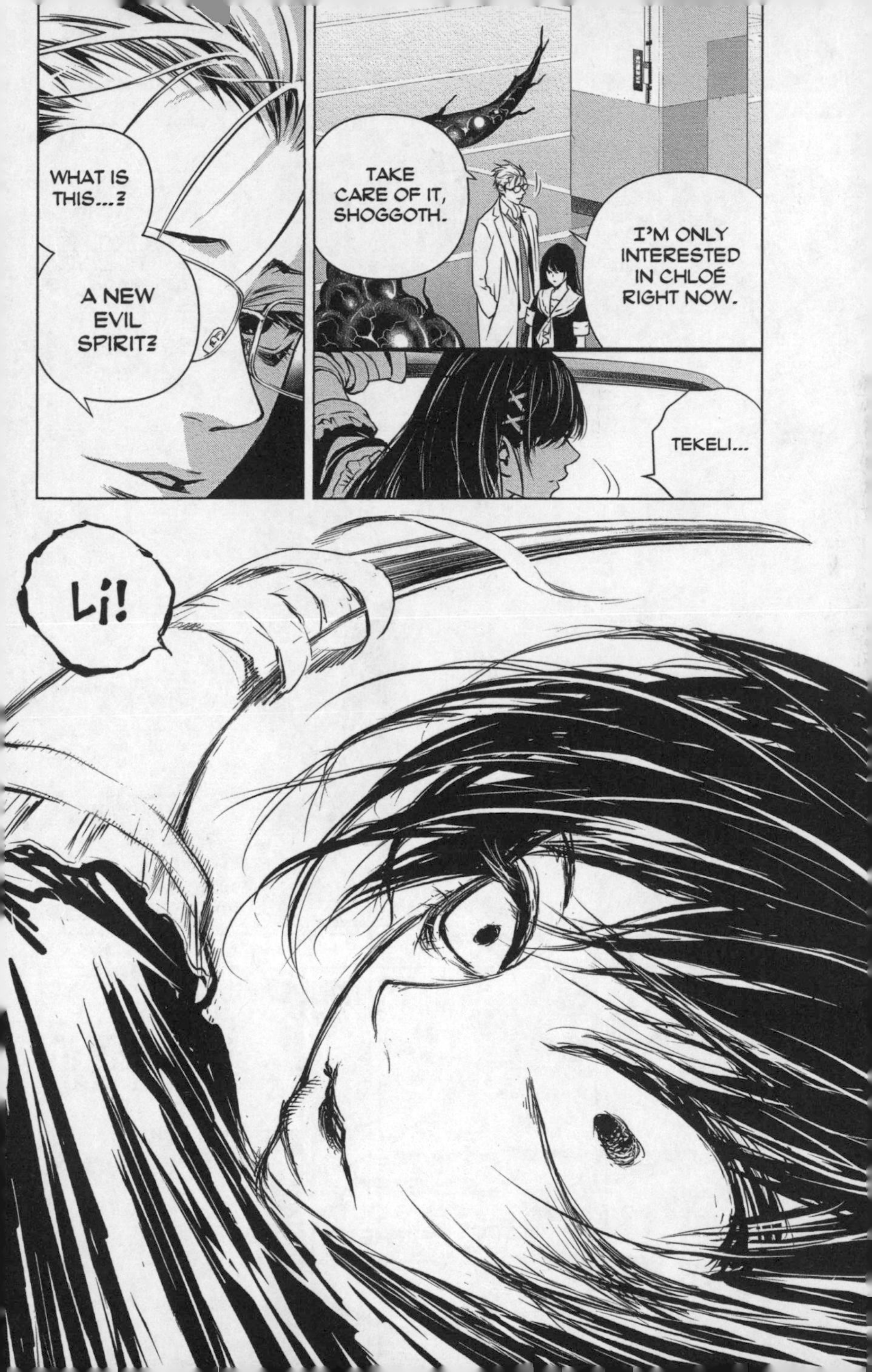
TAKE CARE OF IT, SHOGGOTH.
I'M ONLY INTERESTED IN CHLOÉ RIGHT NOW.
TEKELI...
WHAT IS THIS...?
A NEW EVIL SPIRIT?
Li!

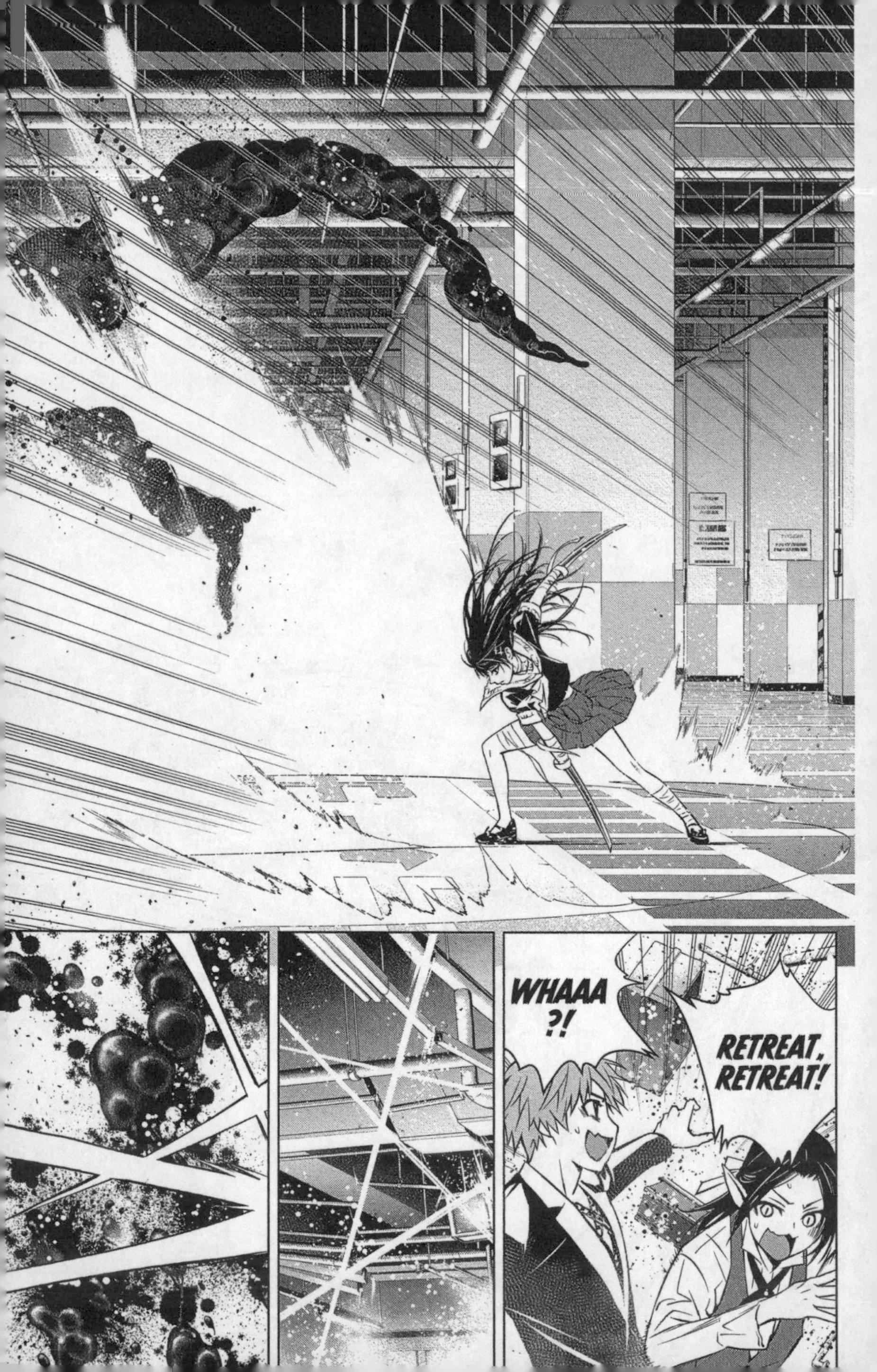
RETREAT, RETREAT!
WHAAA ?!

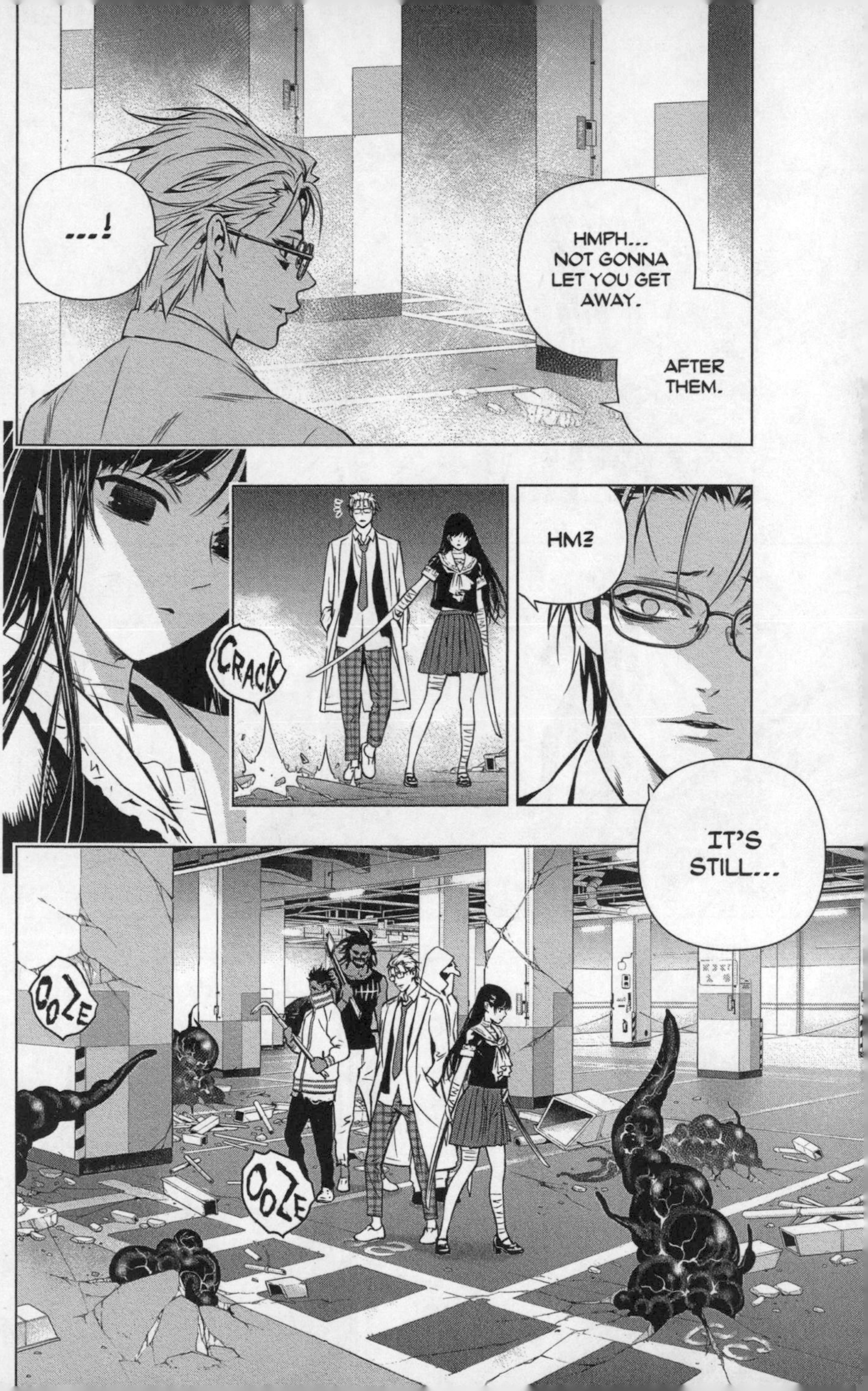
HMPH... NOT GONNA LET YOU GET AWAY.
AFTER THEM.
...!
HM?
IT'S STILL...
CRACK
OOZE
OOZE

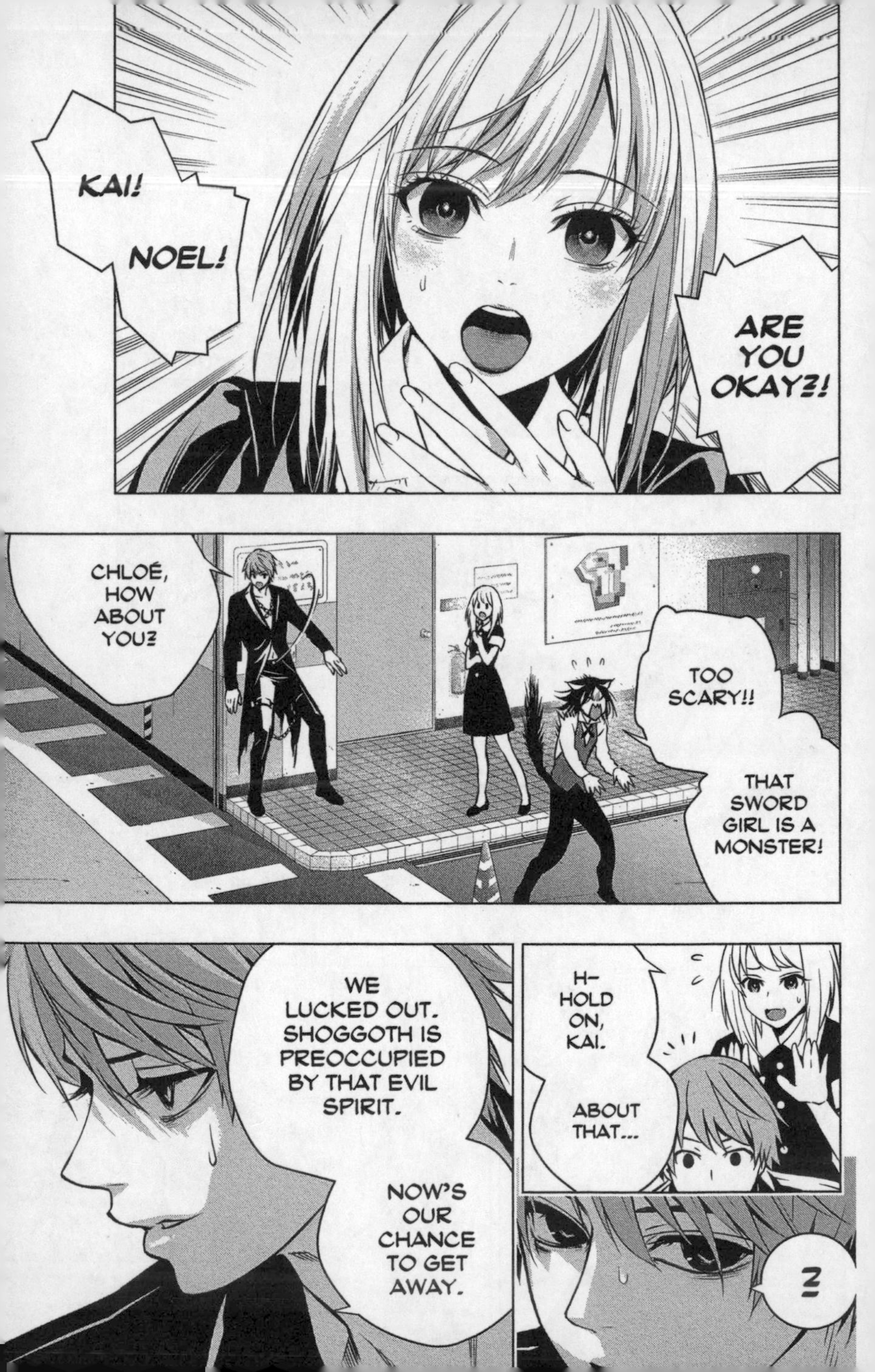
KAI!
NOEL!
ARE YOU OKAY?!
TOO SCARY!!
THAT SWORD GIRL IS A MONSTER!
CHLOÉ, HOW ABOUT YOU?
H-HOLD ON, KAI.
ABOUT THAT...
WE LUCKED OUT. SHOGGOTH IS PREOCCUPIED BY THAT EVIL SPIRIT.
NOW'S OUR CHANCE TO GET AWAY.
?

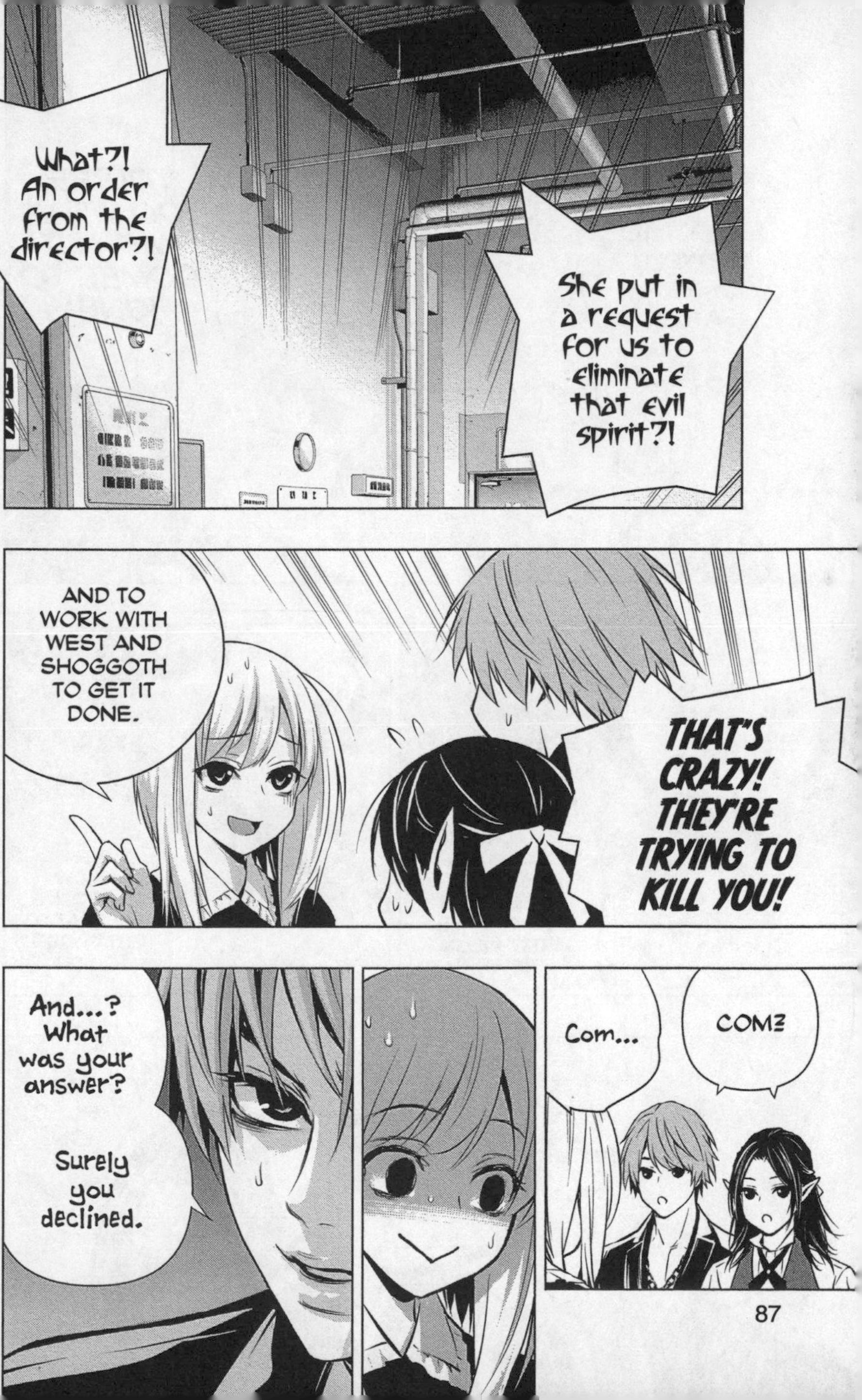
What?! An order from the director?!
She put in a request for us to eliminate that evil spirit?!
AND TO WORK WITH WEST AND SHOGGOTH TO GET IT DONE.
THAT'S CRAZY! THEY'RE TRYING TO KILL YOU!
And...? What was your answer?
Surely you declined.
Com...
COM?

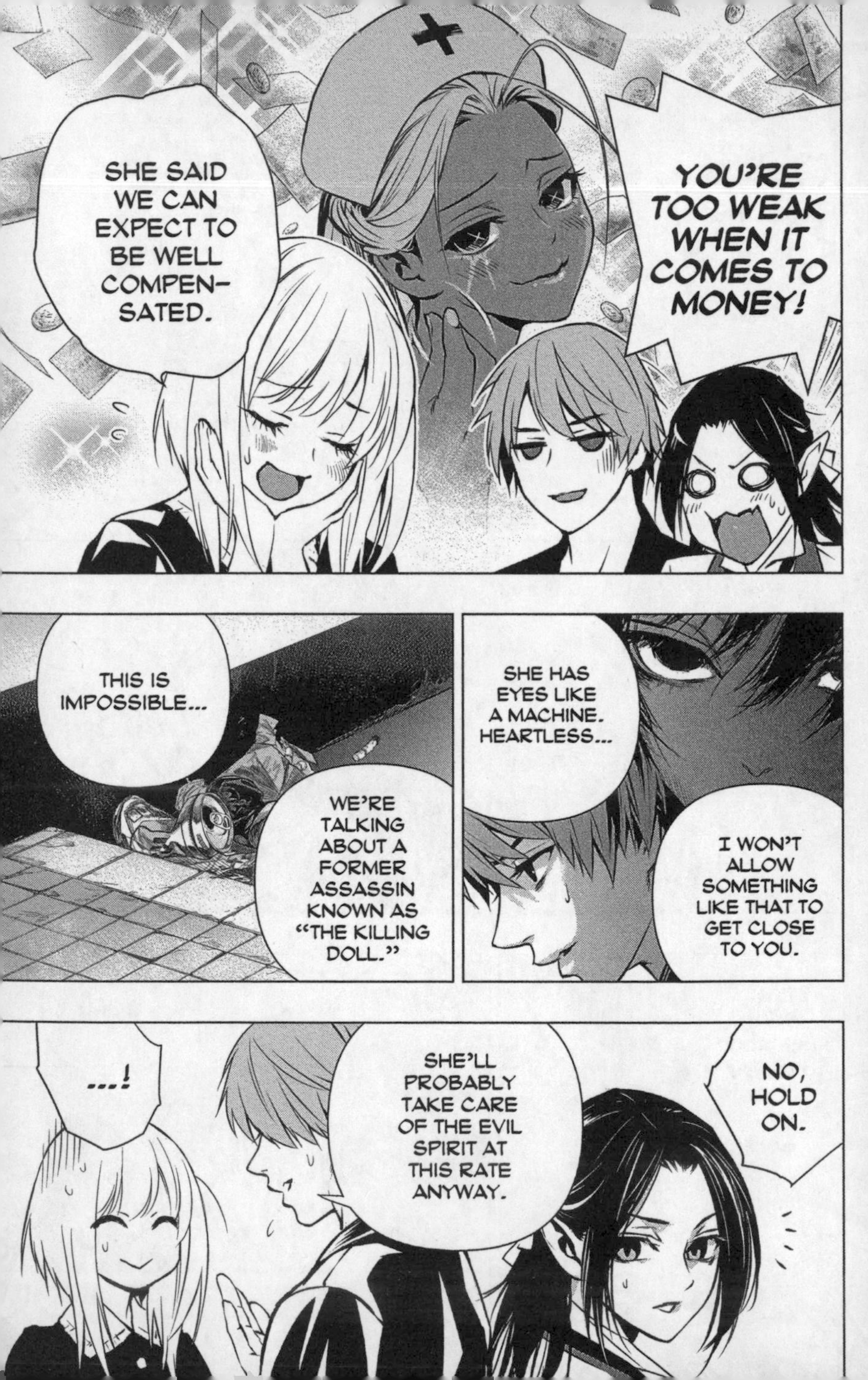
YOU'RE TOO WEAK WHEN IT COMES TO MONEY!
SHE SAID WE CAN EXPECT TO BE WELL COMPEN-SATED.
SHE HAS EYES LIKE A MACHINE. HEARTLESS...
I WON'T ALLOW SOMETHING LIKE THAT TO GET CLOSE TO YOU.
THIS IS IMPOSSIBLE...
WE'RE TALKING ABOUT A FORMER ASSASSIN KNOWN AS "THE KILLING DOLL."
NO, HOLD ON.
SHE'LL PROBABLY TAKE CARE OF THE EVIL SPIRIT AT THIS RATE ANYWAY.
...!

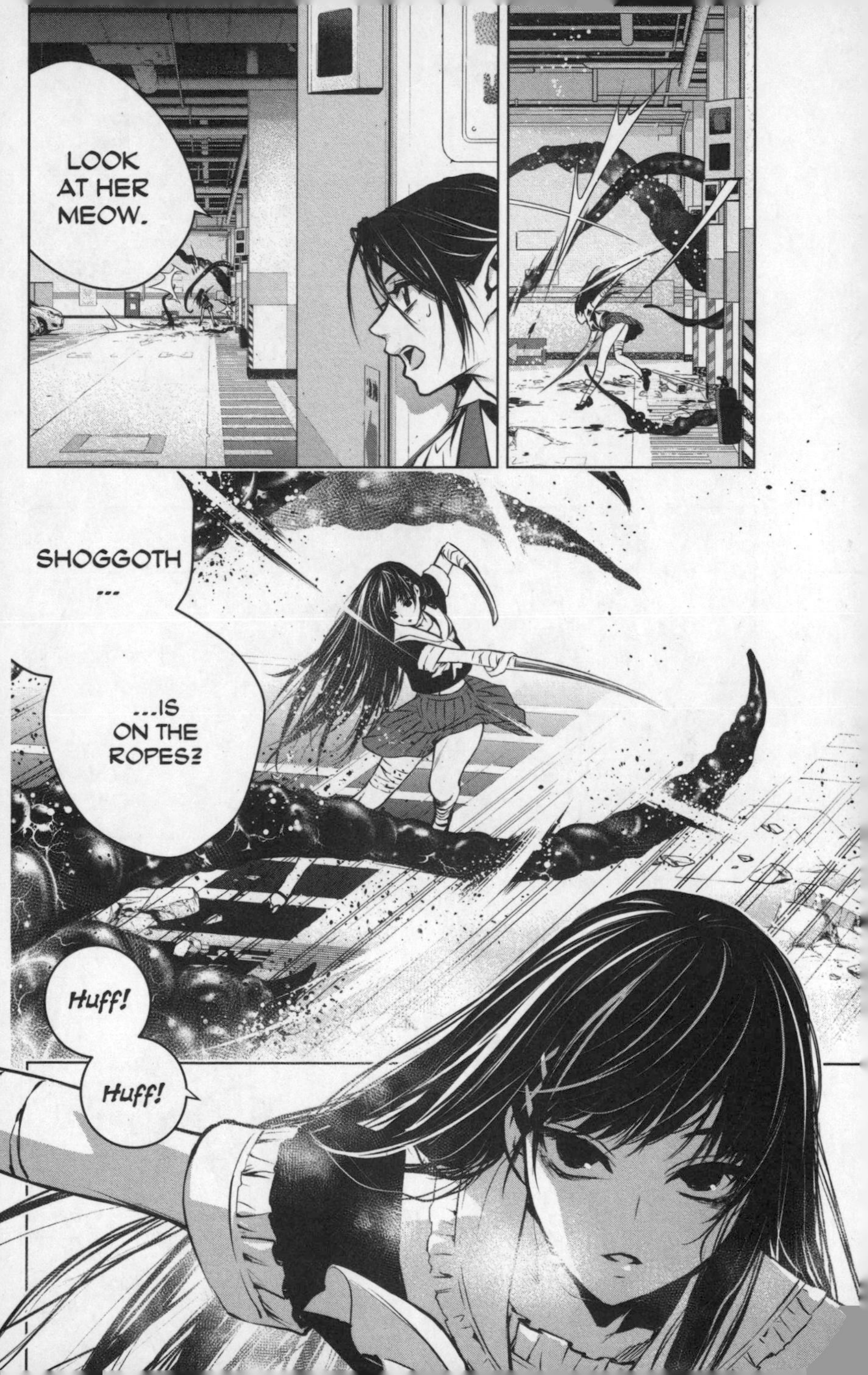
LOOK AT HER MEOW.
SHOGGOTH ...
...IS ON THE ROPES?
Huff!
Huff!

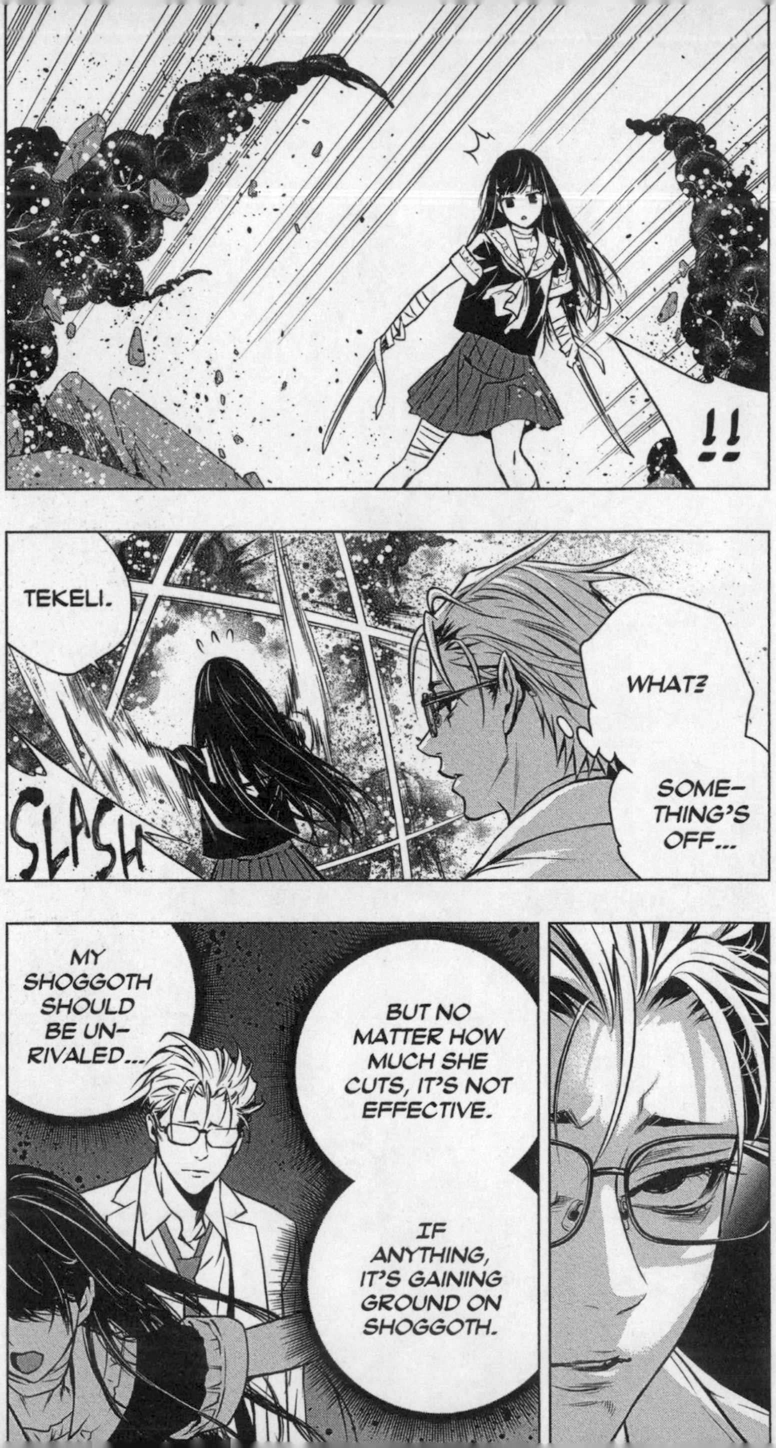
!!
TEKELI.
SLASH
WHAT?
SOME-THING'S OFF...
MY SHOGGOTH SHOULD BE UN-RIVALED...
BUT NO MATTER HOW MUCH SHE CUTS, IT'S NOT EFFECTIVE.
IF ANYTHING, IT'S GAINING GROUND ON SHOGGOTH.

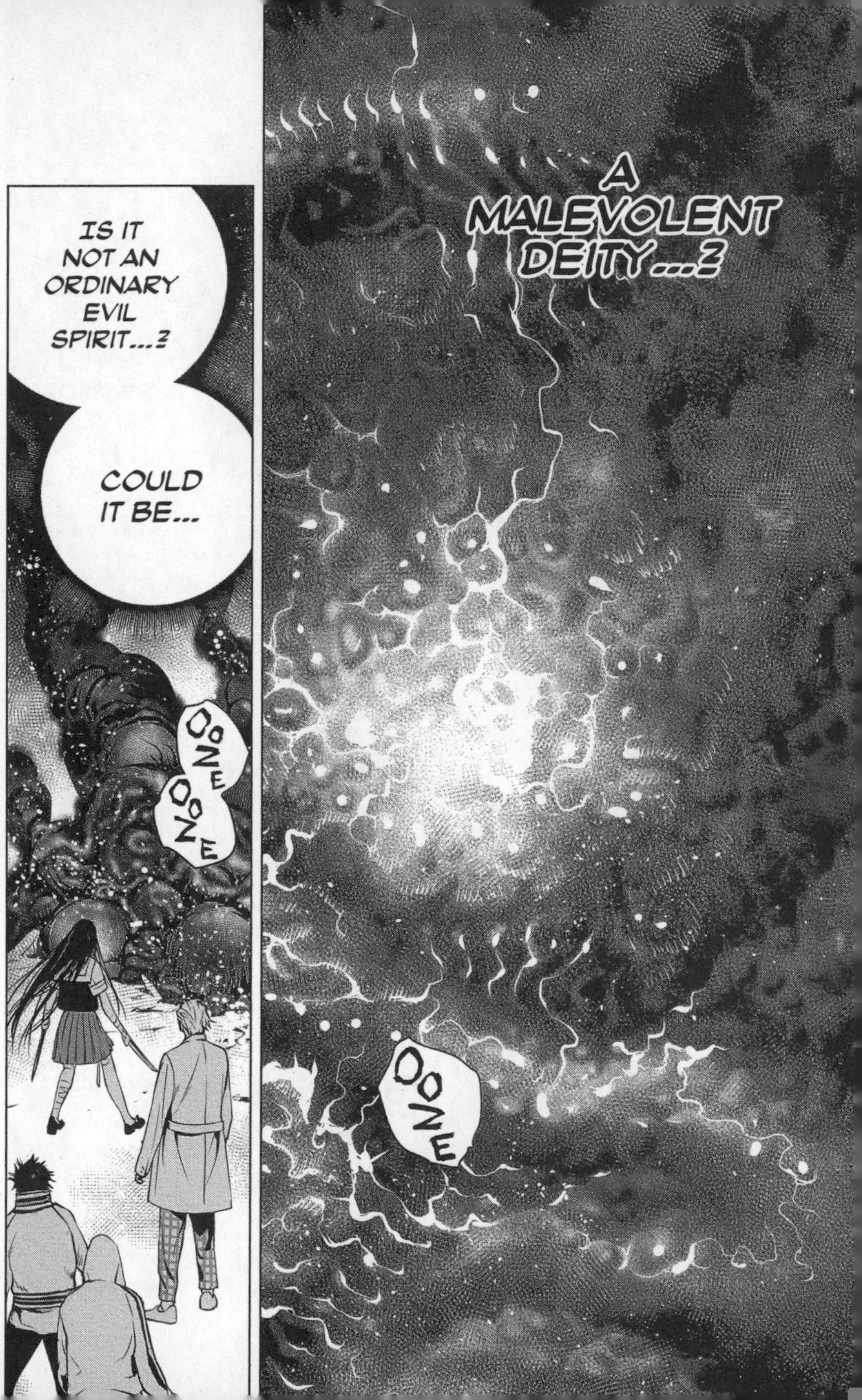
IS IT NOT AN ORDINARY EVIL SPIRIT...?
COULD IT BE...
OOZE OOZE
A MALEVOLENT DEITY...?
OOZE

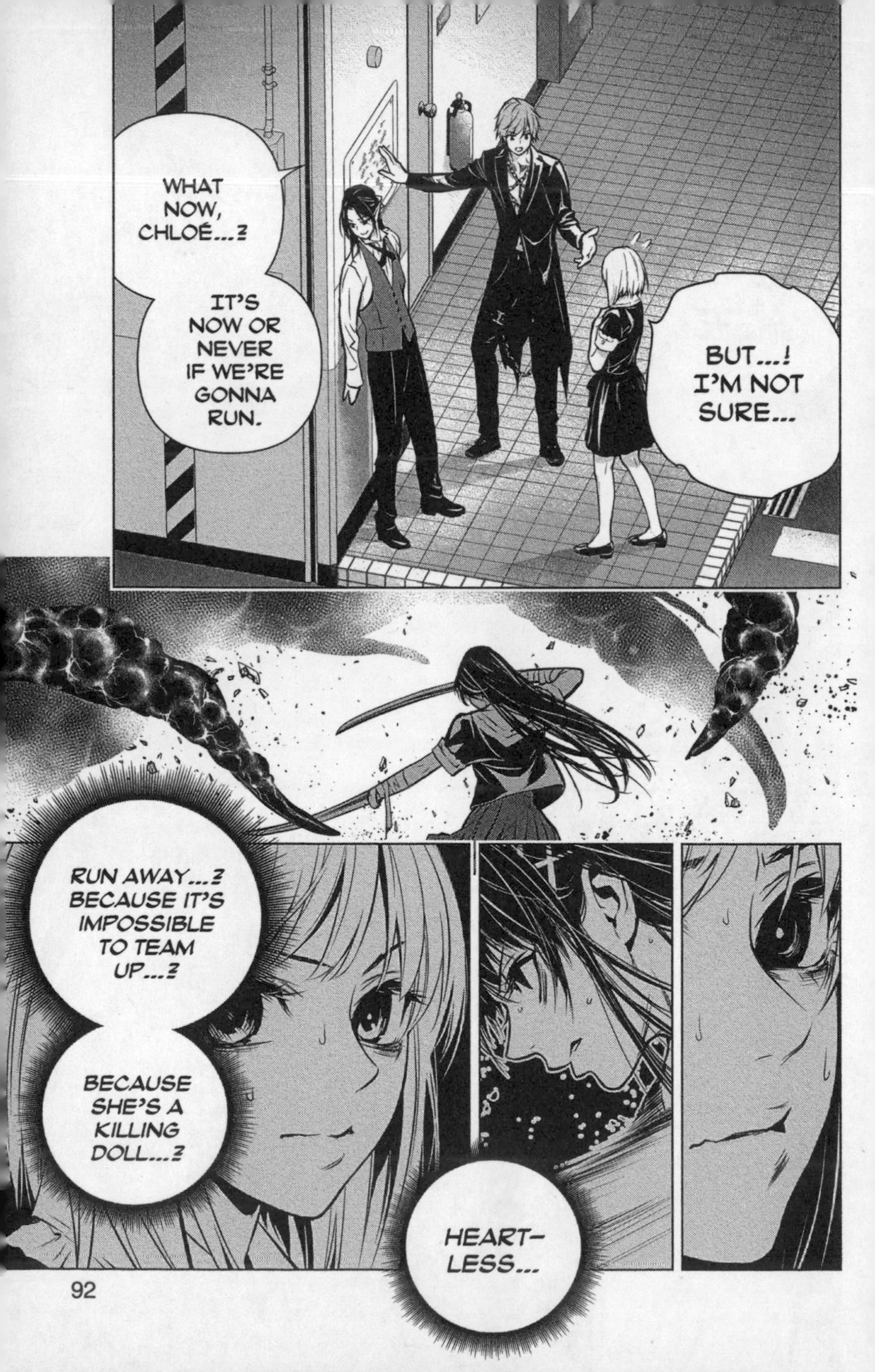
WHAT NOW, CHLOÉ...?
IT'S NOW OR NEVER IF WE'RE GONNA RUN.
BUT...! I'M NOT SURE...
RUN AWAY...? BECAUSE IT'S IMPOSSIBLE TO TEAM UP...?
BECAUSE SHE'S A KILLING DOLL...?
HEART-LESS...

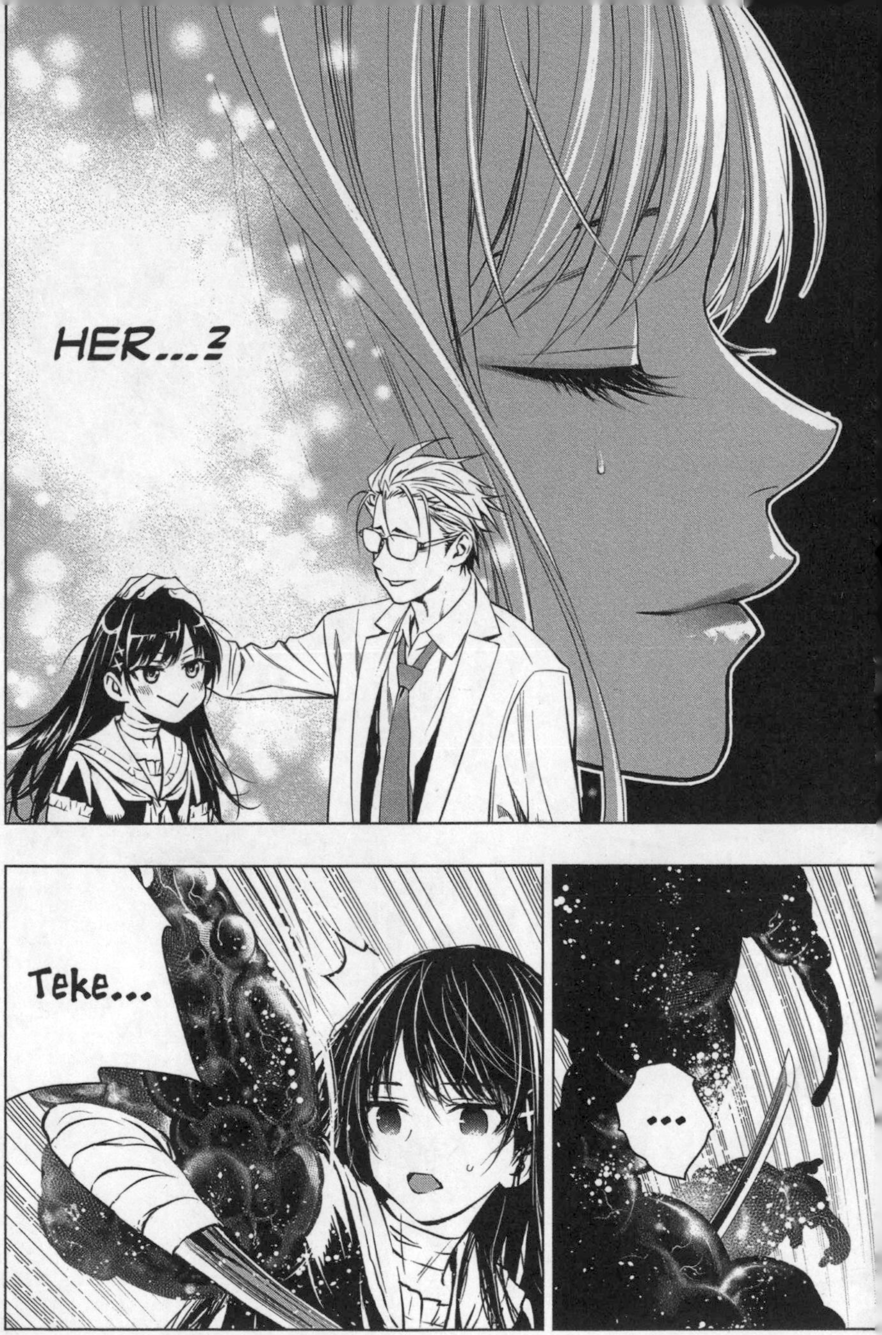
HER...?
...
Teke...

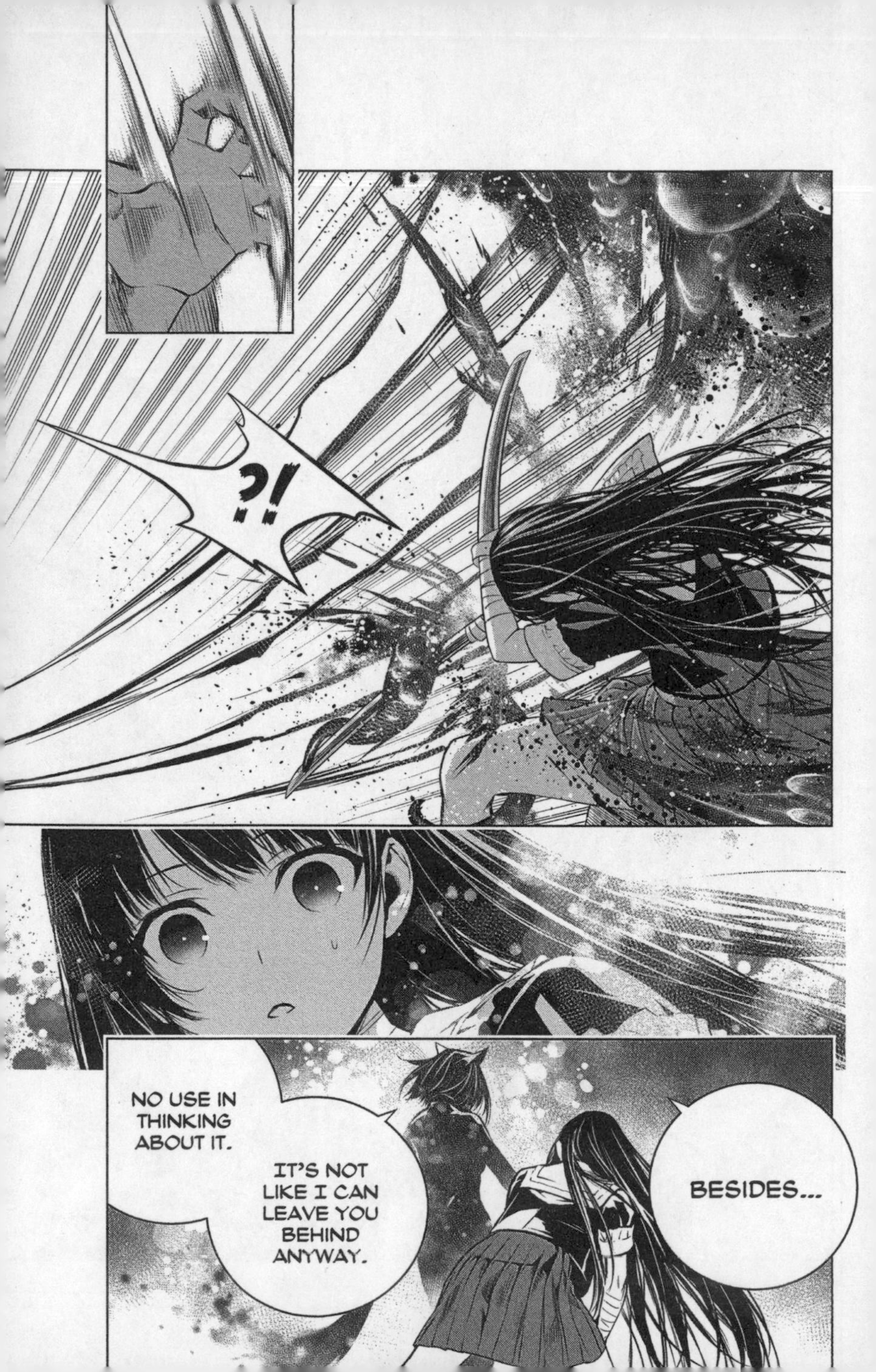
?!
NO USE IN THINKING ABOUT IT.
IT'S NOT LIKE I CAN LEAVE YOU BEHIND ANYWAY.
BESIDES...

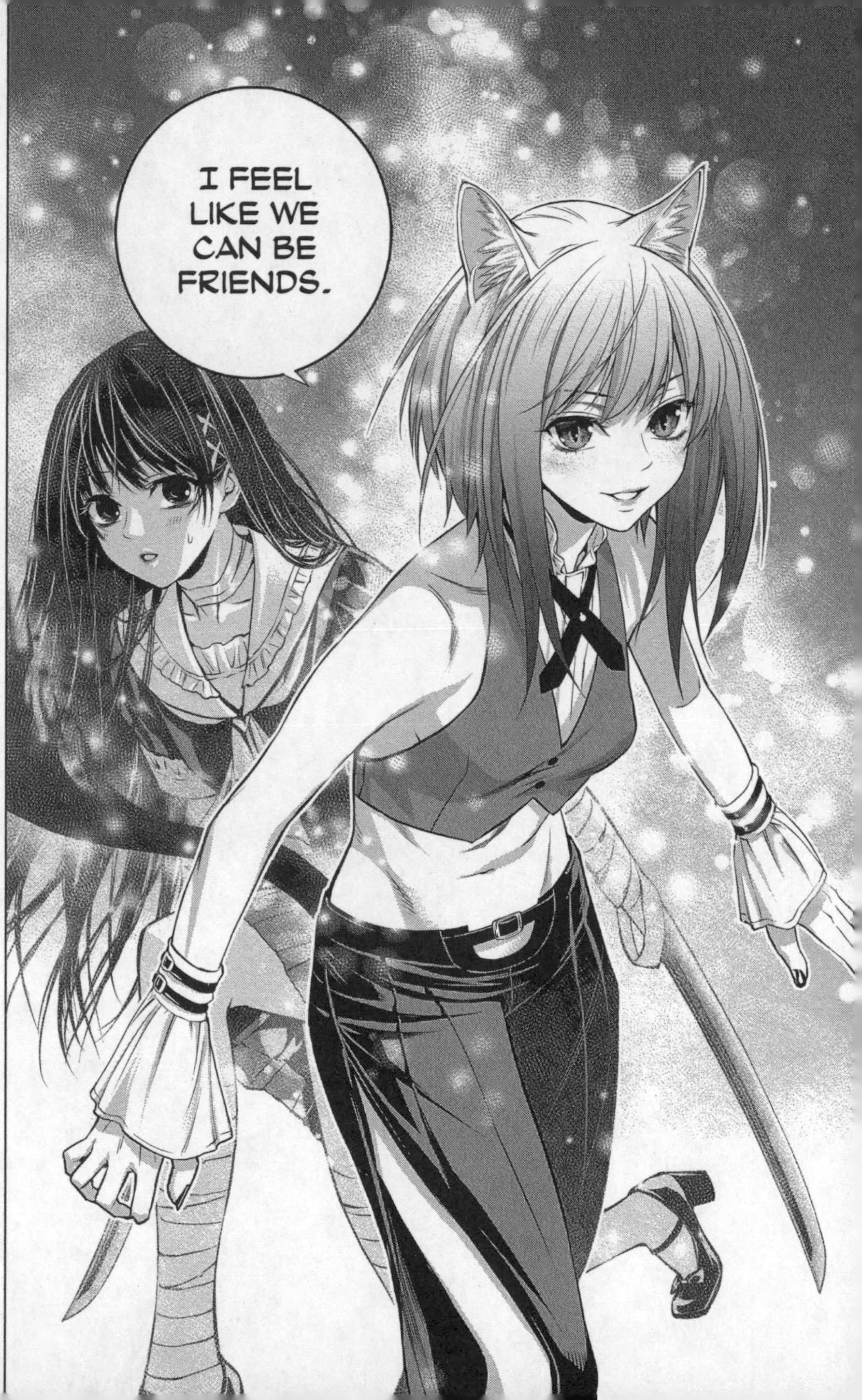
I FEEL LIKE WE CAN BE FRIENDS.

#10: Like Magic

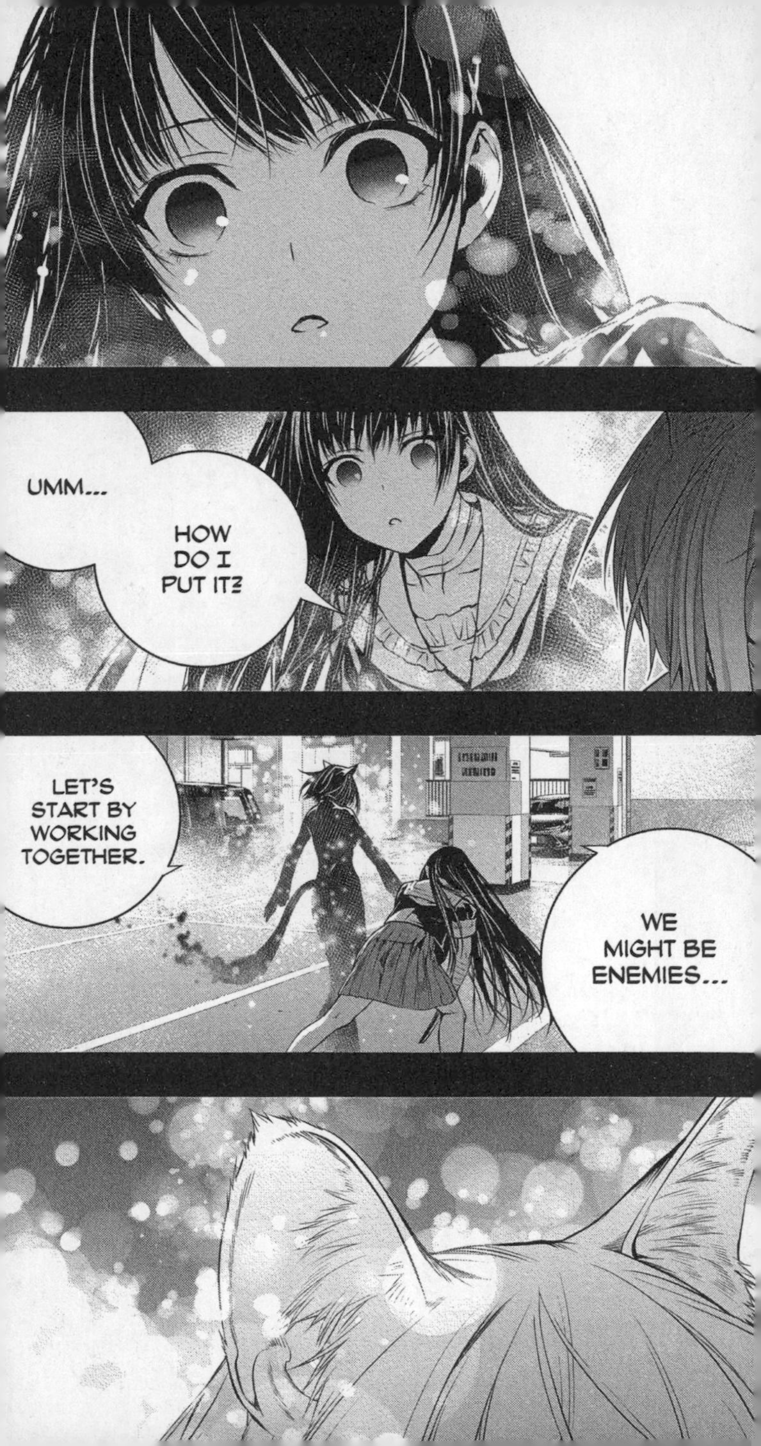
UMM...
HOW DO I PUT IT?
WE MIGHT BE ENEMIES...
LET'S START BY WORKING TOGETHER.

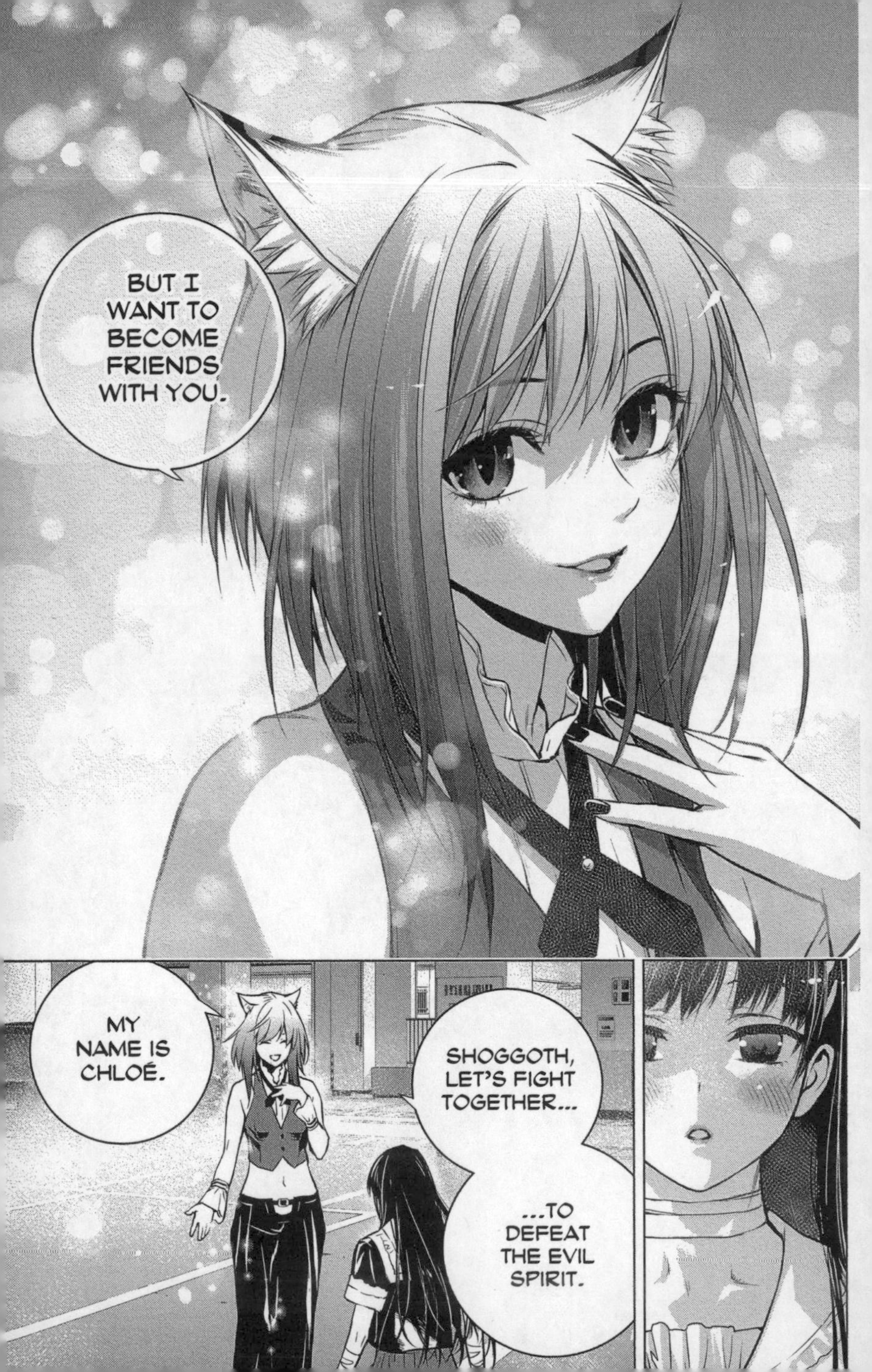
BUT I WANT TO BECOME FRIENDS WITH YOU.
MY NAME IS CHLOÉ.
SHOGGOTH, LET'S FIGHT TOGETHER...
...TO DEFEAT THE EVIL SPIRIT.

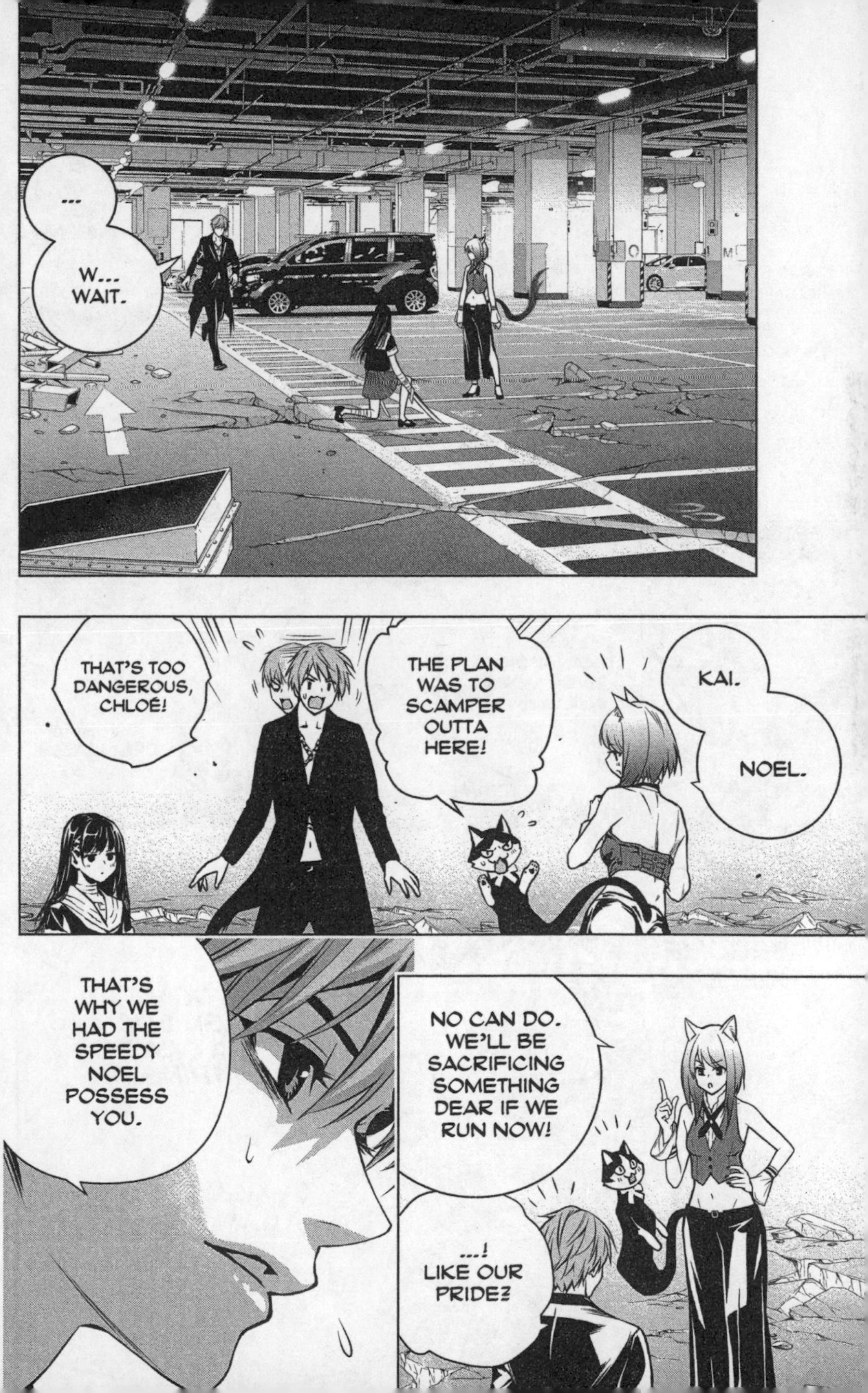
...
W... WAIT.
KAI.
NOEL.
THE PLAN WAS TO SCAMPER OUTTA HERE!
THAT'S TOO DANGEROUS, CHLOÉ!
NO CAN DO. WE'LL BE SACRIFICING SOMETHING DEAR IF WE RUN NOW!
...! LIKE OUR PRIDE?
THAT'S WHY WE HAD THE SPEEDY NOEL POSSESS YOU.

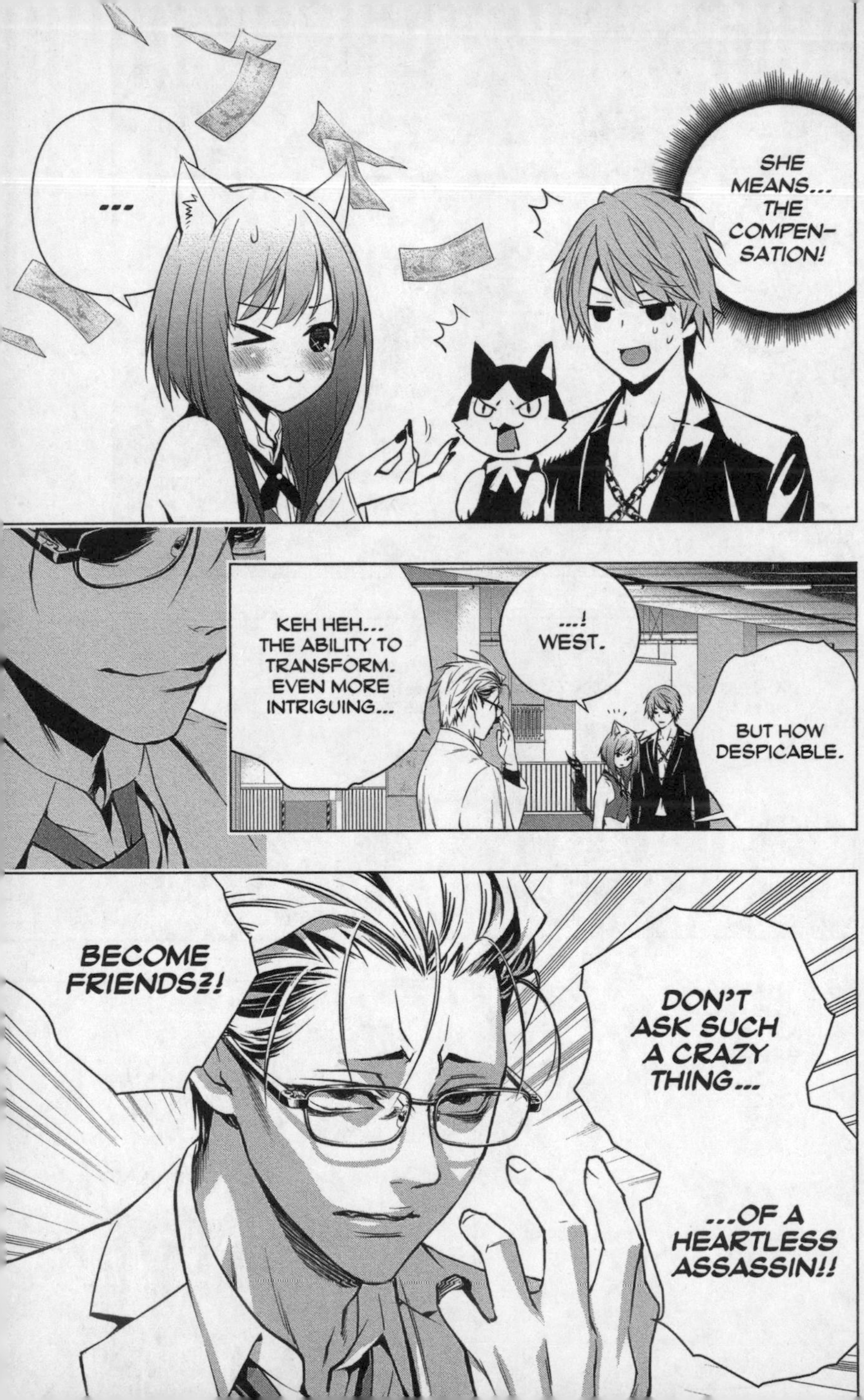
SHE MEANS... THE COMPENSATION!
...
...! WEST.
KEH HEH... THE ABILITY TO TRANSFORM. EVEN MORE INTRIGUING...
BUT HOW DESPICABLE.
BECOME FRIENDS?!
DON'T ASK SUCH A CRAZY THING...
...OF A HEARTLESS ASSASSIN!!

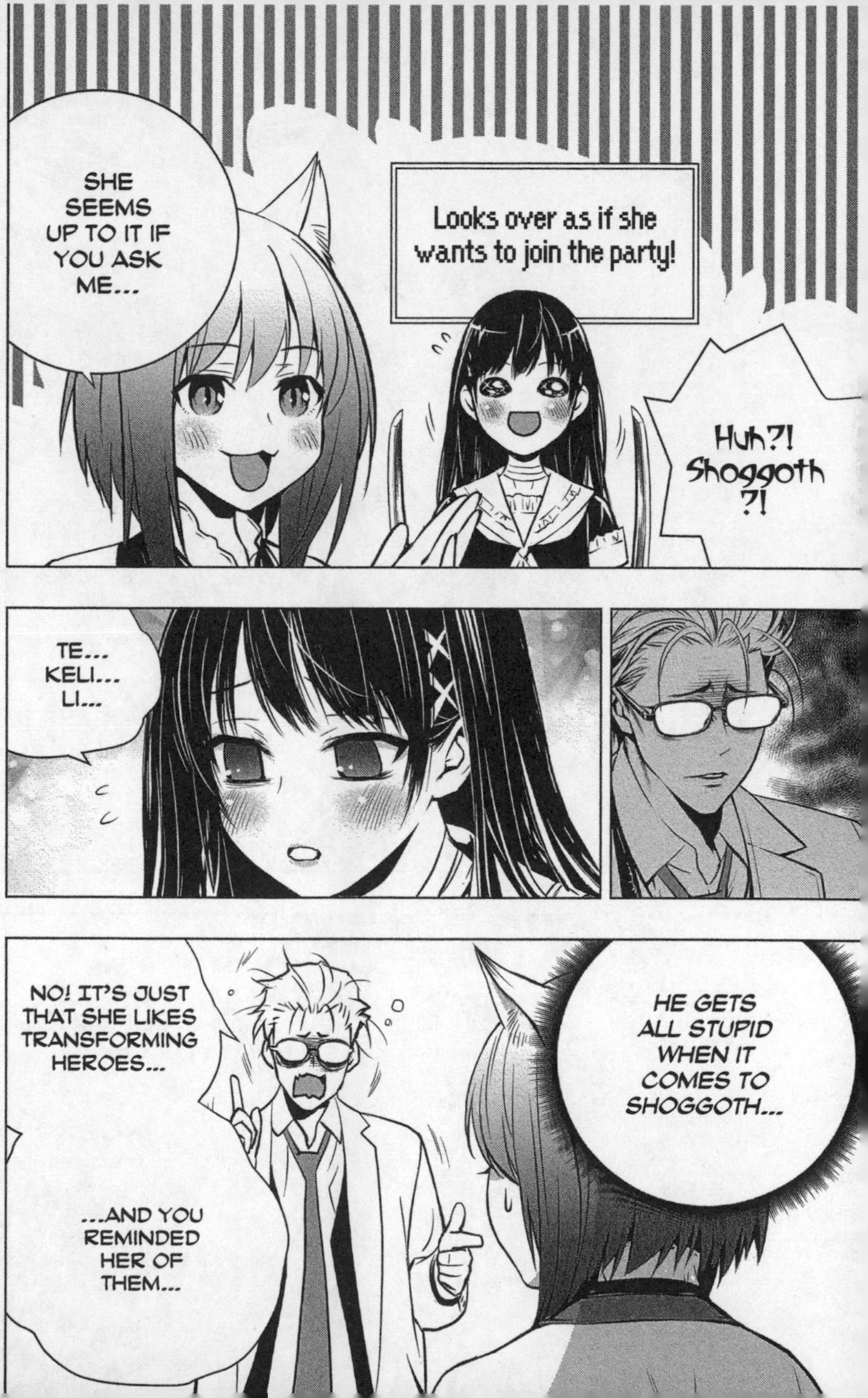

Looks over as if she wants to join the party!
Huh?! Shoggoth ?!
SHE SEEMS UP TO IT IF YOU ASK ME...
TE... KELI... LI...
HE GETS ALL STUPID WHEN IT COMES TO SHOGGOTH...
NO! IT'S JUST THAT SHE LIKES TRANSFORMING HEROES...
...AND YOU REMINDED HER OF THEM...

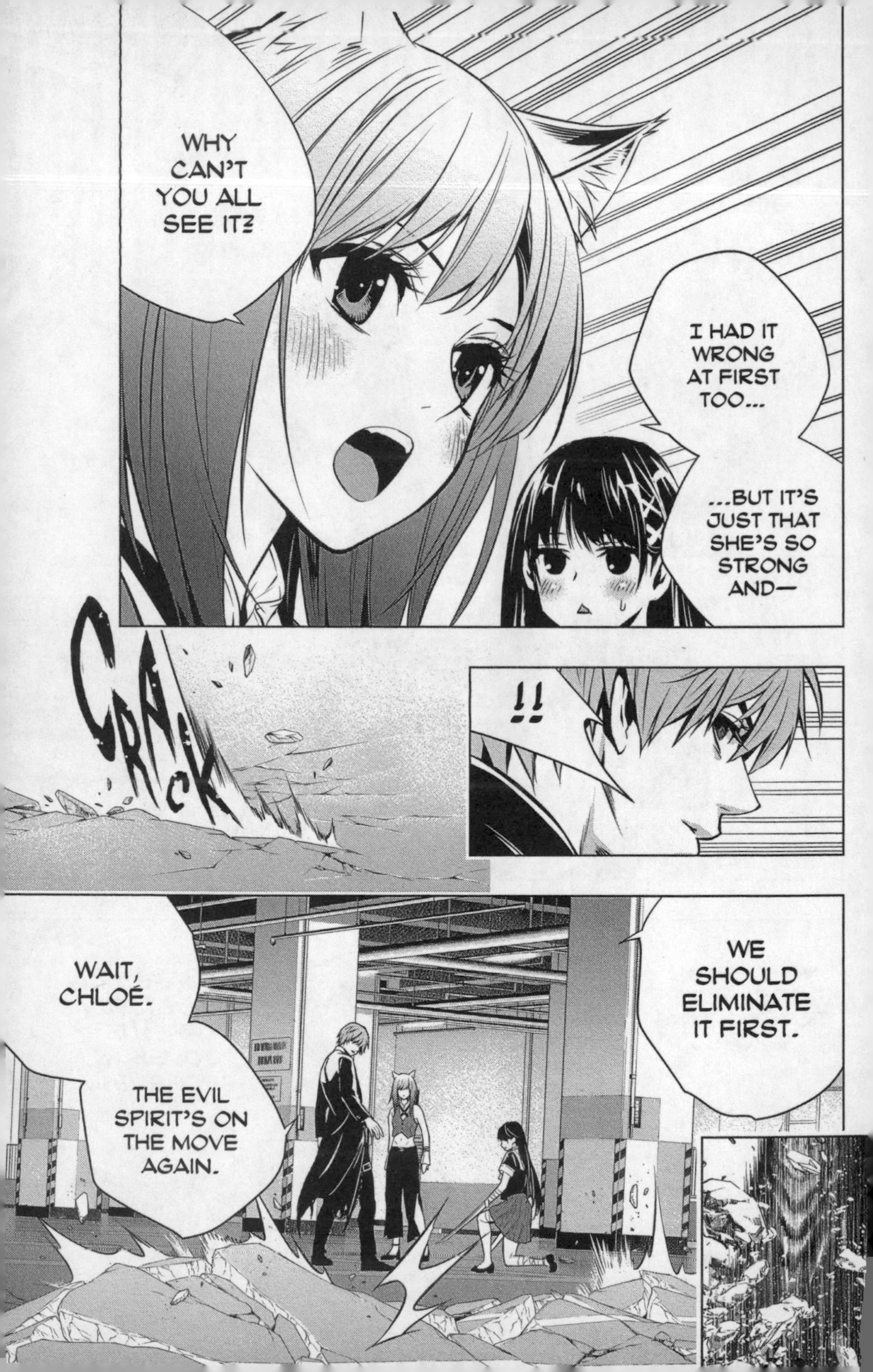
WHY CAN'T YOU ALL SEE IT?
I HAD IT WRONG AT FIRST TOO...
...BUT IT'S JUST THAT SHE'S SO STRONG AND—
!!
CRACK
WAIT, CHLOÉ.
THE EVIL SPIRIT'S ON THE MOVE AGAIN.
WE SHOULD ELIMINATE IT FIRST.

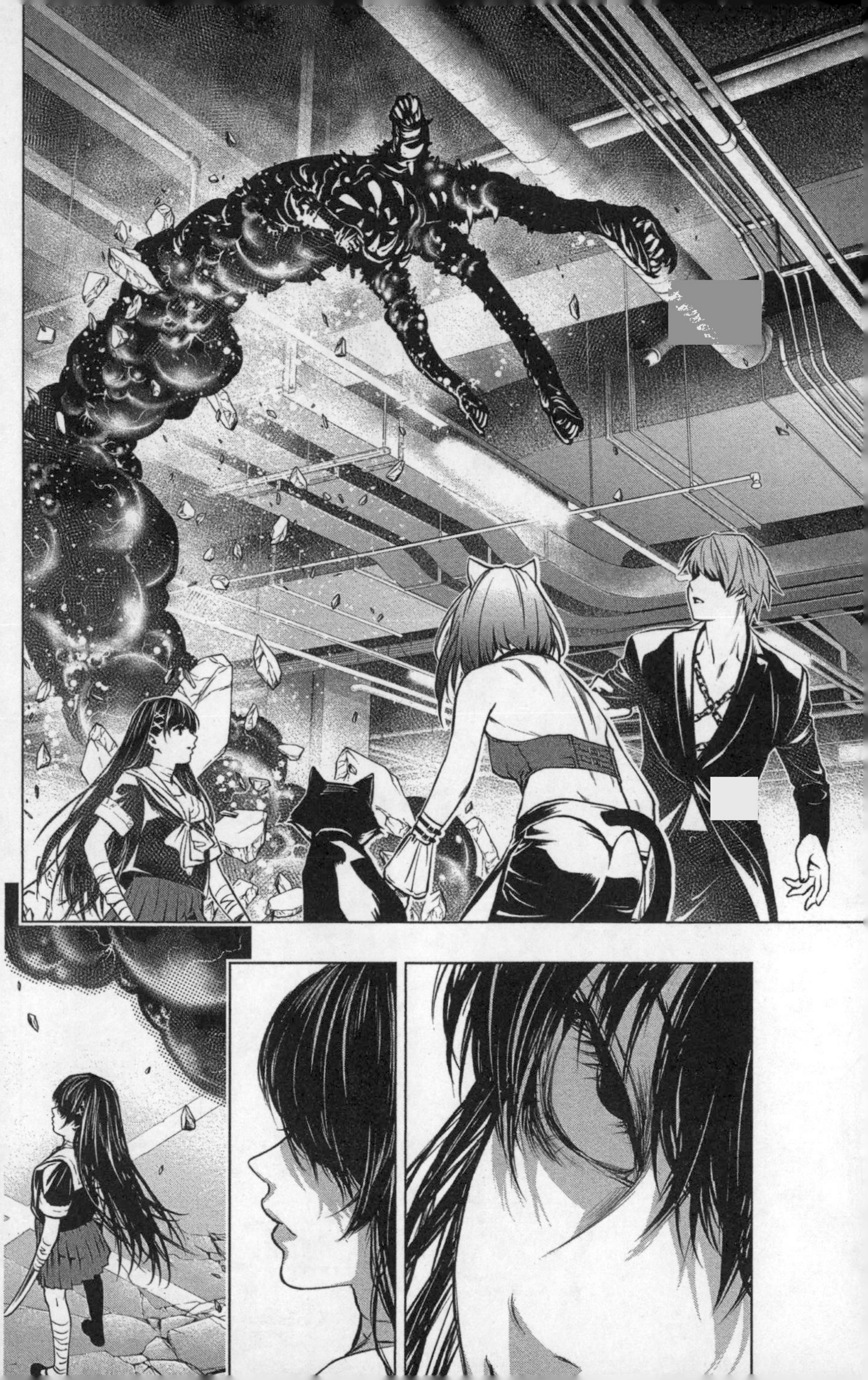

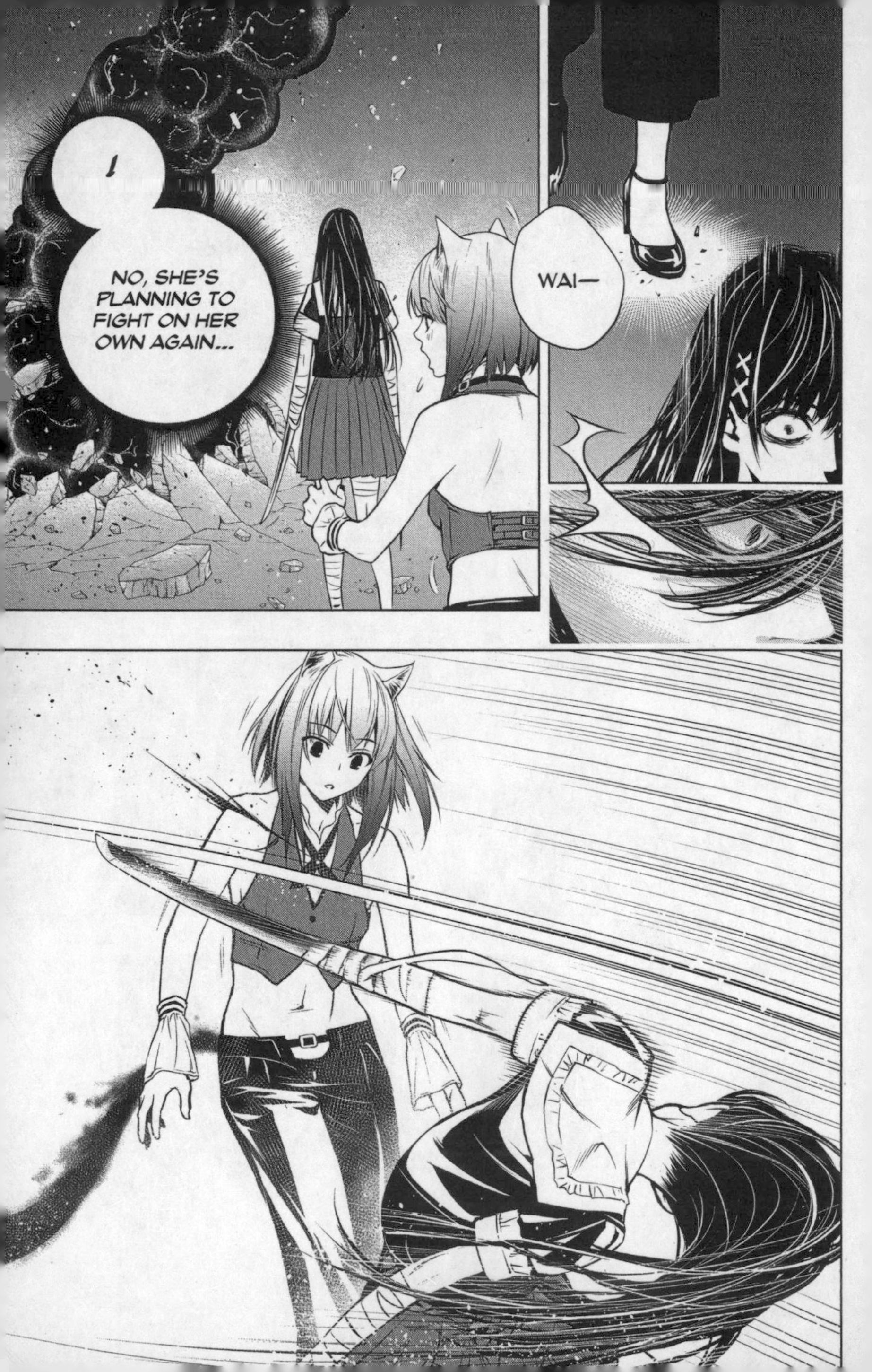
!
NO, SHE'S PLANNING TO FIGHT ON HER OWN AGAIN...
WAI—

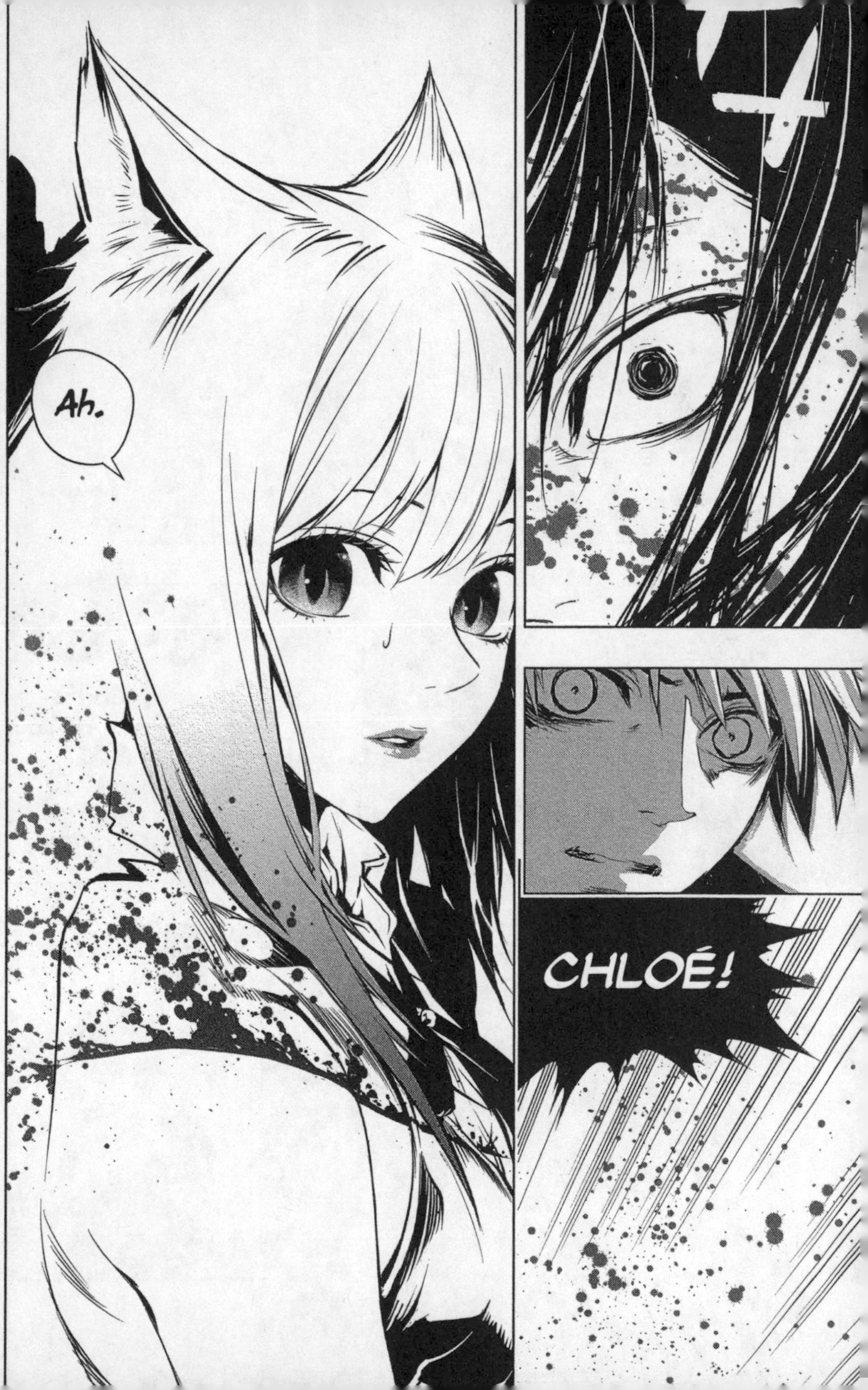
CHLOÉ!
Ah.

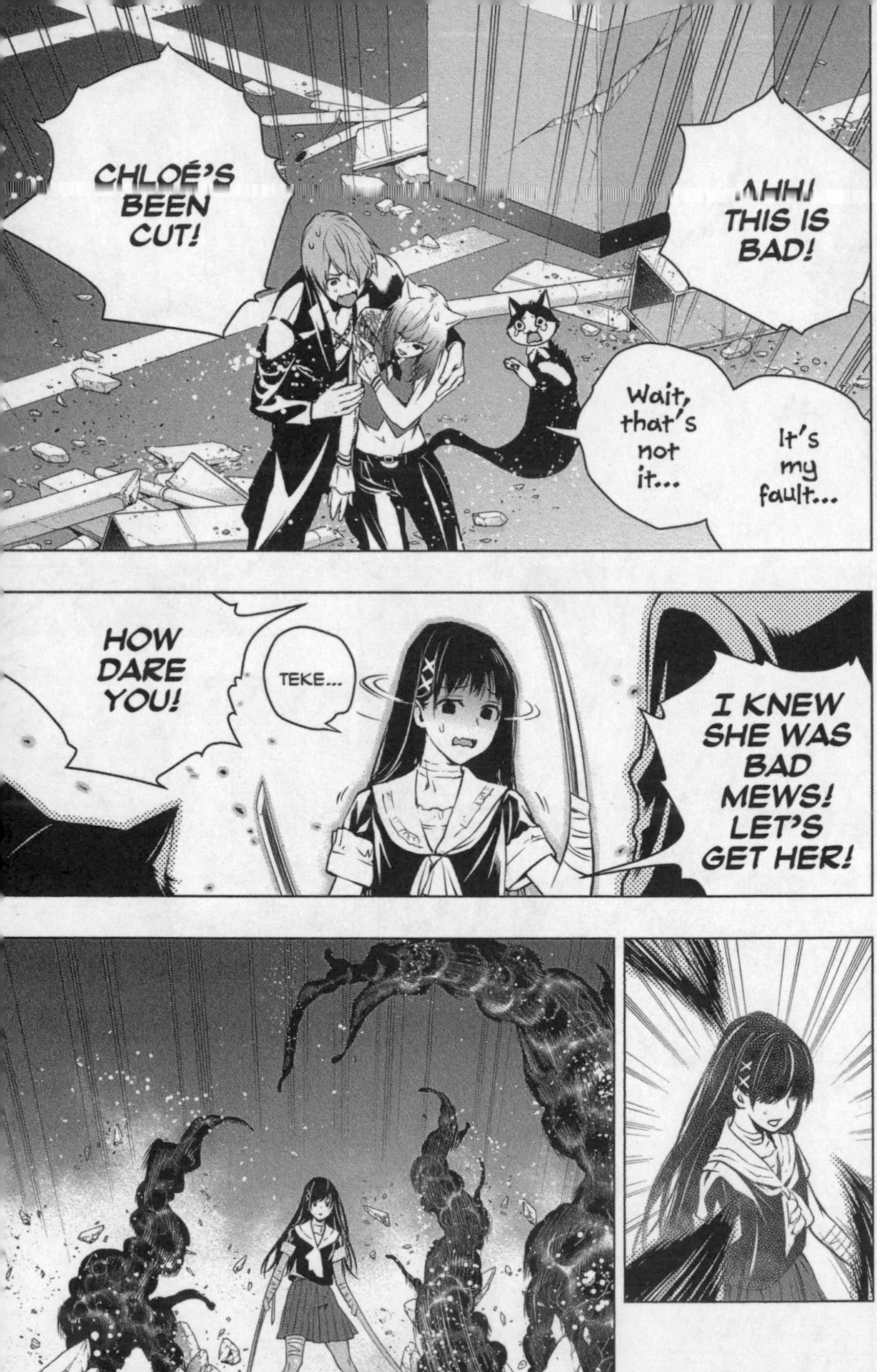
AHH! THIS IS BAD!
CHLOÉ'S BEEN CUT!
Wait, that's not it...
It's my fault...
I KNEW SHE WAS BAD MEWS! LET'S GET HER!
TEKE...
HOW DARE YOU!

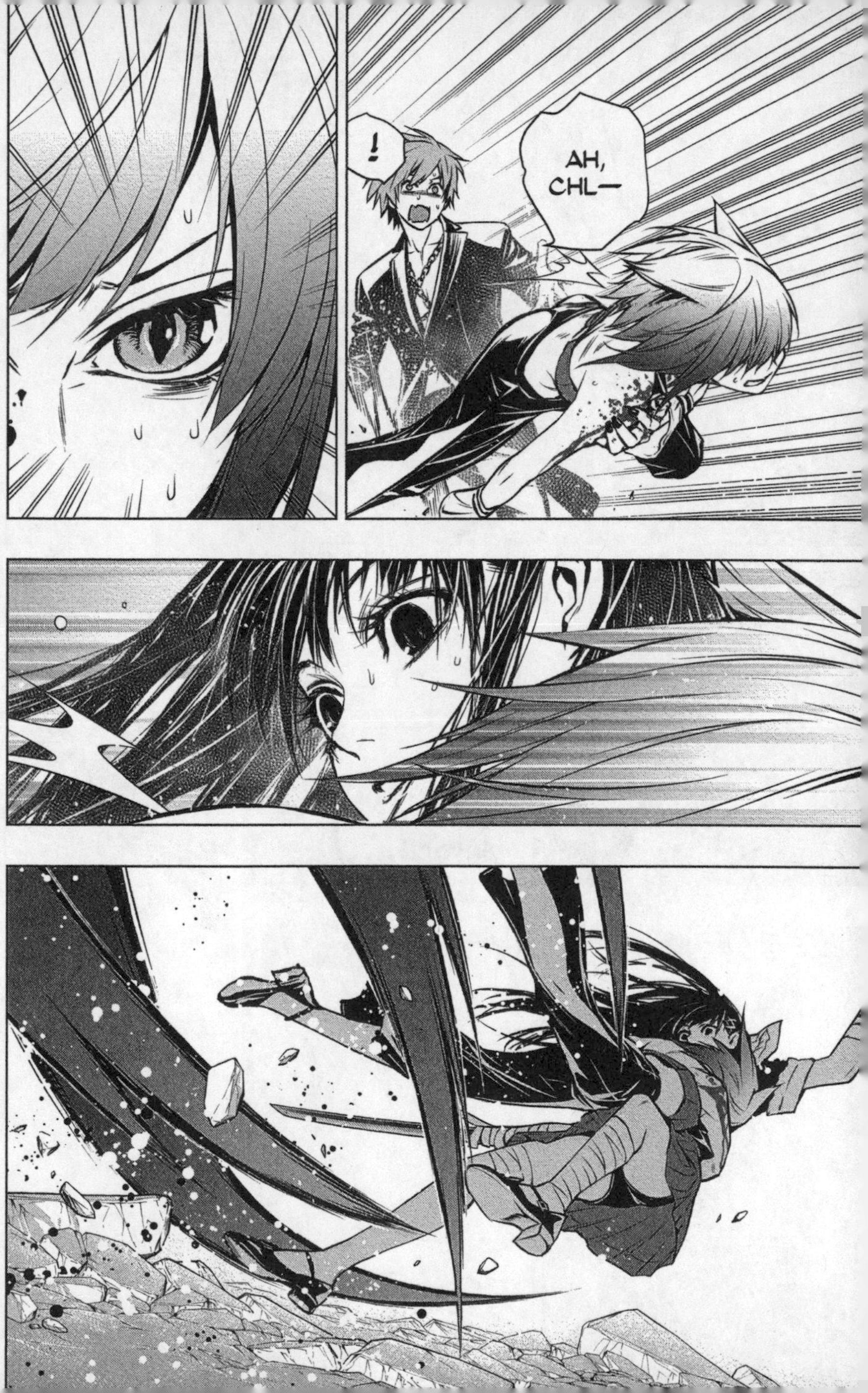
AH, CHL—
!

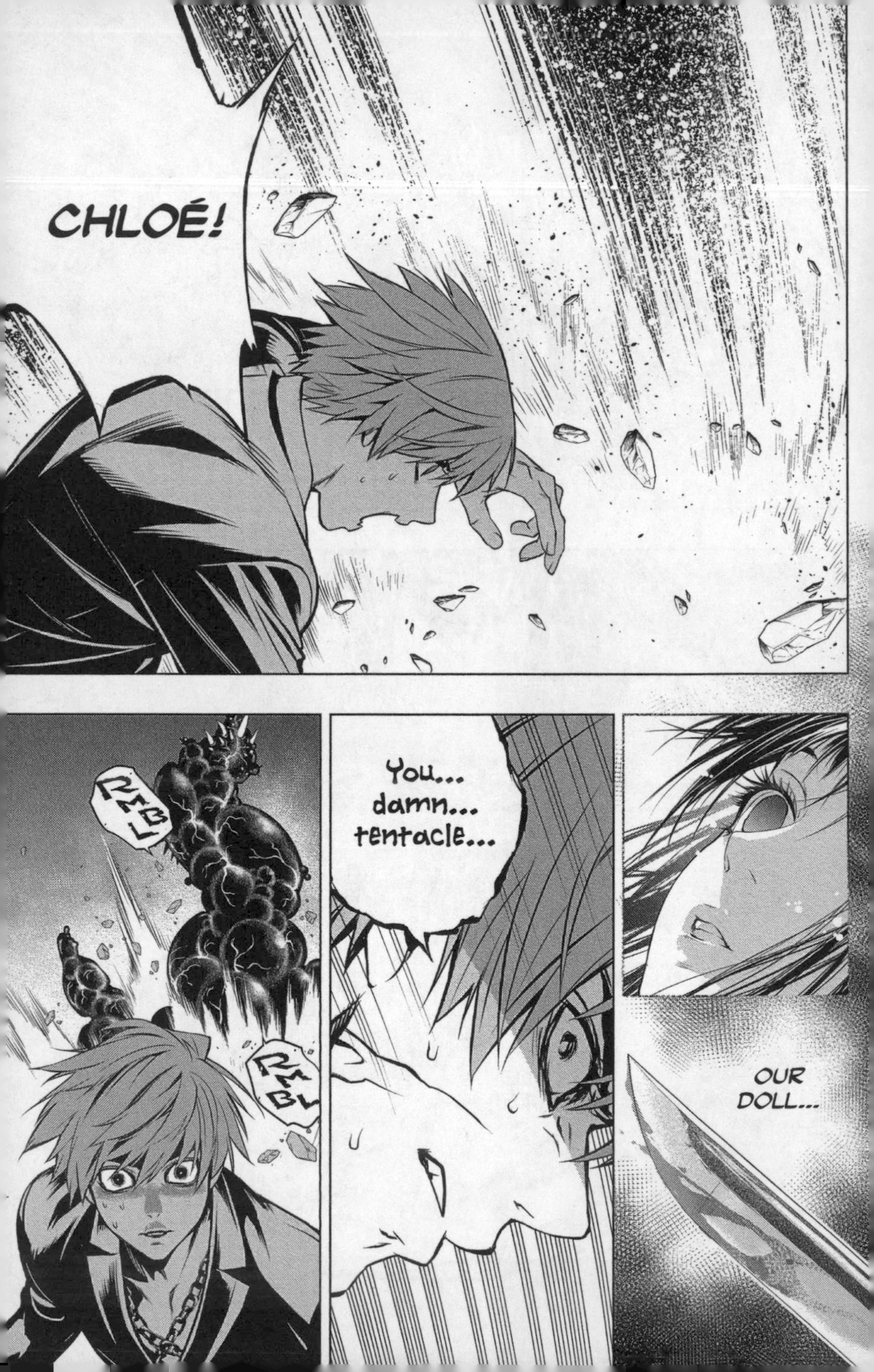
CHLOÉ!
OUR DOLL...
You... damn... tentacle...
RMBL
RMBL

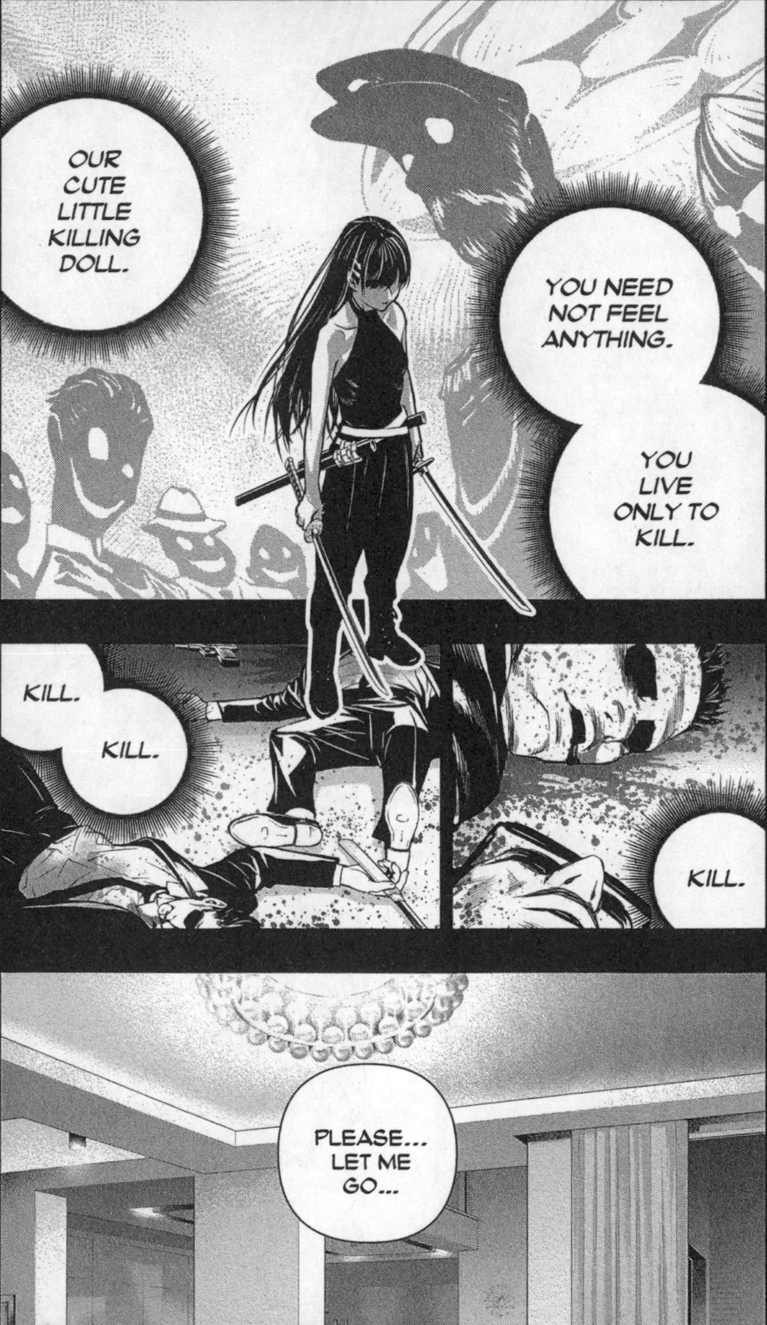
OUR CUTE LITTLE KILLING DOLL.
YOU NEED NOT FEEL ANYTHING.
YOU LIVE ONLY TO KILL.
KILL.
KILL.
KILL.
PLEASE... LET ME GO...

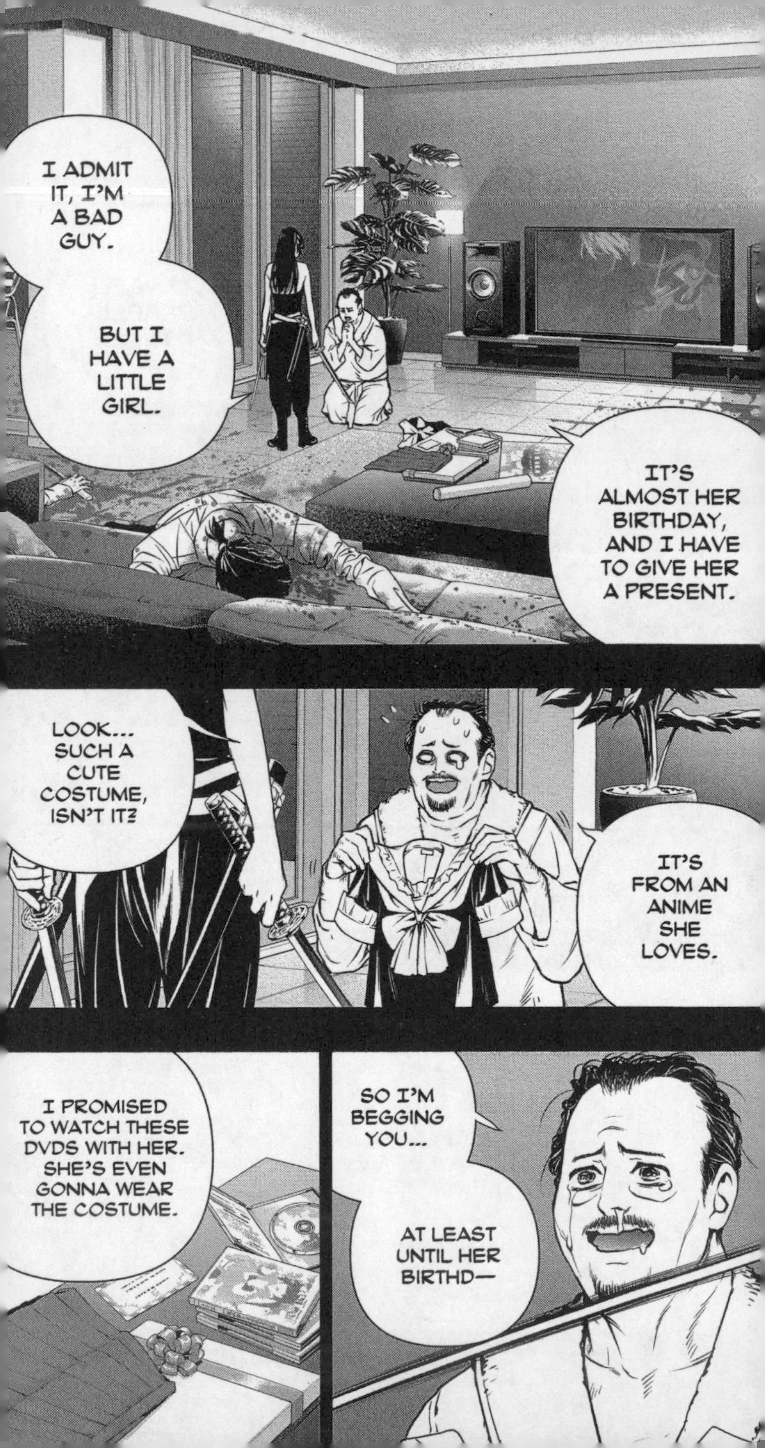
I ADMIT IT, I'M A BAD GUY.
BUT I HAVE A LITTLE GIRL.
IT'S ALMOST HER BIRTHDAY, AND I HAVE TO GIVE HER A PRESENT.
LOOK... SUCH A CUTE COSTUME, ISN'T IT?
IT'S FROM AN ANIME SHE LOVES.
I PROMISED TO WATCH THESE DVDS WITH HER. SHE'S EVEN GONNA WEAR THE COSTUME.
SO I'M BEGGING YOU...
AT LEAST UNTIL HER BIRTHD—

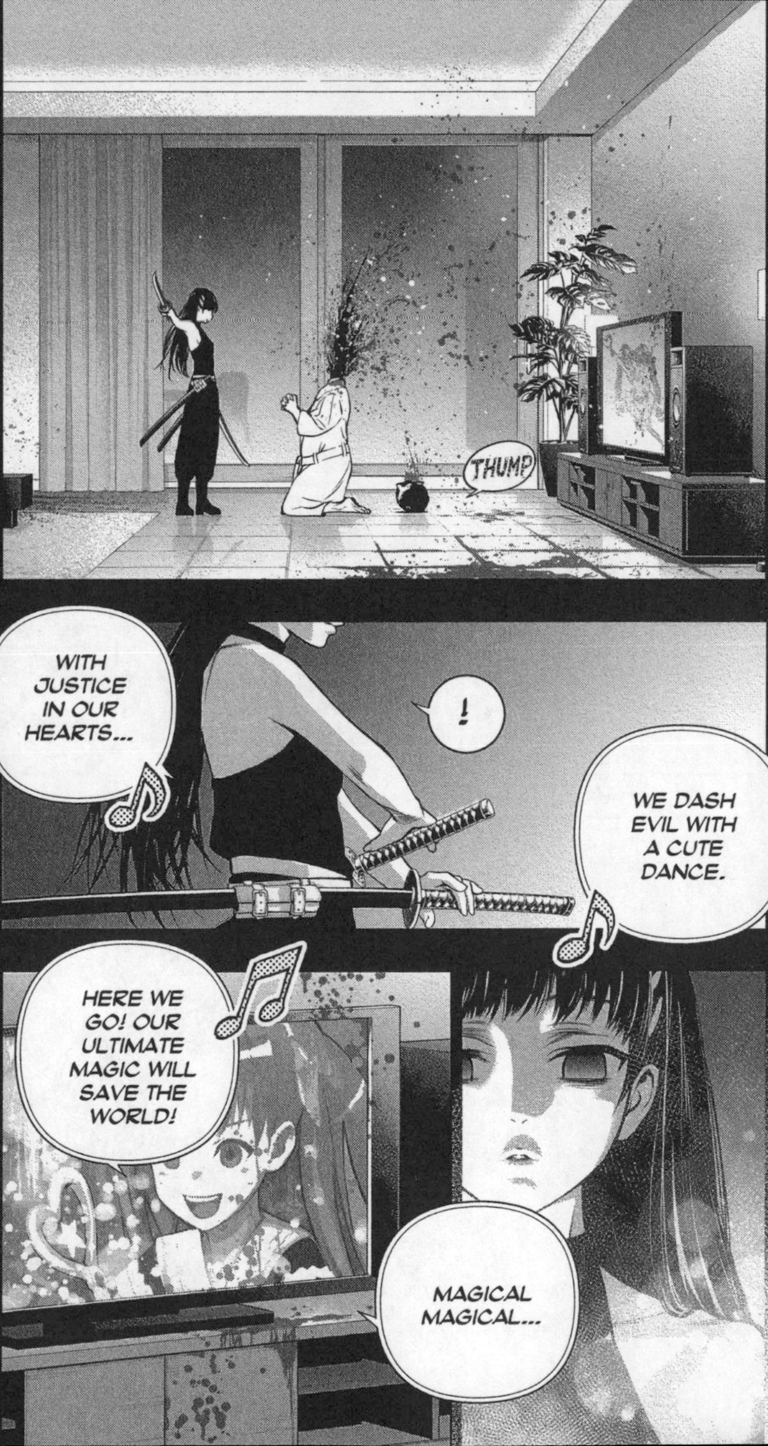
THUMP
WITH JUSTICE IN OUR HEARTS...
!
WE DASH EVIL WITH A CUTE DANCE.
HERE WE GO! OUR ULTIMATE MAGIC WILL SAVE THE WORLD!
MAGICAL MAGICAL...

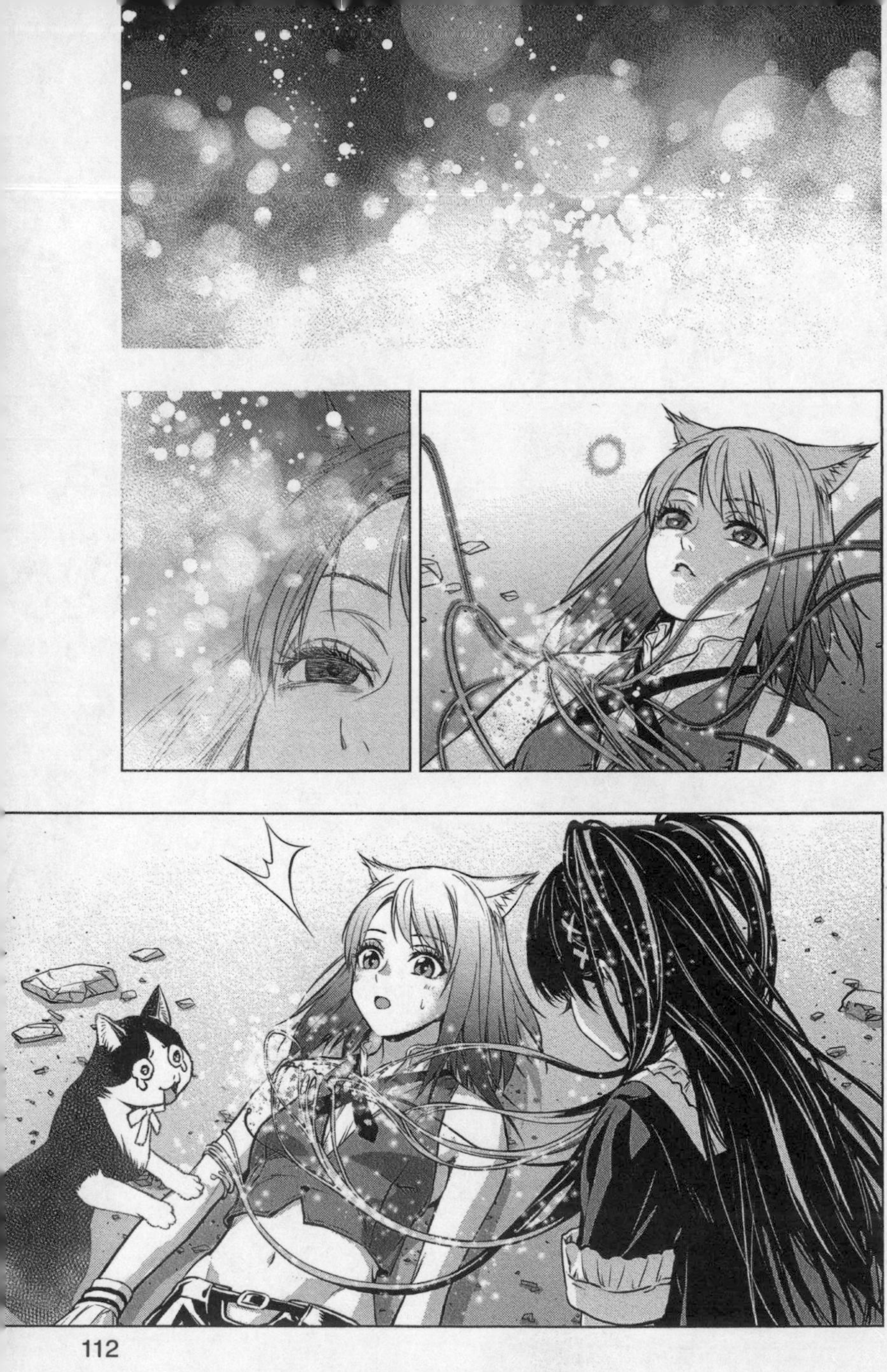

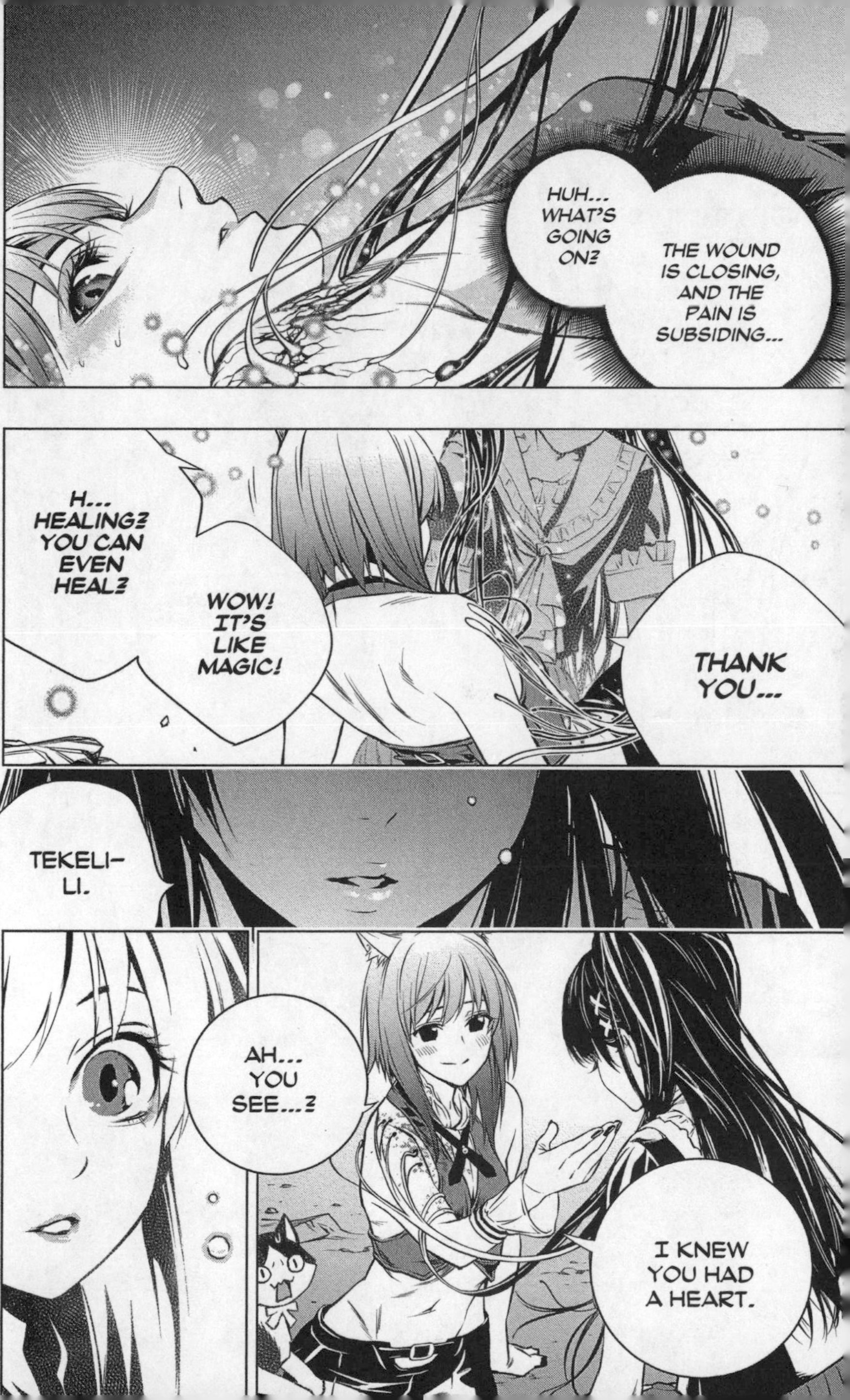
HUH... WHAT'S GOING ON?
THE WOUND IS CLOSING, AND THE PAIN IS SUBSIDING...
THANK YOU...
WOW! IT'S LIKE MAGIC!
H... HEALING? YOU CAN EVEN HEAL?
TEKELI-LI.
I KNEW YOU HAD A HEART.
AH... YOU SEE...?

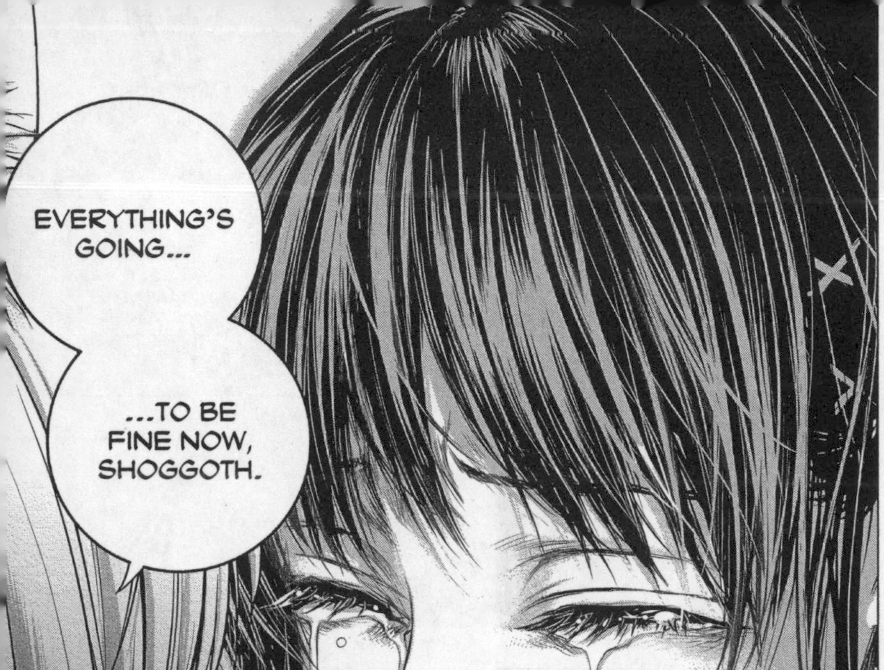
EVERYTHING'S GOING...
...TO BE FINE NOW, SHOGGOTH.
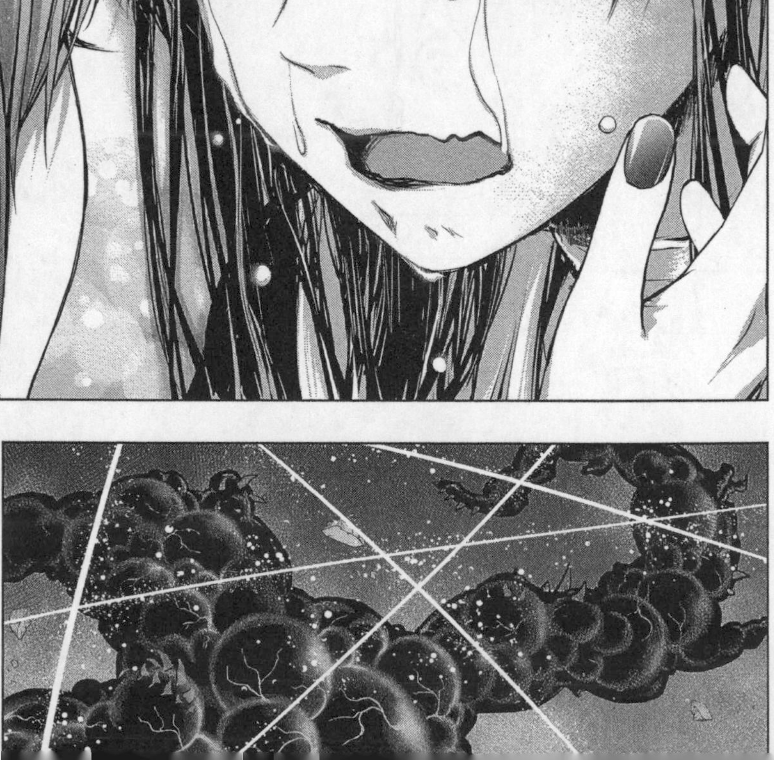

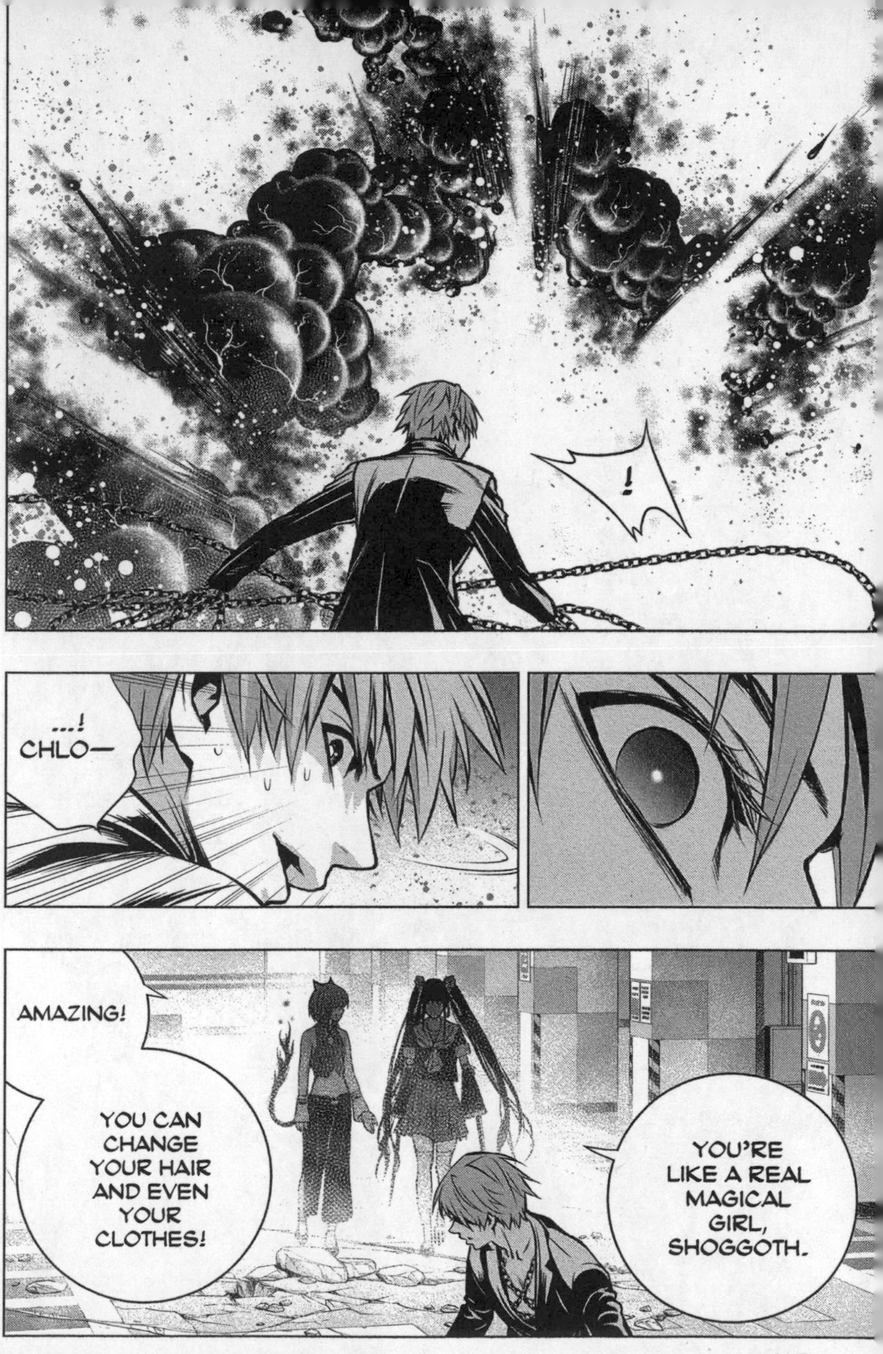
!
...! CHLO—
AMAZING!
YOU CAN CHANGE YOUR HAIR AND EVEN YOUR CLOTHES!
YOU'RE LIKE A REAL MAGICAL GIRL, SHOGGOTH.

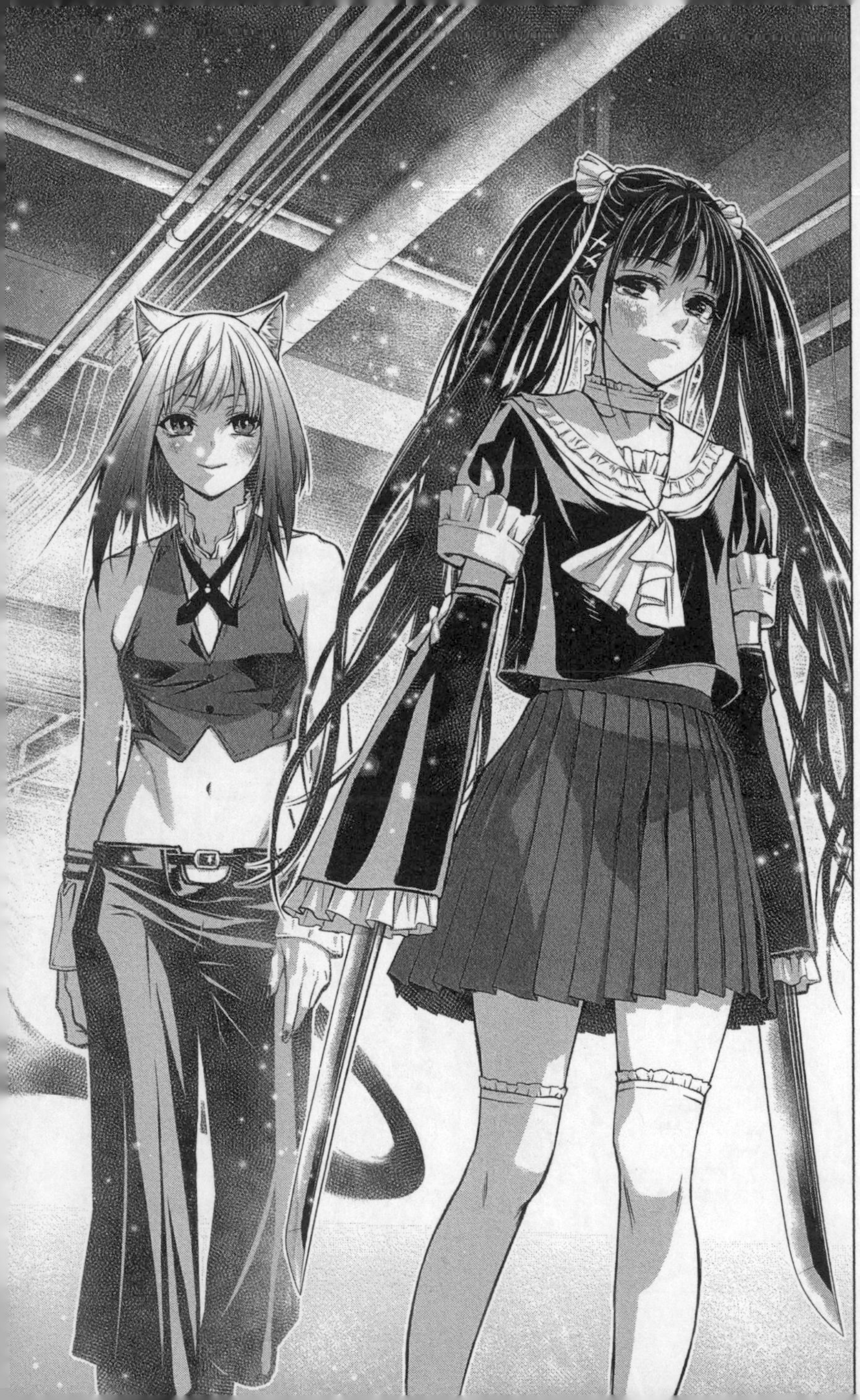

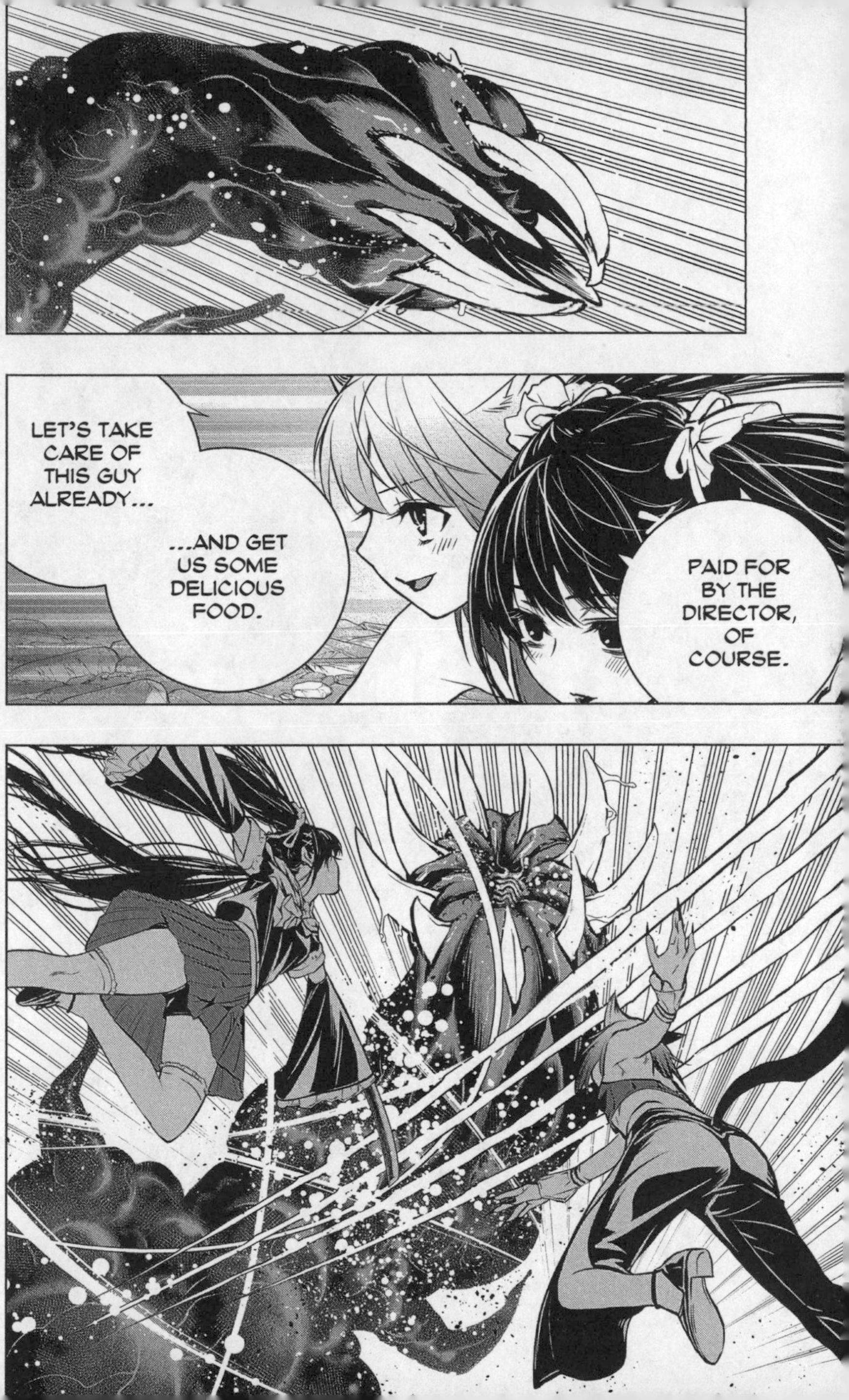
LET'S TAKE CARE OF THIS GUY ALREADY...
...AND GET US SOME DELICIOUS FOOD.
PAID FOR BY THE DIRECTOR, OF COURSE.

#11: Changes

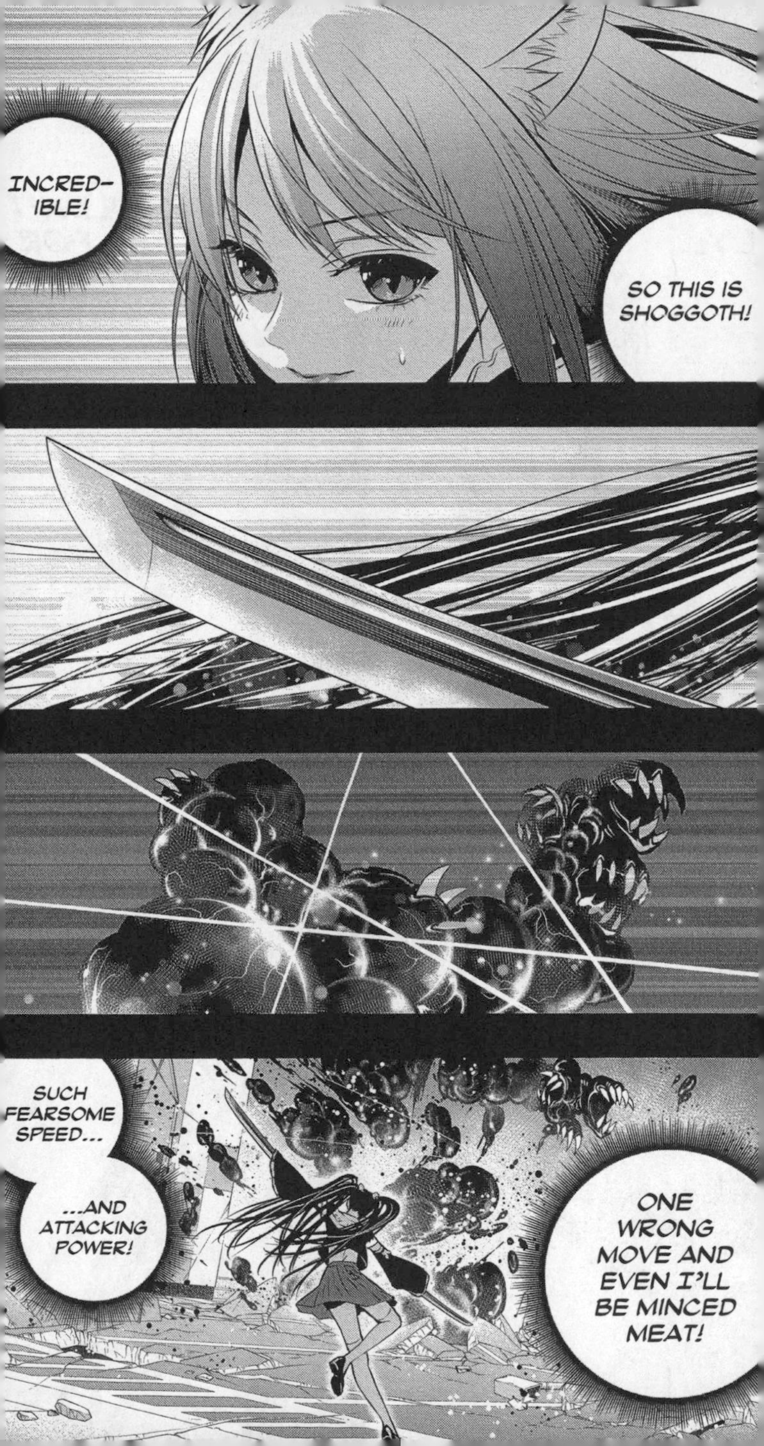
INCRED-IBLE!
SO THIS IS SHOGGOTH!
SUCH FEARSOME SPEED...
...AND ATTACKING POWER!
ONE WRONG MOVE AND EVEN I'LL BE MINCED MEAT!

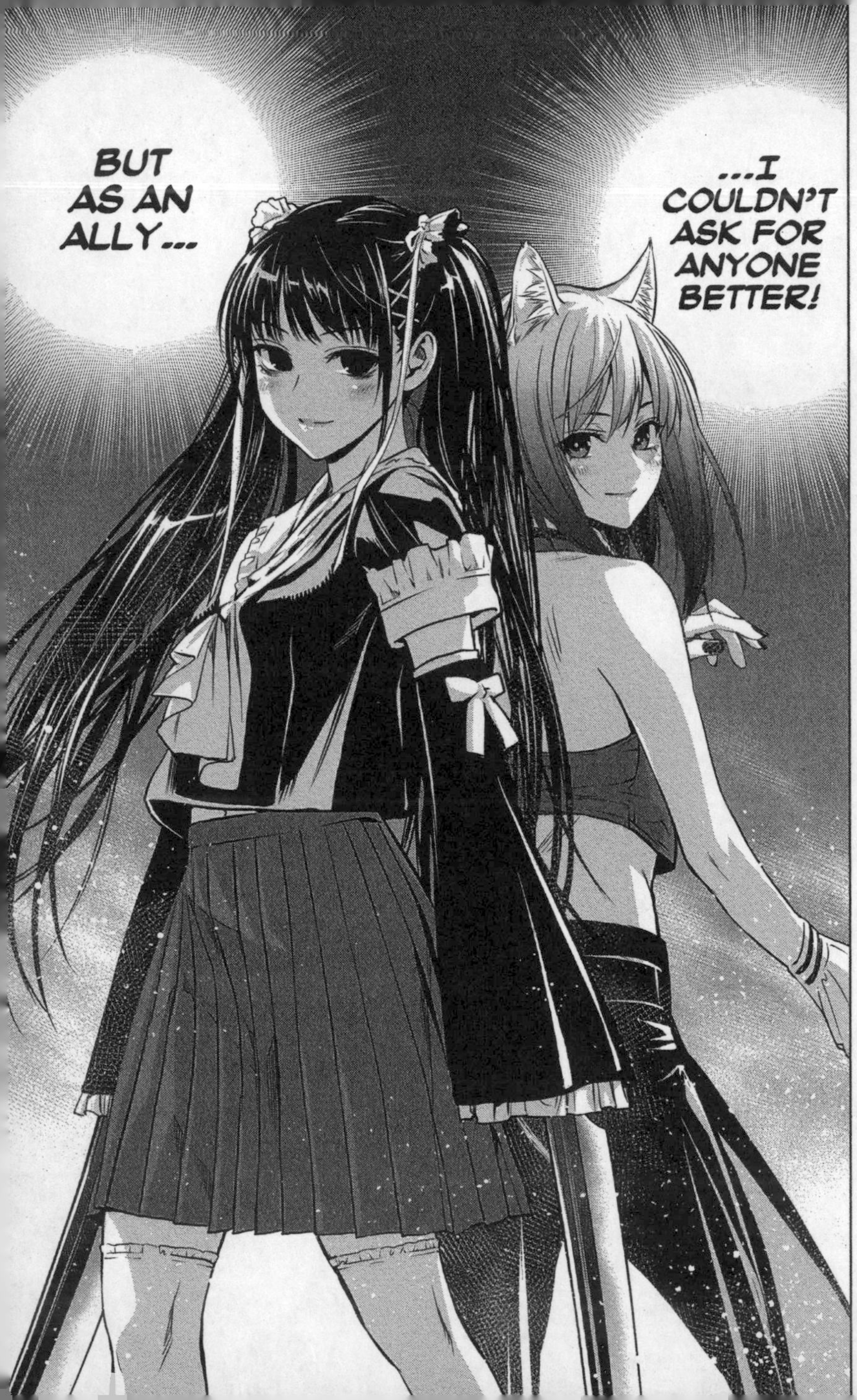
BUT AS AN ALLY...
...I COULDN'T ASK FOR ANYONE BETTER!

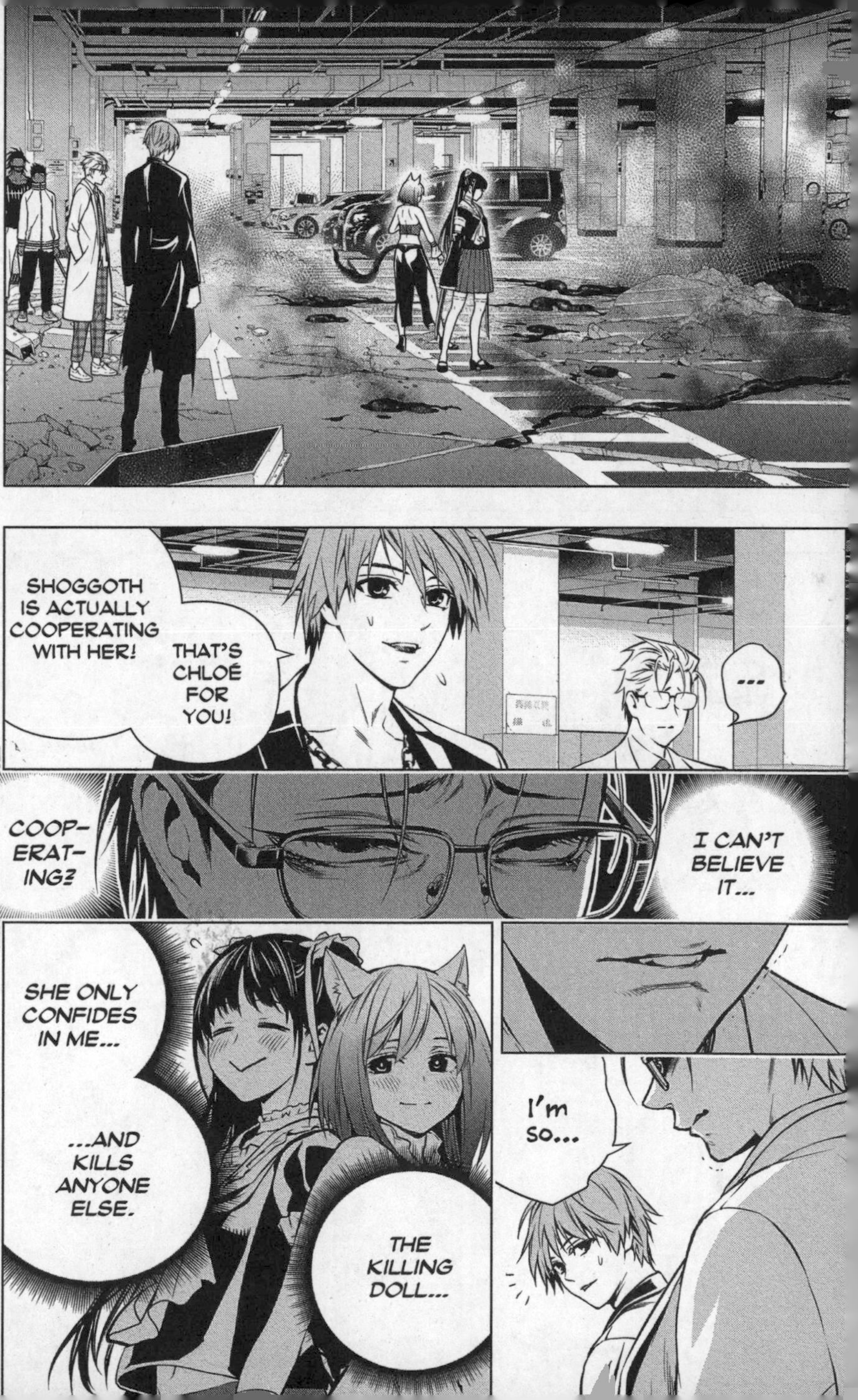
...
THAT'S CHLOÉ FOR YOU!
SHOGGOTH IS ACTUALLY COOPERATING WITH HER!
I CAN'T BELIEVE IT...
COOP-ERAT-ING?
I'm so...
SHE ONLY CONFIDES IN ME...
...AND KILLS ANYONE ELSE.
THE KILLING DOLL...

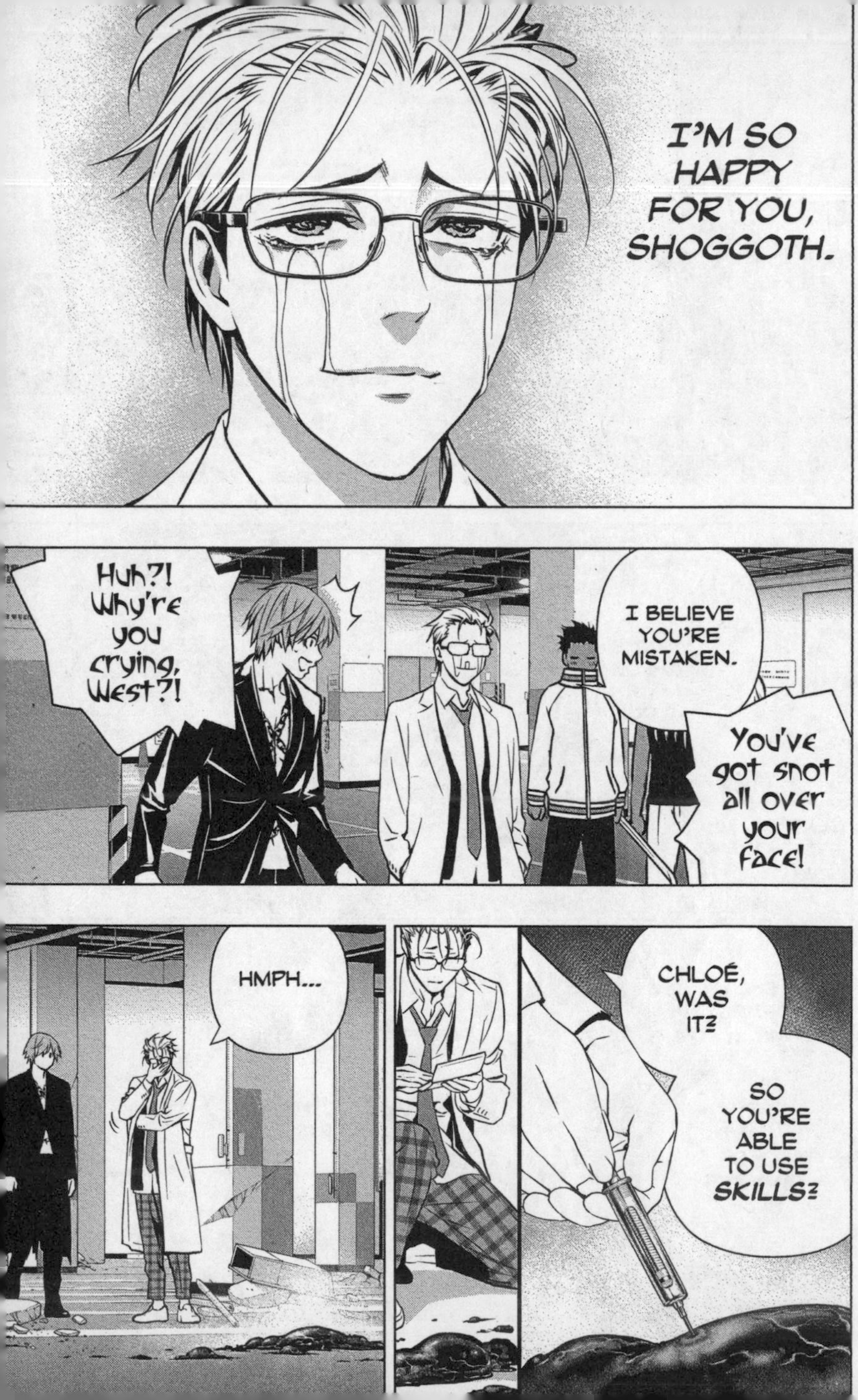
I'M SO HAPPY FOR YOU, SHOGGOTH.
Huh?! Why're you crying, West?!
I BELIEVE YOU'RE MISTAKEN.
You've got snot all over your face!
HMPH...
CHLOÉ, WAS IT?
SO YOU'RE ABLE TO USE SKILLS?

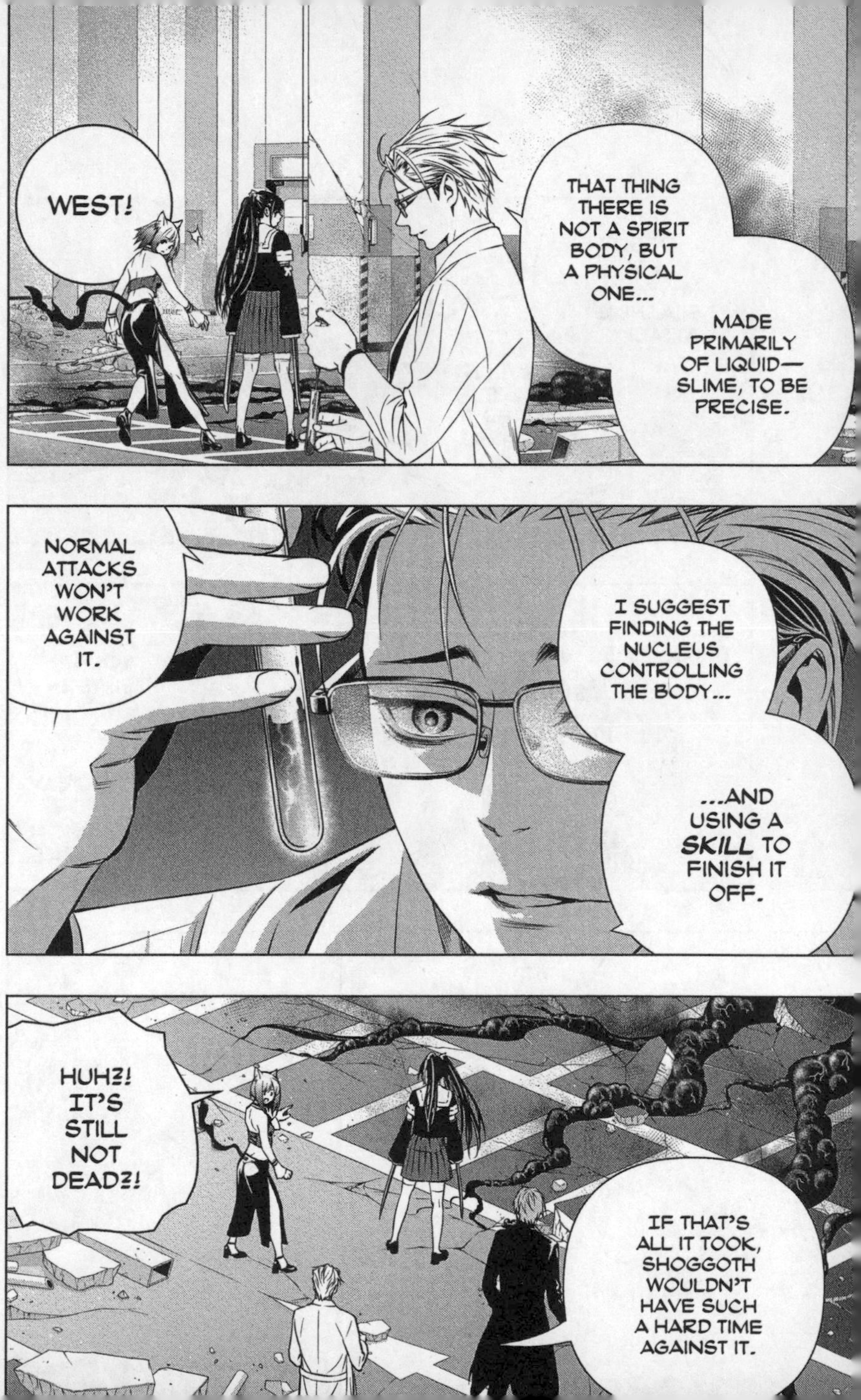
WEST!
THAT THING THERE IS NOT A SPIRIT BODY, BUT A PHYSICAL ONE...
MADE PRIMARILY OF LIQUID—SLIME, TO BE PRECISE.
NORMAL ATTACKS WON'T WORK AGAINST IT.
I SUGGEST FINDING THE NUCLEUS CONTROLLING THE BODY...
...AND USING A *SKILL* TO FINISH IT OFF.
HUH?! IT'S STILL NOT DEAD?!
IF THAT'S ALL IT TOOK, SHOGGOTH WOULDN'T HAVE SUCH A HARD TIME AGAINST IT.

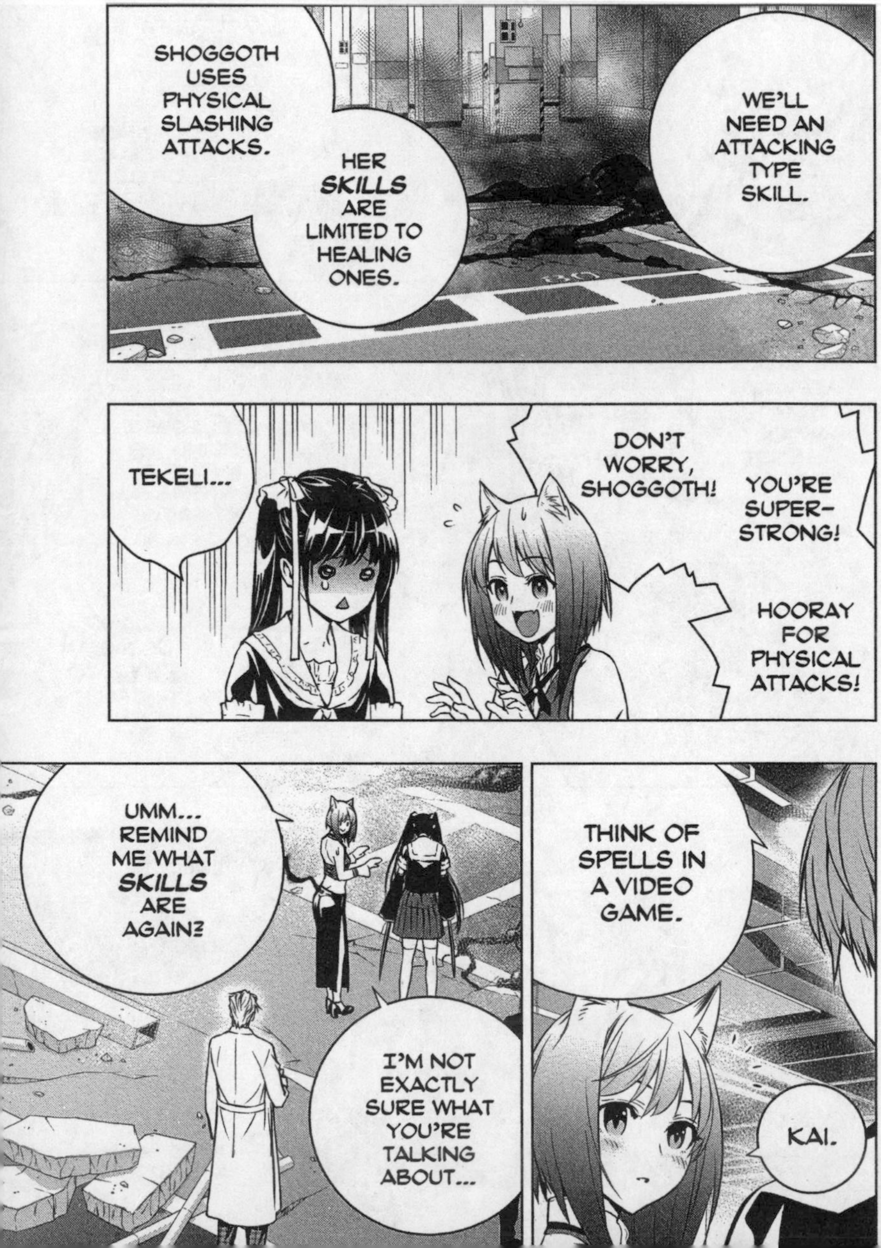
WE'LL NEED AN ATTACKING TYPE SKILL.
SHOGGOTH USES PHYSICAL SLASHING ATTACKS.
HER *SKILLS* ARE LIMITED TO HEALING ONES.
YOU'RE SUPER-STRONG!
DON'T WORRY, SHOGGOTH!
HOORAY FOR PHYSICAL ATTACKS!
TEKELI...
THINK OF SPELLS IN A VIDEO GAME.
KAI.
UMM... REMIND ME WHAT *SKILLS* ARE AGAIN?
I'M NOT EXACTLY SURE WHAT YOU'RE TALKING ABOUT...

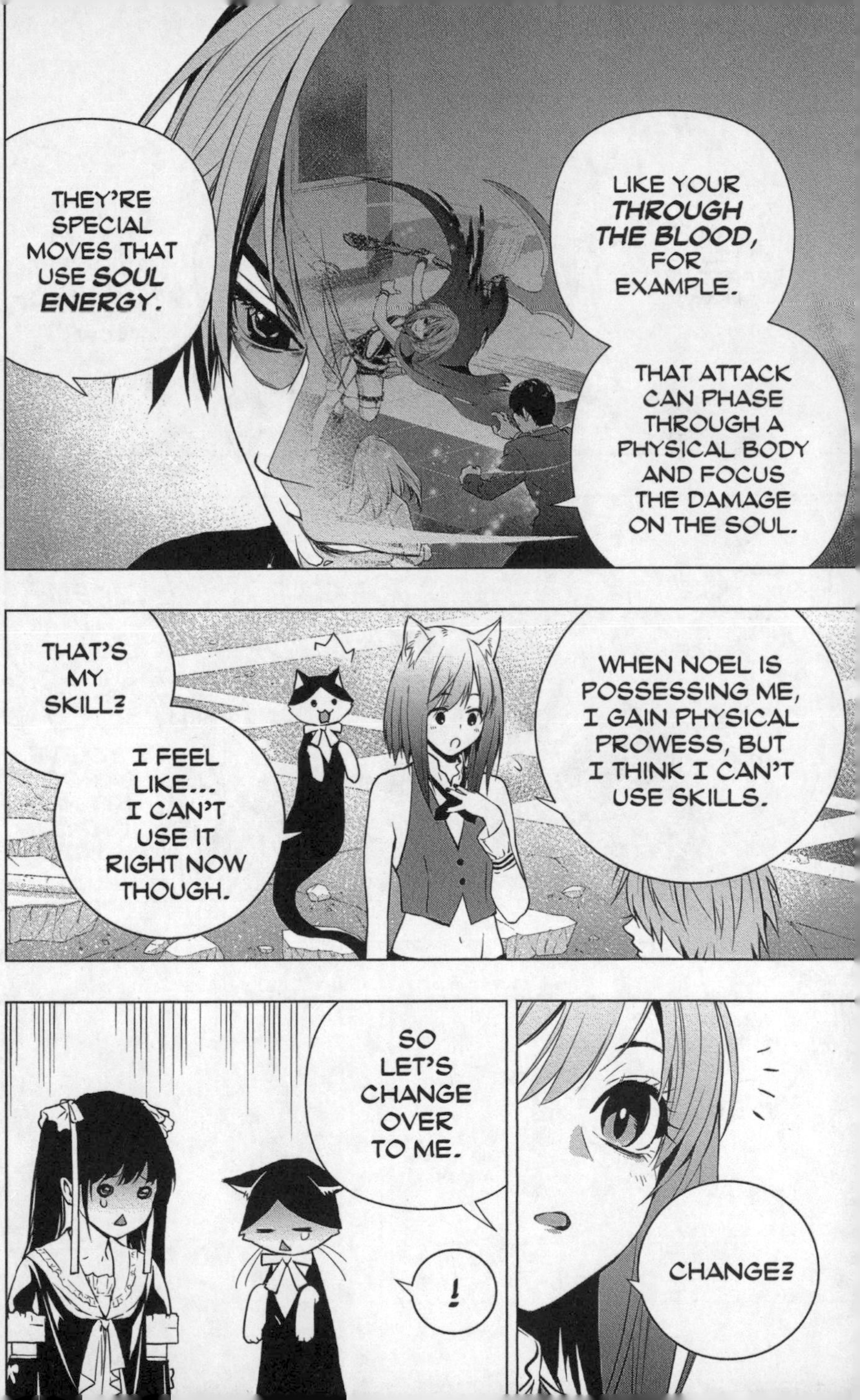
THEY'RE SPECIAL MOVES THAT USE SOUL ENERGY.
LIKE YOUR THROUGH THE BLOOD, FOR EXAMPLE.
THAT ATTACK CAN PHASE THROUGH A PHYSICAL BODY AND FOCUS THE DAMAGE ON THE SOUL.
THAT'S MY SKILL?
I FEEL LIKE... I CAN'T USE IT RIGHT NOW THOUGH.
WHEN NOEL IS POSSESSING ME, I GAIN PHYSICAL PROWESS, BUT I THINK I CAN'T USE SKILLS.
SO LET'S CHANGE OVER TO ME.
!
CHANGE?

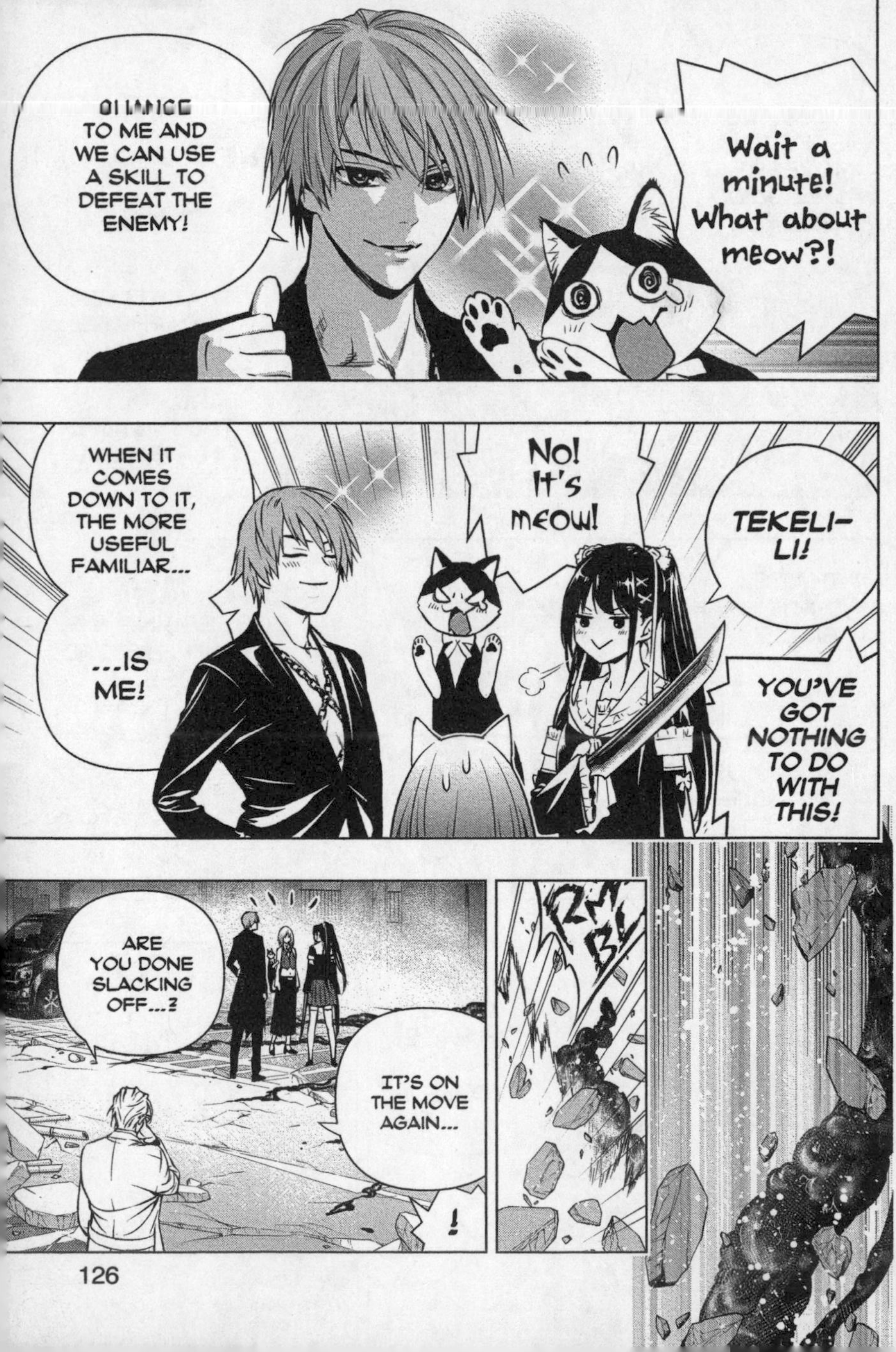
TO ME AND WE CAN USE A SKILL TO DEFEAT THE ENEMY!
Wait a minute! What about meow?!
WHEN IT COMES DOWN TO IT, THE MORE USEFUL FAMILIAR...
...IS ME!
No! It's meow!
TEKELI-LI!
YOU'VE GOT NOTHING TO DO WITH THIS!
ARE YOU DONE SLACKING OFF...?
IT'S ON THE MOVE AGAIN...
!

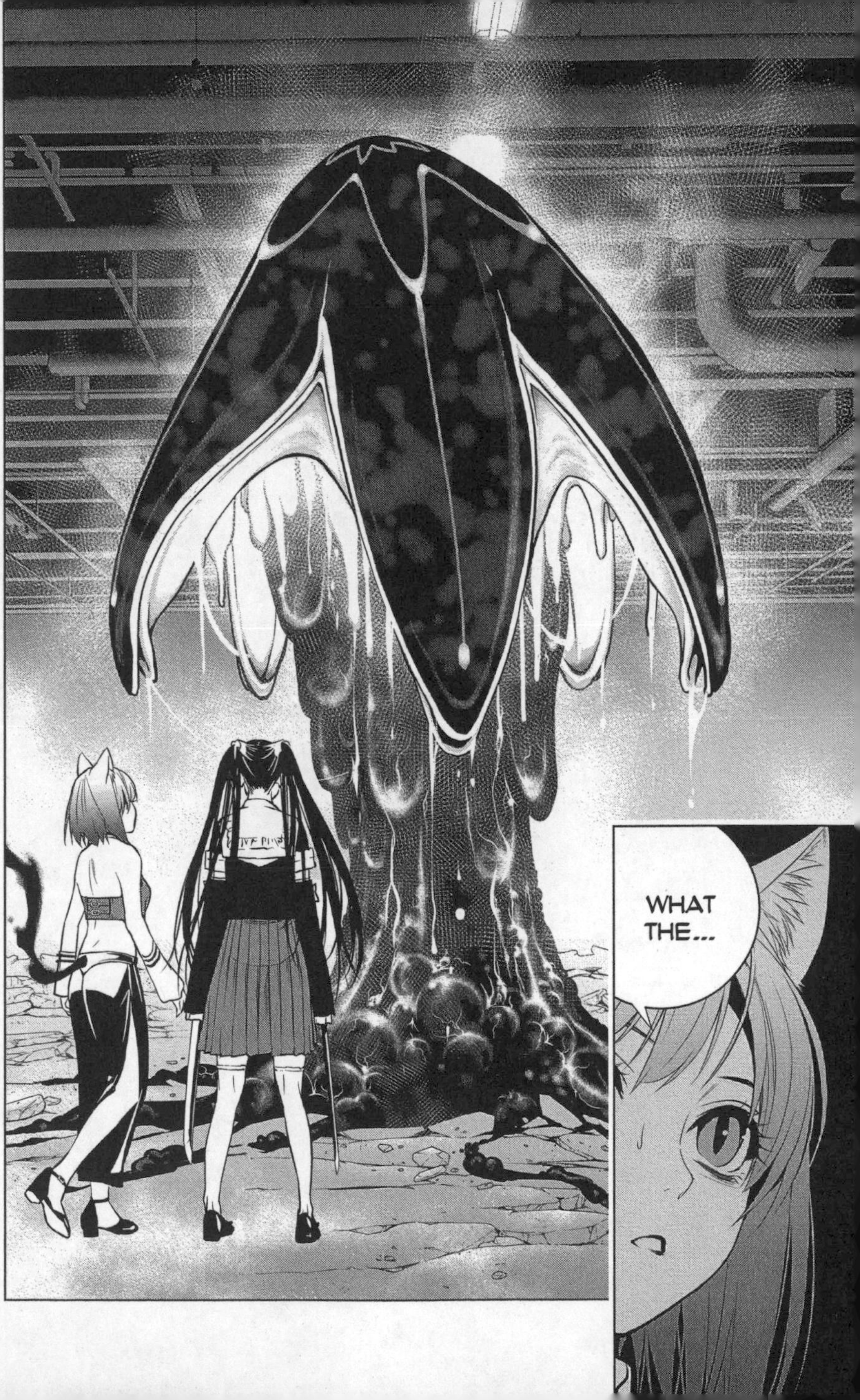
WHAT THE...

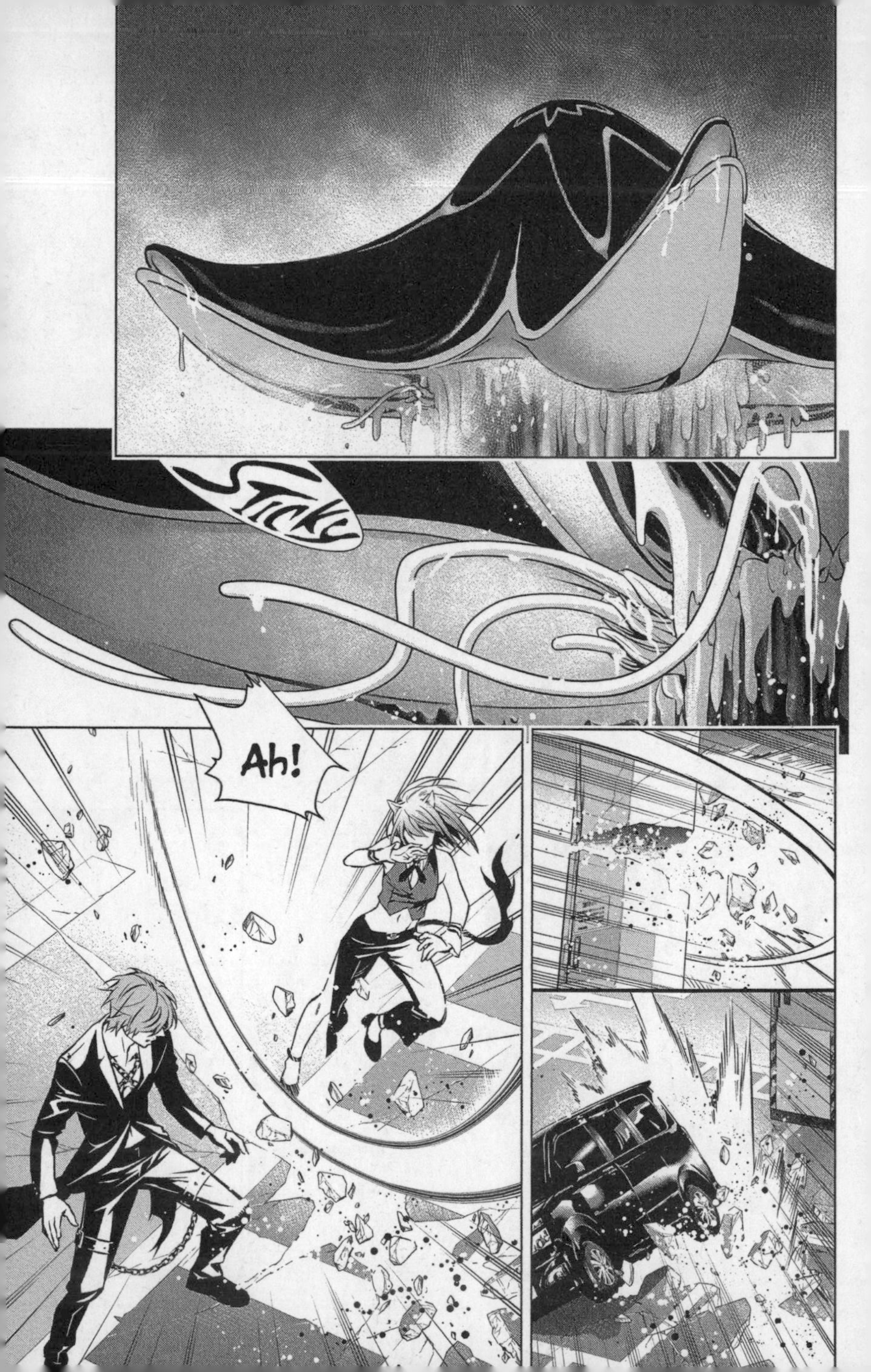
Sticky
Ah!

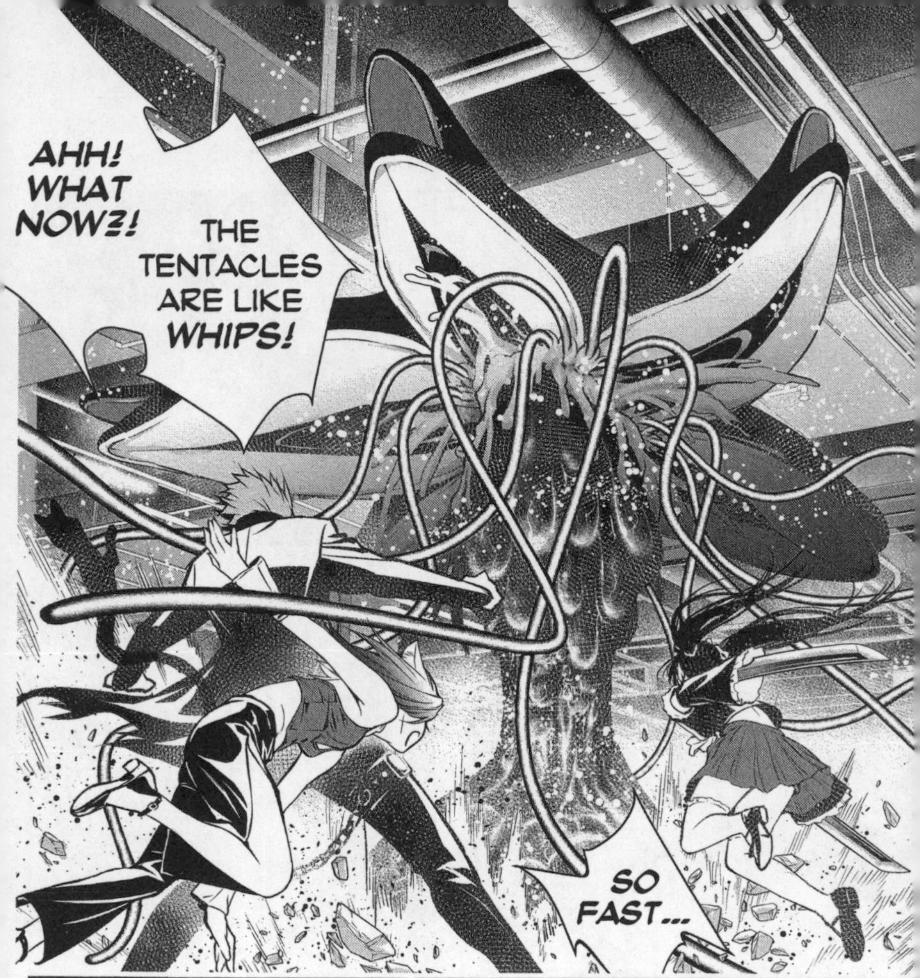
AHH! WHAT NOW?!
THE TENTACLES ARE LIKE WHIPS!
SO FAST...

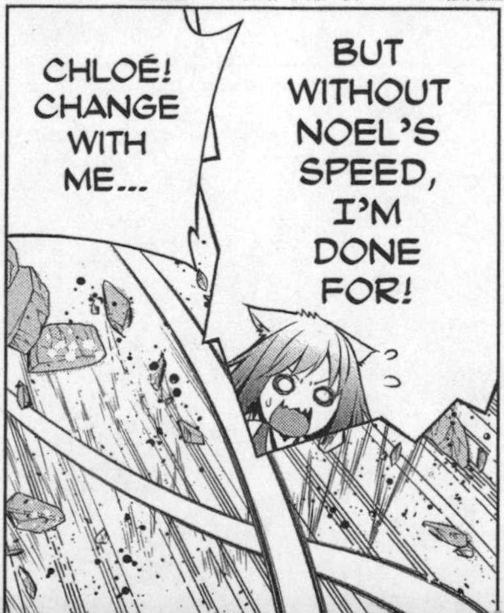
CHLOÉ! CHANGE WITH ME...
BUT WITHOUT NOEL'S SPEED, I'M DONE FOR!

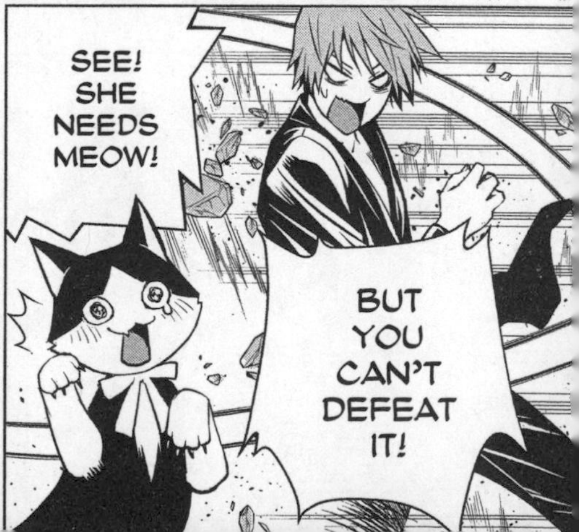
SEE! SHE NEEDS MEOW!
BUT YOU CAN'T DEFEAT IT!

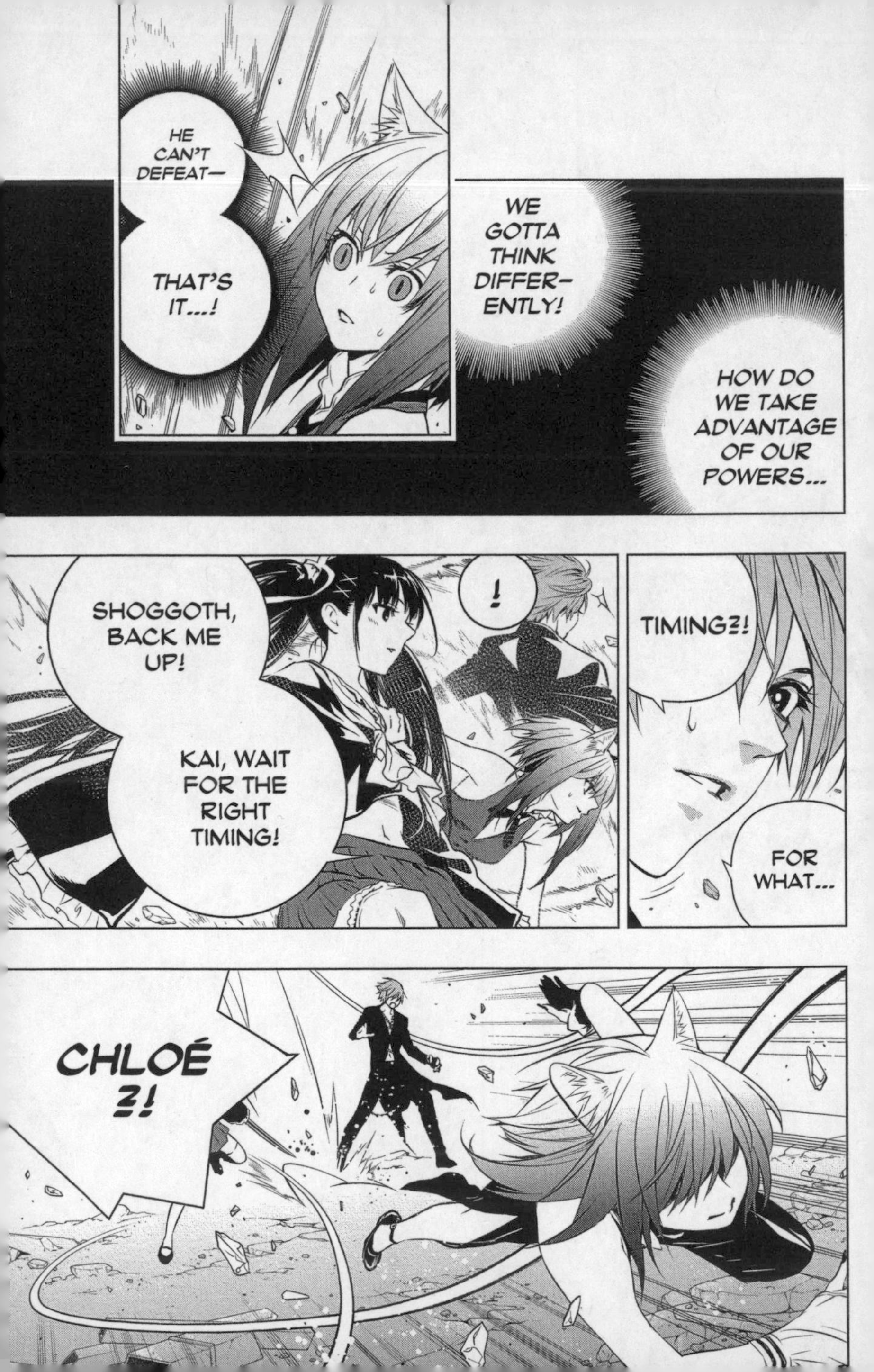
WE GOTTA THINK DIFFER-ENTLY!
HE CAN'T DEFEAT—
THAT'S IT...!
HOW DO WE TAKE ADVANTAGE OF OUR POWERS...
TIMING?!
FOR WHAT...
!
SHOGGOTH, BACK ME UP!
KAI, WAIT FOR THE RIGHT TIMING!
CHLOÉ ?!

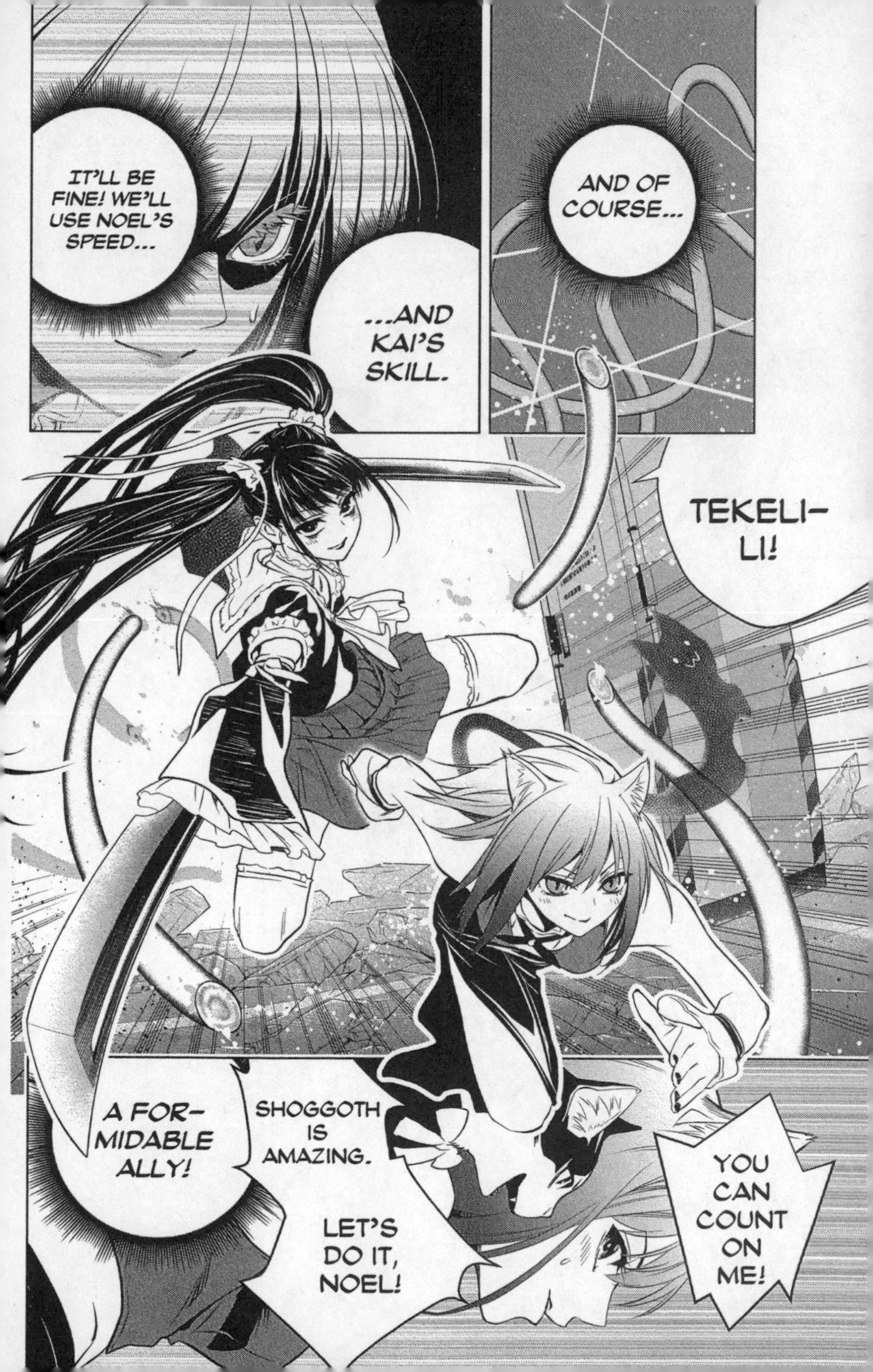
IT'LL BE FINE! WE'LL USE NOEL'S SPEED...
...AND KAI'S SKILL.
AND OF COURSE...
TEKELI-LI!
A FOR-MIDABLE ALLY!
SHOGGOTH IS AMAZING.
LET'S DO IT, NOEL!
YOU CAN COUNT ON ME!

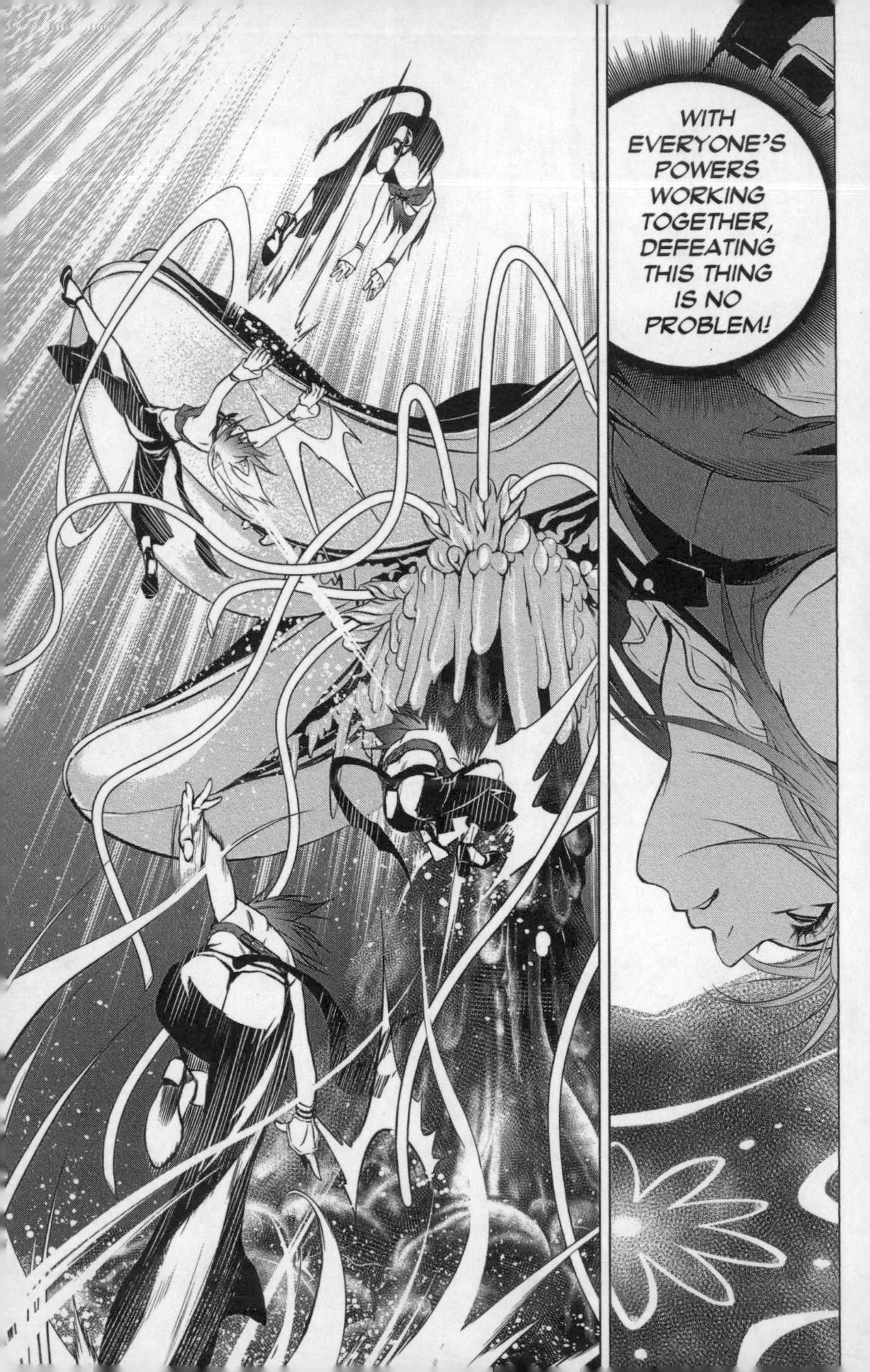
WITH EVERYONE'S POWERS WORKING TOGETHER, DEFEATING THIS THING IS NO PROBLEM!

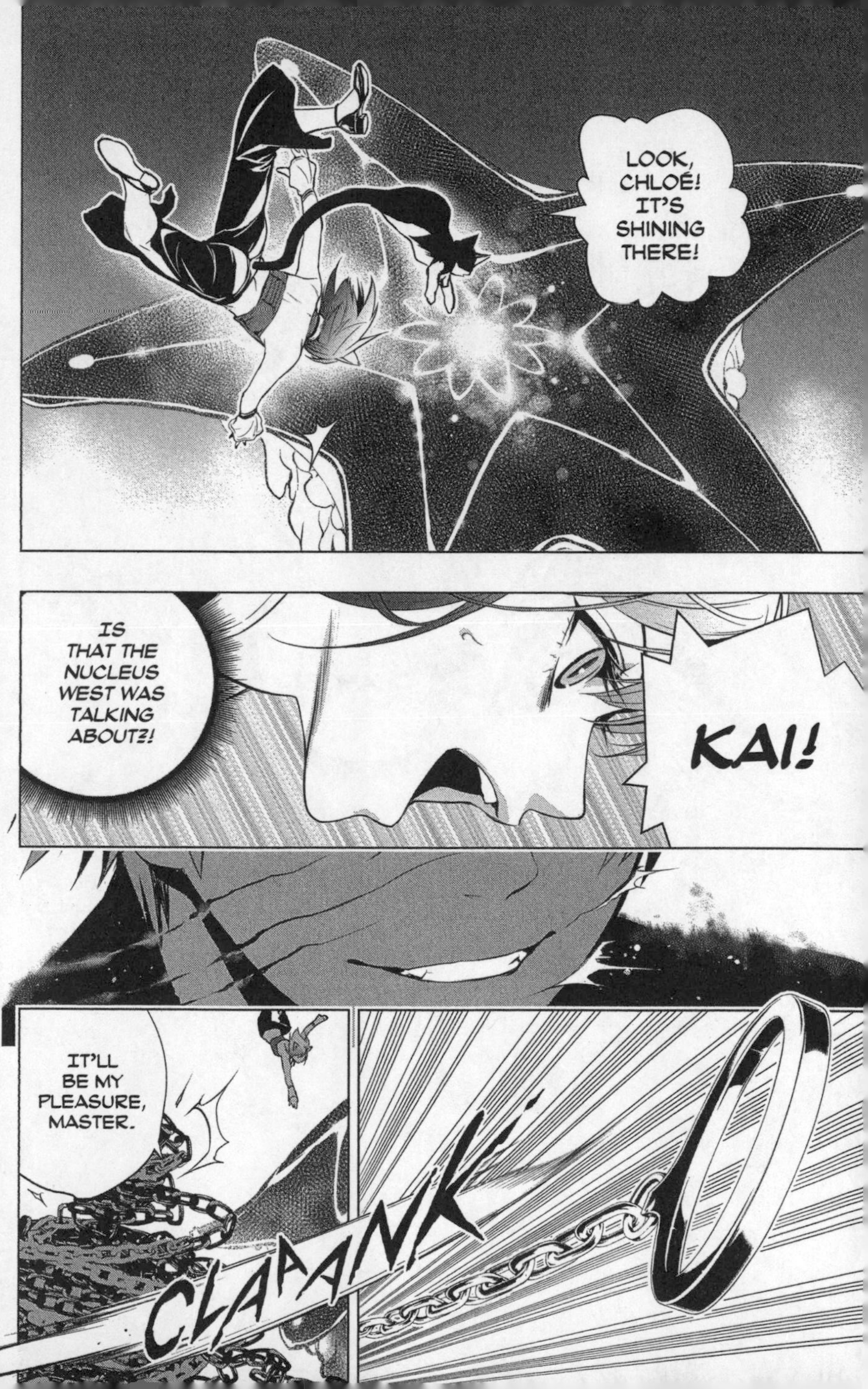
LOOK, CHLOÉ! IT'S SHINING THERE!
IS THAT THE NUCLEUS WEST WAS TALKING ABOUT?!
KAI!
CLAAANK
IT'LL BE MY PLEASURE, MASTER.

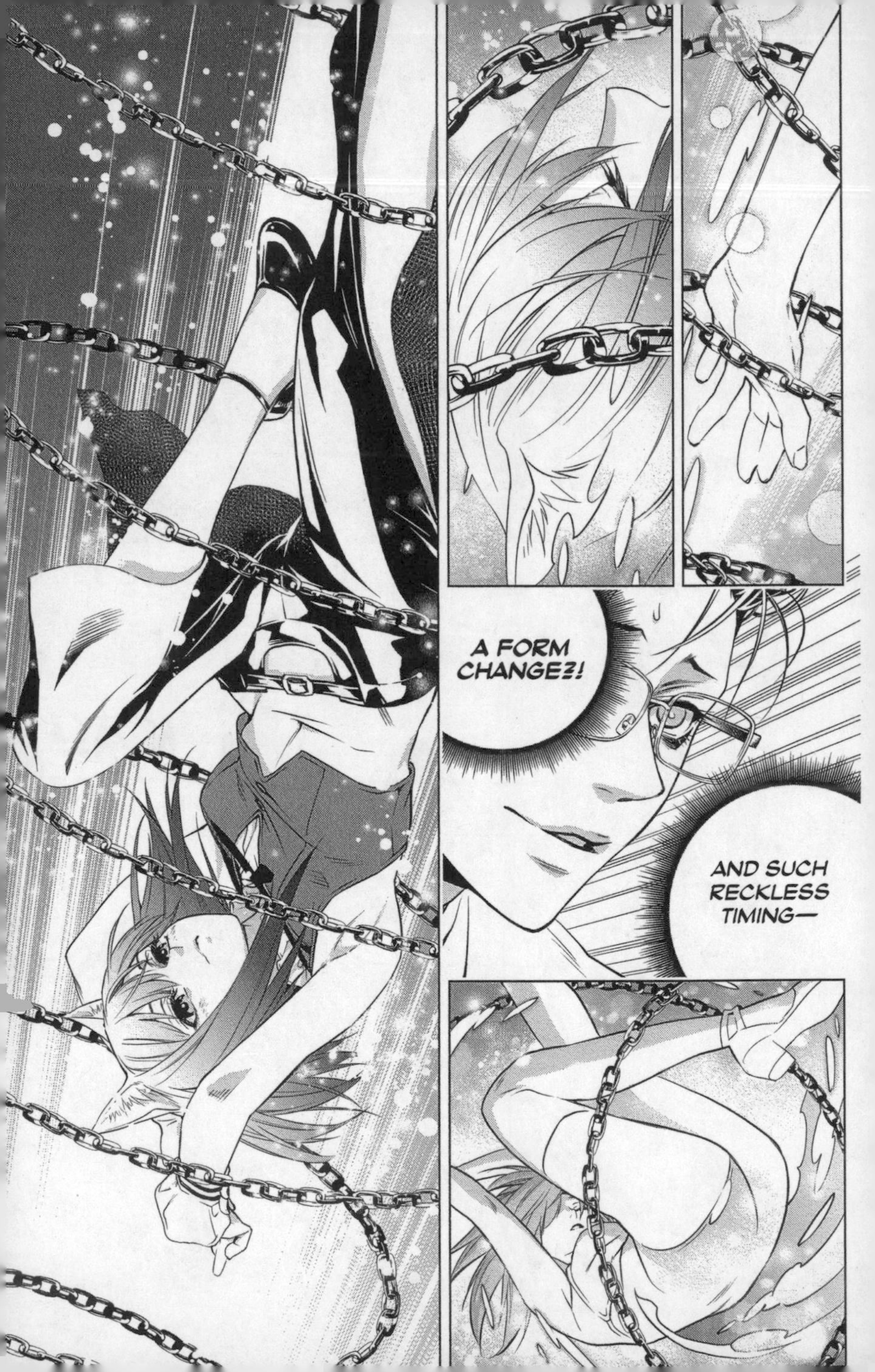
A FORM CHANGE?!
AND SUCH RECKLESS TIMING—

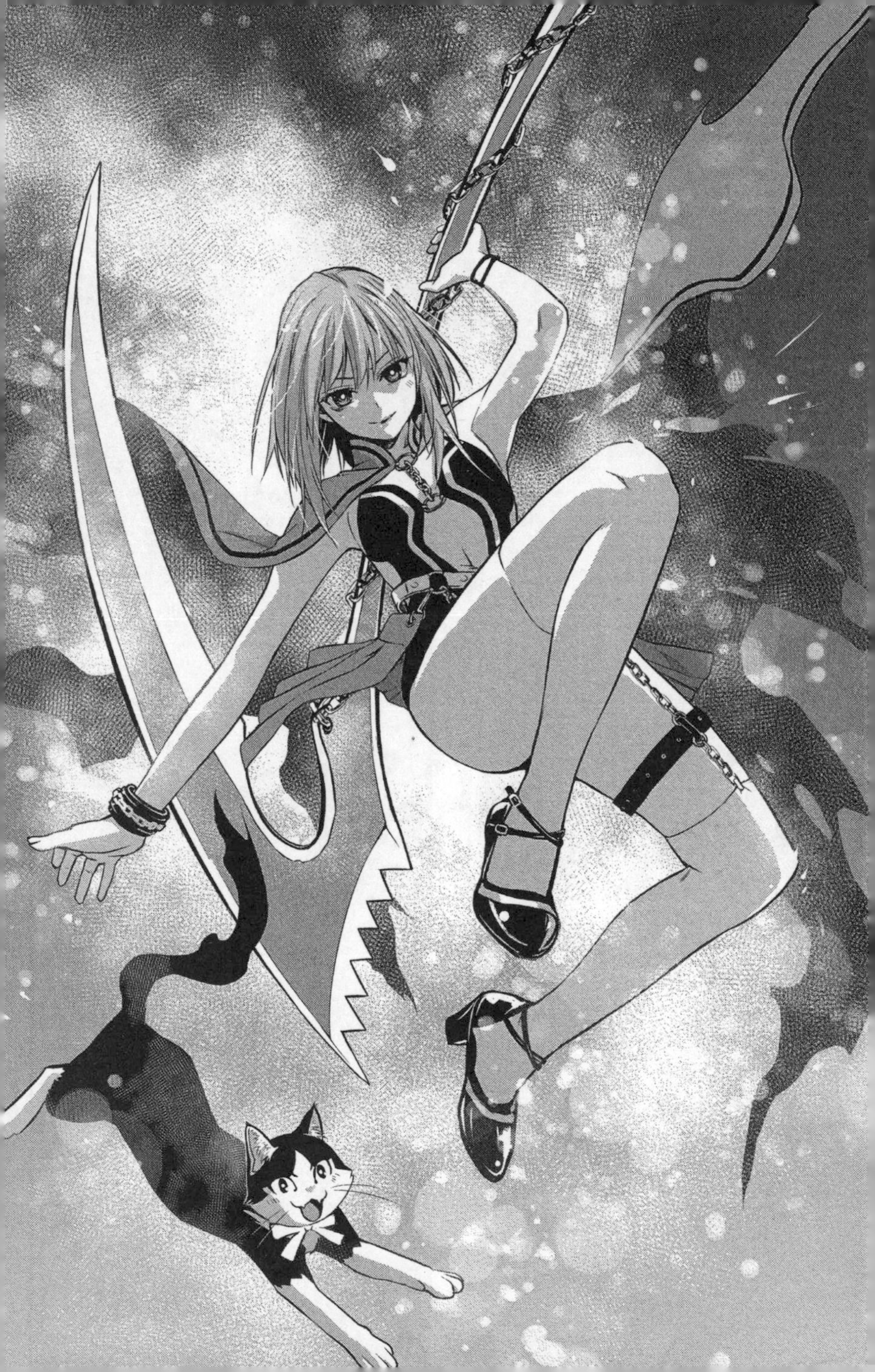

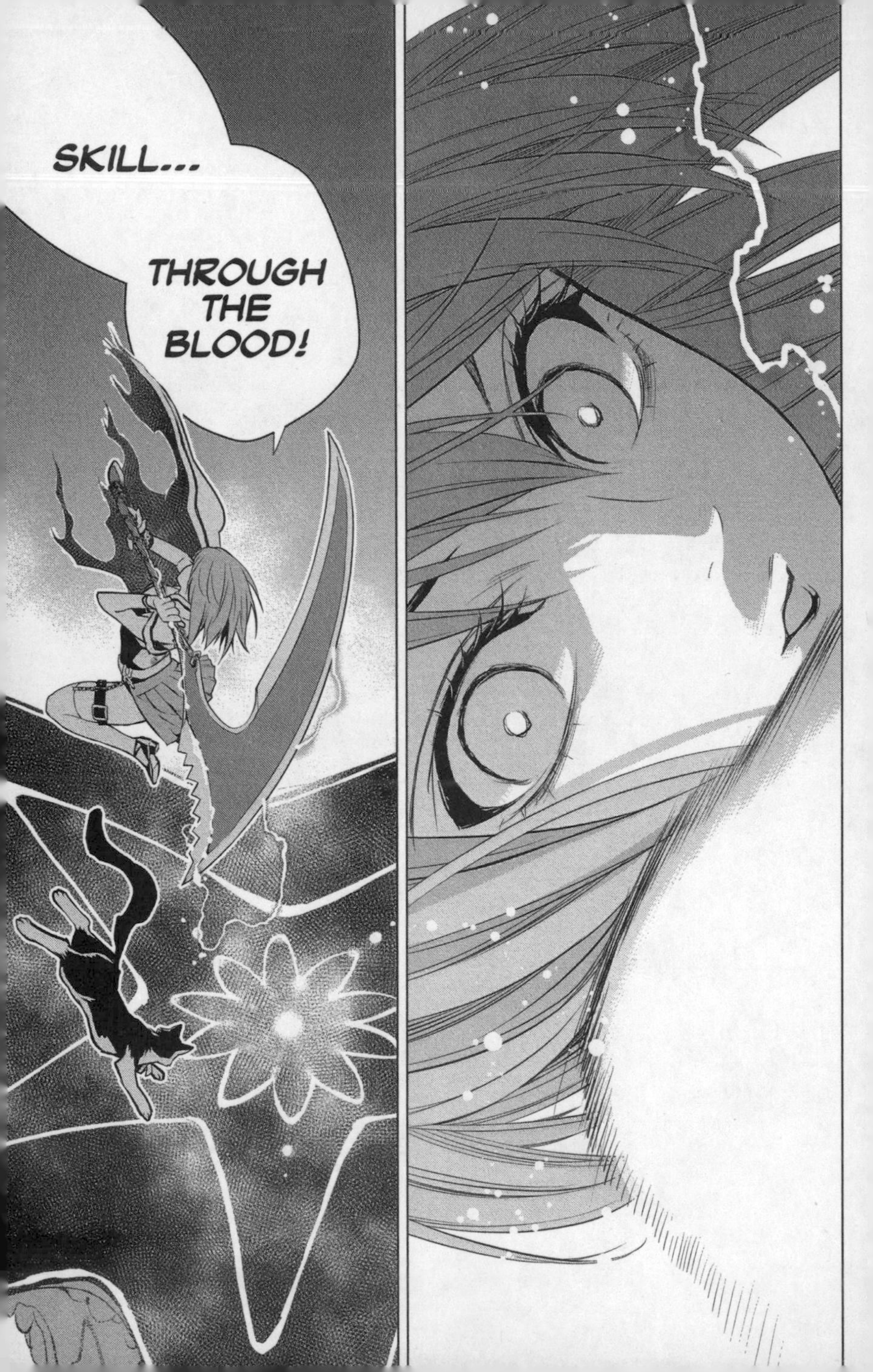
SKILL...
THROUGH THE BLOOD!

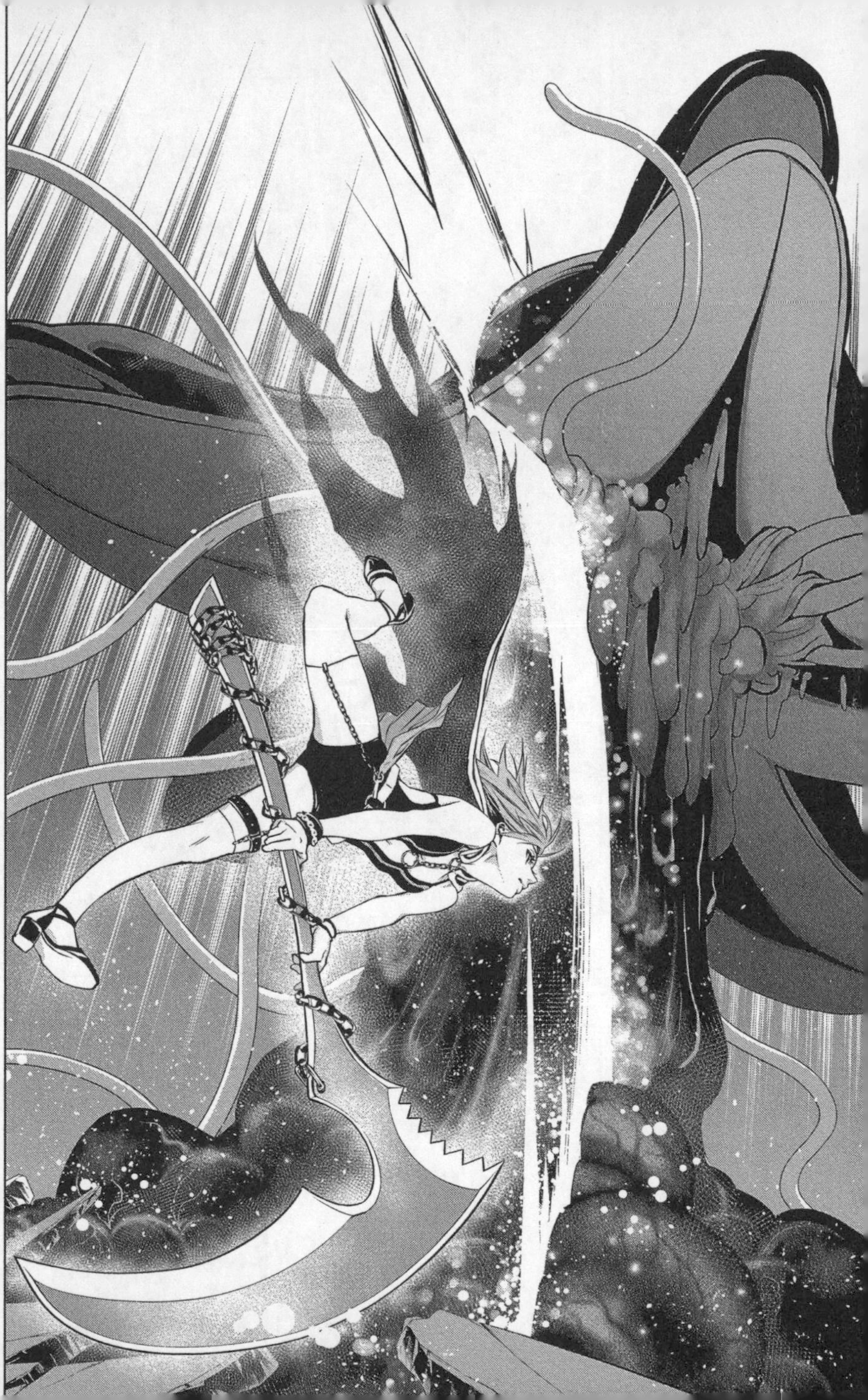

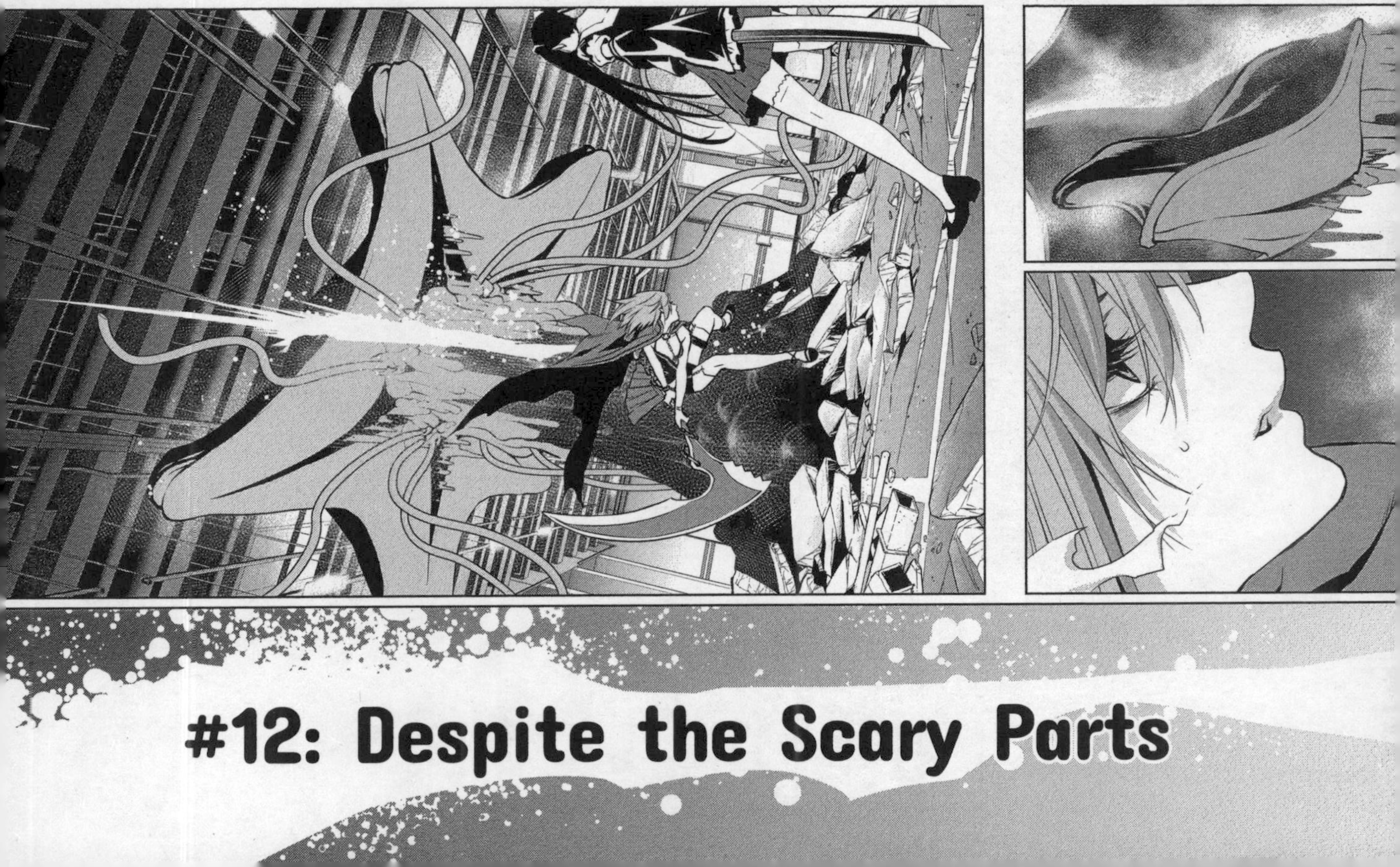

#12: Despite the Scary Parts

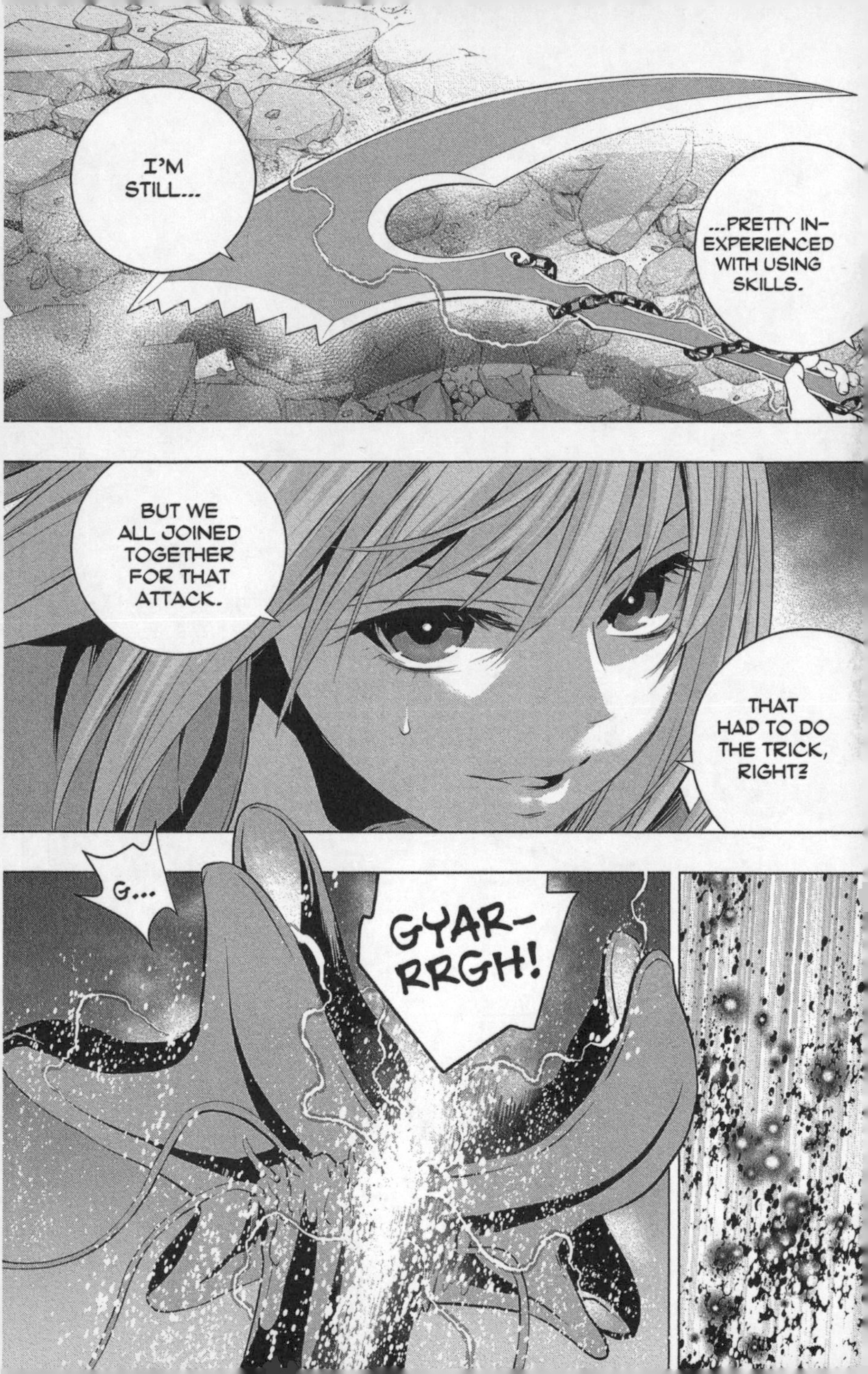
I'M STILL...
...PRETTY IN-EXPERIENCED WITH USING SKILLS.
BUT WE ALL JOINED TOGETHER FOR THAT ATTACK.
THAT HAD TO DO THE TRICK, RIGHT?
G...
GYAR-RRGH!

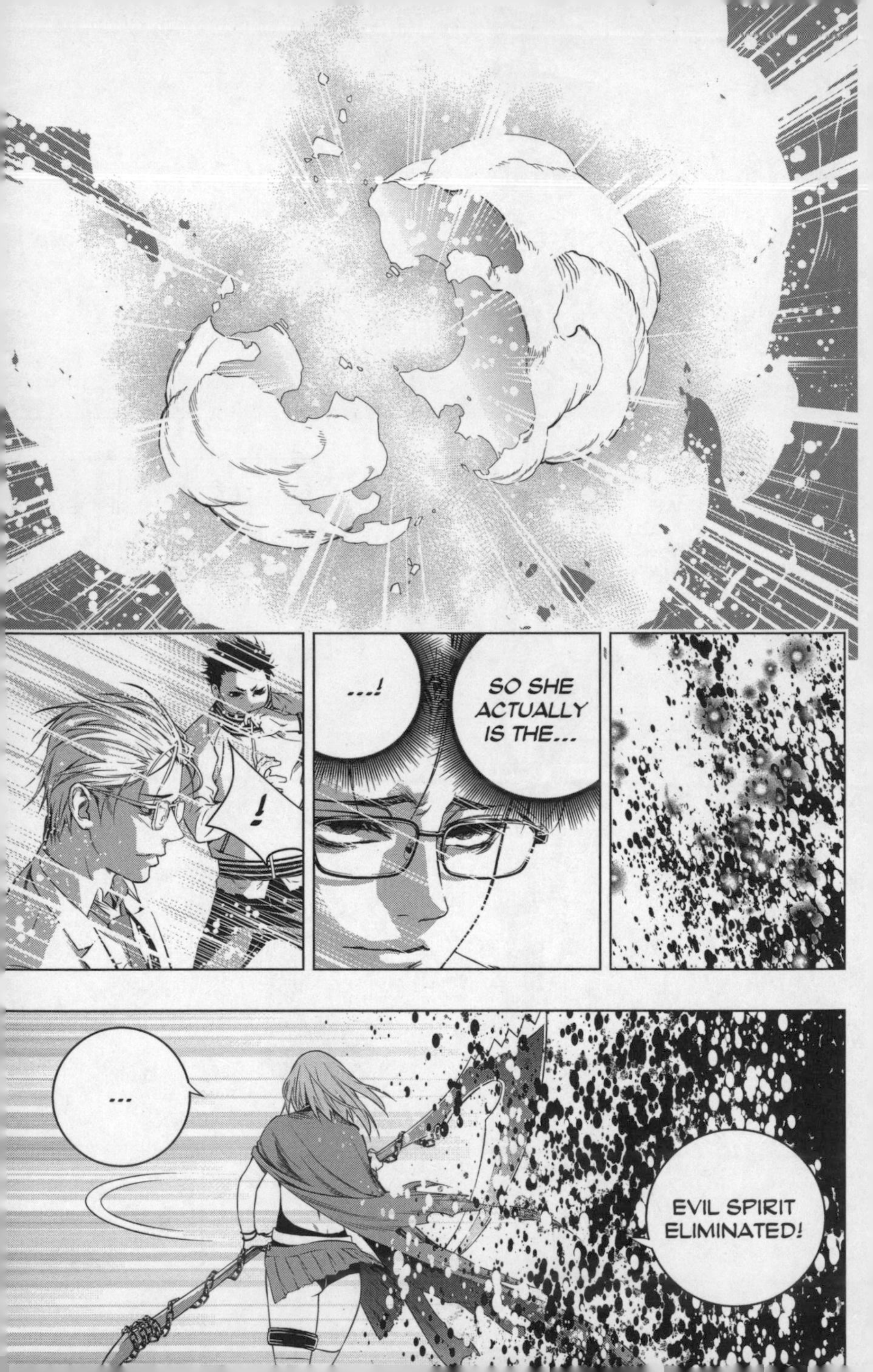
SO SHE ACTUALLY IS THE...
...!
!
EVIL SPIRIT ELIMINATED!
...

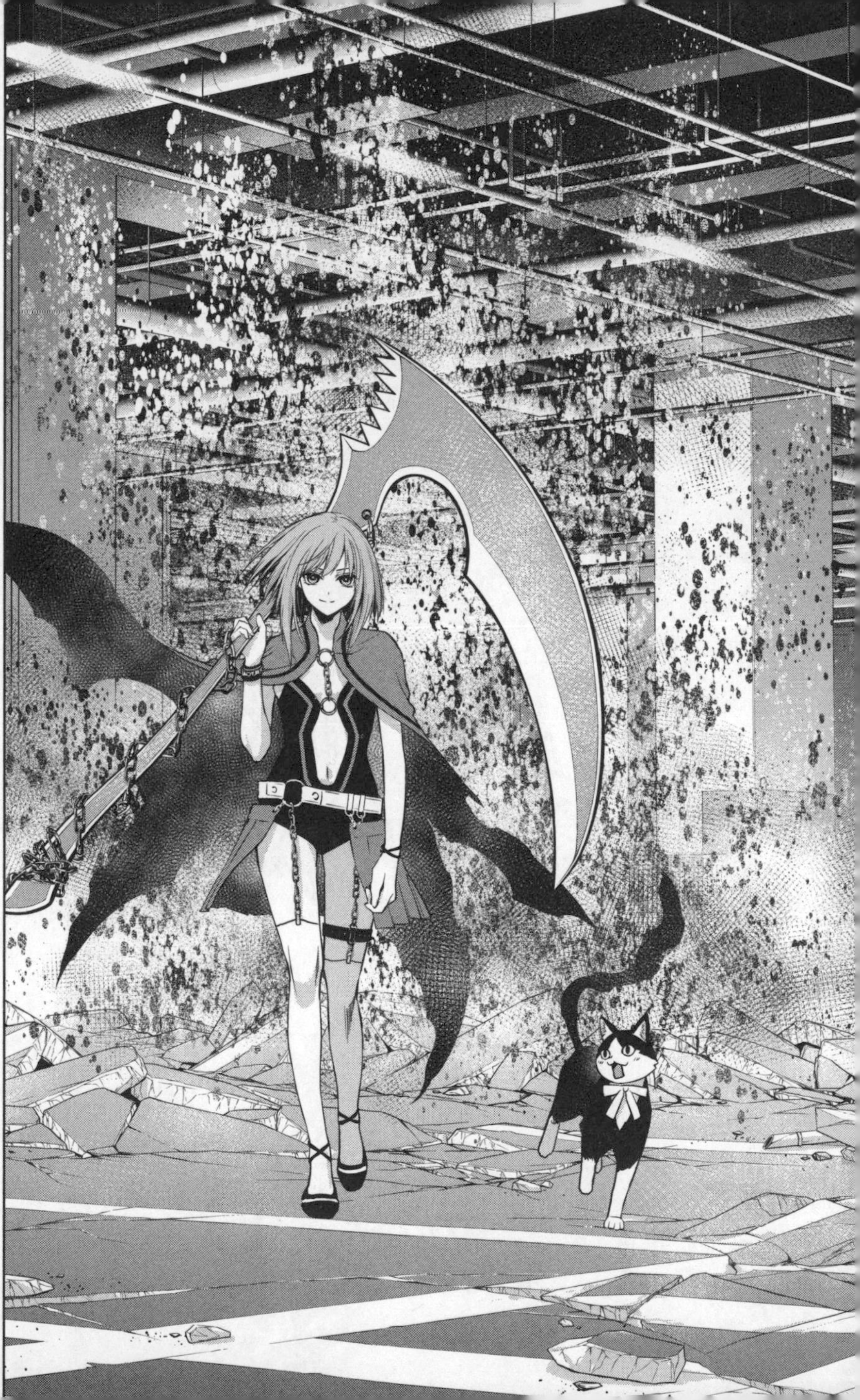

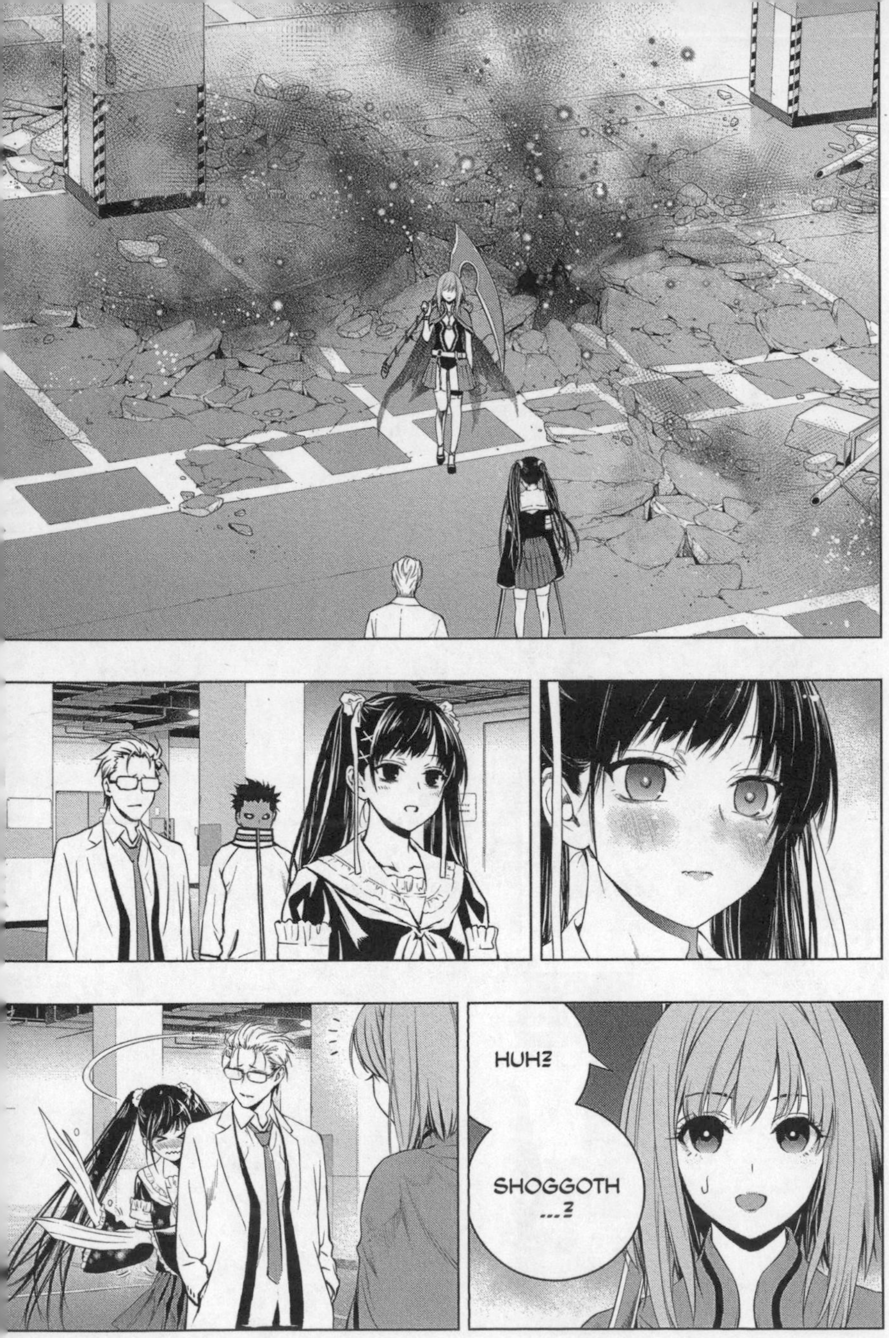
HUH?
SHOGGOTH
...?

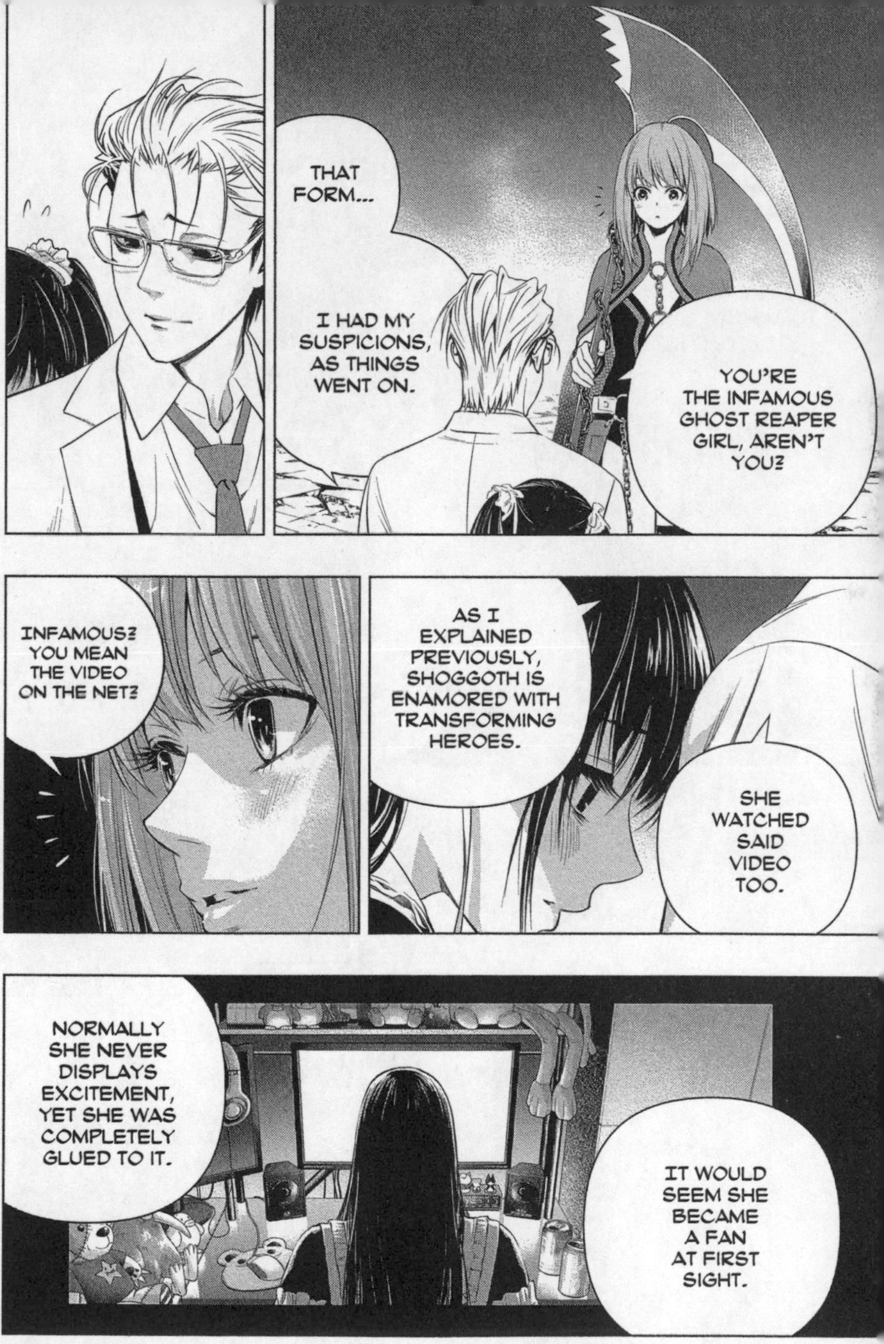
THAT FORM...
I HAD MY SUSPICIONS, AS THINGS WENT ON.
YOU'RE THE INFAMOUS GHOST REAPER GIRL, AREN'T YOU?
INFAMOUS? YOU MEAN THE VIDEO ON THE NET?
AS I EXPLAINED PREVIOUSLY, SHOGGOTH IS ENAMORED WITH TRANSFORMING HEROES.
SHE WATCHED SAID VIDEO TOO.
NORMALLY SHE NEVER DISPLAYS EXCITEMENT, YET SHE WAS COMPLETELY GLUED TO IT.
IT WOULD SEEM SHE BECAME A FAN AT FIRST SIGHT.

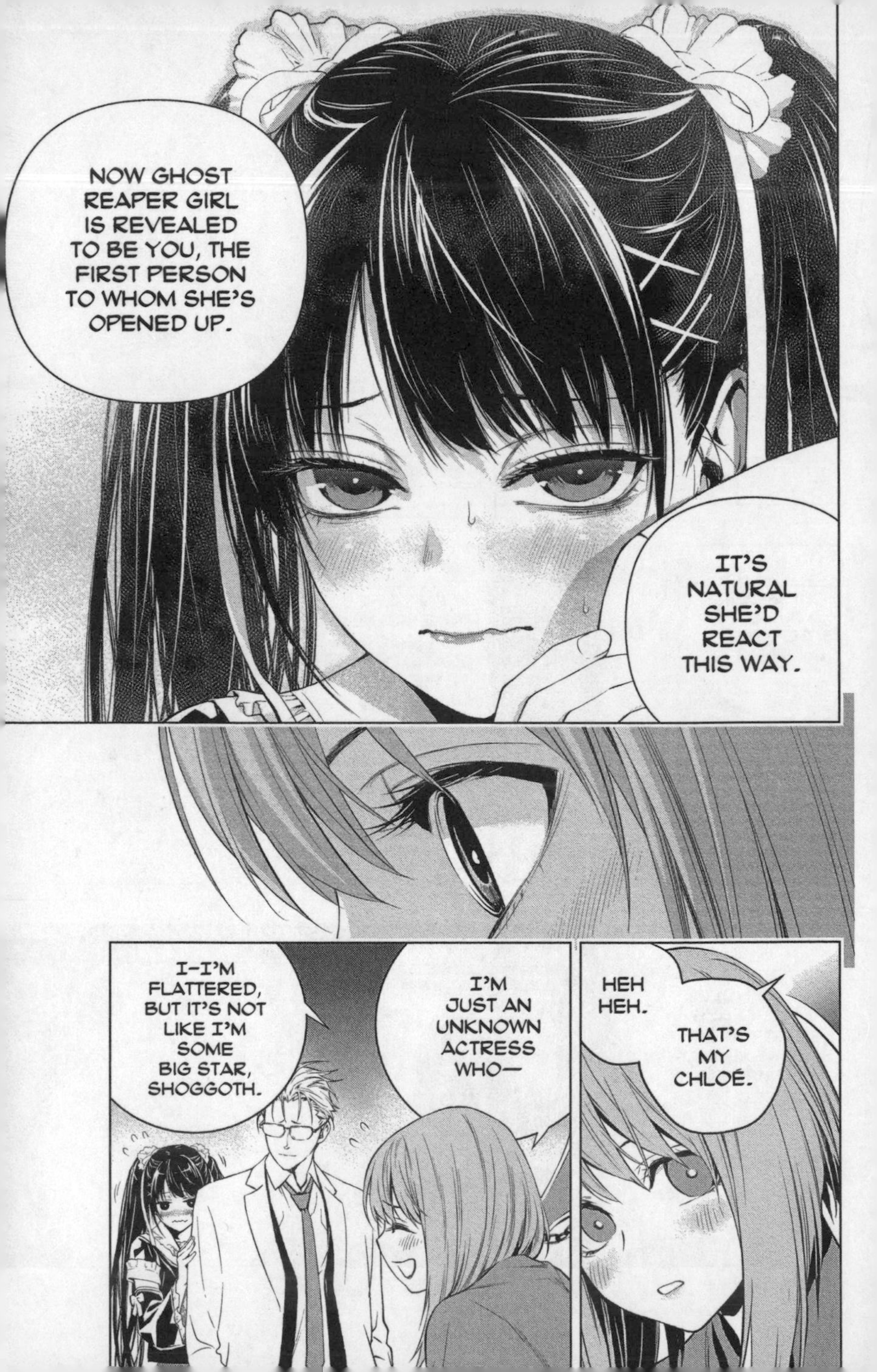
NOW GHOST REAPER GIRL IS REVEALED TO BE YOU, THE FIRST PERSON TO WHOM SHE'S OPENED UP.
IT'S NATURAL SHE'D REACT THIS WAY.
HEH HEH.
THAT'S MY CHLOÉ.
I-I'M FLATTERED, BUT IT'S NOT LIKE I'M SOME BIG STAR, SHOGGOTH.
I'M JUST AN UNKNOWN ACTRESS WHO—

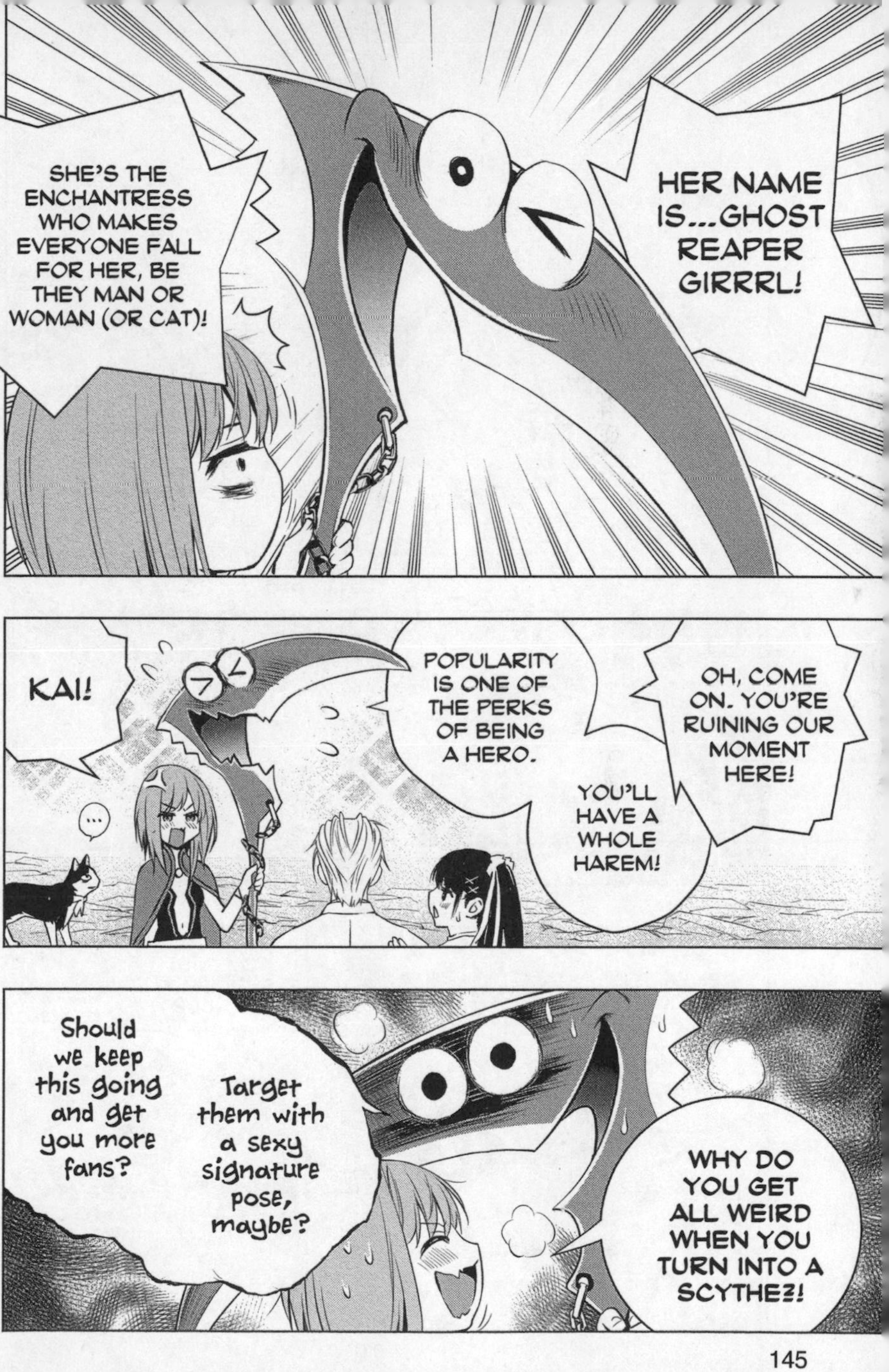
HER NAME IS...GHOST REAPER GIRRRL!
SHE'S THE ENCHANTRESS WHO MAKES EVERYONE FALL FOR HER, BE THEY MAN OR WOMAN (OR CAT)!
OH, COME ON. YOU'RE RUINING OUR MOMENT HERE!
YOU'LL HAVE A WHOLE HAREM!
POPULARITY IS ONE OF THE PERKS OF BEING A HERO.
KAI!
...
WHY DO YOU GET ALL WEIRD WHEN YOU TURN INTO A SCYTHE?!
Target them with a sexy signature pose, maybe?
Should we keep this going and get you more fans?

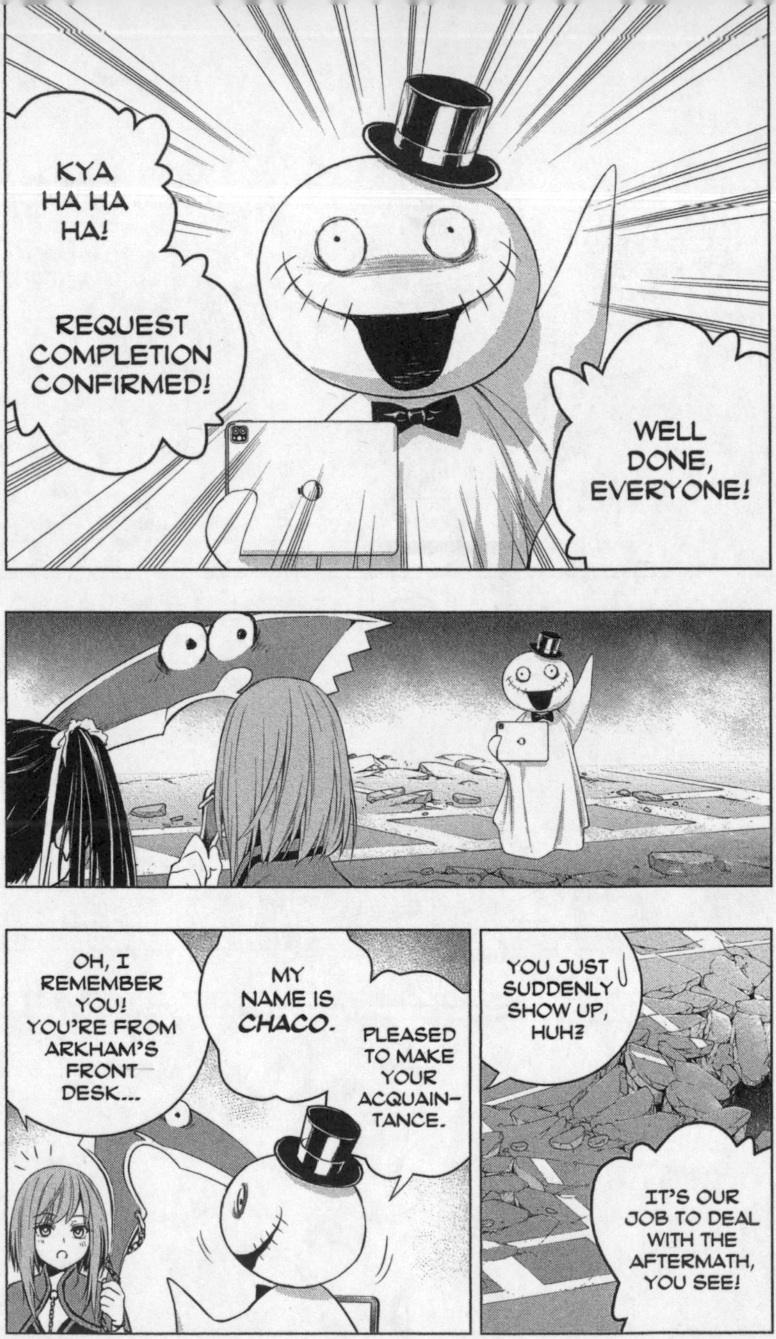
KYA HA HA HA!
REQUEST COMPLETION CONFIRMED!
WELL DONE, EVERYONE!
OH, I REMEMBER YOU! YOU'RE FROM ARKHAM'S FRONT DESK...
MY NAME IS *CHACO*.
PLEASED TO MAKE YOUR ACQUAINTANCE.
YOU JUST SUDDENLY SHOW UP, HUH?
IT'S OUR JOB TO DEAL WITH THE AFTERMATH, YOU SEE!

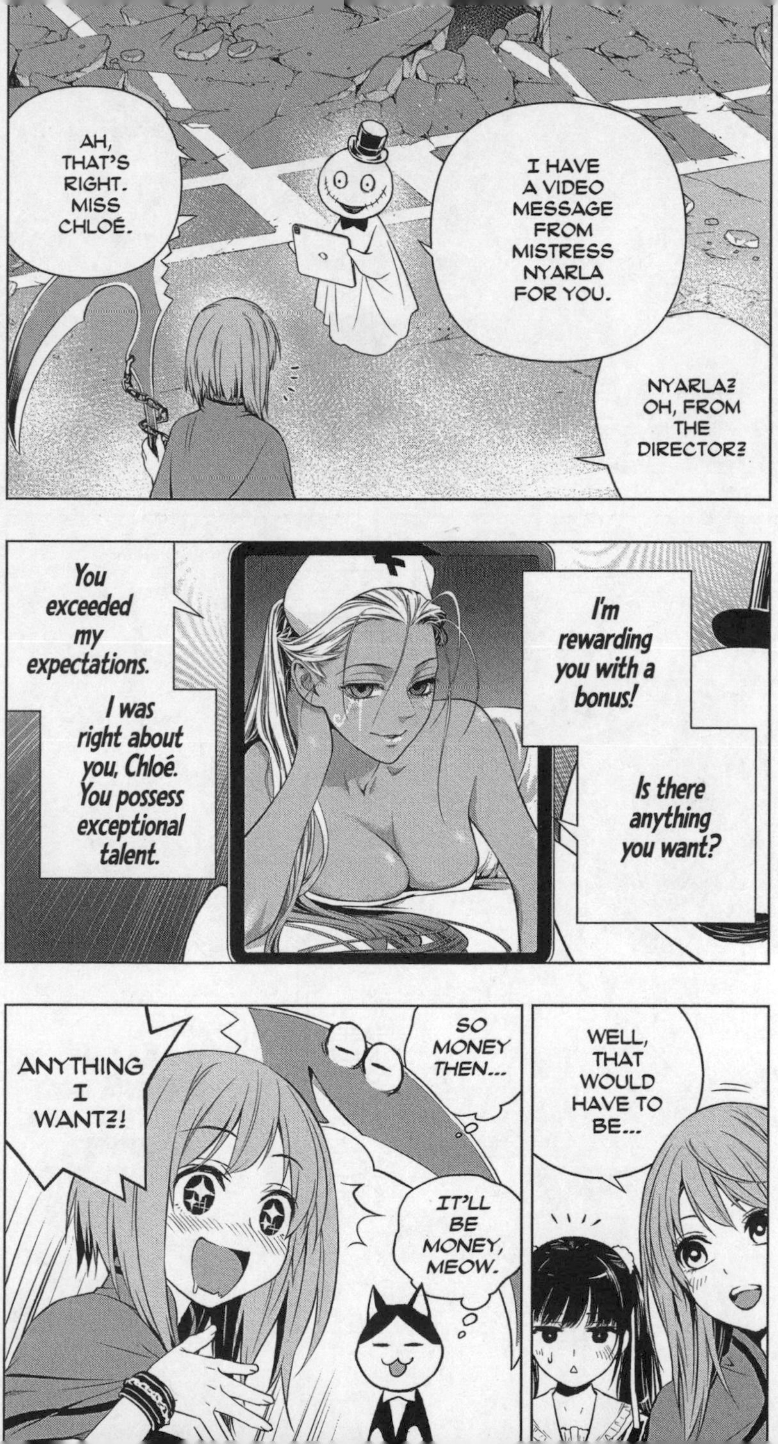
AH, THAT'S RIGHT. MISS CHLOÉ.
I HAVE A VIDEO MESSAGE FROM MISTRESS NYARLA FOR YOU.
NYARLA? OH, FROM THE DIRECTOR?
You exceeded my expectations.
I was right about you, Chloé. You possess exceptional talent.
I'm rewarding you with a bonus!
Is there anything you want?
ANYTHING I WANT?!
SO MONEY THEN...
IT'LL BE MONEY, MEOW.
WELL, THAT WOULD HAVE TO BE...

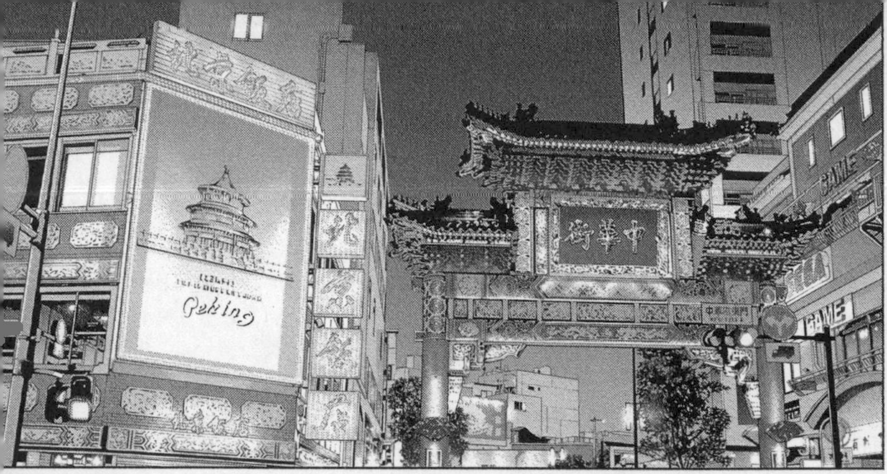
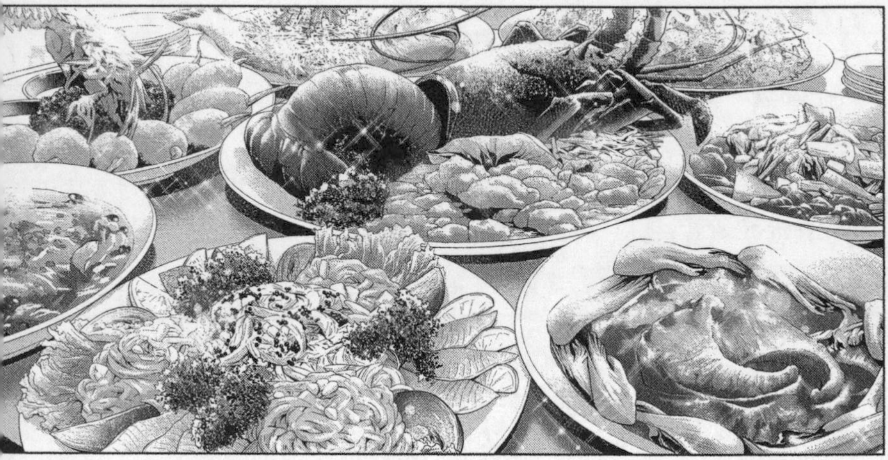
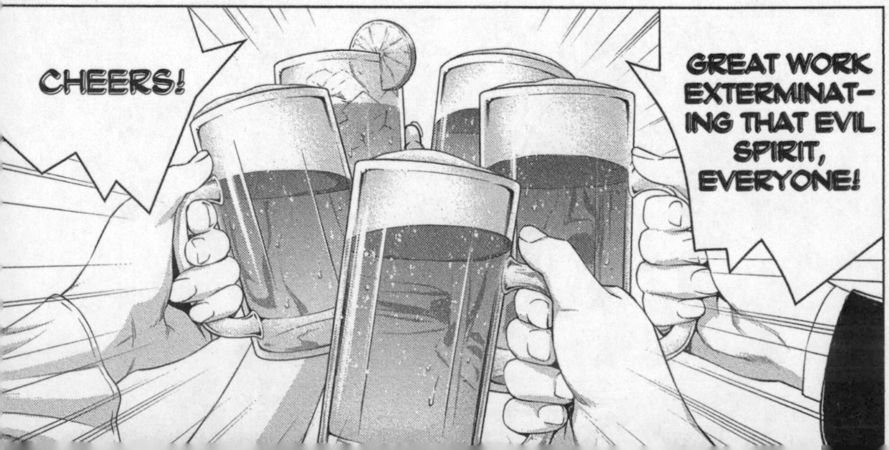
GREAT WORK EXTERMINAT-ING THAT EVIL SPIRIT, EVERYONE!
CHEERS!

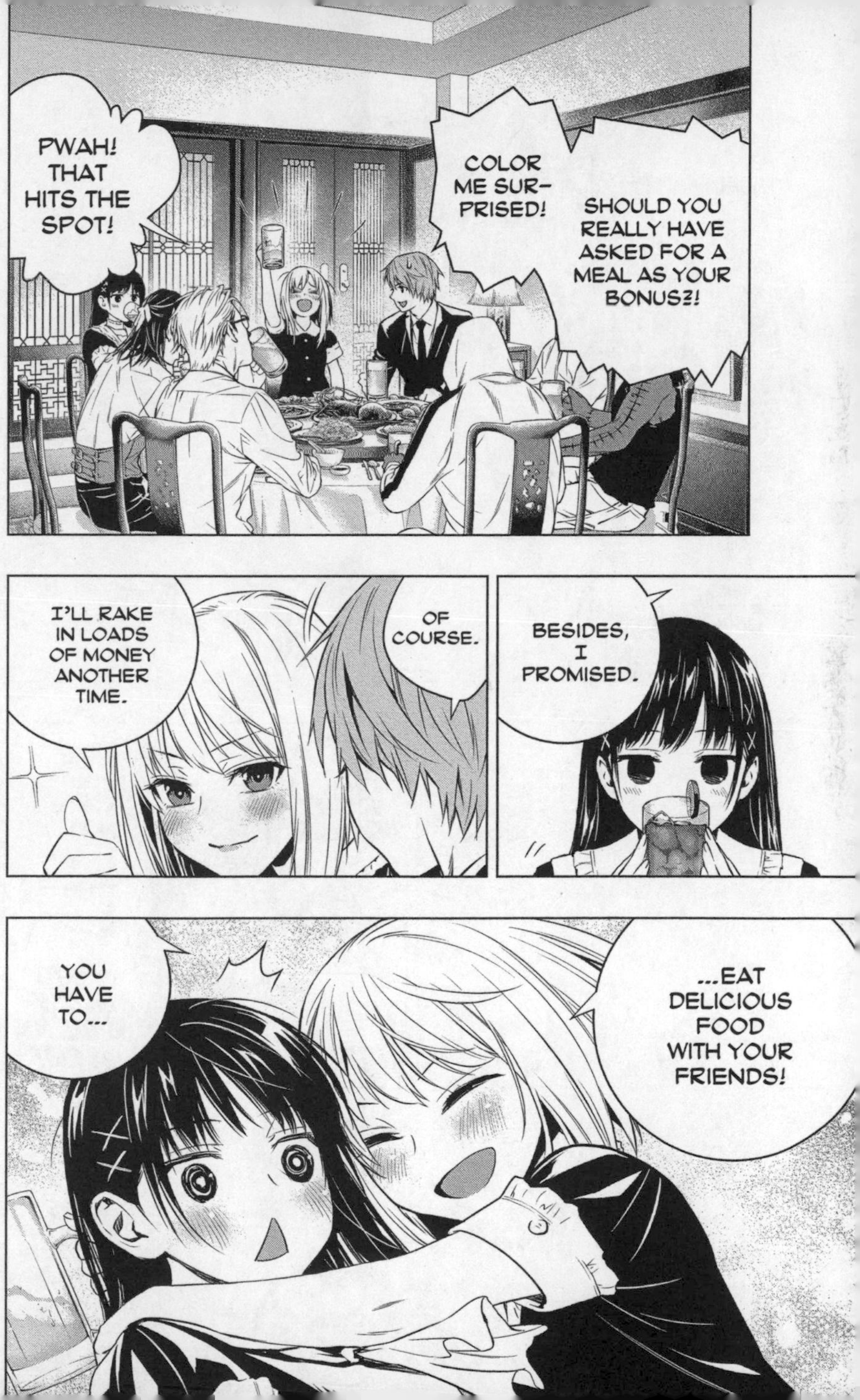
PWAH! THAT HITS THE SPOT!
COLOR ME SUR-PRISED!
SHOULD YOU REALLY HAVE ASKED FOR A MEAL AS YOUR BONUS?!
I'LL RAKE IN LOADS OF MONEY ANOTHER TIME.
OF COURSE.
BESIDES, I PROMISED.
YOU HAVE TO...
...EAT DELICIOUS FOOD WITH YOUR FRIENDS!

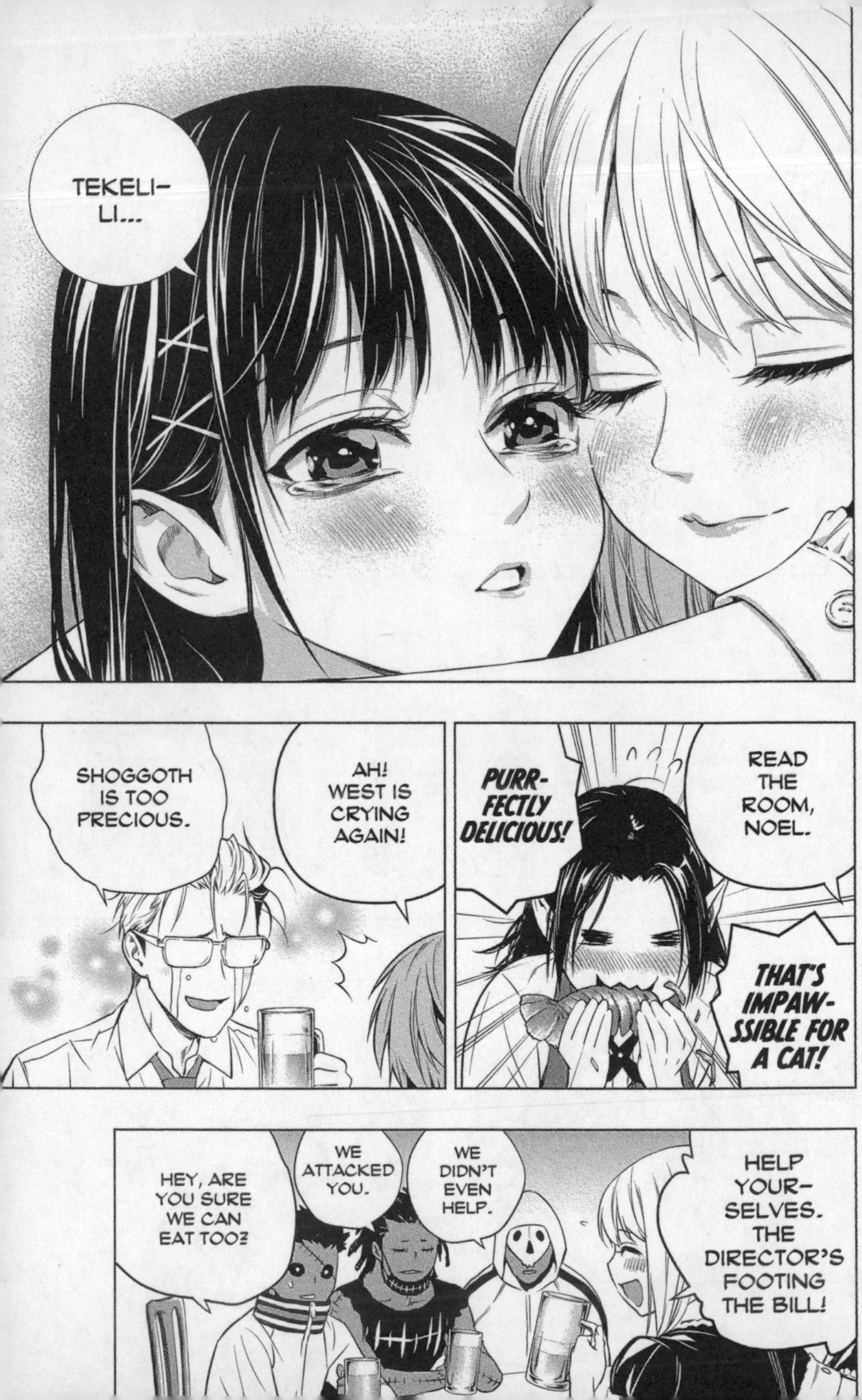
TEKELI-LI...
PURR-FECTLY DELICIOUS!
READ THE ROOM, NOEL.
THAT'S IMPAW-SSIBLE FOR A CAT!
AH! WEST IS CRYING AGAIN!
SHOGGOTH IS TOO PRECIOUS.
HELP YOUR-SELVES. THE DIRECTOR'S FOOTING THE BILL!
WE DIDN'T EVEN HELP.
WE ATTACKED YOU.
HEY, ARE YOU SURE WE CAN EAT TOO?

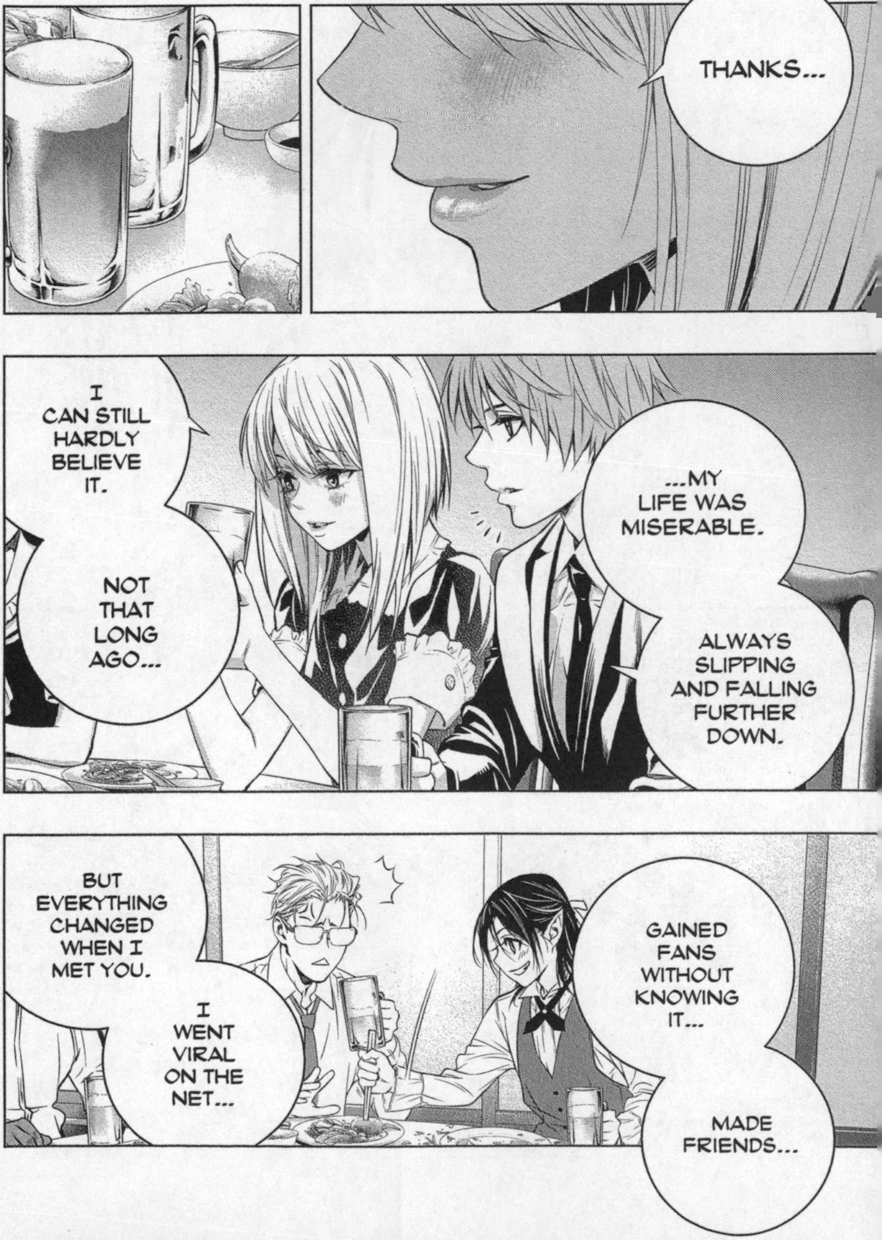
THANKS...
I CAN STILL HARDLY BELIEVE IT.
NOT THAT LONG AGO...
...MY LIFE WAS MISERABLE.
ALWAYS SLIPPING AND FALLING FURTHER DOWN.
BUT EVERYTHING CHANGED WHEN I MET YOU.
I WENT VIRAL ON THE NET...
GAINED FANS WITHOUT KNOWING IT...
MADE FRIENDS...

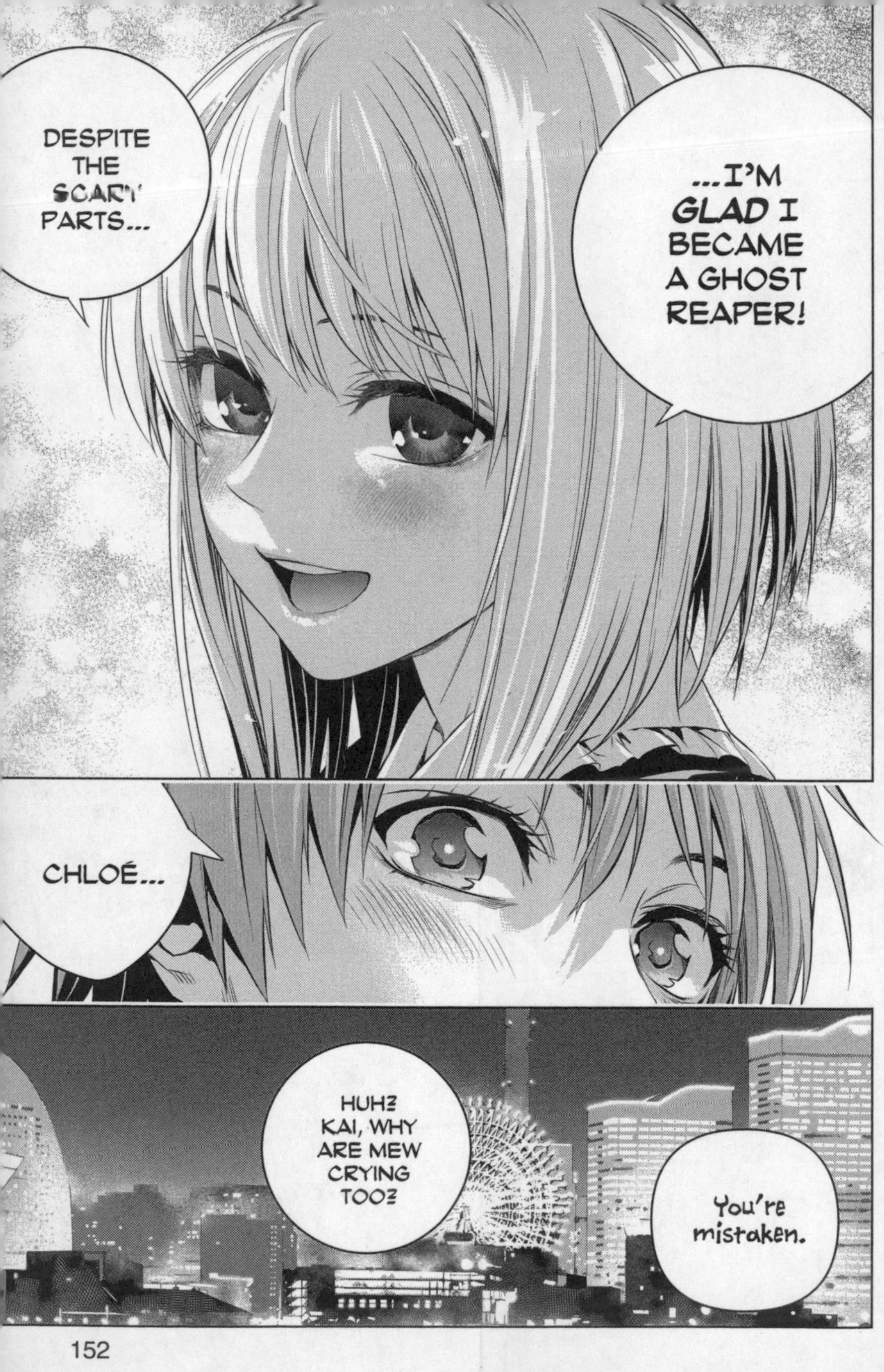
DESPITE THE SCARY PARTS...
...I'M GLAD I BECAME A GHOST REAPER!
CHLOÉ...
You're mistaken.
HUH? KAI, WHY ARE MEW CRYING TOO?

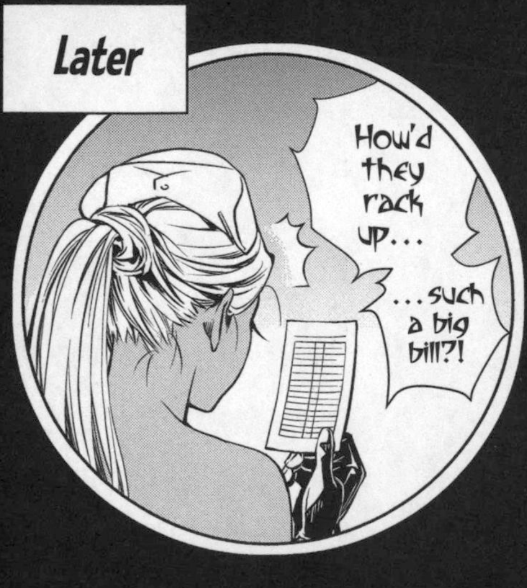
Later
How'd they rack up...
...such a big bill?!

GHOST REAPER GIRL

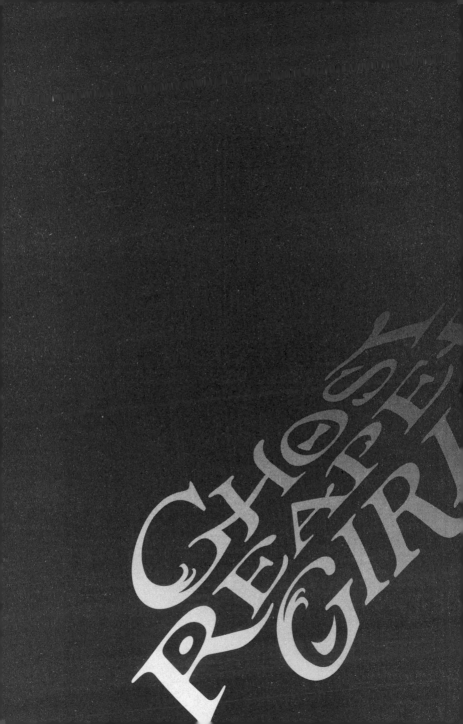

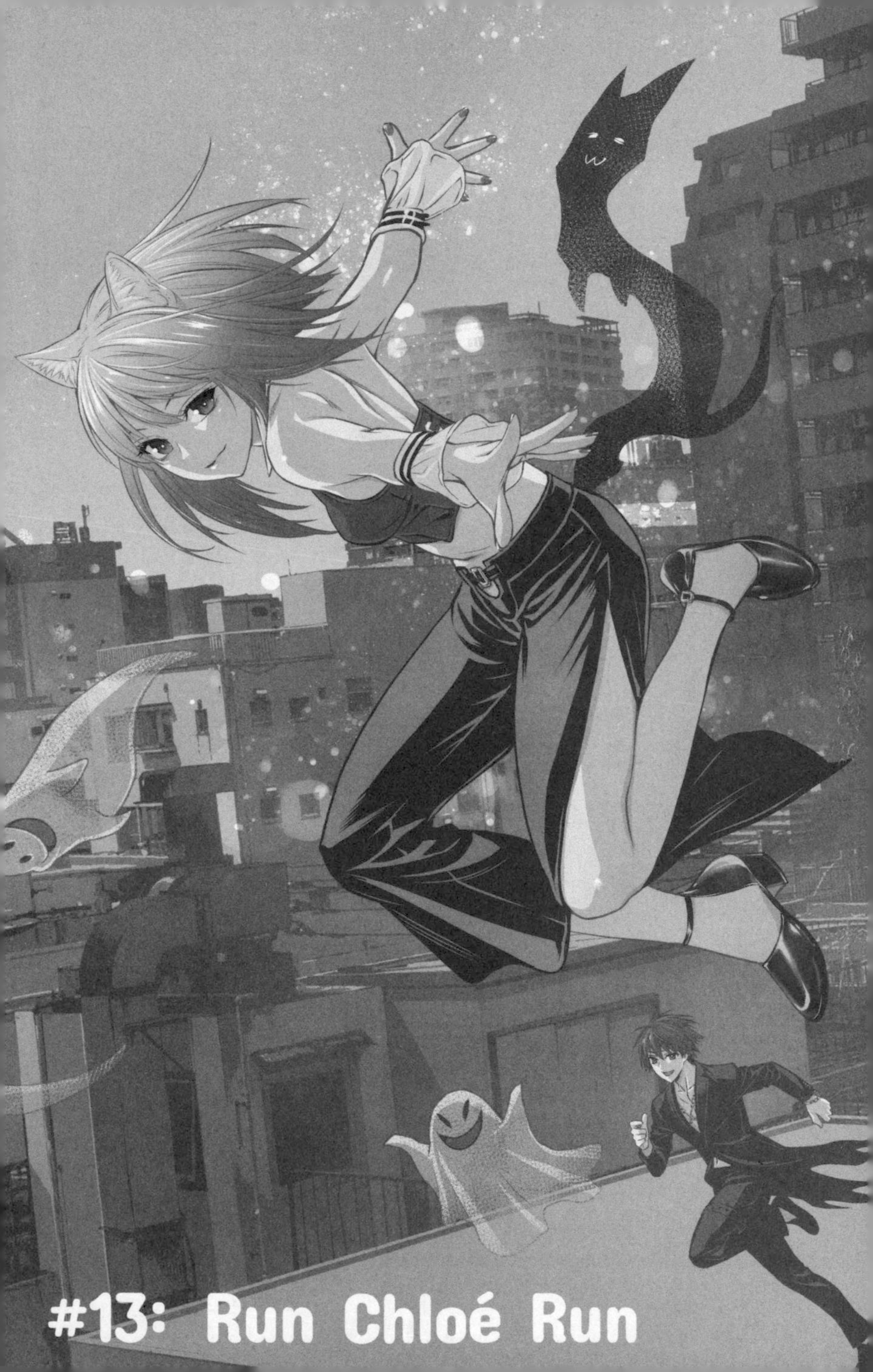

#13: Run Chloé Run

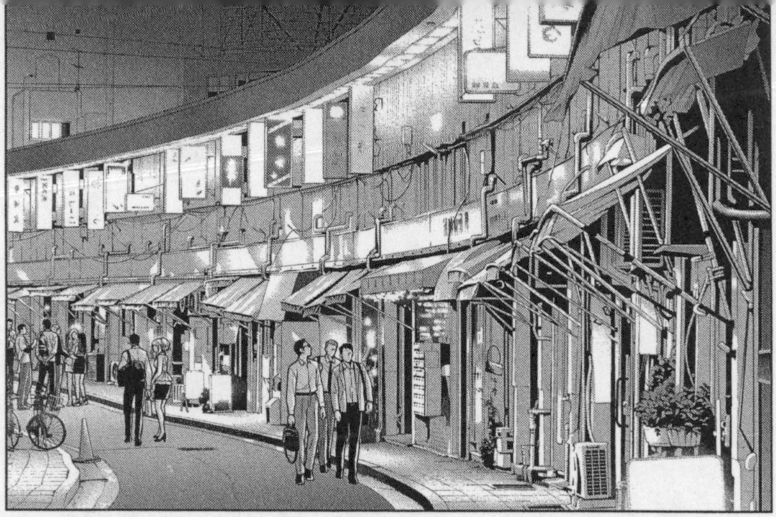
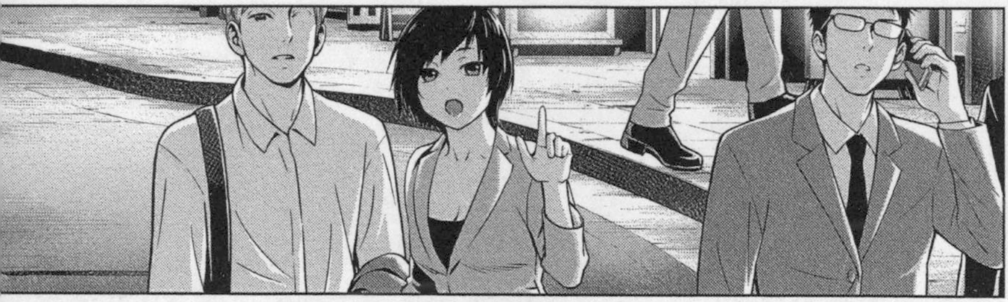
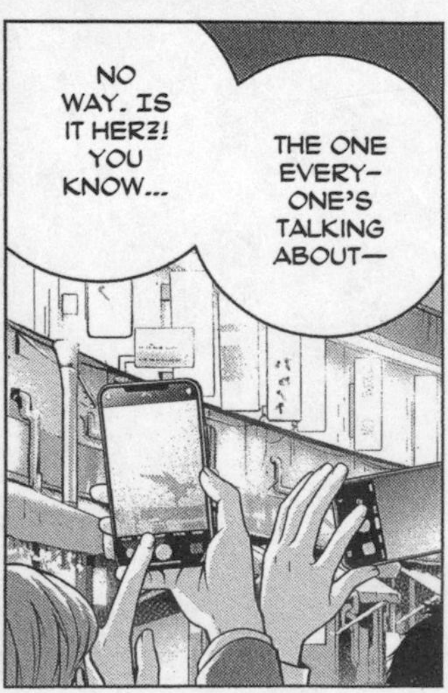
NO WAY. IS IT HER?! YOU KNOW...
THE ONE EVERYONE'S TALKING ABOUT—
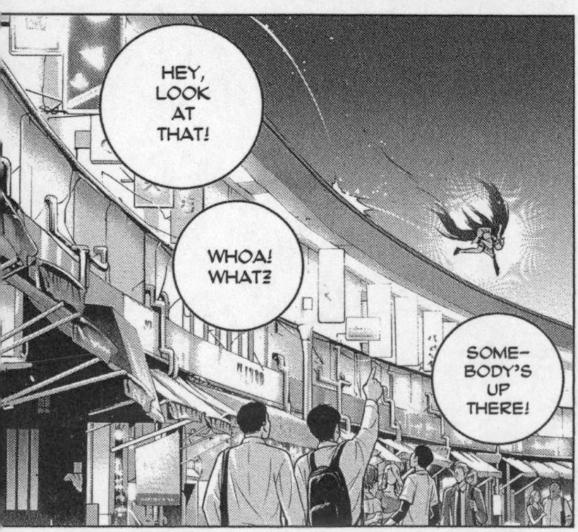
HEY, LOOK AT THAT!
WHOA! WHAT?
SOMEBODY'S UP THERE!

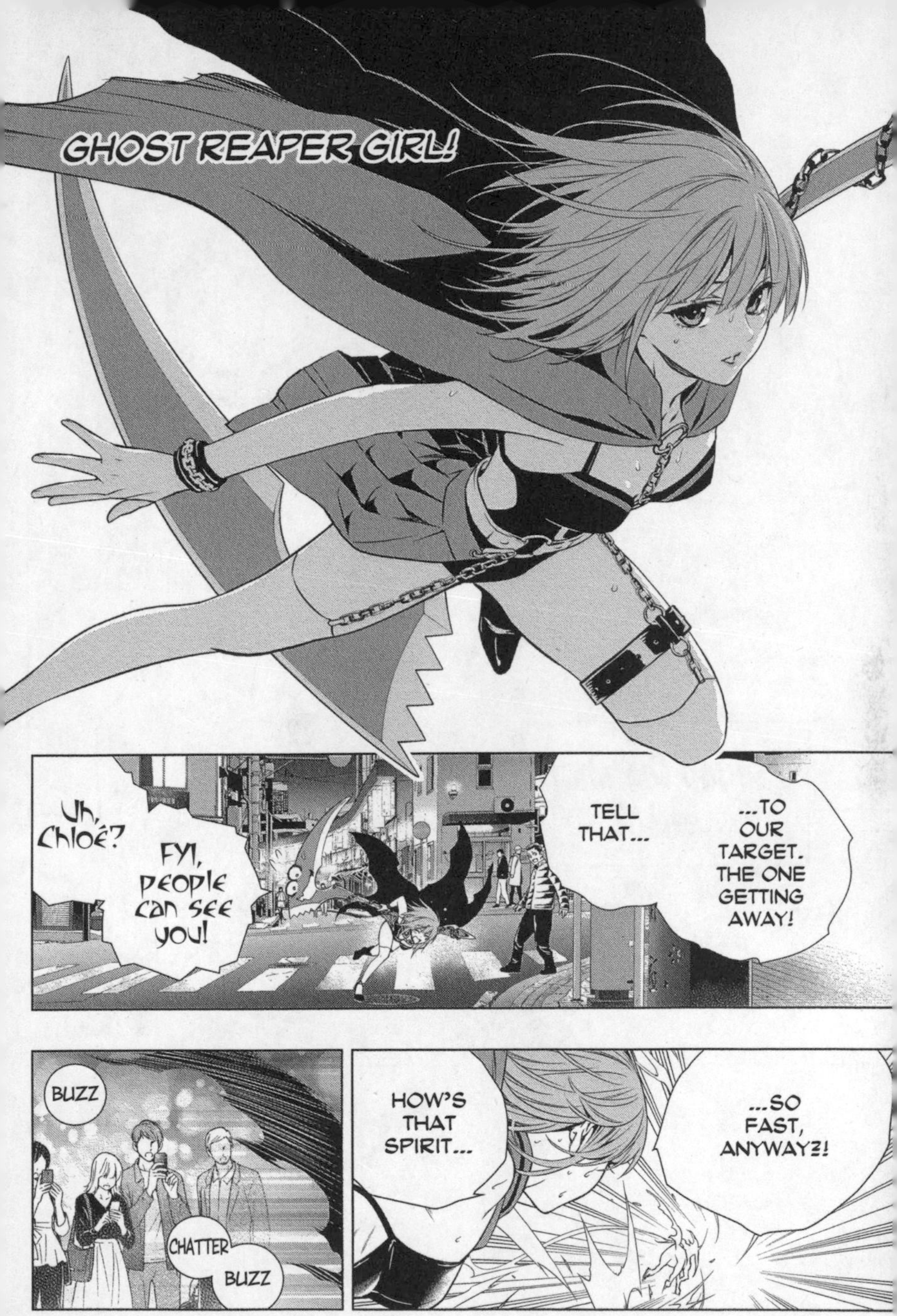
GHOST REAPER GIRL!
Uh, Chloé?
FYI, people can see you!
TELL THAT...
...TO OUR TARGET. THE ONE GETTING AWAY!
BUZZ
CHATTER
BUZZ
HOW'S THAT SPIRIT...
...SO FAST, ANYWAY?!

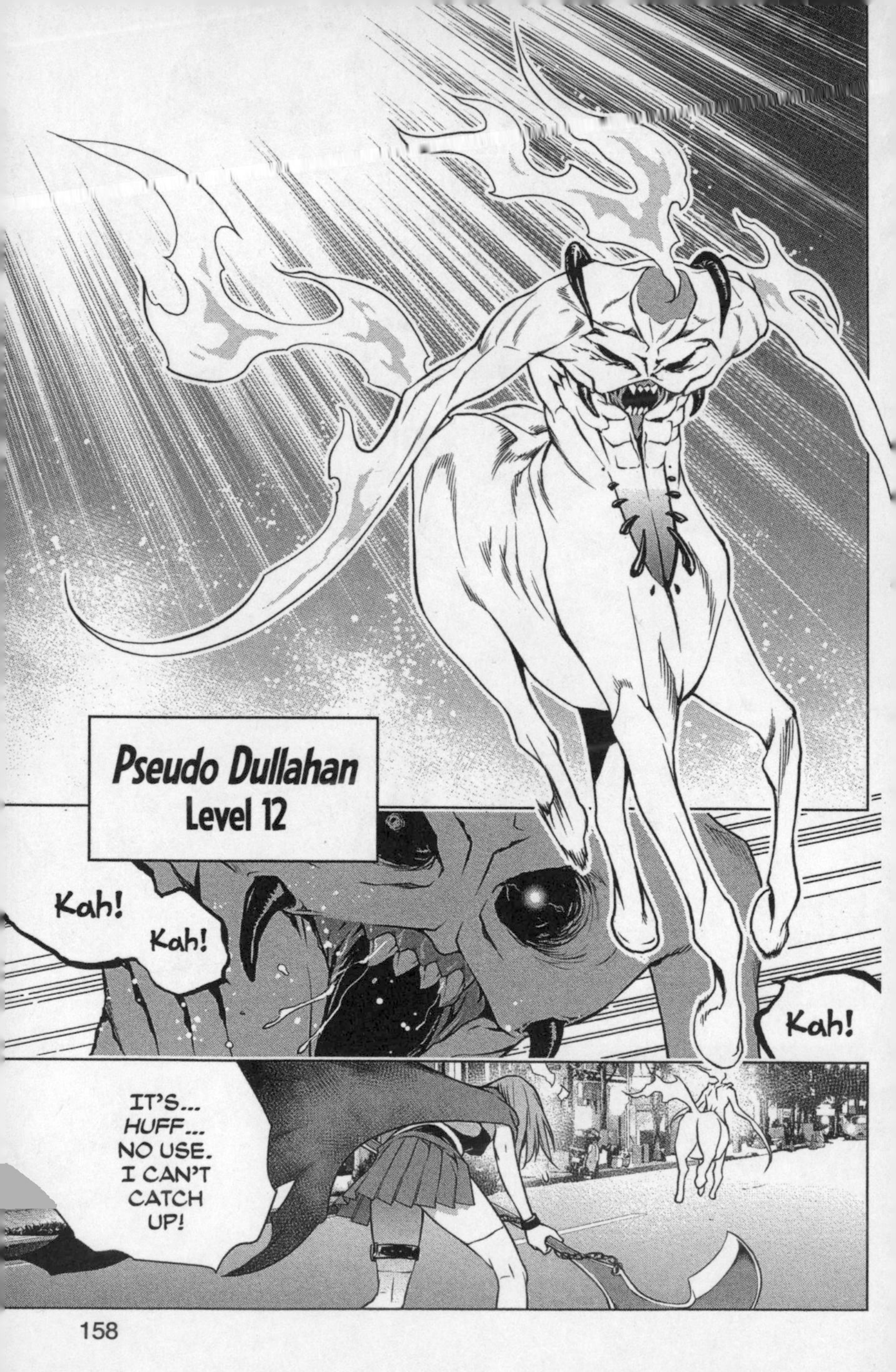
Pseudo Dullahan
Level 12
Kah!
Kah!
Kah!
IT'S... HUFF... NO USE. I CAN'T CATCH UP!

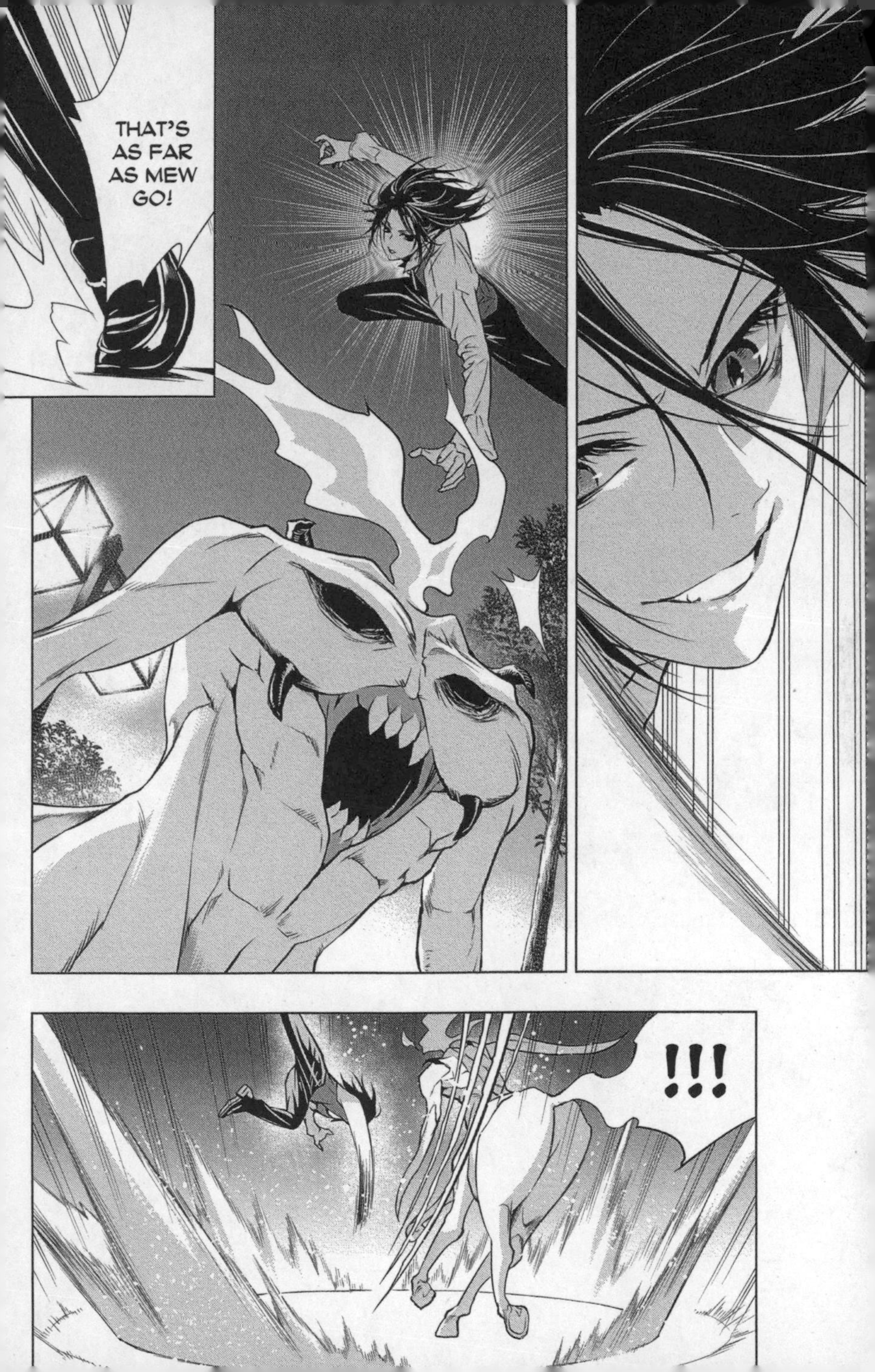
THAT'S AS FAR AS MEW GO!
!!!

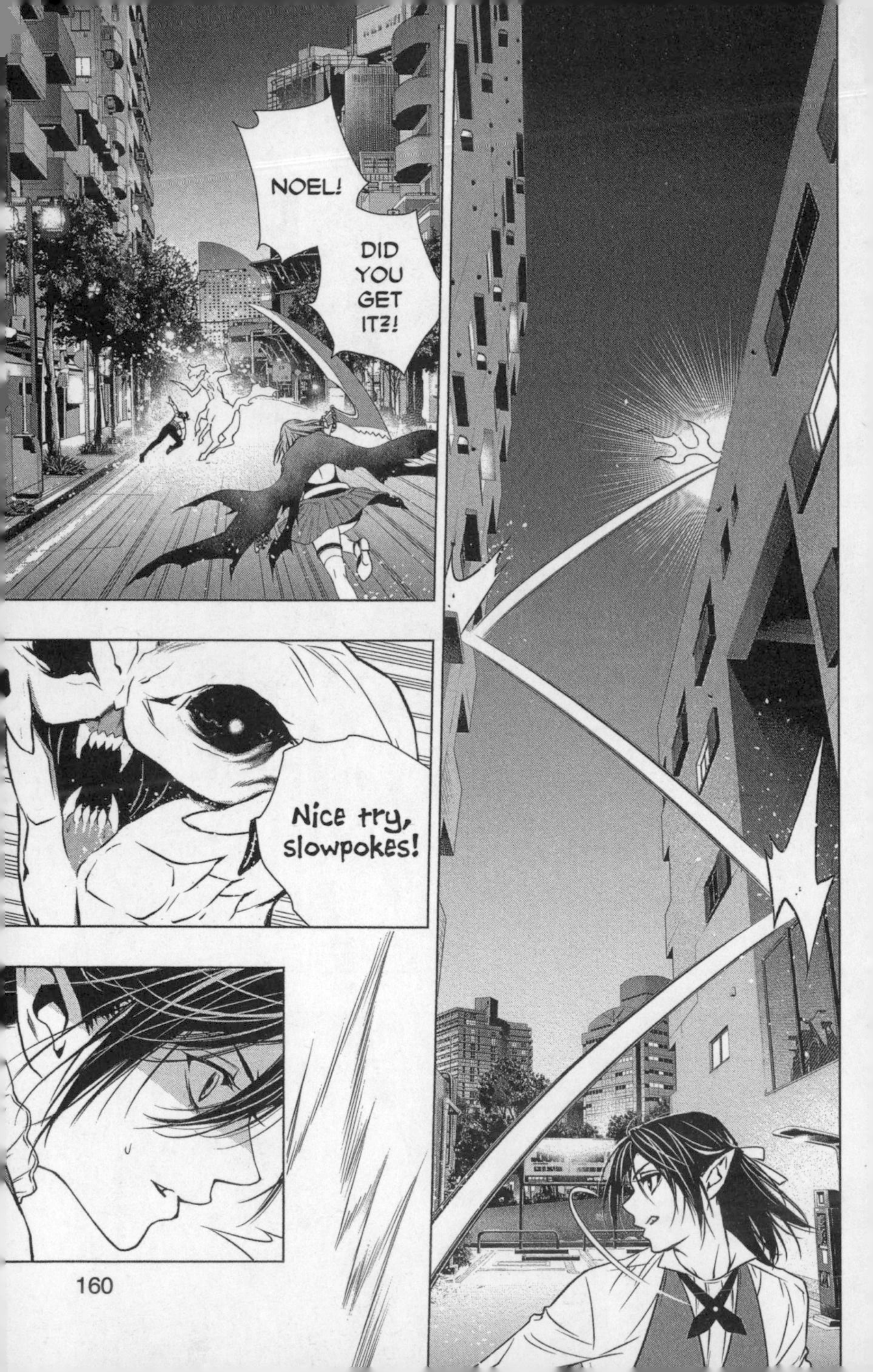
NOEL!
DID YOU GET IT?!
Nice try, slowpokes!

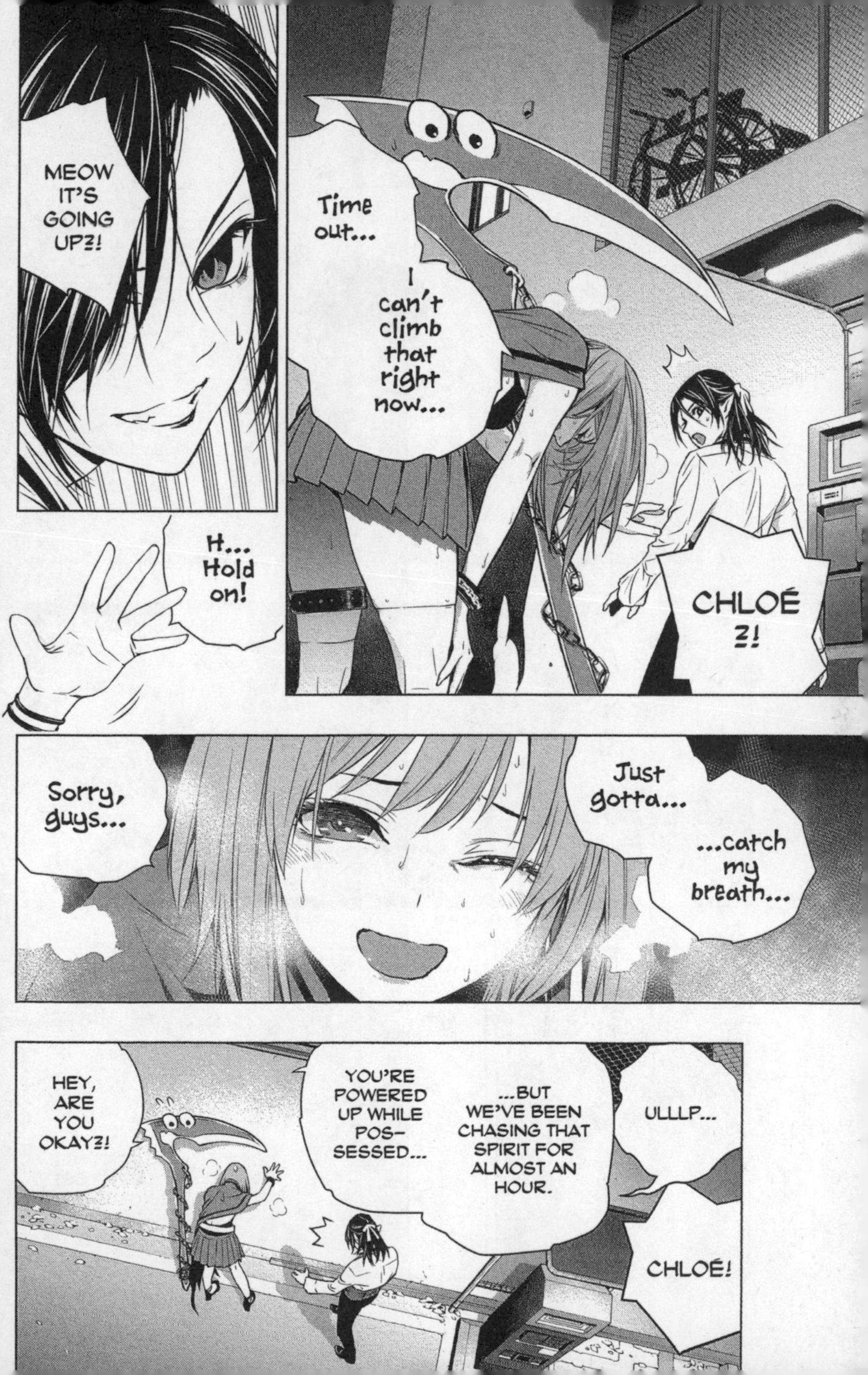
MEOW IT'S GOING UP?!
Time out...
I can't climb that right now...
H... Hold on!
CHLOÉ?!
Sorry, guys...
Just gotta...
...catch my breath...
HEY, ARE YOU OKAY?!
YOU'RE POWERED UP WHILE POS-SESSED...
...BUT WE'VE BEEN CHASING THAT SPIRIT FOR ALMOST AN HOUR.
ULLLP...
CHLOÉ!

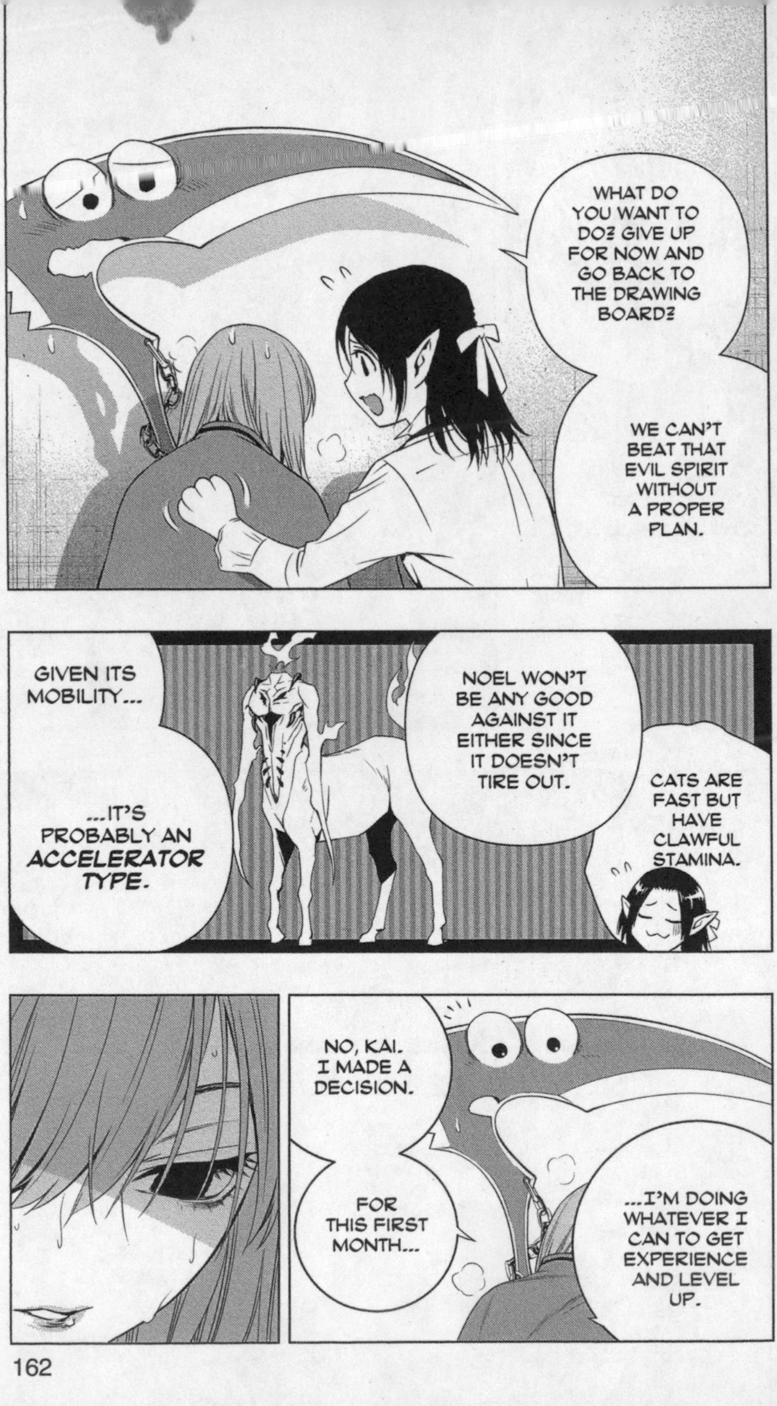
WHAT DO YOU WANT TO DO? GIVE UP FOR NOW AND GO BACK TO THE DRAWING BOARD?
WE CAN'T BEAT THAT EVIL SPIRIT WITHOUT A PROPER PLAN.
NOEL WON'T BE ANY GOOD AGAINST IT EITHER SINCE IT DOESN'T TIRE OUT.
CATS ARE FAST BUT HAVE CLAWFUL STAMINA.
GIVEN ITS MOBILITY...
...IT'S PROBABLY AN ACCELERATOR TYPE.
NO, KAI. I MADE A DECISION.
FOR THIS FIRST MONTH...
...I'M DOING WHATEVER I CAN TO GET EXPERIENCE AND LEVEL UP.

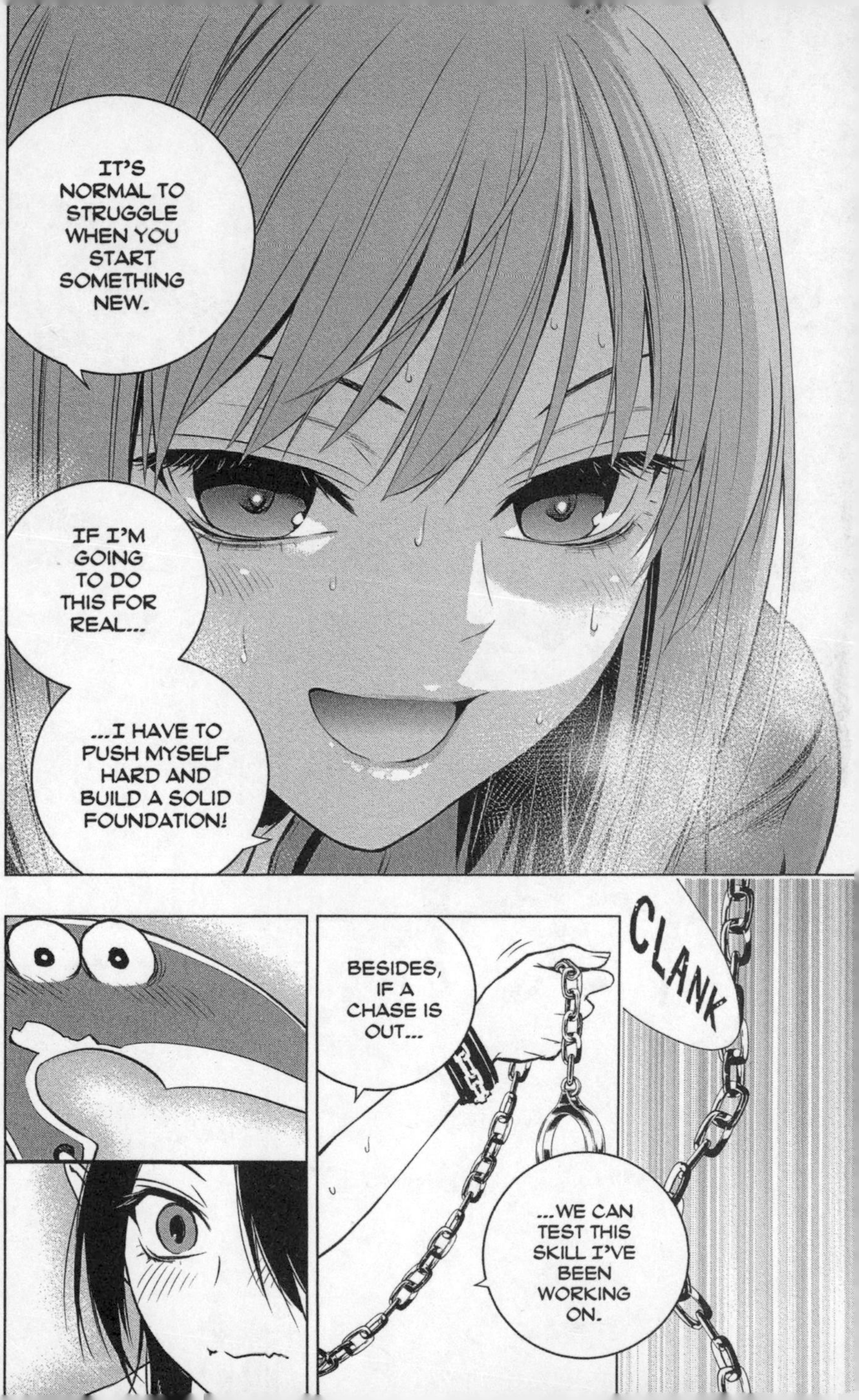
IT'S NORMAL TO STRUGGLE WHEN YOU START SOMETHING NEW.
IF I'M GOING TO DO THIS FOR REAL...
...I HAVE TO PUSH MYSELF HARD AND BUILD A SOLID FOUNDATION!
CLANK
BESIDES, IF A CHASE IS OUT...
...WE CAN TEST THIS SKILL I'VE BEEN WORKING ON.

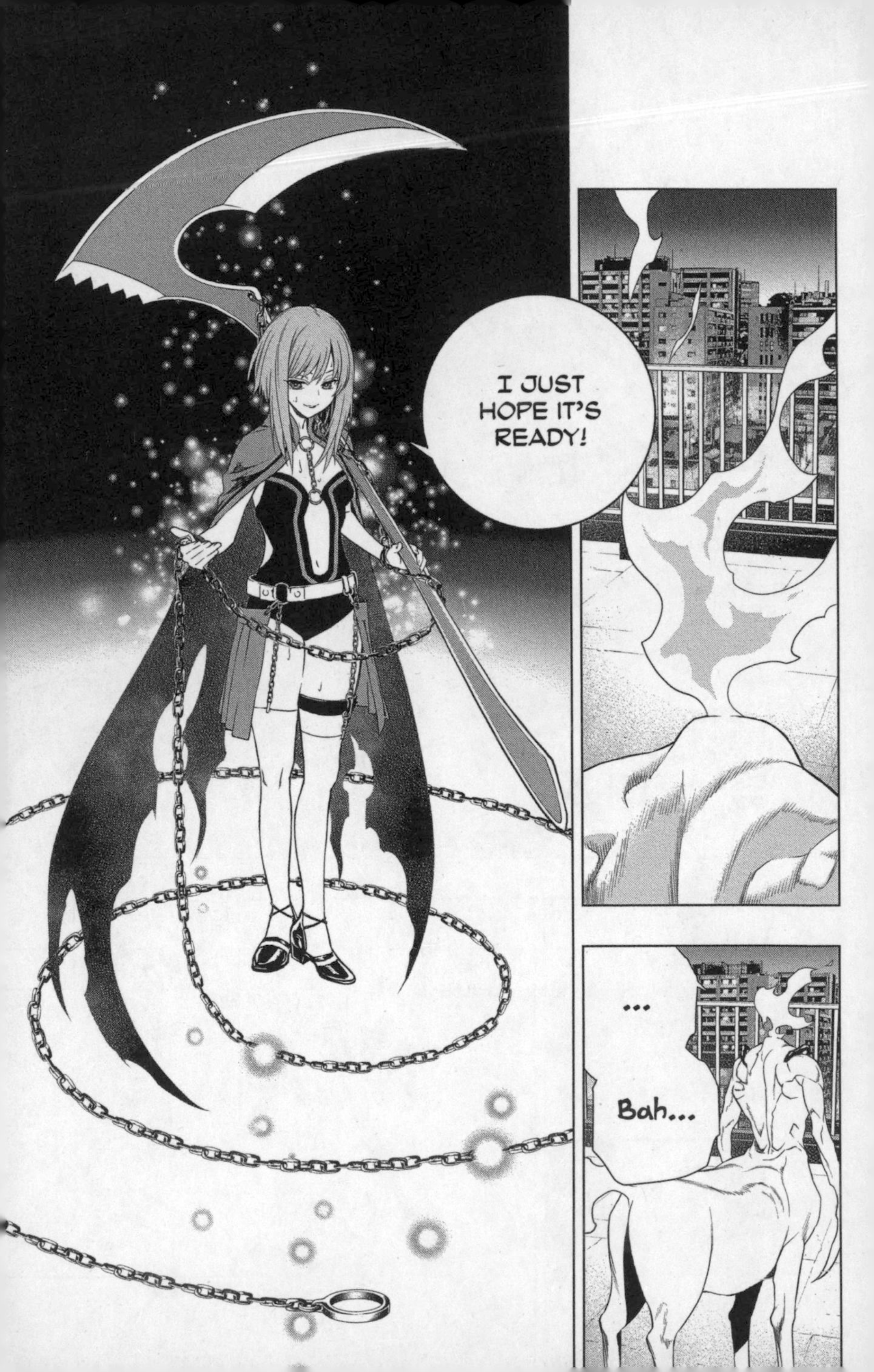
I JUST HOPE IT'S READY!
...
Bah...

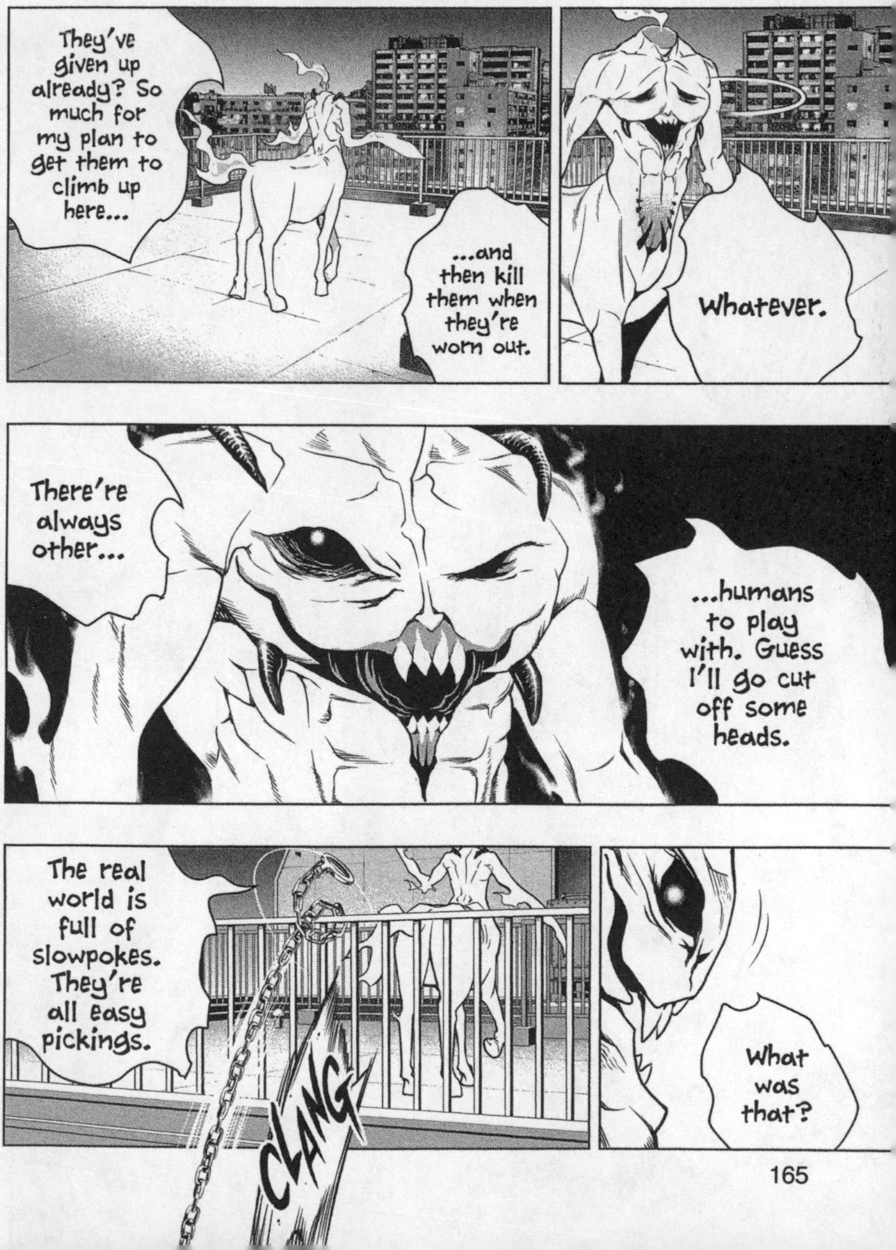
They've given up already? So much for my plan to get them to climb up here...
...and then kill them when they're worn out.
Whatever.
There're always other...
...humans to play with. Guess I'll go cut off some heads.
The real world is full of slowpokes. They're all easy pickings.
CLANG
What was that?

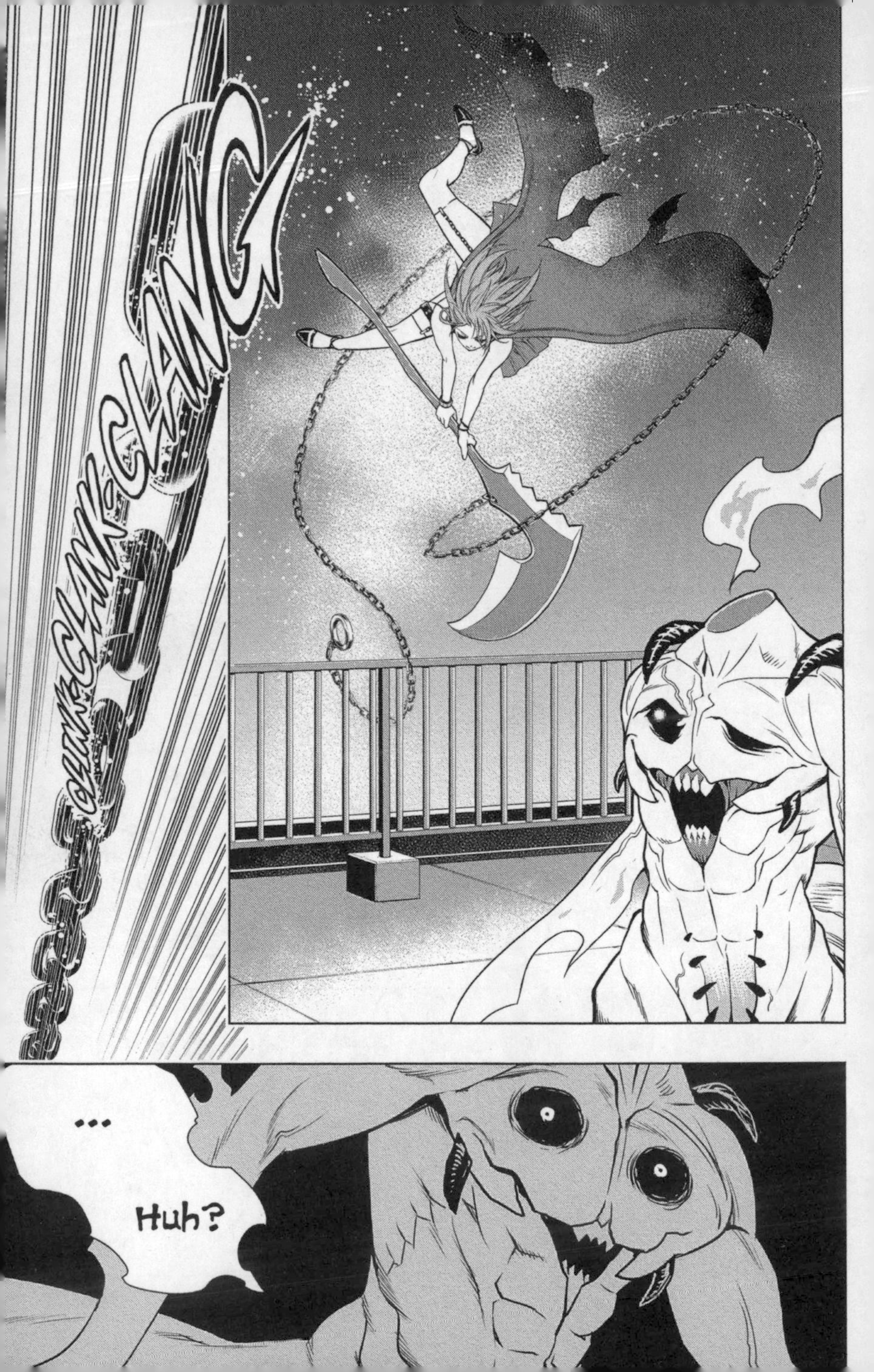
CHINK CLINK CLANG
...
Huh?

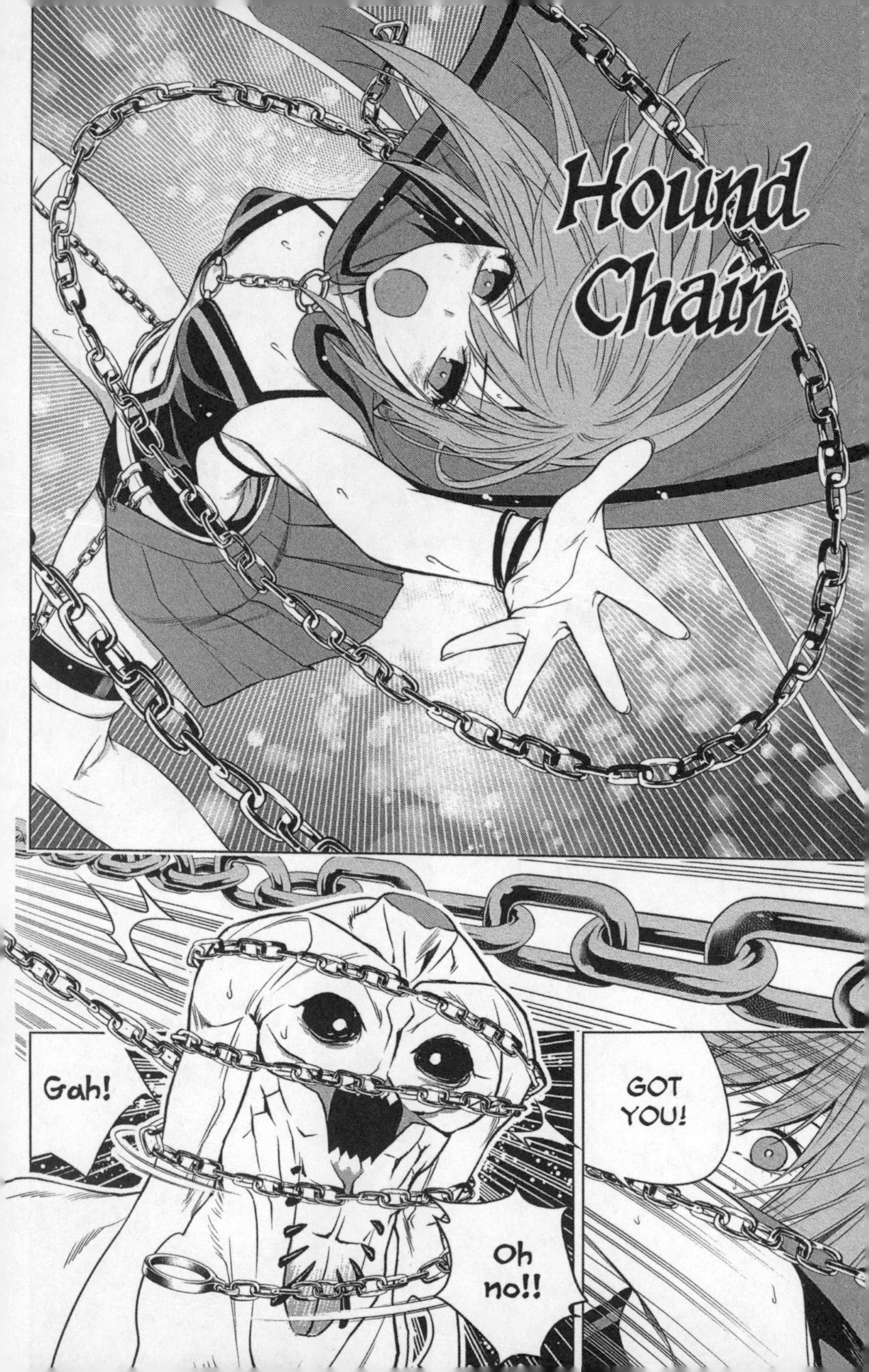
Hound Chain
GOT YOU!
Gah!
Oh no!!

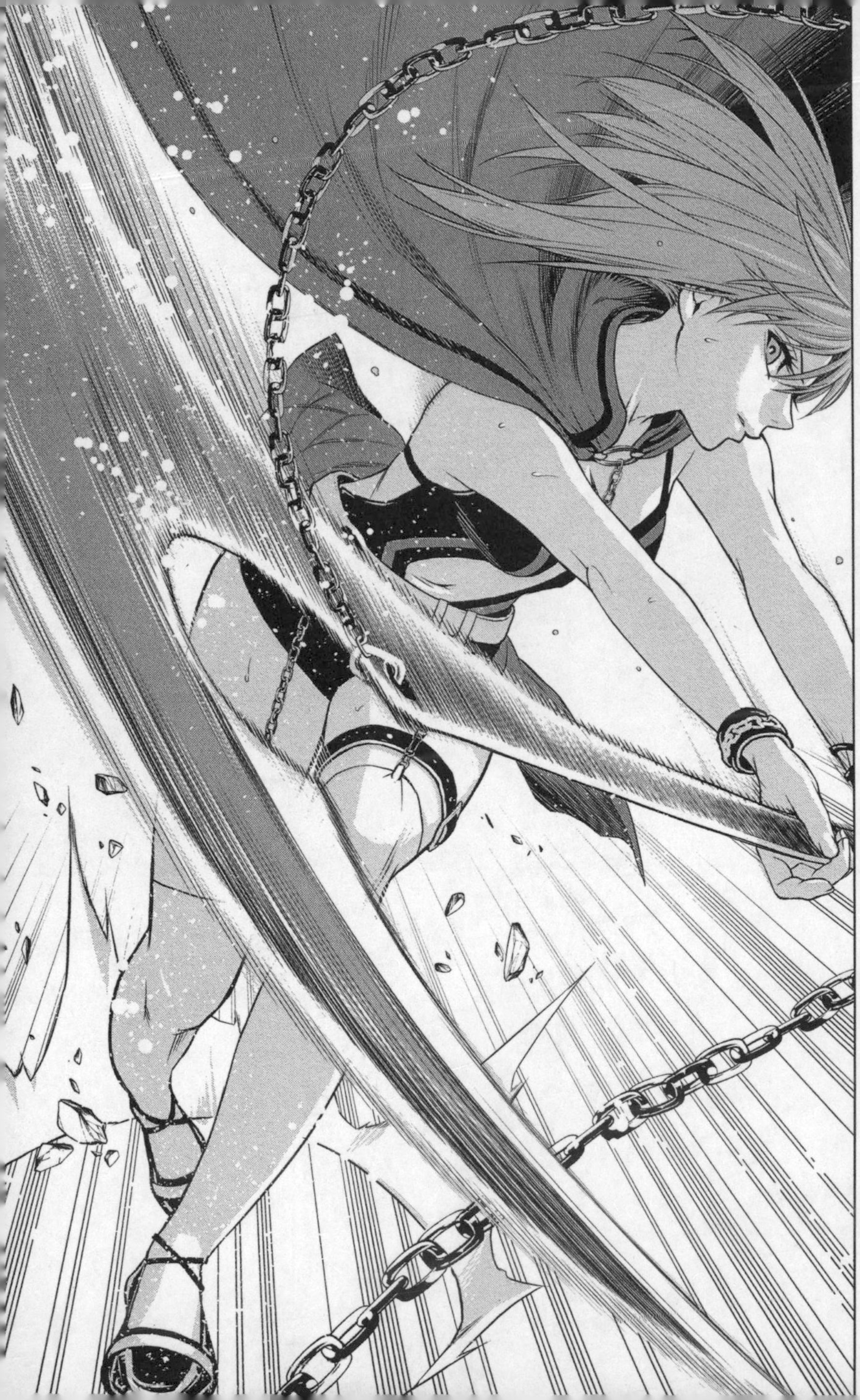

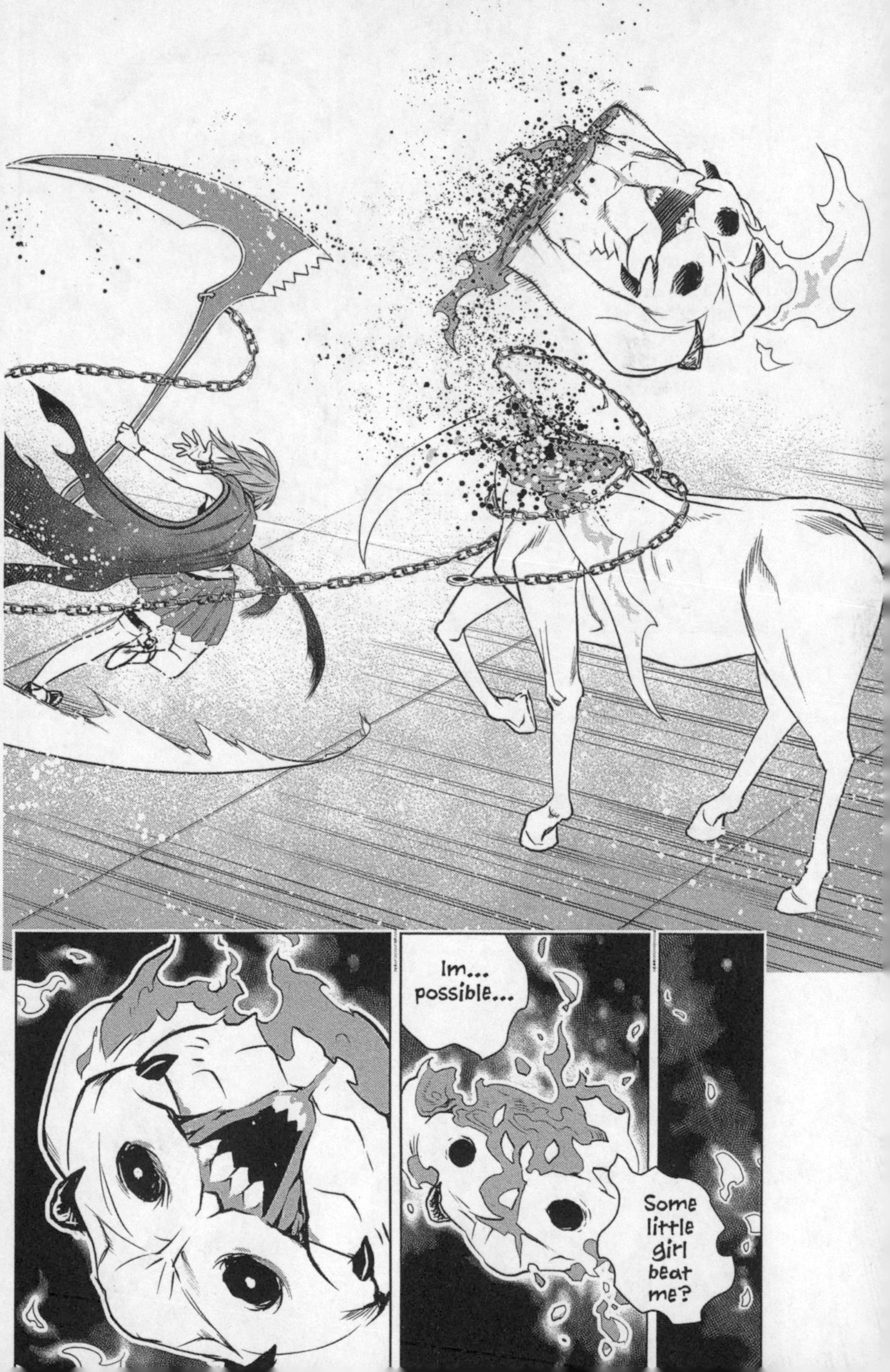

Im...
possible...
Some little girl beat me?

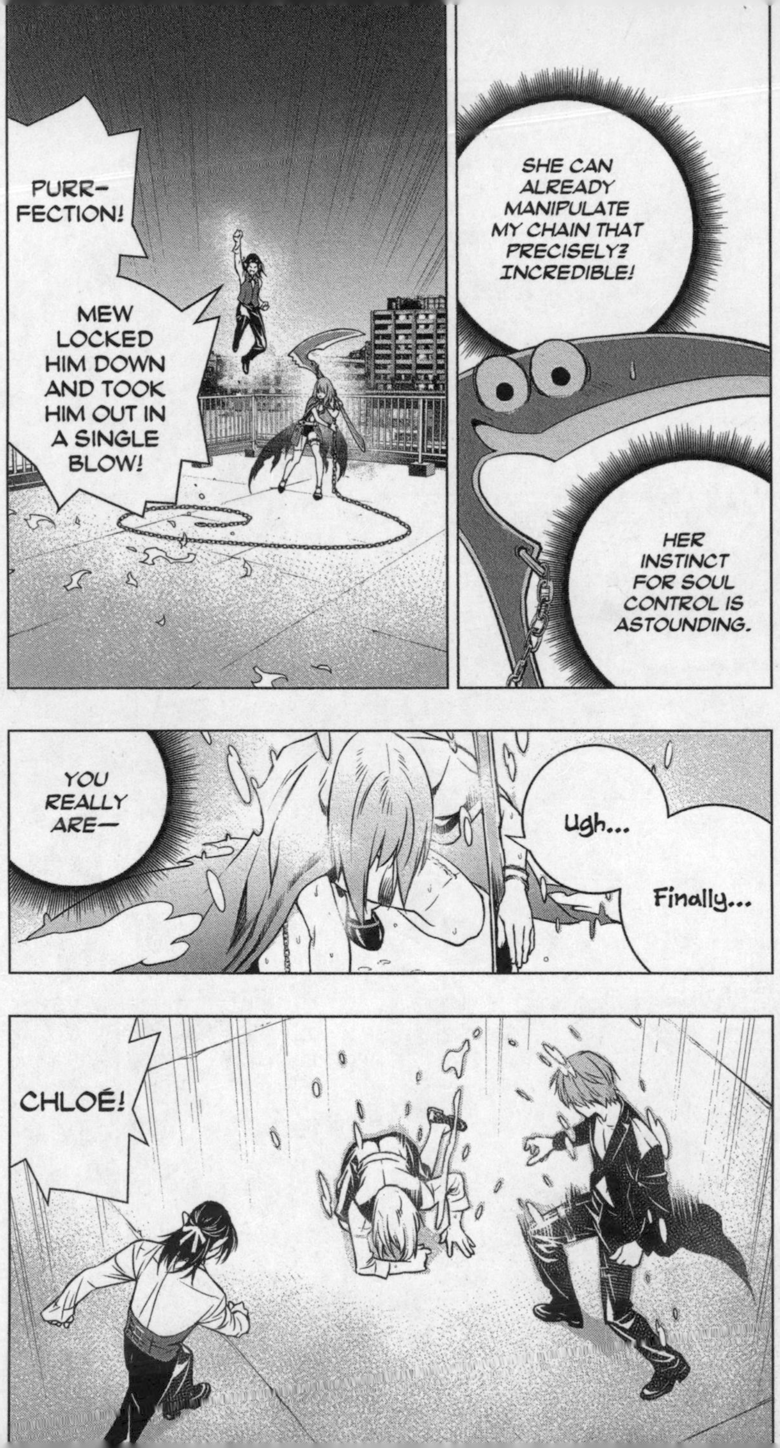
SHE CAN ALREADY MANIPULATE MY CHAIN THAT PRECISELY? INCREDIBLE!
HER INSTINCT FOR SOUL CONTROL IS ASTOUNDING.
PURR-FECTION!
MEW LOCKED HIM DOWN AND TOOK HIM OUT IN A SINGLE BLOW!
Ugh...
Finally...
YOU REALLY ARE—
CHLOÉ!

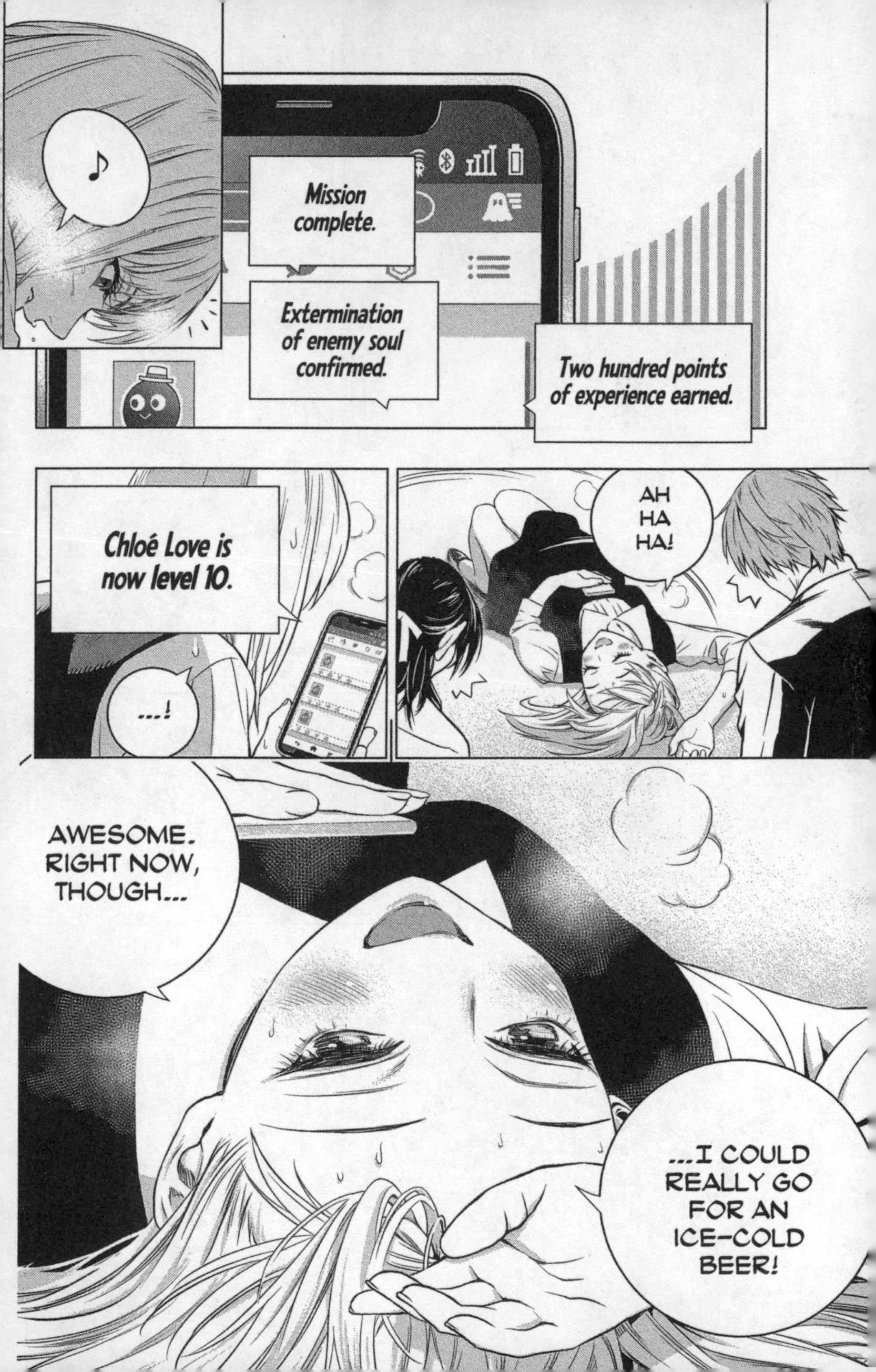
Mission complete.
Extermination of enemy soul confirmed.
Two hundred points of experience earned.
♪
AH HA HA!
Chloé Love is now level 10.
...!
AWESOME. RIGHT NOW, THOUGH...
...I COULD REALLY GO FOR AN ICE-COLD BEER!

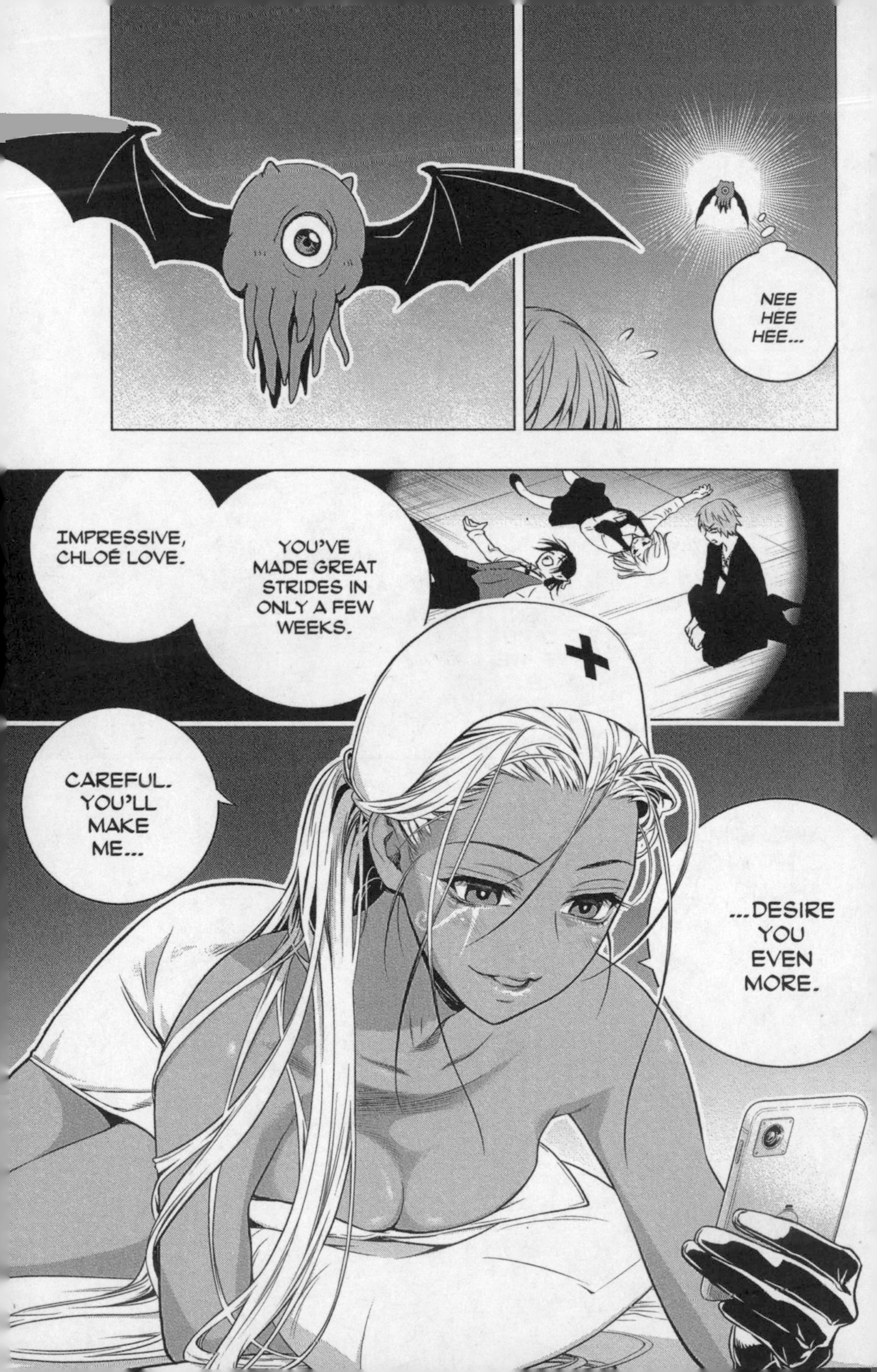
NEE HEE HEE...
IMPRESSIVE, CHLOÉ LOVE.
YOU'VE MADE GREAT STRIDES IN ONLY A FEW WEEKS.
CAREFUL. YOU'LL MAKE ME...
...DESIRE YOU EVEN MORE.

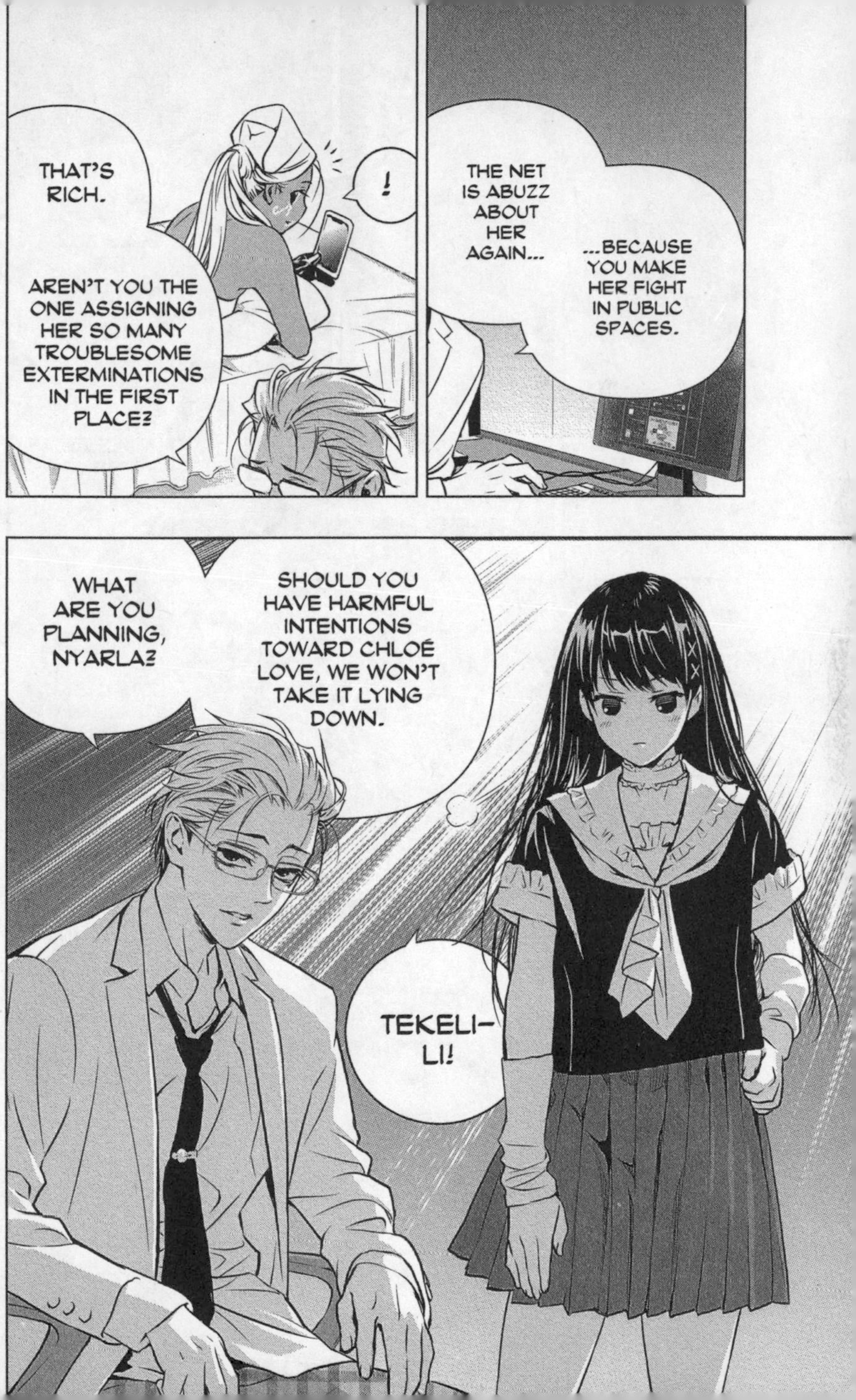
THE NET IS ABUZZ ABOUT HER AGAIN...
...BECAUSE YOU MAKE HER FIGHT IN PUBLIC SPACES.
!
THAT'S RICH.
AREN'T YOU THE ONE ASSIGNING HER SO MANY TROUBLESOME EXTERMINATIONS IN THE FIRST PLACE?
WHAT ARE YOU PLANNING, NYARLA?
SHOULD YOU HAVE HARMFUL INTENTIONS TOWARD CHLOÉ LOVE, WE WON'T TAKE IT LYING DOWN.
TEKELI-LI!

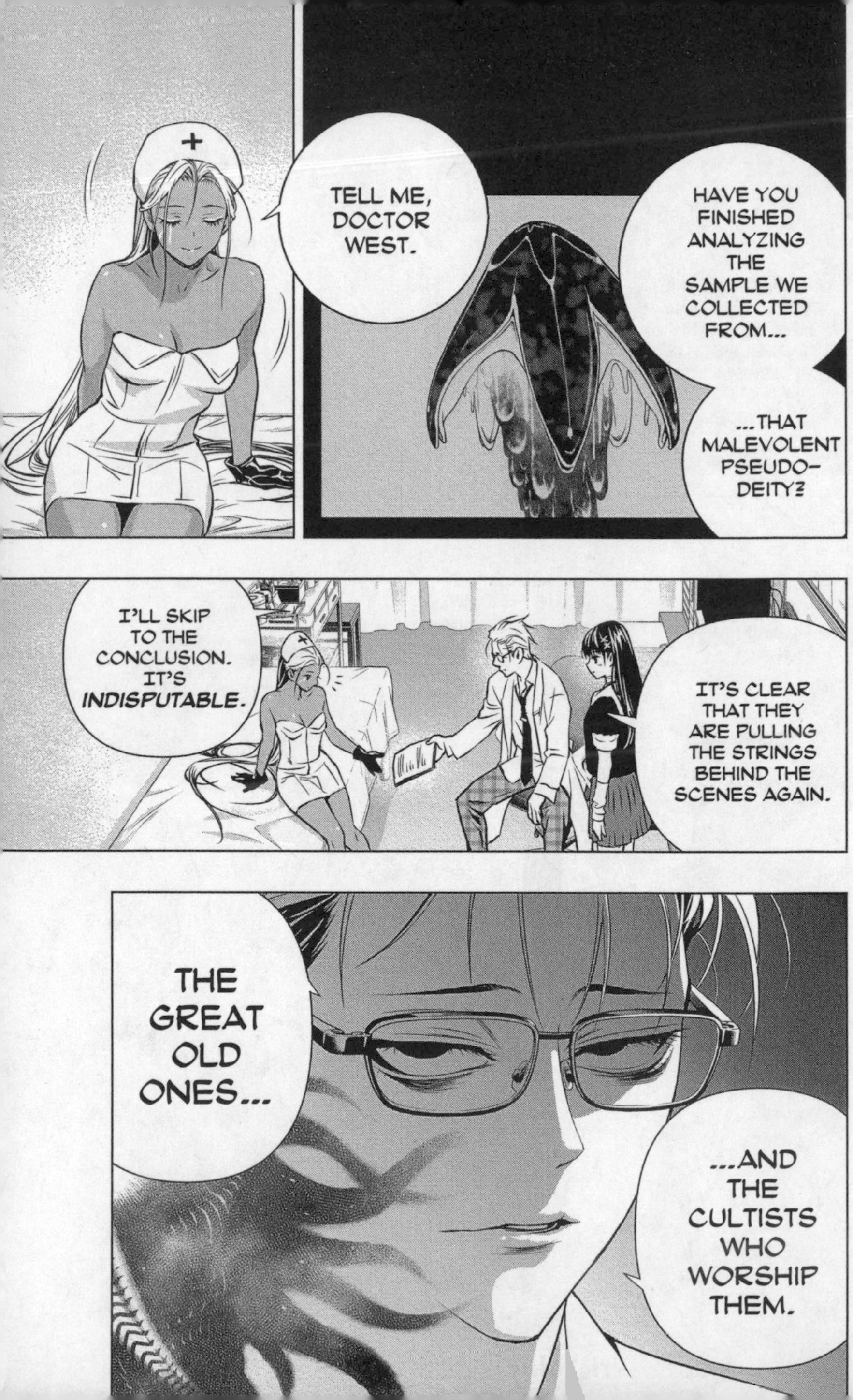
TELL ME, DOCTOR WEST.
HAVE YOU FINISHED ANALYZING THE SAMPLE WE COLLECTED FROM...
...THAT MALEVOLENT PSEUDO-DEITY?
I'LL SKIP TO THE CONCLUSION. IT'S INDISPUTABLE.
IT'S CLEAR THAT THEY ARE PULLING THE STRINGS BEHIND THE SCENES AGAIN.
THE GREAT OLD ONES...
...AND THE CULTISTS WHO WORSHIP THEM.

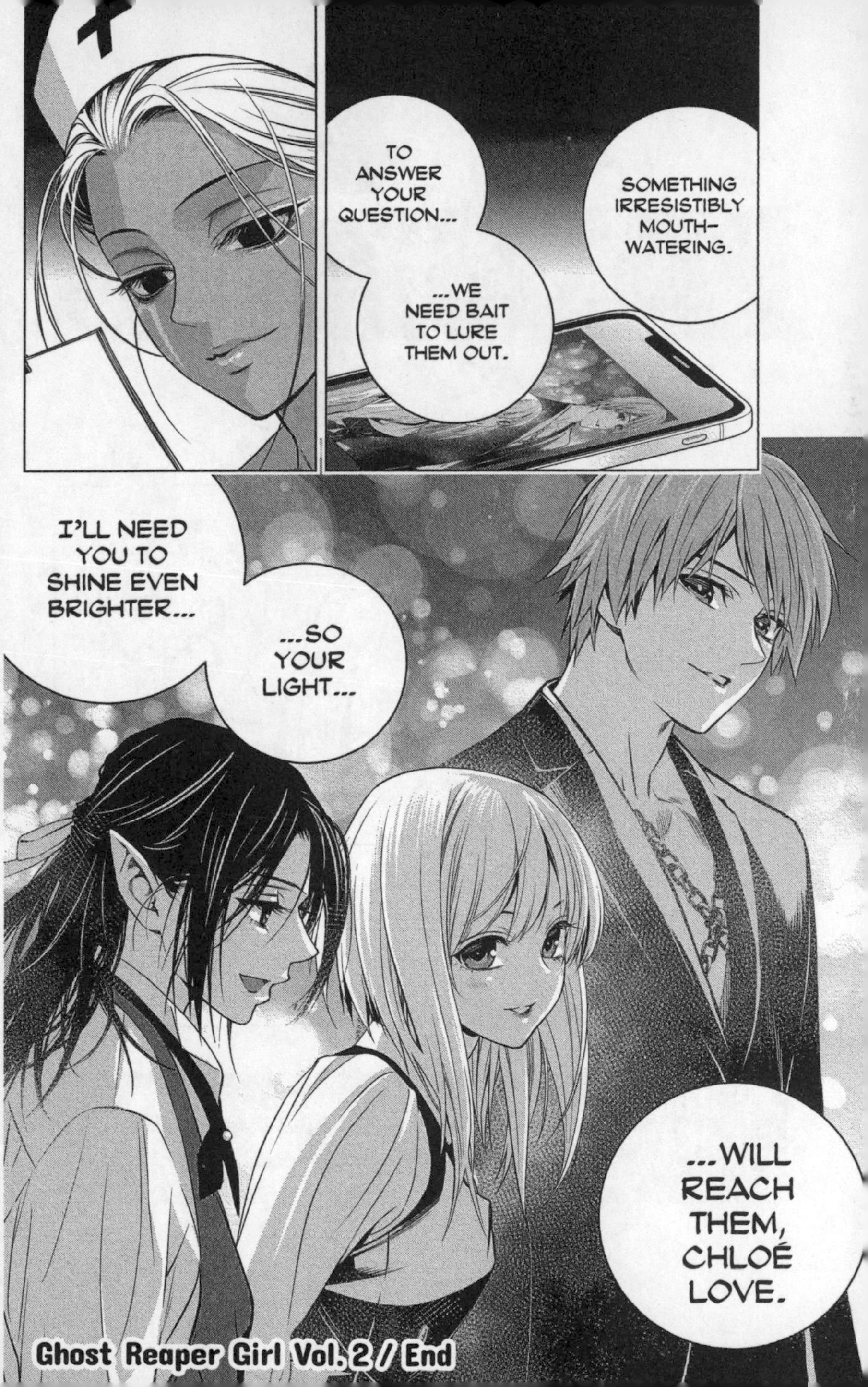
TO ANSWER YOUR QUESTION...
...WE NEED BAIT TO LURE THEM OUT.
SOMETHING IRRESISTIBLY MOUTH-WATERING.
I'LL NEED YOU TO SHINE EVEN BRIGHTER...
...SO YOUR LIGHT...
...WILL REACH THEM, CHLOÉ LOVE.
Ghost Reaper Girl Vol. 2 / End

Carefree Bonus Theater

Bonus Chapter 2:
Never Let a Drunk Person Spend Your Money

*All persons depicted in this story are of legal drinking age.

I'M SHO DRUUUNK. ♡
Pace yourself, Chloé!

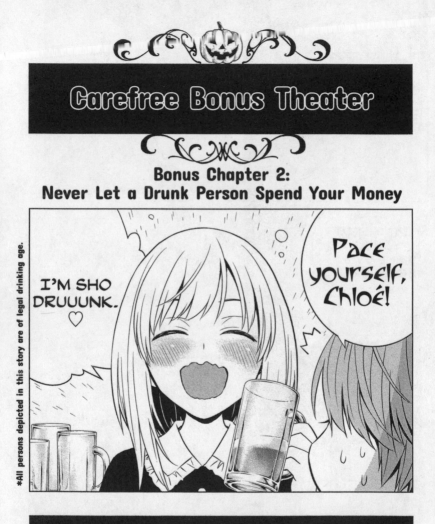

This bonus chapter is a continuation of the dinner the director paid for as Chloé's bonus in chapter 12.

Bleed the Powerful Dry

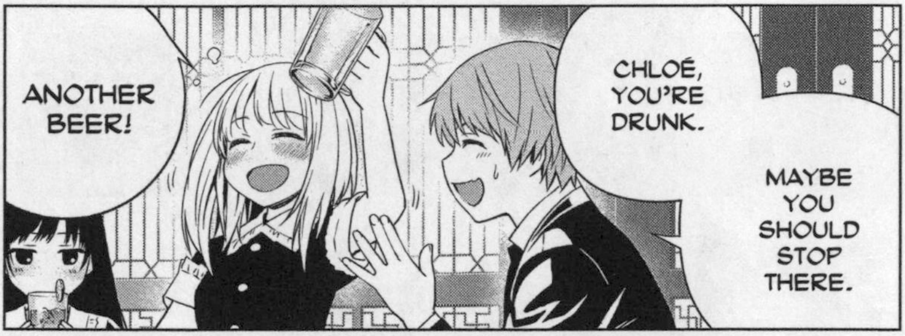
ANOTHER BEER!
CHLOÉ, YOU'RE DRUNK.
MAYBE YOU SHOULD STOP THERE.

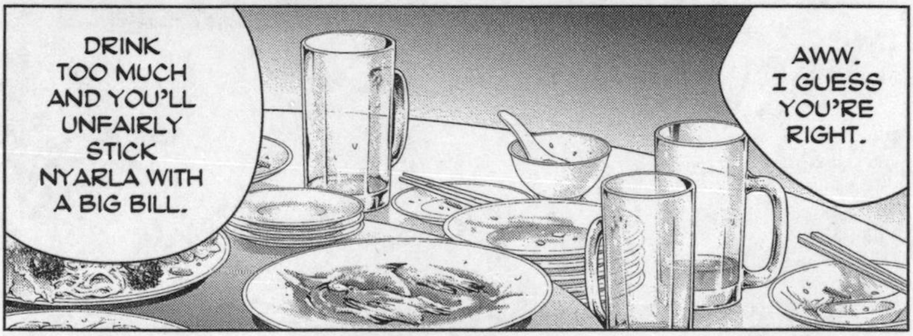
DRINK TOO MUCH AND YOU'LL UNFAIRLY STICK NYARLA WITH A BIG BILL.
AWW. I GUESS YOU'RE RIGHT.

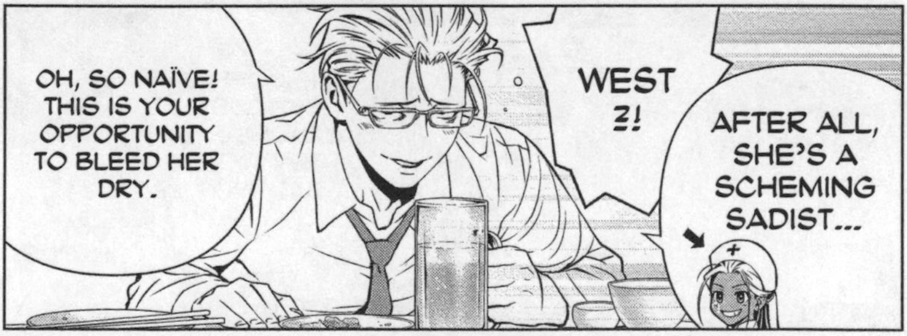
OH, SO NAÏVE! THIS IS YOUR OPPORTUNITY TO BLEED HER DRY.
WEST ?!
AFTER ALL, SHE'S A SCHEMING SADIST...

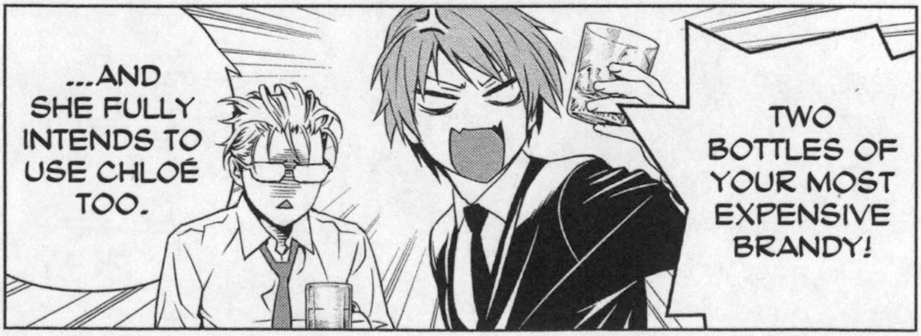
...AND SHE FULLY INTENDS TO USE CHLOÉ TOO.
TWO BOTTLES OF YOUR MOST EXPENSIVE BRANDY!

A Bad Feeling

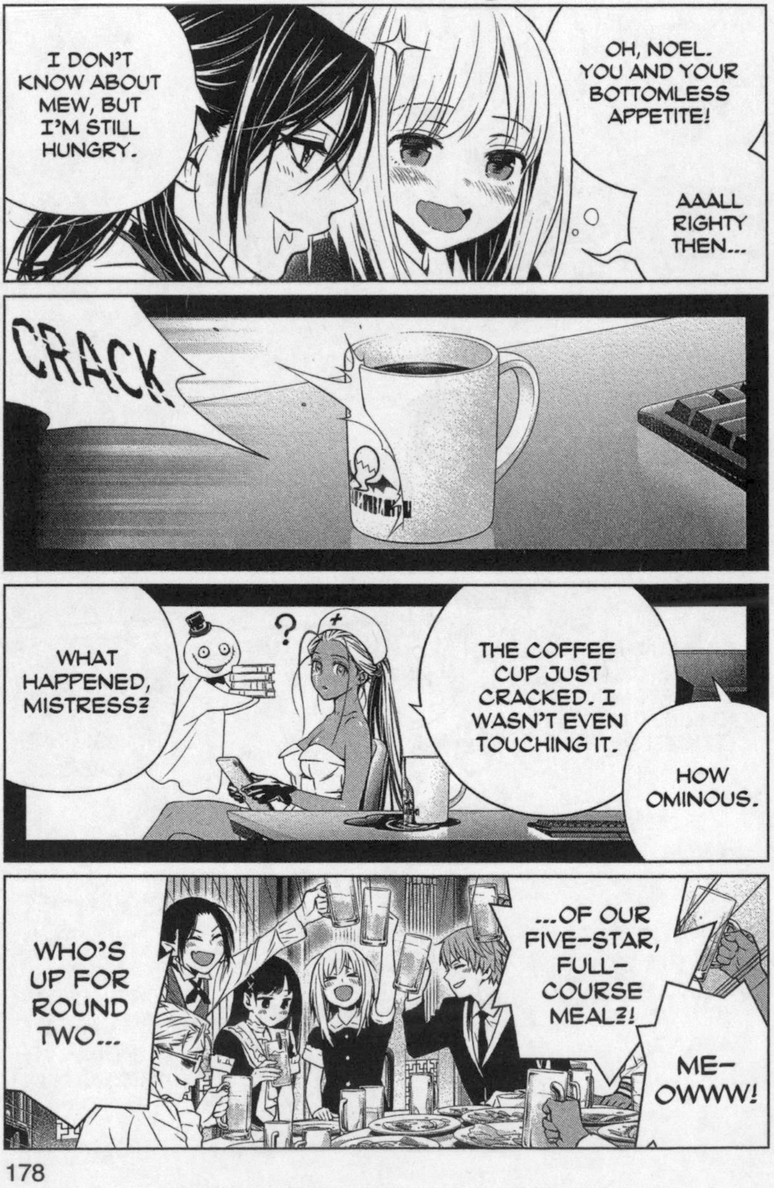
I DON'T KNOW ABOUT MEW, BUT I'M STILL HUNGRY.
OH, NOEL. YOU AND YOUR BOTTOMLESS APPETITE!
AAALL RIGHTY THEN...
CRACK!!
WHAT HAPPENED, MISTRESS?
THE COFFEE CUP JUST CRACKED. I WASN'T EVEN TOUCHING IT.
HOW OMINOUS.
WHO'S UP FOR ROUND TWO...
...OF OUR FIVE-STAR, FULL-COURSE MEAL?!
ME-OWWW!

A First

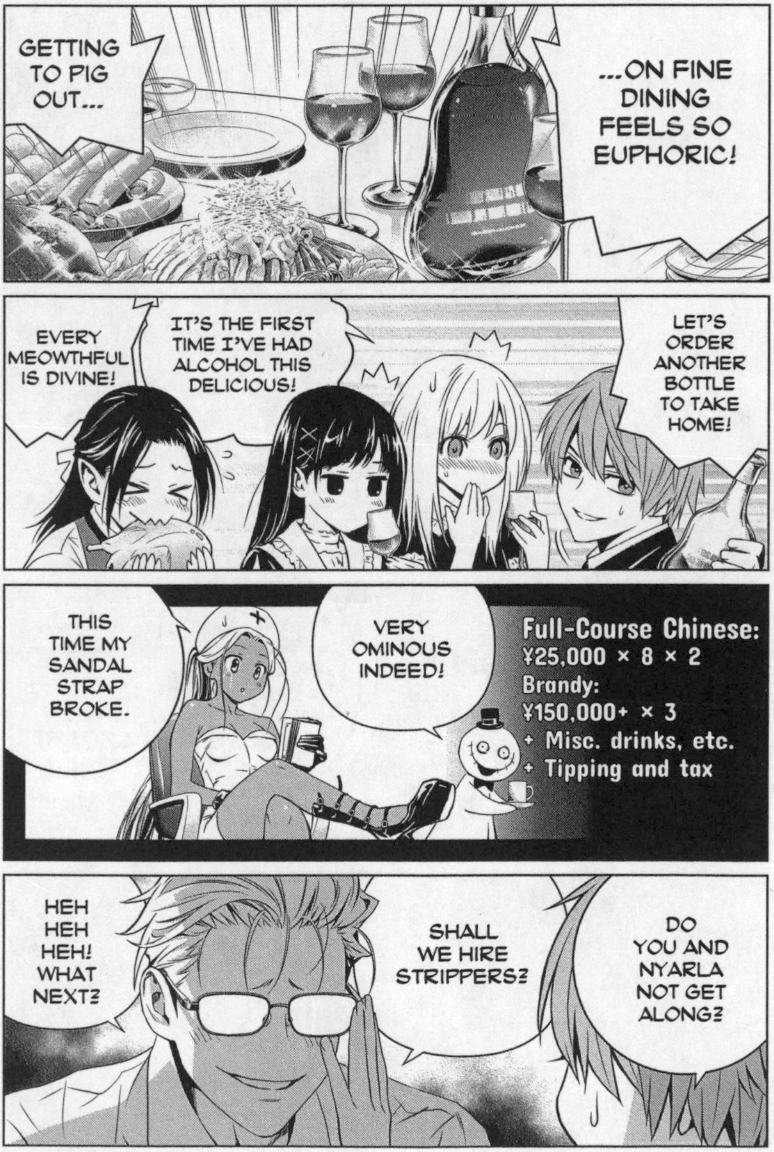
GETTING TO PIG OUT...
...ON FINE DINING FEELS SO EUPHORIC!
EVERY MEOWTHFUL IS DIVINE!
IT'S THE FIRST TIME I'VE HAD ALCOHOL THIS DELICIOUS!
LET'S ORDER ANOTHER BOTTLE TO TAKE HOME!
THIS TIME MY SANDAL STRAP BROKE.
VERY OMINOUS INDEED!
Full-Course Chinese: ¥25,000 × 8 × 2
Brandy: ¥150,000+ × 3
+ Misc. drinks, etc.
+ Tipping and tax
HEH HEH HEH! WHAT NEXT?
SHALL WE HIRE STRIPPERS?
DO YOU AND NYARLA NOT GET ALONG?

An Invitation?

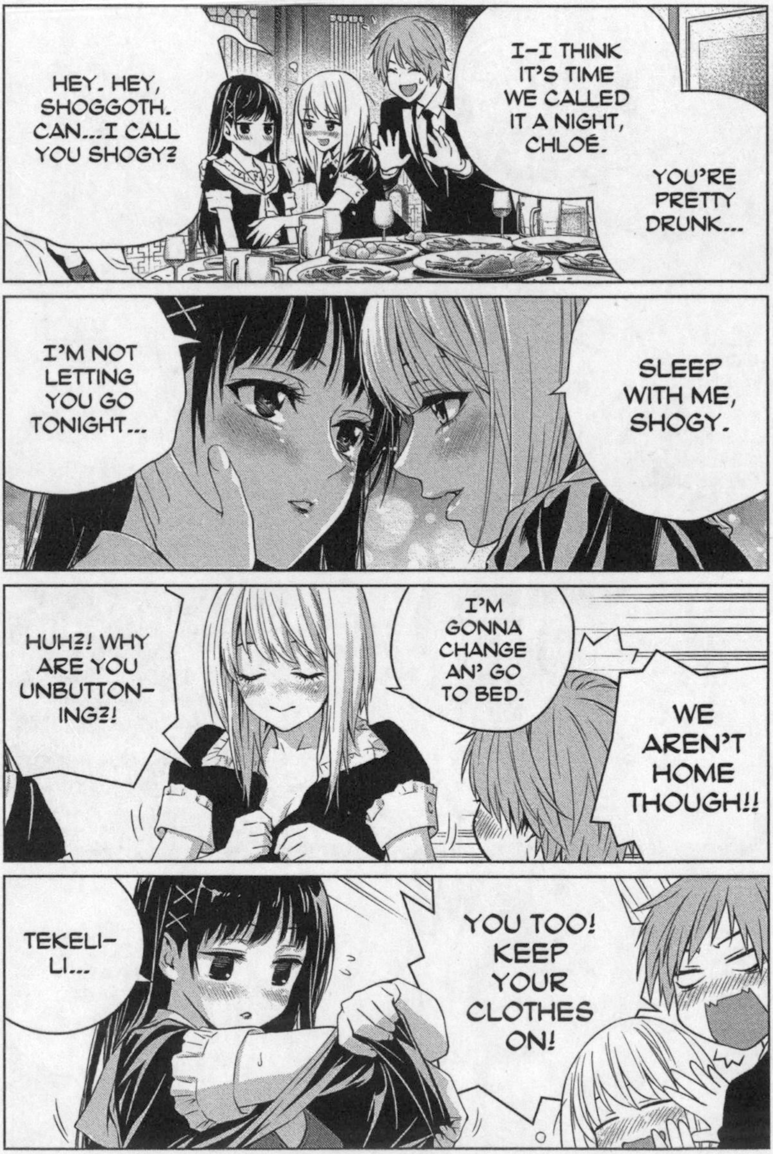
I-I THINK IT'S TIME WE CALLED IT A NIGHT, CHLOÉ.
YOU'RE PRETTY DRUNK...
HEY. HEY, SHOGGOTH. CAN...I CALL YOU SHOGY?
SLEEP WITH ME, SHOGY.
I'M NOT LETTING YOU GO TONIGHT...
I'M GONNA CHANGE AN' GO TO BED.
HUH?! WHY ARE YOU UNBUTTONING?!
WE AREN'T HOME THOUGH!!
TEKELI-LI...
YOU TOO! KEEP YOUR CLOTHES ON!

The Morning After

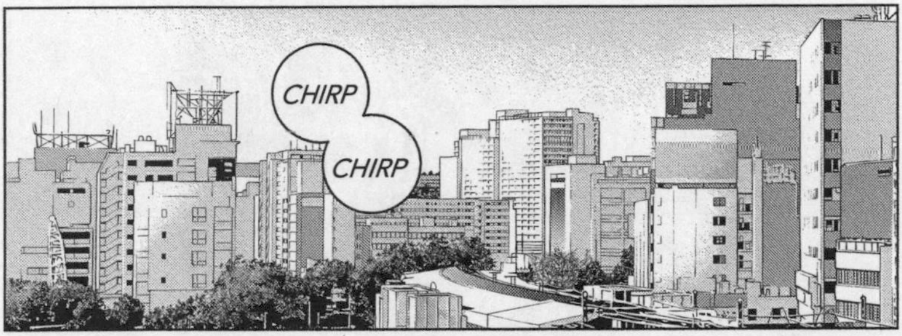
CHIRP
CHIRP

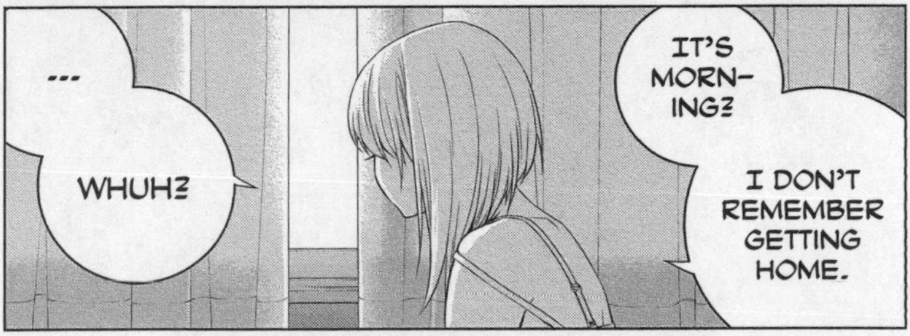
... WHUH?
IT'S MORN-ING?
I DON'T REMEMBER GETTING HOME.

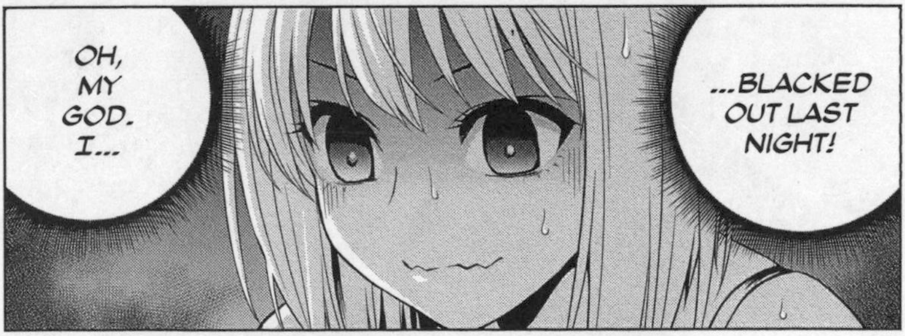
OH, MY GOD. I...
...BLACKED OUT LAST NIGHT!

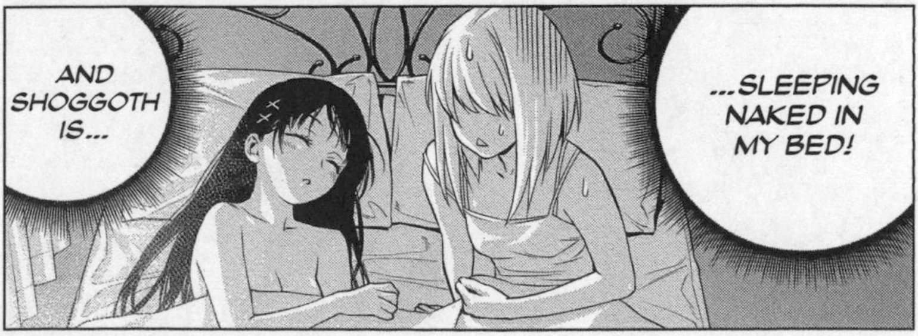
AND SHOGGOTH IS...
...SLEEPING NAKED IN MY BED!

Drunken Mistakes Can't Be Undone

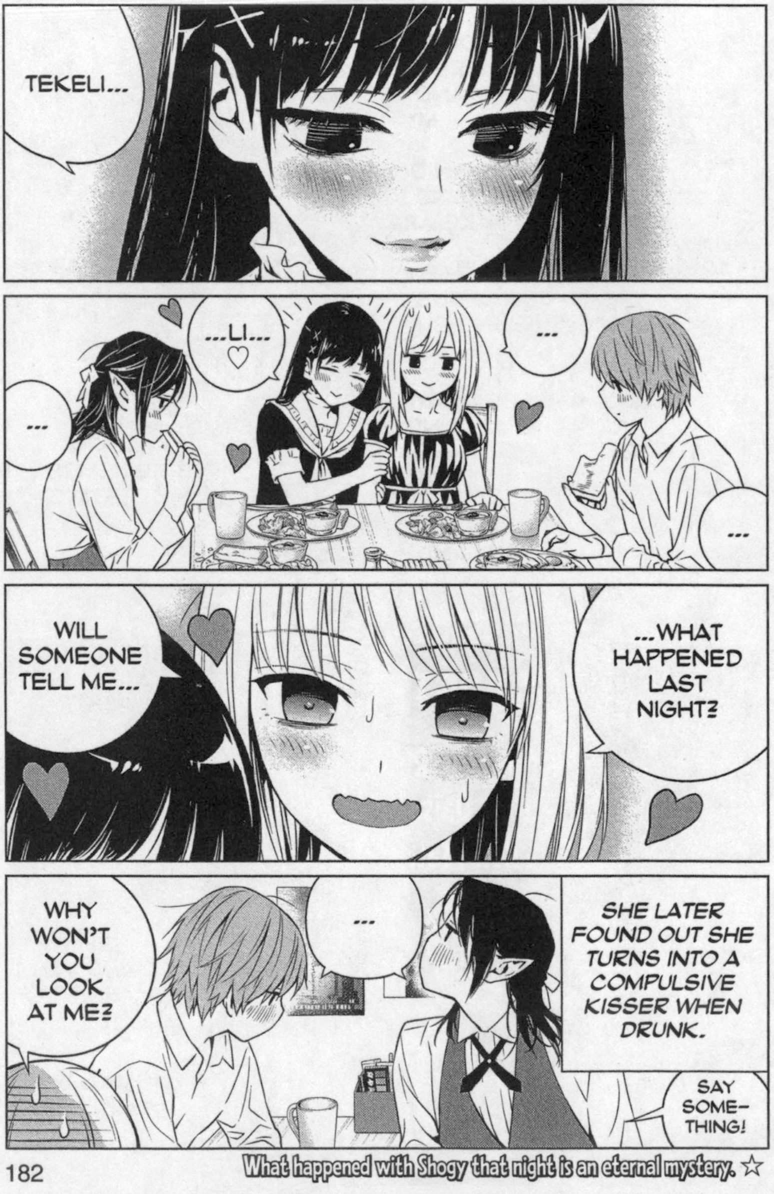
TEKELI...
...
...LI... ♡
...
...
WILL SOMEONE TELL ME...
...WHAT HAPPENED LAST NIGHT?
WHY WON'T YOU LOOK AT ME?
...
SHE LATER FOUND OUT SHE TURNS INTO A COMPULSIVE KISSER WHEN DRUNK.
SAY SOME-THING!

What happened with Shogy that night is an eternal mystery. ☆

AFTERWORD

GHOST REAPER GIRL IS SET IN A MORE DIVERSE YOKOHAMA.

I'VE LIVED IN YOKOHAMA FOR OVER 20 YEARS. I'VE SPENT MORE TIME IN YOKOHAMA THAN IN MY HOMETOWN, AND IT HAS A SPECIAL PLACE IN MY HEART.

MY USUAL RAMEN JOINT, MY FAVORITE MOVIE THEATER, THE EXOTIC PORT, THE STUDIO WHERE I TAKE ART CLASSES...

I STARTED THIS MANGA IN 2020, WHEN THE CORONAVIRUS STRUCK THE WORLD WITH UNPRECEDENTED MISFORTUNE. DOWNTOWN YOKOHAMA IS NOW DESERTED AND QUIET.

I'LL JUST BE DRAWING CHLOÉ AND FRIENDS RUNNING AROUND THE CITY I LOVE WHILE PRAYING FOR THE SAFETY AND HEALTH OF MY DEAR READERS.

MAY A NEW NORMAL COME TO YOU IN DUE TIME, AND HOPE ALONG WITH IT!

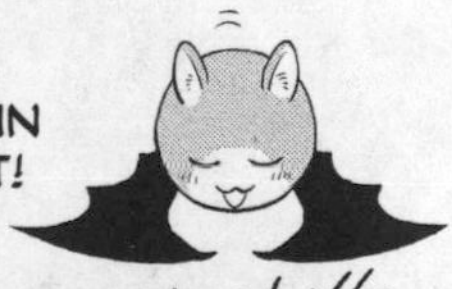

2021. akissa

GHOST REAPER GIRL

Akissa Saiké Rika Shirota Hashimoto
Shu Nagata Daisuke Nogishi Higoro Tomori
Editors: Harukata Kasai, Satoshi Watanabe Designer: Daiju Asami

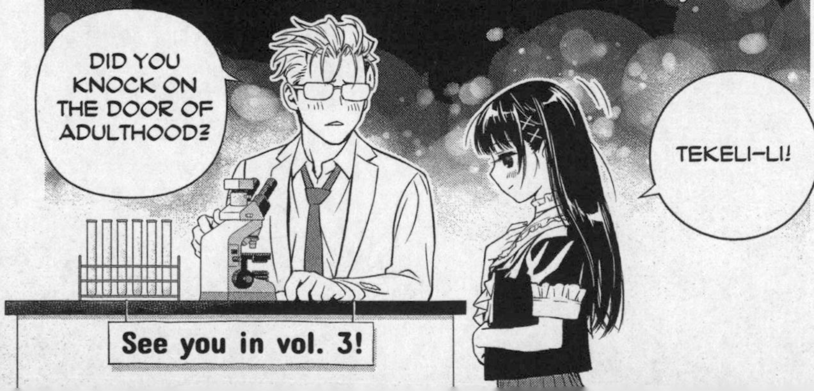

TEKELI-LI!
DID YOU KNOCK ON THE DOOR OF ADULTHOOD?
See you in vol. 3!

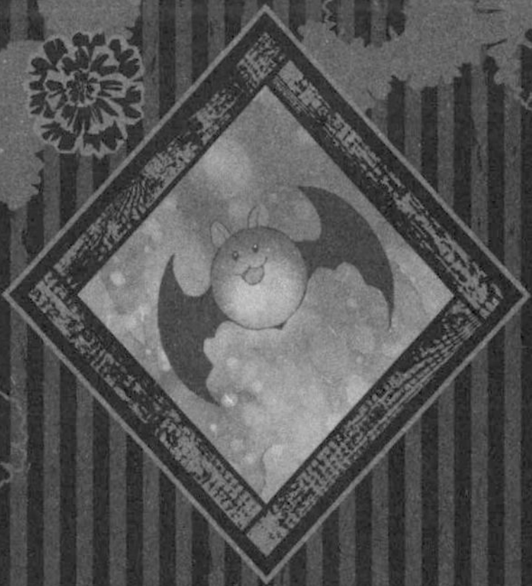

AKISSA SAIKÉ

Before *Ghost Reaper Girl*, I drew a manga called *Rosario+Vampire* under my real name, Akihisa Ikeda. I get asked more often than I expected about why I changed pen names.

You see, when I drew under my real name, the following episode took place. A delivery person looked at my name on a package and said, "Aren't you the artist of *Rosario+Vampire*?" That was when I knew I'd have to change pen names someday.

It would have sounded cool if the reason was that I'd given the name Akihisa Ikeda over to *Rosario+Vampire* though.

Akissa Saiké began working professionally as a manga artist with the four-volume magical-warrior fantasy series *Kiruto* in 2002, which was serialized in *Monthly Shonen Jump*. *Rosario+Vampire* began serialization in *Monthly Shonen Jump* in March of 2004 and continued in *Jump SQ* as *Rosario+Vampire: Season II*. In 2020, he changed his pen name from Akihisa Ikeda and launched *Ghost Reaper Girl* on the Jump+ platform.

GHOST REAPER GIRL

Volume 2

SHONEN JUMP Edition

STORY AND ART BY **Akissa Saiké**

GRAPHIC NOVEL TRANSLATION **Amanda Haley**
TOUCH-UP ART & LETTERING **Annaliese "Ace" Christman**
DESIGN **Joy Zhang**
EDITOR **Alexis Kirsch**

First published in Japan in 2020 by SHUEISHA Inc., Tokyo.
English translation rights arranged by SHUEISHA Inc.

Printed in the U.S.A.

Published by VIZ Media, LLC
P.O. Box 77010
San Francisco, CA 94107

10 9 8 7 6 5 4 3 2 1
First printing, September 2022

ratings.viz.com RATED T+ OLDER TEEN

PARENTAL ADVISORY
GHOST REAPER GIRL is rated T+ for Older Teen and is recommended for ages 16 and up. This volume contains fantasy violence and gore.

VIZ MEDIA
viz.com

SHONEN JUMP

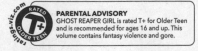

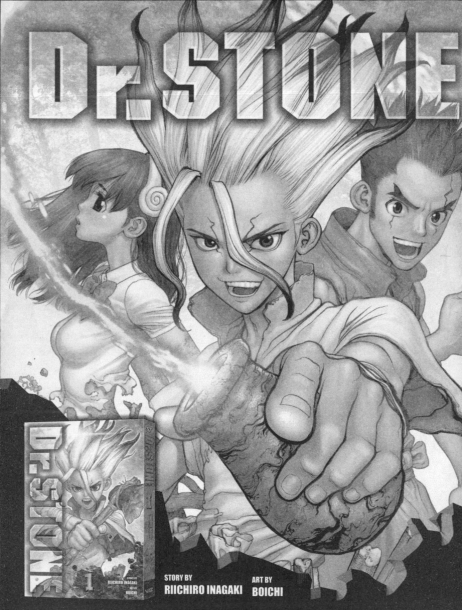

Dr. STONE

STORY BY
RIICHIRO INAGAKI

ART BY
BOICHI

One fateful day, all of humanity turned to stone. Many millennia later, Taiju frees himself from petrification and finds himself surrounded by statues. The situation looks grim—until he runs into his science-loving friend Senku! Together they plan to restart civilization with the power of science!

DEMON SLAYER
KIMETSU NO YAIBA

Story and Art by
KOYOHARU GOTOUGE

In Taisho-era Japan, kindhearted Tanjiro Kamado makes a living selling charcoal. But his peaceful life is shattered when a demon slaughters his entire family. His little sister Nezuko is the only survivor, but she has been transformed into a demon herself! Tanjiro sets out on a dangerous journey to find a way to return his sister to normal and destroy the demon who ruined his life.

DEMON SLAYER
KIMETSU NO YAIBA
1

Story and Art by
KOYOHARU GOTOUGE

VIZ

Black ✳ Clover

STORY & ART BY YŪKI TABATA

Asta is a young boy who dreams of becoming the greatest mage in the kingdom. Only one problem—he can't use any magic! Luckily for Asta, he receives the incredibly rare five-leaf clover grimoire that gives him the power of anti-magic. Can someone who can't use magic really become the Wizard King? One thing's for sure—Asta will never give up!

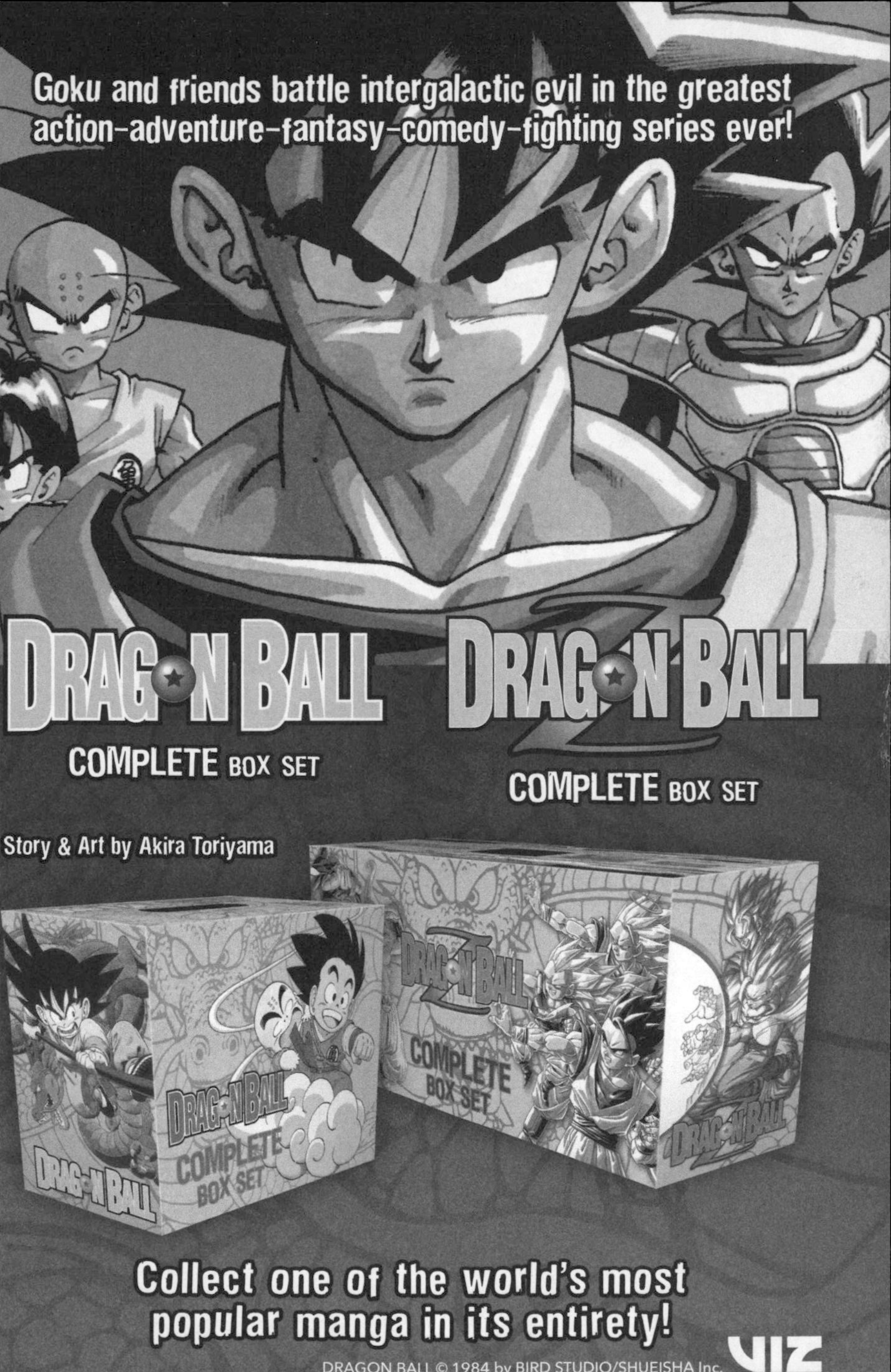
Goku and friends battle intergalactic evil in the greatest action-adventure-fantasy-comedy-fighting series ever!
DRAGON BALL
COMPLETE BOX SET
DRAGON BALL Z
COMPLETE BOX SET
Story & Art by Akira Toriyama
Collect one of the world's most popular manga in its entirety!
VIZ

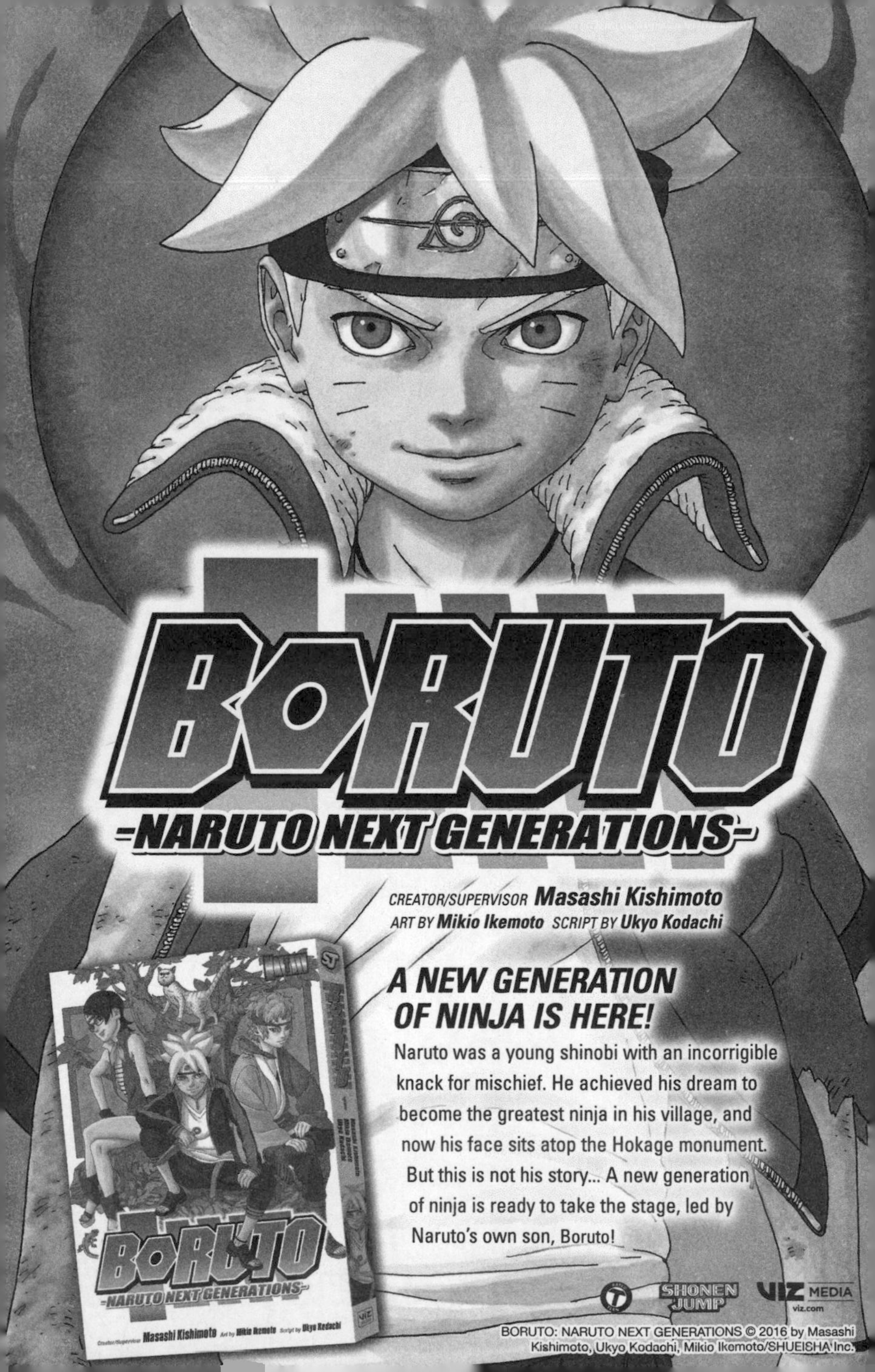
BORUTO
-NARUTO NEXT GENERATIONS-
CREATOR/SUPERVISOR Masashi Kishimoto
ART BY Mikio Ikemoto SCRIPT BY Ukyo Kodachi
A NEW GENERATION OF NINJA IS HERE!
Naruto was a young shinobi with an incorrigible knack for mischief. He achieved his dream to become the greatest ninja in his village, and now his face sits atop the Hokage monument. But this is not his story... A new generation of ninja is ready to take the stage, led by Naruto's own son, Boruto!
BORUTO
-NARUTO NEXT GENERATIONS-
Creator/Supervisor Masashi Kishimoto Art by Mikio Ikemoto Script by Ukyo Kodachi
SHONEN JUMP
VIZ MEDIA
viz.com
BORUTO: NARUTO NEXT GENERATIONS © 2016 by Masashi Kishimoto, Ukyo Kodachi, Mikio Ikemoto/SHUEISHA Inc.

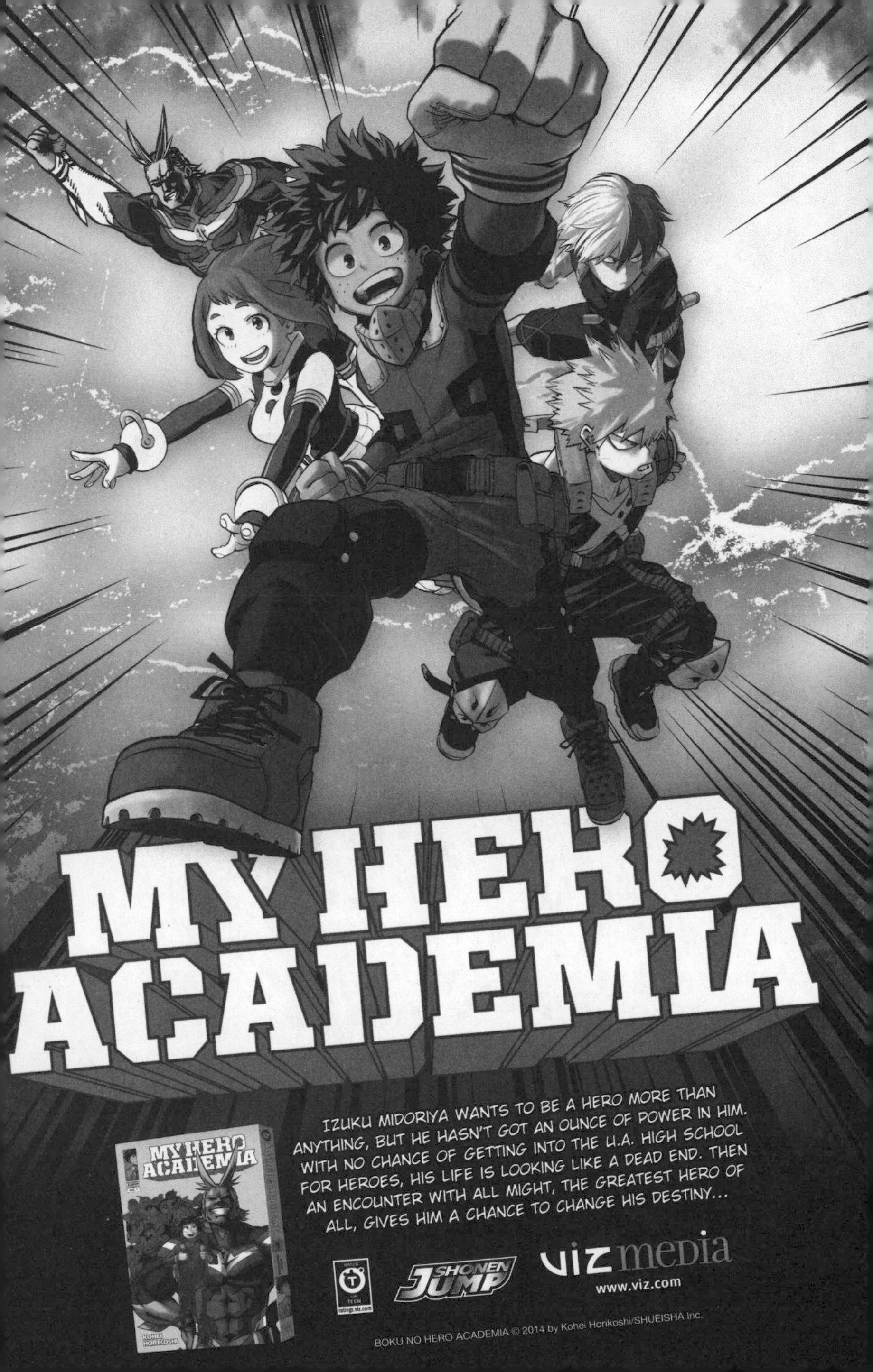
MY HERO ACADEMIA
IZUKU MIDORIYA WANTS TO BE A HERO MORE THAN ANYTHING, BUT HE HASN'T GOT AN OUNCE OF POWER IN HIM. WITH NO CHANCE OF GETTING INTO THE U.A. HIGH SCHOOL FOR HEROES, HIS LIFE IS LOOKING LIKE A DEAD END. THEN AN ENCOUNTER WITH ALL MIGHT, THE GREATEST HERO OF ALL, GIVES HIM A CHANCE TO CHANGE HIS DESTINY...
SHONEN JUMP
viz media
www.viz.com
BOKU NO HERO ACADEMIA © 2014 by Kohei Horikoshi/SHUEISHA Inc.

YOU'RE READING THE
WRONG WAY!

Have evil spirits taken over this manga?!
How can this be the wrong way?

Unlike most manga, *Ghost Reaper Girl*
reads left to right in traditional English
order, as requested by Akissa Saiké,
creator of the series.